Through their apathy
people become accomplices
to their own disempower-
ment,

Albert Bandura
2004

CAMPUS, INC.

CAMPUS, INC.

Corporate Power
in the
Ivory Tower

edited by
Geoffry D. White, Ph.D.
with Flannery C. Hauck

 Prometheus Books

59 John Glenn Drive
Amherst, New York 14228-2197

Published 2000 by Prometheus Books

Campus Inc.: Corporate Power in the Ivory Tower. Copyright © 2000 by Geoffry D. White. All rights reserved. No part of this publication may be reproduced, stored in a retrieval system, or transmitted in any form or by any means, digital, electronic, mechanical, photocopying, recording, or otherwise, or conveyed via the Internet or a Web site, without prior written permission of the publisher, except in the case of brief quotations embodied in critical articles and reviews.

Inquiries should be addressed to
Prometheus Books
59 John Glenn Drive
Amherst, New York 14228–2197
VOICE: 716–691–0133, ext. 207
FAX: 716–564–2711
WWW.PROMETHEUSBOOKS.COM

04 03 02 01 00   5 4 3 2 1

Library of Congress Cataloging-in-Publication Data

Campus, Inc.: corporate power in the ivory tower / edited by Geoffry D. White with Flannery C. Hauck.
    p. cm.
Includes bibliographical references.
ISBN 1–57392–810–0 (cloth : alk. paper)
    1. Education, Higher—Economic aspects—United States. 2. Industry and education—United States. I. White, Geoffry D. II. Hauck, Flannery C.

LC67.62 .C36 2000
371.19'5—dc21   99–045208
                                                                                  CIP

Printed in the United States of America on acid-free paper

CONTENTS

5

PART FOUR. TAKE BACK THE NIKE!
CAMPUS COMMUNITIES BATTLE
THE CORPORATE GIANTS

PART FIVE. EDUCATION WITH REPRESENTATION:
UNION ORGANIZING ON THE
CAMPUS, INCORPORATED

PART SIX. MUCKRAKING 101:
ADVICE AND RESOURCES
FOR CAMPUS ORGANIZERS

Contents

9

ACKNOWLEDGMENTS

Irst and foremost I want to thank my children for inspiring my political and humanitarian projects. I wrote this poem for my daughter, Lauren, on the occasion of her Bat Mitzvah. Of course it applies equally to my son, Eric.

Peril or No

Peril or no,
I must let you go.
But what if you choke on a piece of meat?
Or try some particularly perilous feat?
What if you step in front of a car?
Or your boyfriend tries to go too far?
Peril or no,
I must let go.
If I couldn't stand your perilous play,
I knew I'd drive you quickly away.
But if I can't keep you next to me,
I'll make the world a safer place to be.
Peril or no,
We must let go.

Thanks to my wife, Judy, for holding down the fort during my brief absences.

I owe a debt of gratitude to my mother, who helped me through a midlife crisis by teaching me the fine art of oil paint. An excellent teacher, always encouraging, she created a space for me to love my paintings.

My father, a physician still in practice after almost sixty years, showed me that projects could be taken on and completed. Dad built a hospital, an airplane, and even a bomb shelter during the Cuban Missile Crisis.

To Prometheus's Steven Mitchell and Meghann French: midwives to the birth of an idea.

To Jennifer Horsman—my unofficial writing coach—for her generosity, humor, and unique ability to lay it on the line without being the least bit offensive. To Terri, who coaxed me into putting more of myself into my writing. To the friends who helped me believe in myself: Anna, Eliane, Charlie, Ira, Jean, Jeff, Judy, Martine, Nancy, and Rush.

Finally, to Yvonne and the people of Malawi and Bosnia, who taught me the meaning of love and courage.

PREFACE
Geoffry D. White

All it takes for evil to exist is for good people to do nothing.

—Edmund Burke

A man was walking upstream along a riverbank. Suddenly, he heard the screams of people drowning. He jumped in and rescued one grateful person, then another. As the man continued his journey up the river he encountered and saved more and more drowning people. Soon a crowd gathered to watch the man's valiant efforts. Then, inexplicably, the man began to run upstream, seeming to ignore the pleas of the next victim. Shocked at his apparent act of indifference, someone from the crowd yelled out, "How can you abandon this person?" The man shot back, "I'm going upstream to see who's pushing them all in!"

For decades as a psychologist I've tried with varying degrees of success to pull people from the maelstroms of their lives. By helping individuals, I thought I was doing something significant to alleviate the suffering in the world. Eventually, through a series of crises and coincidences, I was swept toward the realization that I was not addressing the primary source of human suffering. Psychotherapy can certainly be useful in helping people cope with certain emotional and interpersonal difficulties, but it does little to correct the primary causes of large-scale human misery.[1]

So I moved upstream to have a look.

13

On my journey, I beheld some tragic sights: the corporate takeover of the health-care delivery system through managed care and HMOs; Americans rendered ignorant and pliable as the media were taken over by a few superwealthy corporations, notably, General Electric, Disney, Westinghouse, and Time Warner;[2] the welfare system maimed almost beyond recognition; elections for sale to the highest bidder through a system of legalized bribery; and countless other catastrophes. The hallmarks and foundations of democracy were being stripped away by the power and greed of big business.

Part of what helped me figure this out was getting involved with several ballot initiatives in California. My first involvement was with an attempt to establish a Canadian-style, single-payer health-care system in the state. The plan was to take the huge profit being reaped by private insurance companies and use it to cover health benefits for the millions of uninsured. If the initiative had passed, all health insurance companies in California would have become extinct. The initiative lost because of the tidal wave of money spent by insurance companies to defeat it. Nonetheless, the ballot measure helped educate Californians about a humane health-care delivery system. More than one-third of the voters endorsed it. Not bad for the first attempt to humanize health care in one of the most politically corrupt states in the union.

I had an even more eye-opening experience a few years later, when I joined the Common Cause–backed campaign finance reform initiative for California, one of the few remaining states in which there were no limits on contributions and spending for state elections. The initiative passed overwhelmingly, only to be declared unconstitutional by a federal judge. Court challenges are currently in progress. Recently, however, the U.S. Supreme Court declared that a similar law passed in another state was constitutional, hopefully paving the way for the same result in California.

These and other experiences taught me the difference between democracy and capitalism, captured so clearly by Lester Thurow, professor of economics at MIT:

> Democracy and capitalism have very different beliefs about the proper distribution of power. One believes in a completely equal distribution of political power, "one man, one vote," while the other believes that it is the duty of the economically fit to drive the unfit out of business and into economic extinction. To put it in its starkest form, capitalism is perfectly compatible with slavery. The American South has such a system for more than two centuries. Democracy is not compatible with slavery.[3]

Recently I began to notice the privatization trend metastasizing into academia. Having spent the better part of my life in the ivory tower, I was alarmed to see big business nurturing a new form of corporate welfare in one of the core institutions of democracy. It was unclear to me why more hadn't been written on this topic; so began a four-year project. This collection of essays is the result.

My goal was to bring together a wide range of individuals and organizations who would provide a broad perspective on the problems and remedies unique to this single issue: the growing corporatization of the university. Some of the contributors are among the best-known and most active progressive thinkers and organizers in the country. Others are well-known within the academic and union-organizing traditions.

Since college and university students play a prominent part in the pro-democracy movement, it was especially important to include them in *Campus, Inc.* These are our future leaders, and it has been my longtime belief that campus newspapers are an underutilized resource for raising the consciousness and mobilizing campaigns both on and off campus. This resource is vital because the (corporate-owned) media provide scant coverage of the extensive and growing corporate activity on college campuses.

Ultimately, I wanted *Campus, Inc.* to be a source of inspiration. I wanted to create a book that does something to show how to prevent the university from becoming another source of corporate welfare[4] and, even more important, how we can democratize higher education. I was heartened to find so many examples of successful campaigns and approaches to return higher education to the people it was originally designed to serve. The reader is welcome to contact any of the contributors to this volume for more information.

Returning now to the story of the fellow who was headed upstream to prevent the drownings, the essential question to me is this: Did the people lining the riverbanks remain passive bystanders, or were they inspired to join him in preventing future drownings? This book represents my fervent hope that they joined in.

NOTES

1. J. Hillman and M. Ventura, *We've Had a Hundred Years of Psychotherapy—And the World Is Getting Worse* (San Francisco: HarperCollins, 1992).
2. M. Miller, "Free the Media," *Nation*, June 3, 1996, pp. 9–15.
3. L. Thurow, *The Future of Capitalism* (New York: William Morrow, 1996), p. 242.
4. M. Zepezauer and A. Naiman, *Take the Rich Off Welfare* (Tucson, Ariz.: Odonian Press, 1996).

INTRODUCTION
The Struggle That Matters the Most

Ronnie Dugger

"Corporate, foundation, and tycoon money has had a major, deleterious impact on universities." With these words, Larry Soley, a professor at Marquette University in Wisconsin and a contributor to this volume, summarized the consolidating situation in his 1995 book, *Leasing the Ivory Tower.* "Financial considerations have turned around educational priorities, reduced the importance of teaching, degraded the integrity of academic journals, and determined what research is conducted at universities. The social costs of this influence have been lower-quality education, a reduction in academic freedom, and a covert transfer of resources from the public to the private sector."

"In short," concludes student leader Ben Manski of the University of Wisconsin–Madison, in his essay for this volume, "education is being reconstructed to serve the priorities of corporate profit, and in the process is being destroyed as an institution of democracy."

Campus organizing was in a sorry state as the 1990s began, but has recently taken "an expressly countercorporate pro-democracy direction," Manski writes in his impressive study of campus activism. The Center for Campus Organizing in Cambridge, Massachusetts, has served as an anchor and resource center. In the larger society, the Program on Law, Corporations, and Democracy—a collective of about a dozen people, including Richard Grossman and Ward Morehouse—has taken the lead in laying an intellectual foundation on the inherent incompatibility between corporate power and democracy. The national anticorporate Alliance for Democracy has emerged with fifty-five chapters nationwide; the New, Green, and Labor Parties have taken sharp anticorporate turns; and United for a Fair Economy is advancing an innovative critique of concentrated wealth and corporate power. Meanwhile, as Manski reports, at forty-five campuses in 1997 and more than a hundred in 1998 students conducted "Democracy Teach-Ins" against corporate domination of universities. Student actions against sweatshop labor were a feature of life on some two hundred U.S. campuses in the fall of 1999 because, for example, of some schools' multimillion-dollar exclusive-use contracts with corporations that sell athletic shoes made by exploited low-wage workers in the Third World. Rebelling against tuition hikes, students at the University of Wisconsin–Madison, demonstrated under the banner "Education as a Right." As this book was going to the press, a new chapter-based multicampus student organization, the 180 Movement for Democracy and Education ("180" signifying a 180-degree turn), was organizing university teach-ins against the manifold plans implying the corporate domination of the world that are embodied in the World Trade Organization.

"On North American campuses," Manski writes, "democracy is coming into its own as a radical challenge to corporate power." In Ontario, college students on various campuses are striking, occupying bank and government buildings against education cuts; students at the University of Mexico are striking in what has become a drive for university self-government; and, Manski observes, millions of students and workers at universities in Israel, Korea, Indonesia, Zimbabwe, Puerto Rico, Turkey, France, and other countries have taken part in general strikes.

Student activism runs in cycles. From the evidence in this book and elsewhere it does appear that a student revolt has begun in the United States against corporate attacks on higher education and the corporate domination of democracy, and that an international student movement for democracy on the campus is struggling to emerge. None too soon!

The university is the conscience of the culture—and should be the most independent established institution in civilization—but corporations, especially the transnationals, have become the ruling powers of the age. As we enter the new millennium, corporate CEOs and the major owners behind them are the royalty of our era, succeeding by the brutal logic of power to the divine right of kings, and the administrators of the universities are rolling over for these new worldly gods. In October 1999, the *New York Times* reported "a growing trend in which institutions of higher education see themselves as generators of business," raising the question, "What happens if the pursuit of money competes with the pursuit of knowledge," as between, for example, a money-making engineering department and an English department? Like our elections, our political parties, and our government, our universities have been seduced and penetrated by the giant corporations.

One doesn't mean the universities are whoring—does one? Clark Kerr, the president of the University of California until he became top man at the Carnegie Commission on Higher Education, surely suggested that when he recited:

> "There was a young lady from Kent,
> Who said that she knew what it meant
> When men took her to dine,
> Gave her cocktails and wine,
> She knew what it meant—but she went."

To this, Kerr added, "I am not so sure that the universities and their presidents always knew what it meant, but one thing is certain—they went."

Thomas Jefferson's ideal university was based on "the illimitable freedom of the human mind to explore and to expose every subject susceptible of its contemplation." Today, corporate-dominated higher education in America employs a set of instruments, blunt and subtle, to discourage and suppress basic challenges to the economic system of gigantic-corporation capitalism, which I believe should be called not capitalism, but *gigantalism.* The regents and trustees govern the universities. Far from representing the people, they come disproportionately from the corporate and professional classes. Regents and trustees are the masters of the administrators, especially the academic deans who control what is taught and how and what each professor is paid, and the regents and trustees have set limits—by direct action and by sinister methods that often are difficult to either discern clearly or to resist—on what professors, especially those in the social sciences dealing with economics, power, and ethics, can teach. The professors deny they are under pressure, or avoid the taboos and teach what they can, or try to stand up to the pressure and suffer their losses, or just sell out. They have no unions or professional associations that are strong or sophisticated enough to challenge the whole systemic crisis, so they keep losing ground.

Although most college students are eighteen or older and therefore have all the constitutional rights of citizens, the university's regents or trustees and their hired administrators count heavily on the students being too busy going to class, studying, and just being with each other to worry about how their university is run. Many in the faculty simply drift into serving corporate interests, values, and projects, or stand aside for them and concentrate on their own cul-de-sacs in the academy. The university that once was the best shelter for independence and humane values, freedom from fear of ideas, and enjoyment of thinking and debate—the place where, collectively, we meditated in freedom on what kind of people and what kind of society we should be—has become instead a kind of orphanage where students look for mentors and find, as often as not, distracted corporate consultants.

In the country at large the giant, overmastering corporations dominate our jobs; our wages; our working conditions; our health care; our pensions; our farming and food; our small businesses; our book publishers; and our newspapers, magazines, radio, and television. The CEOs and major owners of the few dominant media corporations control what we, the masses, are invited in the mass media to think about each day and, far more significantly, what we are *not* invited to think about each day.

By their political contributions, the wealthy elite and the gigantic corporations control what candidates appear on television; determine who is not to be permitted to have any chance to win; select those candidates we are permitted to choose among; limit and shape what the sanctioned candidates are permitted to talk about; and then leave to us the privilege of deciding which of their marionettes we prefer.

Thus the major corporations control our government—the legislatures, the Congress, the White House, and, through the presidents' appointments, the uppermost judges of the federal judiciary. The regulatory agencies have fallen under the control of the very industries they are supposed to regulate. Our democracy has become a Potemkin village. We have all the forms of self-government in place, but the elected officials who are permitted to occupy those forms and what those officials are permitted to pass into law are controlled by the corporate oligarchy.

Corporations are taking control of the universities, too, say the professors and students in this book. Hell, if they've already got the country why shouldn't they have the universities? Why worry? Why worry?

In the round, because the top fifth of American households now get half the national income while the bottom fifth get one-twenty-fifth of it. Because the richest one out of one hundred Americans has more wealth than ninety-five out of one hundred of the rest of us. Because the average net worth of each of the four hundred richest Americans has been growing at about a million dollars a day. Because in 1999 the average big-company CEO was paid 419 times the pay of the average manufacturing worker, a gross disparity unique in the world. Because after inflation, between 1990 and 1998, average worker pay eased upward 5.5 percent while average CEO pay skyrocketed 420 percent. Because if average major-corporation CEO pay in 1998 is represented by the Washington Monument, which rises to a height of 555 feet, the

Washington Monument that represents the average full-time worker's pay is just 16 inches high.

Why worry? Because just one of us, Microsoft CEO Bill Gates, has $73 billion all by himself. How much money is that? Well, if you earned $1 million free and clear every year, you would accumulate $73 billion in seventy-three thousand years.

Because in 1999 Gates, Berkshire Hathaway's CEO Warren Buffett, and Microsoft cofounder Paul Allen—three guys you can imagine having a cup of coffee together at a small table in a cafe—had more wealth than the combined gross domestic products of the poorest forty-three nations on earth.

Because in 1999 the world's 475 billionaires, who would hardly fill up the tables in the banquet hall of a good hotel, had more wealth among them than the combined incomes of half the people on earth.

Why worry? Because three billion people live on $2 a day each or less, two billion people have no toilets, two billion people have no schools, and one out of every three people has no access whatsoever to medical care. And because universities should be the places where people are free enough to give a damn.

The university campus is the enclave, the sanctuary, the last free place where, as populist historian Howard Zinn says in his essay for this book, students are permitted to gather under a mentor who, while observing the educational probities, is free to say anything, get them to read anything, and join them in thinking and discussing anything, with the entire process sanctioned by the larger society.

The traditions and the diversity of these free places assure that no single point of view or ideology dominates. Their operating moral law, academic freedom, also guarantees, when it is respected, that important truths cannot be glossed over or suppressed and that important ideas, old or new, reactionary or visionary, which may be misrepresented, ignored, or anathematized in the outside society, can get full and fair consideration.

As the corporations conquer the universities, too, they attempt to turn students into consumers, education into training for jobs, professors into hired-out consultants and researchers, and campuses into corporate research and profit centers. All this is done on premises and through employees who are maintained at the public expense. The liberal arts don't bring in the corporate grants, so they are basically starved in the budgets prepared by the regents' administrators. After another generation or two of once-higher education at the Campus, Inc., nearly all of us, college graduates or not, may become expendable integers in a gigantalism that regards the billions of poor people on earth as no subject at all and will continue to devour the resources and foul the water and heat up the air of Mother Earth.

Fight back! That we must do. The fight is developing quickly now in the strengthening rejection of corporate domination in North America, Europe, and the Third World. Replacing gigantalism with new forms of economic and political democracy will require idealism, ideas, and youthful leadership. These will come in sufficient strength not from the unions that are necessarily grounded in the giant-corporation power system—not from small-business owners those corporations can crush, not from the former family farmers who have been turned into subcontractors for agribusiness, not from the demoralized poor, and certainly not from the bought-and-paid-for politicians. Most of all, those inspirations and youthful leadership will come from the students in our universities. That is why the struggle for the freedom and self-governance of the university is the struggle that matters the most.

The reports, articles, and essays in this book have been composed by professors and students in the very midst of social combat on what one San Francisco student group calls "The Last Front: Corporatization and the End of Public Education." Students abetted by allies among their teachers are fighting for educational standards and human values, and therefore against corporate misuses, violations, and perversions of the universities. The essays here about these struggles are not more bleatings from the intellectuals, they are primary documents in the American showdown between democracy and the mobile corporate giants who are gathering in everything they need for their perfectly objective goals of endless profit and endless growth.

In his essay, graduate student leader Thomas Reifer, of the State University of New York (SUNY) at Binghamton, repeats John Dewey's warning that healthy democratic societies must eliminate the most exclusive and dangerous oligarchy of all, the one "that attempts to monopolize the benefits of intelligence and the best methods for the profit of a few privileged ones."

Corporate influence in universities, says government professor Jeffrey Lustig of California State University (CSU), Sacramento, thwarts the development of "the kind of intelligence that makes a well-rounded person and democratic citizen possible." Donald W. and Marjorie Woodford Bray of CSU, Los Angeles, expostulate against "the corporatization trap" in U.S. higher education, and graduate student Todd Alan Price of UW–Madison reports on the role and the ulterior motive of Ameritech, a Fortune 500 company, in designing superschools in middle America.

"A university for hire is no university at all," declare Professors Henry Steck of SUNY Cortland and Michael Zweig of SUNY Stony Brook, in the course of making their strong case that traditional unions can best represent and defend college teachers against the arrayed administration and the elitist, "I'm no worker" self-image of some senior professors. "In the entrepreneurial university," they ask, "what happens to knowledge that is inconvenient to those with power and money? It cannot thrive. . . . People cannot do creative work looking over their shoulders for signals in the smiles or frowns of the rich and powerful."

The commercialization of the faculty's teaching and research—turning professors into "profit centers"—is explored by Sheila Slaughter and Larry Leslie of the Center for the Study of Higher Education at the University of Arizona. Lawrence Soley, in his essay here, illustrates the sinister implications of corporations and conservative foundations designing and funding pro-corporation courses and of corporations endowing chairs that pay professors to do research of interest to the corporations paying for it. "Universities accept funding from conservative front organizations . . . and allow their faculty positions, curricula, and research priorities to be transformed," writes Sonya Huber, a journalist and former director of the Center for Campus Organizing.

Let's sample some of the startling data regarding the corporate takeover that these writers provide. Huber shows us that U.S. and Canadian universities made almost $600 million from licenses and research sold in 1996 to corporations and that products from university research generated about $25 billion in the two countries that year. Further, more than half of university scientists who received funds from drug or biotech companies said the companies expected to influence their work. Marriott is the food contractor for more than five hundred campuses; Coke and Pepsi fight over campus "pouring rights," which can be worth more than $10 million per year at a big school. Barnes and Noble manages more than 340 campus bookstores, as University of Pennsylvania graduate student Matthew Ruben informs us. Nationwide, CEOs of corporations are the largest single group of trustees of universities. SUNY Binghamton graduate student Kevin Kniffen found twenty-four of fifty presidents of top national universities serving on corporate boards. At the personal level, there are inevitably conflicts of interest. Kniffen reports creative ideas to hold trustees at SUNY schools with corporate ties in check: requiring them to take an oath that they will uphold the university's charter; prohibiting them, and all university officers, from serving on for-profit corporate boards; and, if driven to it, forming an alternative board of trustees.

Students fighting back on the front lines are well represented in this volume. Kniffen and John E. Peck both advise students on how to conduct research about their own institutions—the administrations of universities, even public ones, are notoriously secretive about their funding from private sources and the exact facts about their spending. Ben Manski's essay constitutes a guide to student organizing—how to do it while taking into account race, gender, and class considerations that are too easily overlooked. Professor Neil Wollman suggests that students should promote among themselves a simple pledge, first proposed at Humboldt State University in California, to consider social and environmental issues in any job they might take.

In his chapter on activism against unethical investments at Stanford University, Seth Newton outlines a number of tactical suggestions, such as starting a class with a faculty sponsor that lets students research their university for credit; researching corporations one's university is invested in, engaging faculty in the work; forming an investment responsibility student group and networking with other such groups at other universities; using teach-ins, guerrilla theater, and sit-ins; and proposing to regents and trustees socially responsible investment and selective ethical purchasing regulations and the establishment of a socially responsible endowment fund alumni can support.

At Rochester Institute of Technology (RIT), long involved in collaboration with the Central Intelligence Agency, students conducted a mock trial of the president of the institute and declared him an embarrassment to the university and the human race, as educator Ali Zaidi reports here. Professor Corey Dolgon reports that activists supporting campus workers whose union was threatened at Worcester State College made it a point to leaflet and demonstrate when parents and alumni were on the campus.

A blatant for-profit, ten-year proposal of four corporations—Microsoft, Fujitsu, GTE, and Hughes—that they be locked into a $350-million-a-year technology infrastructure at the twenty-three campuses of CSU provoked an ultimately successful resistance by a multicampus coalition. This intriguing fight is recounted here by student leaders Burt Levy, Adam Martin, and Joshua Wolfson. Student Zar Ni and Professor Michael W. Apple emphasize in their account of building the Free Burma Coalition, an alliance of students and educators at UW–Madison and people in the community, the strength a movement gets by doing its research thoroughly.

Ultimately, the question of democracy is the question of governance. Universities, whether public or private, are governed—that is, ruled—by the trustees or regents who, through their administrators, have not only the right to hire and fire, but also the right not to hire. In his reflections on ideological control of the universities, Michael Parenti emphasizes that concepts of proper professorial conduct are often applied selectively against leftists. Rebuffed student demands for an elected board of regents at UW–Madison led the students to conduct a wildcat election of their own regent. The regents in place fled their own monthly meeting rather than deal with the insistence of the students' choice of a seat at the table.

Thus, writes Ben Manski in a pamphlet on the corporate takeover, "the central lesson learned in any democratic society, that all people are fit to govern," is contradicted in the university.

This book's originator and editor, Dr. Geoffry White, is a practicing psychologist and a social-action polymath. His chosen causes and his ventures in social activism embody the same broad ethical cultivation that led him to produce the systematic advocacy within these covers for the independence of higher education from corporate domination. He was drawn by compassion for a suicidal client into cofounding a nonprofit public benefit corporation for the victims of drunk driving. He has worked on California initiatives for campaign finance reform and single-payer health care. He proposes the treatment of what he calls Political Apathy Disorder with something like France's Good Samaritan Law, whereby not helping someone in trouble is considered illegal. A specialist in post-traumatic stress and compassion fatigue, White developed programs in Malawi, Africa, to help health-care workers struggling with victims of cervical cancer. Then he organized and carried out treatment training programs in the Balkans, first for Bosnian and Croatian refugees in refugee camps in Croatia, then in Sarajevo.

Now, this book. Citizens' attention comes and goes. State legislators and congresspersons come and go. And students come and go. As one student activist at RIT remarked concerning successful student resistance to an administration initiative, in three or four years, when all the current were gone, the administration would simply try again. The immortal corporations count on the inconstancy of mere individuals. So student activists might consider maintaining a print, audio, and visual record of their efforts and what they learn, an activist archive for their own university. There could be alumni associations of former student activists, an Activist Alumni Homecoming Weekend.

Perhaps the citizens of universities need a comprehensive theory of what kind of community they constitute so they can exist as genuinely self-governing subdivisions of society. In the corporate model for higher education, the regents or trustees are perceived as the boards of directors, the administrators as the trustees' managerial brigades, and the faculty and students as the grunts. Like the high incomes of corporation executives, those of top university administrators point to their supremacy over the workers. To totally reject that model for their communities, perhaps universities could reconstitute themselves as cities for education.

As I wrote in 1973, in *Our Invaded Universities*, the eighteen-year-old vote clearly signifies the extension of adult citizenship to the group between eighteen and twenty-one. All the political and constitutional rights of the people now belong (or, to those under eighteen, will soon belong) to university students—free speech, press, assembly, petition for redress of grievances, equal protection, and due process. The students are part of the body politic and the rights of the people are the rights of the students.

In the old elitist concept in Europe, students and faculty constituted "the community of scholars," and they are still the mainline members of the community of learning, the brain workers. But other campus workers and the trustees and administrators are citizens in the same city alongside the students and teachers. The locus of university democracy is the city that is the university. In the private university the self-perpetuating boards of trustees have to deal with a community whose citizens know they have the rights of self-governance—elections of the trustees, ballot initiatives on conditions of employment, impeaching derelict trustees, suing administrators who forget they work for the citizens. Likewise, in the public university the trustees appointed by the governor of the state would represent the state government in just one more of its relationships with a local community, all of whose citizens (at least those eighteen and over) have all the rights of self-government.

The university is not a corporate personnel training agency, a research subcontractor, a business, a state agency, a graft machine, or an instrument for oppressing unwelcome facts and opinions. As Jacques Barzun said, "The university is a city, or a city within a city." If our universities fail, our society probably will, too. We want not a University of Utopia, but a university worthier of our lives; not a cocoon of privilege, but a realization of the right relation between democracy and knowledge; not a survival of the master-slave relationship, but the university as the self-governing city, deriving its powers from the consent of the governed.

The largest question about educational institutions comes forward to us from ancient times. Somewhere in his *History of Education in Antiquity*, Professor H. L. Marrou observes that education in Greece and Rome was essentially passive, a bowl into which the cultures of the times and places were poured. The corporate takeover of universities is succeeding essentially because corporations are taking over society and education is still passive. The students, the faculty, and the other workers of the university can evolve now beyond the ancient cultural passivity of education, reconceive themselves as citizens of a community with self-governing rights, reject not only corporate domination but any violative intrusion from corporations or government, and proceed as active and independent communities for the cultivation of the mind, the arts and sciences, the spirit, and the just democracy. In the university city the ancient traditions of the independent university and the modern traditions of American democracy can occupy and vivify their common ground.

Such a vision is what this book is about.

Part One

POWER TENDS TO CORRUPT; CORPORATE POWER CORRUPTS ABSOLUTELY

1

THE TRICKS OF ACADEME

Lawrence C. Soley

The House Ethics Committee investigated former Speaker Newt Gingrich's teaching of a course titled "Renewing American Civilization" at Reinhardt and Kennesaw State colleges in Georgia. The course was beamed by satellite to other colleges and universities, which offered it for college credit.[1]

Gingrich's critics charged that the course's purpose was indoctrination rather than instruction. The accusations were given substance by a letter sent by Gingrich soliciting contributions for the course. The letter, sent before the controversy began, suggested that the House Speaker intended to use the course to recruit Republican activists for the 1996 campaign. "Our goal is to have 200,000 committed citizen activists nationwide before we're done," Gingrich wrote.[2]

Another solicitation letter invited corporate contributors to "participate in the course development process," and contributors like Hewlett-Packard and Scientific Atlanta were mentioned favorably during lectures. The former House Speaker described Hewlett-Packard Corporation as "one of the great companies in American history." In another lecture, Gingrich described Scientific Atlanta as "a model of the spirit of invention and discovery."

Lawrence Soley, Colnik Professor of Communication at Marquette University, is the author of *Leasing the Ivory Tower* (Boston: South End Press, 1995). An earlier version of this essay was published in *CAQ* (spring 1997) and received a "project censored" award.

Critics also charged that the course was improperly funded by a Republican political action committee and corporate contributions, which were tax deductible because they were given to a college rather than a political organization. The House Ethics Committee eventually agreed with these criticisms, and fined Gingrich $300,000 and reprimanded him for using tax-exempt contributions for political purposes.

The criticism directed at Gingrich's course and his agreements with Reinhardt and Kinnesaw State Colleges leaves the impression that arrangements such as these are unusual in academe. They aren't. In reality, colleges and universities will turn tricks for anyone with money, and about the only ones with money are corporations, corporate foundations, tycoons, and the Defense Department.

Using universities to further political or corporate objectives didn't start with Newt Gingrich. Beginning in the late 1970s, Hammermill Paper Company designed and funded courses in economics for high school teachers at Gannon University in Pennsylvania and Springfield College in Massachusetts. The courses presented economics from a pro-business perspective.

At Boston University (BU), the John M. Olin Foundation,[3] founded and funded by an ultraconservative munitions manufacturer, underwrites a journalism course, "Reporting Military Affairs." According to a former BU dean, the course is designed "to make journalists more sympathetic to the military," rather than train future journalists.

Even foreign governments and fat cats have found that a small contribution goes a long way in garnering influence on college campuses. The U.S.-Japan Foundation,[4] which is funded by Ryoichi Sasakawa, a Japanese businessman and nationalist who was jailed by the allies after World War II as a war criminal, has given grants for Japanese Studies programs to Duke University, the University of Kansas, the University of Arkansas, and other colleges. *New Republic* writer John B. Judis and *Agents of Influence* author Pat Choate maintain that this funding promotes pro-Japanese attitudes at universities.

Germany and France underwrite German and French studies courses at Harvard, Princeton, Georgetown, and other universities. And the Saudi government has recently given $5 million to Harvard, which will teach classes in Islamic law.[5]

Some of the agreements between universities and their patrons are comical. A wealthy Texas couple, seeking prestigious titles so they could impress their friends, gave $150,000 to a Harvard University–affiliated center and were thereafter appointed as lecturers at the Harvard Medical School, where they taught a psychiatry course titled "Love's Body in the Western World." Neither had a degree in psychiatry or psychology.

Most agreements between universities and their patrons have not been as harmless as the one at the Harvard Medical School. Some donors have tried and succeeded in influencing the direction of entire disciplines. For example, the John M. Olin Foundation funds programs of study in "Law and Economics" at several universities, including the University of Chicago, Yale, Stanford, Harvard, Columbia, George Mason, Georgetown, and Duke Universities. In *The Politics of the Rich and Poor*, Kevin Phillips, a Republican critic of the ultra-right, described Law and Economics as a neo-Darwinist "theology" reminiscent of the views of Herbert Spencer and William Graham Sumner. According to Phillips, Law and Economics preaches that "commercial selection processes in the marketplace could largely displace government decision-making."[6]

The movement was an extremist, fringe philosophy until the John M. Olin Foundation began underwriting programs at universities, which sometimes pay students for attending Law and Economics seminars, provide research funding to professors who use a Law and Economics framework,[7] and give monetary awards to students who write papers on Law and Economics. As a result of the Olin Foundation's sponsorship, Law and Economics has become a mainstream legal philosophy, accounting for "roughly 25% of the scholarship in the Yale, Harvard, Chicago, and Stanford law reviews," according to a study published in the *Antitrust Law and Economics Review*.[8]

Directly funding courses is just one way that corporations, millionaires and foundations wield influence at universities. Other ways include the funding of endowed chairs and the sponsoring of "research centers." Contributions to universities for these purposes, as was the case with Gingrich's course, are tax deductible.

Endowed chairs, also called *endowed professorships*, were first established by universities to honor nationally known scholars who taught at or graduated from them. For example, Harvard University's Charles Eliot Norton Professorship of Poetry honors the university's first professor of the history of art, who died in 1898. Other professorships are named for deceased alumni who bequeathed their estates to their alma maters.

Increasingly, however, endowed chairs are funded by and named for corporations, conservative foundations, and wealthy patrons rather than deceased scholars and alumni. The chairs have names such as the Bell South Professor of Education through Telecommunication (at the University of South Carolina); the Reliance Corporation Professor of Free Enterprise (at the University of Pennsylvania); the Carlson Travel Tour and Hospitality Chair (at the University of Minnesota); and the Lamar Savings Professorship of Finance (at Texas A & M), named for a defunct savings and loan whose operators were convicted of embezzling $85 million.

Most of these endowed professorships come with strings attached. The initial agreement between the University of Pennsylvania and Saul Steinberg, head of the Reliance Corporation, stipulated that the Reliance Corporation Professor of Free Enterprise was to be "a spokesperson for the free enterprise system" and engage "twice a year in employee training or another aspect of Reliance operations."[9]

The Carlson Chair at the University of Minnesota was endowed by the owner of the Carlson Travel Network,[10] the university's preferred travel agency. The endowment provides money for the Carlson Chair to do research on issues of interest to the travel industry. Arnold Hewes, the executive vice president of the Minnesota Restaurant, Hotel, and Resort Associations, praised this research funding, saying, "We'll have data on who comes to Minnesota and why; why people fail to return; and other statistics that we need to make decisions about advertising, marketing, and promotion."

Cal Bradford, a former fellow at the University of Minnesota's Humphrey Institute for Public Policy, is critical of endowed professorships, saying that such funding determines "what universities will teach and research, what direction the university will take. If universities would decide that they needed an endowed chair in English, and then try to raise the money for it, it would be one thing. But that's not what happens. Corporate donors decide to fund chairs in areas that they want research done. Their decisions determine which topics universities explore and which aren't [explored]." Bradford's contract at the University of Minnesota wasn't renewed after he criticized university-corporate ties.[11]

Research centers also allow well-heeled patrons to influence universities. A research center is typically funded by a single corporation or tycoon and bears the name of its sponsor. The University of Wisconsin–Milwaukee houses the Johnson Controls Institute for Environmental Quality in Architecture, which is funded by Johnson Controls, Inc., a manufacturer of electrical controls for heating and air conditioning. Johnson Controls provides $200,000 a year to support the center, whose professors work on research projects of interest to the corporation. A company spokesperson said the purpose of the institute is to discover how "workers and students can be more productive when a building's heating, cooling, lighting and sound systems are properly controlled."[12]

Southern Methodist University in Dallas is home to the Maguire Oil and Gas Institute, named for and funded by Cary M. Maguire, the CEO of the Maguire Oil Company. The institute's purpose "is to advance productive working relations with key industrial and government leaders, and with academic departments and programs."[13] The institute achieves this goal by producing reports such as "Oil and Environmentalism Do

Mix," which laments that "instead of harmonizing oil and gas discoveries with environmental goals, [environmental laws] have resulted in an extravagant amount of federal land being placed off-limits to oil and gas leasing. Experience in Alaska, Michigan, and Wyoming shows that oil and gas activity, with proper care and supervision, can be compatible with the environment." Such opinionated writings gain an aura of objectivity because they are produced at universities rather than corporate public-relations departments.

Most universities have similar centers. The University of Utah is home to the Garn Institute of Finance, which functions as a psuedononymous lobby group for the banks and savings and loans (S & Ls) that fund it. The institute is named for former Senator Jake Garn,[14] who cowrote the legis-lation that deregulated the S & L industry, opening it to recklessness and fraud. The Garn Institute's chairman is Richard T. Pratt of Merrill Lynch Mortgage Capital, who was President Reagan's first head of the Federal Home Loan Bank Board, which oversaw S & Ls. In *The Greatest Bank Robbery Ever*, author Martin Meyer wrote that Pratt "had fired the guards and suspended the rules. If you had to pick one individual to blame for what happened to the S & Ls and to hundreds of billions of dollars in tax-payer money, Dick would get the honor without even campaigning."

The University of Minnesota houses the *China Times* Center for Media and Social Studies, which seeks "humbly to promote China's democracy."[15] The center's funding comes from Taiwan, China's arch-enemy, and it is named for Taiwan's largest circulation, progovernment newspaper, owned by a member of the central committee of Taiwan's ruling Kuomintang political party.

To help Taiwan achieve its objectives of embarrassing and isolating its enemy, the center sponsors conferences and research critical of China, and its associates pump out articles condemning China's policies. On a sab-batical leave in Hong Kong, a professor associated with the *China Times* Center wrote numerous articles criticizing China's impending takeover of Hong Kong. His articles assert that "the party will be over at one minute after midnight," when the Communists come in. The professor boasts that his writings have probably put him on China's blacklist.[16]

The funding of research centers, endowed chairs, and courses of study are just three ways that corporations, business mandarins, and for-eign countries exert influence at universities. They exercise their influ-ence in many other ways, too, such as hiring professors as consultants and contracting with universities for research. Although all of these practices are widespread, magazines and newspapers have been silent about corpo-rate-university relations; instead, they have dwelled on the issue of "polit-ical correctness." One explanation for the media's silence about corporate investments is that numerous media corporations, including Knight-Ridder, the *New York Times*, and the Belo and Cowles Corporations, have themselves invested money in universities. Many of their investments in academia have paid off. For example, at the University of Texas at Austin, the dean of the College of Communication ordered the chair of the Department of Journalism not to testify in a lawsuit against the owner of the *Dallas News*, the Belo Corporation, which had donated $300,000 to the University of Texas's College of Communication. The lawsuit stemmed from Belo's alleged unfair business practices, which drove the competing Dallas *Times Herald* out of business. Maxwell McCombs, the journalism department chair, had studied the effects that the *Dallas News'* monopoly on popular syndicated features had on the *Times Herald*.

To rationalize his order, the dean dipped into his academic bag of tricks, saying, "There is an unwritten rule in the Department of Journalism, and the college in general, that says a professor should not testify in a trial against a newspaper."

There is another unwritten rule in academe, which explains why universities now attend to the interests of their well-heeled patrons rather than students. It's the old adage, "Whoever pays the piper calls the tune."

NOTES

1. Timothy Mescon, dean of Kennesaw's business school, claims that he recruited Gingrich to teach the class. Mescon's father, Michael, was a former dean and free enterprise chair holder at Georgia State before retiring to set up the Mescon Group, a consulting firm with ties to Gingrich; see Doug Cumming, "Newt Gingrich at Kennesaw State," *Atlanta Journal and Constitution*, September 19, 1993, p. F1. Kennesaw's business school also houses the Georgia Cobb Free Enterprise Chair.

2. Charles Walston, "Gingrich College Class Raises Questions," *Atlanta Journal and Constitution*, September 2, 1993, p. A1.

3. The John M. Olin Foundation is one of six conservative foundations that collectively have assets of about $925 million and pour about $40 million annually into conservative on- and off-campus think tanks, many of which promote the idea that political correctness, rather than corporate influence, is rampant on college campuses. The other foundations that fund the think tanks are the Sarah Scaife, Smith Richardson, J. M. Earhart, and Lynde and Harry Bradley Foundations.

4. *The Center for International Security and Strategic Studies Annual Report 1990* (Mississippi State, Miss.: Mississippi State University, 1991), p. 2.

5. "Saudi Gift Sets Up Islamic Law Center," *New York Times*, June 11, 1993, p. B8.

6. Kevin Phillips, *The Politics of Rich and Poor* (New York: Random House, 1990), p. 65. Phillips further relates, "One intellectual frontiersman,

Richard Posner, University of Chicago law professor turned federal appeals court judge . . . suggested making a market for babies so that it would be easier for couples to adopt. A second prominent Chicago legalist, Richard A. Epstein, leader of the movement's 'economic rights' faction, deplored most government economics regulation as unconstitutional." Phillips contends that the Law and Economics movement was a fringe ideology before Reagan's inauguration, but has since moved into the mainstream.

7. John M. Olin Progam in Law and Economics, *1989–90 Annual Report* (Stanford, Calif.: Stanford Law School, n.d.).

8. Nan Aron, Barbara Moulten, and Chris Owens, "Economics, Academia, and Corporate Money in America: The 'Law and Economics' Movement," *Antitrust Law and Economics Review* (1993): 27–42.

9. From the Chair, Senate, "Documents Relating to the Endowment of the Reliance Professorship/Deanship," *Almanac*, January 27, 1981, p. 3. As a result of faculty protests at the University of Pennsylvania, the wording of the agreement between Steinberg and the university was eventually changed.

10. Mike Kaszuba, "Critics Say Gift Influenced 'U' Choice of Travel Agency," *Minnesota Star Tribune*, July 9, 1990, p. 3B.

11. Telephone interview with Cal Bradford, February 12, 1992.

12. Johnson Controls, Inc., *Company Fact Sheet* (Milwaukee: Johnson Controls, 1993), p. 2. James Keyes is also a trustee of Marquette University.

13. *Graduate Bulletin of Southern Methodist University* (Dallas: Southern Methodist University, 1992), pp. 101–102.

14. Steven Pizzo, "Utah Officials Hit on S & Ls" *National Mortgage News*, March 23, 1992, p. 1.

15. *Messenger, Report from the* China Times *Center for Media and Social Studies*, August 1, 1990, p. 1

16. Brenda Rotherham, "China to Offer Veneer of Reform, Scholar Says," *Minneapolis Star Tribune*, October 8, 1989, p. 13A. In May 1991, Taiwan's president, Lee Teng-hui, terminated the "Period of National Mobilization for the Suppression of the Communist Rebellion," which reduced the level of hostility between Taiwan and China.

2

THE GOODS AT THEIR WORST
Campus Procurement
in the Global Pillage

Kevin Kniffin

INTRODUCTION

"**F**ollowing the money" is a time-honored tradition among investigative reporters. Similarly, campus-based investigators are increasingly "following the university T-shirts," "following the college gift register," and "following the coffee." Creating consciousness about the university's consumption patterns is a way in which students and other community members are moving toward local change while simultaneously getting more acquainted (if not involved) with broader political-economic pressures.

As mergers, acquisitions, downsizing, and outsourcing have become the most recent "fashions" in the business world, so it is in the university world. Indeed, the contributions to this volume should suffice to prove the point to doubters that "the campus" is increasingly a part of the business world. The fact that at least one university, on the heels of its "Renaissance Program," recently transformed one of its student affairs offices into a "Customer Service Department" represents only one tip of the profit iceberg that increasingly encroaches upon the space of the campus.[1]

BRANDS MARK THE DAY

Ever since Spike Lee's Air Jordan™ commercials, it has been an American fixation to look at other people's sneakers—and the logos that appear on them. This preoccupation, in fact, would appear to be largely responsible for the steep increase in sneaker prices over the past two decades. As advertisers have basked in the growth of this industry, stories about people killing others for "the right sneakers" have been seen on television newscasts in many large American cities.

Universities have fallen to this fashion as well. Always looking to create new "revenue streams," universities have become welcome hosts over the past decade as companies such as Nike and Reebok compete to expand their relative market shares. In exchange for forcing all of its student-athletes to wear Brand X, the school receives a kickback as determined in a contract with the logo company. In short, the school administrators are selling advertising space on the shoes of their players and on their uniform sleeves. The corporations pay for this kind of advertising with the hundreds of millions of dollars in their advertising budgets—an amount that often stands in stark contrast to their allowances for the needs of the workers who make the company's products.

The Nike Corporation is sometimes described in its bare bones as a marketing and design company. Shoes were manufactured in Maine and New Hampshire in the 1980s, but since then, Nike has subcontracted almost all of its manufacturing outside the United States.[2] It is this organizational division that Nike and other such conglomerates have invoked as a division of responsibility. They retain control of the cultural capital of the logo while the raw materials are assembled by others in conditions typically disavowed by the logo companies.

Indeed, behind the veneer of Nike's slick advertising is a complex of stories that would offend most believers in any kind of universal human right to dignity. For example, in China, the British-based group Christian Aid has estimated that Nike and other shoe companies spend an average of less than 4 percent of the retail price of their shoes on manufacturing labor costs.[3] In spite of Nike's outspoken support of women's sports, an International Labor Organization study found that in Indonesia, 88 percent of the Nike workers making the minimum wage—most of whom are women—are malnourished.[4] Reporting on conditions elsewhere in the Nike pseudoempire, an Ernst and Young survey found air inside factories containing levels of the carcinogen toluene that were between 24 and 708 times higher than levels accepted under U.S. laws.[5] And Thuyen Nguyen of Vietnam Labor Watch related an incident—on International Women's Day—in which a Vietnamese manager took out his entire crew of fifty-

six female workers and made them run laps around the factory because
some of them did not follow the factory's dress code. Bob Herbert
reported that twelve of the women collapsed before the manager relented
the punishment.[6]

For its part, Reebok is sure not to be left behind in the rush to slap
logos on the buildings and residents of the ivory tower. At the University
of Wisconsin (UW)–Madison, Reebok attempted to buy the freedom of
speech of UW student-athletes and coaches. Not content with being
allowed to brand all student-athletes with its logo, Reebok wanted the
UW board of regents to agree that coaches from UW would not be
allowed to make any disparaging comments about Reebok or any of its
employees. As is often—but by no means always—the case, however,
once enough noise was made by community members, UW chancellor
David Ward announced the deletion of the clause.[7]

Even without the infamous no-disparagement clause, the main body
of the UW-Reebok contract maintains that "Teams, Coaches, and Staff
shall use Endorsed Goods exclusively during all athletic workouts, practices, tournaments, games, exhibitions, media interviews, and at all other
events and public appearances when it is reasonable and appropriate or
customary to wear athletic apparel or footwear." In fact, *only* if the stu-
dent-athlete has a doctor's note about a foot problem that Reebok considers itself unable to accommodate, may non-Reebok shoes be worn and
then only if the competitor's logo is sufficiently hidden from public view.
When asked how such rules are enforced, Vince Sweeny, UW's lead
negotiator, remarked that since the contract is still relatively new, the university has yet to become the "logo cops"[8] implied by the contract.

As with many of the fashionable partnerships between universities
and big corporations, UW and other universities receive monies in addition to free sporting goods from companies such as Nike and Reebok.
Lowell Reese, however, has written that about 90 percent of the monies
paid by Nike to the University of Kentucky will be disbursed in the basketball and football programs—primarily to supplement coaches'
salaries.[9] University athletic departments do not need the money from the
big contracts; instead, it appears to be the runaway marketing costs and
salary increases for college athletics that is fed by the revenue chasing.
One basketball coach, Georgetown's John Thompson, has been more
directly a part of Nike in his role, shared with two other university professors, on the board of directors of Nike.

At the University of Oregon (UO), Philip Knight's alma mater, Nike
has endowed professorial chairs, sponsored building construction, and
involved the university's athletic program in a multimillion-dollar sponsorship deal. Julia Fox, a UO sociology instructor, is critical of these ties

with Nike. Fox believes that the acceptance of major donations weakens the integrity of the university and constrains the university's missions. Citing a specific case, Fox recounted an organizational meeting for a conference on labor at UO in which the planners decided that talking about Nike labor rights would not be wise given the university president's recent acceptance of so many Nike dollars.[10] Fox argues that such constraint infringes upon the needs of the university to have no limits to its critical approaches.

In more common but lower-profile relations, universities give companies, such as the College Licensing Company (CLC), permission to make official university apparel in return for an agreed-upon fee. Indeed, since the CLC is the licensing agent for more than 150 universities, and since relatively few other companies are licensed to distribute college apparel, students and others concerned about sweatshop labor have often had a shared target. Other contributions to this volume will make clear that United Students Against Sweatshops (USAS) appears to have emerged in a rather short period of time as a vigorous national group whose primary mission is taking on these fights. The efforts of people involved in this group have already gained national attention for the issues at hand, as well as major steps toward full disclosure of the manufacturing plants used for college apparel.

THE BOOK CORPORATION

College students represent a captive market for booksellers. Given that books are required for almost every college course, there is an attendant need for booksellers on or near campuses. Increasingly, however, one company is trying to fill that need at every campus across the nation. Barnes and Noble (B&N) College Bookstores presently operates on approximately 350 campuses, having increased at a steady rate of fifteen to twenty new colonies in each of the last ten years. It is the effects of this kind of growth, both on campuses and off, that prompted the 1998 lawsuit filed by the American Booksellers Association (representing about thirty-five hundred independent stores) against Barnes and Noble and Borders (which each operate about one thousand stores) for antitrust practices.[11] In response to this kind of criticism, CEO Len Riggio, who holds 90 percent of the B&N College corporation (which is separate from Barnes and Noble Inc.) told *Business Week*, "I don't shed a tear for the little guy."[12]

B&N College Bookstores' marketing director, Stan Frank, considers the chain a service to most universities.[13] Frank says that the chain can almost always give the university more money than it is already making, because the B&N expertise helps them to sell more per square foot once the company takes over. Frank states that "there's hardly any reason why a school should run [the bookstore]" except, perhaps, for pride. What is often not questioned in this worldview, however, is obsession with the bottom line. Barnes and Noble often can pay more in rent for bookstore space than local cooperatives, but the assumption that more is better should not be taken for granted—for example, nonlocal ownership usually translates to increased capital flight from local communities. Frank credits much of B&N's growth to the fact that "the idea of privatization has taken off." The effects of privatization with regard to wealth distribution, diversity of selection, and labor rights are not addressed.

While Barnes and Noble may have a more direct line to professors ordering books, it is often the case that there are off-campus options for professors and others to place their orders. At the University of Pennsylvania, however, the primary competition to the new, "official" Barnes and Noble bookstore is being displaced by the university trustees. The independently owned and operated Penn Book Center is located on property owned by the university, property the trustees now want to free for development. The co-owner, a Penn alum, says that the rent for the new location offered by the trustees for his store is prohibitively expensive and claims that the university is effectively putting his shop out of business. Former English department chair John Richetti told the *Philadelphia Inquirer,* "I am outraged by the university's indifference to the fostering of intellectual life. This is a big campus with many students, and this means one of two independent bookstores will be forced to shut down. This is just corporate gangsterism."[14]

MALLING THE COMMONS

The model for Barnes and Noble's presence on campuses may well be the campus branch of Marriott Management Services (MMS). Following a merger in early 1998 with the North American branch of Sodexho, a French-based food services conglomerate, the new entity, which services nine hundred campuses, is called Sodexho Marriott. In addition to its reputation in food services, Judith Evans reports that the new company recently signed a contract with the Virginia State University that gives Sodexho Marriott the job of building maintenance for the campus.[15] Following this merger, many analysts predict that Sodexho Marriott will aggressively pursue greater market penetration in the next decade in the "outsourcing industry."

Simply dealing with the company's current market reach, however, is not a matter of simple math. Given that there were only 3,706 colleges and universities in the United States in 1995, and more specifically, 2,244 four-year colleges and universities,[16] one can estimate Sodexho Marriott's market share to be somewhere around 24–40 percent. This rough calculation is necessary because Sodexho Marriott claims that market share is proprietary information and would not confirm a figure.[17] Max B. Sawicki and Alex Molnar identify this kind of thinking as one of the more general problems of outsourcing. Stressing the importance of information about private vendors seeking public business, the authors state that "[i]n a democratic society, such information is the basis for open evaluation and discussion. Confidentiality of such information is thus the bane of informed, effective, democratic decision-making."[18] In the case of Sodexho Marriott, knowing the company's market share would, among other things, provide new and current clients with increased leverage to demand discounts based on the company's economy of scale.

Comfortable with their capture of the market, Sodexho Marriott's Web page, like the pre-merger MMS page, touts the company's service as creating "an environment that offers students the quality, value, convenience and excitement of mall-style dining, pizza delivery, branded catering and other *off campus revenue robbers*, giving students what they want right on campus."[19] With this criminalization of independent, off-campus entrepreneurs, the rhetoric of inclusiveness, diversity, and tolerance preached by the university administrators with whom Sodexho Marriott is so popular suddenly rings hollow.

Likewise, the "open competition" administrators cite when asked why Sodexho Marriott is on campus is a weak concept. The usual scenario is that universities send out a request for proposals (RFP) for a company to service the entire university. Since this requires a very large and diversified company, local entrepreneurs often cannot compete. The result is that Sodexho Marriott (and sometimes Aramark and a few other companies) is the only viable competitor. If the RFP were framed differently, the competition would thrive, diversity would reign, and more monies would remain in the local economy as local community members are given more stake in the nonprofit, non-tax-paying campus.

Sodexho has very little history in the United States, but San Francisco Local 2 of the Hotel Employees and Restaurant Employees Union (HERE) has produced an excellent background history on the Marriott "family" of corporations. Identifying Marriott as the sixteenth largest employer in the United States, the HERE pamphlet also reports that Marriott International contributed $25,000 to the "Alliance to Protect Small Businesses and Jobs" in 1996, when champions of capital were working to stop a ballot initiative to raise the minimum wage in California. Writing about Marriott's successful plays to gain tax credits for its head-quarters in Maryland, Russell Mokhiber and Robert Weissman argue that because such credits typically have a direct effect on school budgets, it is fair in this regard to compare Marriott to a bully who is taking others' lunch money.[20] Sodexho Marriott's major role as a lead investor of the private prison industry is also deeply problematic, but not surprising, in these contexts.

Not only is 51 percent of Sodexho Marriott's corporate "parentage" known for its aggressive antiunionism, but the company is also closely aligned with partisan interests typically considered inimical to support for education. In 1996, for example, various members of the Marriott family made donations of more than $250,000 to Republicrat politicians, typically of the Republican persuasion. This is not surprising, but is nonetheless indicative of the role that this food services empire plays in a broader context. The idea of privatization gaining popularity has not happened in a vacuum; instead, we see clearly that the Marriott family is one of the companies paying for that popularity, which is being sold very cheaply by "public" servants on Capitol Hill.

"I'D LIKE TO BUY THE WORLD A COKE"

Soda companies are also chomping to gain relative advantages in the "schools market." An article in the March 10, 1998, *New York Times* features the increasingly aggressive attempts by cola bottlers to gain exclusive access to students in public school districts.[21] Winning brand loyalty to phosphoric-acid, tooth-rotting concoctions at an early age is the noble goal driving the game. To that end, companies attempt to lure people unsure about the "partnership" into thinking that the perks make the compromise worthwhile—for example, in one case, a car was awarded to a high school senior with perfect attendance and high grades. Despite the millions involved in the deals, Marianne Manilov of the Center for Commercial-Free Public Education says "When you break down [the company's offer], it is nothing [per student/young undecided consumer]."[22]

In addition to contracts gained for exclusive pouring rights on campus, Coke and Pepsi (and sometimes other companies) also invite curricular changes with essay contests and other "innovative" programs designed to get elementary and high school students to do the marketing for the multinational. In fact, Michael Cameron was suspended from Greenbrier High School in Evans, Georgia, on March 20, 1998, for unveiling a Pepsi T-shirt on a day that the school principal had designated

"Coke Day." The principal was hoping for an elusive $10,000 prize from Coca-Cola in exchange for showing the tooth-decay marketeers that his students were the most loyal and creative Coke advocates. Despite the principal's claims that this "was not a Coke-Pepsi thing," the facts illustrate a school desperate for funds and overly anxious about freedom of speech when companies like Coke are looking to buy the thought-space of the students.[23] As a poster from the Center for Commercial-Free Public Education (CCFPE) states, "Our children should be treated as future leaders, not future consumers—these deals are stealing away classroom time and replacing it with corporate indoctrination. Students need more quality education, more reading, more real math and science skills—not more advertising."

Two recent cases near Binghamton, New York, illustrate the issues that are repeated across the country in one form or another. In the winter 1998–1999, after significant public debate, a local school district's board voted down a proposed agreement with either Coke or Pepsi for exclusive access to its campuses. The superintendent stated that he was "not comfortable initiating contracts which have brand recognition as a primary motive."[24] At approximately the same time, the nearest center of public higher education, the State University of New York at Binghamton, was entering agreements with PespiCo that, among other things, allowed for the company to plaster its logo on a new baseball-field scoreboard. The university's decision, unlike the local school district's vote, was not informed by anything resembling widespread public debate.

At the University of Minnesota (UM), Twin Cities campus, a contract was signed with the Miller Brewing Company in 1994 that allowed Miller to use the UM mascot in its advertisements. When the contract recently came up for renewal, however, McKinley Boston, the vice-president for student development and intercollegiate athletics for the UM system, said the relationship would be ending. Boston said, "I just felt like we were sending students a mixed message."[25] While the National Collegiate Athletic Association (NCAA) does not presently have any plans to sever this kind of university relationship with corporations that promote and sell alcoholic beverages, an increasing number of schools, including the University of North Carolina at Chapel Hill, Brigham Young, and California State University, Fresno, are quitting the habit on their own initiative after being pressed to recognize the harms that can be caused by alcohol abuse—a situation arguably fostered by advertising images of college students drinking alcoholic beverages.

"THERE'S NO SUCH THING AS A FREE LUNCH"

Using sneakers and other "giveaways" as their wedges, corporations are increasingly encroaching upon the space of universities. Given the narrow, profit-oriented goals that dictate a corporation's actions, one may be well served to know the saying that "gifts make slaves like whips make dogs." This saying is indicative of a human universal: Whether it's campaign financing or university-industry relations, gifts make the receiver beholden in specific ways. Another way of saying it is, "He who pays the piper calls the tune."

Nowhere might this relationship be clearer than Channel One's offer of free audiovisual equipment in return for free access to adolescents' open minds. CCFPE reports that 40 percent of U.S. middle and high school classrooms presently have contracts with Channel One that mandate two minutes of advertising each day. The total time required by the not-so-special "news" coverage of Channel One takes the equivalent of six school days each year, which Molnar and Sawicki estimate to be a cost of $1.8 billion in lost (or sold) instructional time each year. The $17,000 worth of audiovisual equipment and regular maintenance that these schools have sold out for amounts to no more than $2,000 per year.[26] In turn, Channel One reportedly charges its client advertisers approximately $200,000 per thirty-second commercial.

Despite the 40 percent market share owned by Channel One, the CCFPE and other groups around the country have successfully resisted many of these kinds of encroachments into taxpayer-subsidized public spaces. For example, New York State remains the largest untapped market for Chris Whittle's "direct pipeline" to teenage consumers (as Channel One is pitched to potential advertisers). Because of protests against the profiteers, the New York State Board of Regents has made it illegal for public school boards in the state to sign on with Channel One.

Indicative of constant tension on this issue, however, is the fact that the trustees of the State University of New York (SUNY) have orchestrated an end run around the regulations and agreed to produce some special college programs with Channel One, "the leading provider of news and information-based programming to young people."[28] This backdoor loan of support to Channel One would seem to be evidence of the ways in which money-rich lobbying pressures can find the TV network friends. In fact, the SUNY press release on this matter describes Channel One in detail with no mention of commercials, profits, or restrictions on its "twelve-minute program" reaching youth in New York State public schools.

Channel One may have some competition soon, however. As the

Internet begins to replace television as the primary information medium, a new company called ZapMe has emerged. ZapMe effectively applies the Channel One model of free equipment in exchange for mandatory advertisements to the Internet. Schools contracted with ZapMe must actively use the company's browser for at least four hours each day. In return for "helping" to wire the nation's classrooms, the company sells advertising that remains in the corner of the browser for the duration of its use.[28] A less obvious but still relevant case of possible "strings-attached" free gifts can be found in the $4.1 million in contributions made to the SUNY system over the past decade in an attempt to foster the development of computer-based long-distance learning systems.[29] The donations have come from the Sloan Foundation—whose current president is director of a multinational computer equipment company and a former senior researcher at IBM. To some people, this kind of gift—in which universities are given awards to make signficant changes in direction with little reason to expect the award will continue once the change is complete—is reminiscent of a protracted and indirect bait-and-switch.

The California State University (CSU) system was recently the focus of a consortium of corporations, including Microsoft, GTE, Fujitsu, and Hughes, that wanted to set up the California Educational Technology Initiative (CETI), a for-profit organization that would service the twenty-three-campus university system under a ten-year contract.[30] Because the proposed partnership was much more intimate than a traditional vendor/customer relationship, the plan was a target of outrage among people who considered it more appropriately tagged the "Corporate Educational Takeover Initiative."[31] CSU administrators claimed that the lack of state support was an underlying reason for negotiating a contract, but students, faculty, and other citizens made it clear that selling the integrity of the university was not a legitimate source of revenue.

THE CAMPUS SHOPPING CHANNEL

Credit card companies need not worry about finding new customers on the campuses of the City University of New York (CUNY), where administrators are phasing in new ID cards on which the CUNY logo—and Citibank's logo—are displayed. Under this arrangement, the new student ID cards may also be used as Citibank ATM cards upon written agreement of the student/customer. With approximately two hundred thousand students, CUNY's twenty-one campuses provide a large, captive audience for Citibank. Dean Stojkovic reported that Baruch College students and staffers were upset because after the new ID cards were introduced,

Citibank adopted a more stringent check cashing policy and refused to cash CUNY checks—even those underwritten by Citibank—for individuals who did not have an account with the bank.[33]

CUNY's arrangement with Citibank may be new, but it is by no means special. Over the past decade, hundreds of schools have "upgraded" their ID cards to provide a variety of conveniences to the students. The result is a proliferation of agreements between universities, banks, and long-distance telephone carriers that provide the companies with advertising on ID cards, and some basic infrastructure (for example, magnetic strips in the cards) that requires activation in the form of a few signatures, to be transformed into ATM or credit cards.

These mergers evoke concerns not simply because they narrow the think-space of the university's students, but because the university becomes forced by the contract to promote Company X in a very intimate way. These ties symbolically bind the university to the corporation on the ID card, but they are also bound in other ways. One subtle technique to make the distance between the campus and corporate headquarters seem shorter has been employed at SUNY Albany, where those with questions about their campus-based Citibank accounts are directed to a phone number whose last four digits are identified as "SUNY." Indeed, the state's own SUNY Card Web page provides a link to the homepage of MCI WorldCom, another "partner" corporation advertised on the card.

Absent the luxuries offered to the companies involved with the ID card systems, credit card companies remain vigilant in their struggles to gain as many new customers as possible. One strategy is to "help" student groups through companies such as Campus Dimensions, a business focused on giving modest "finder fees" to student groups in return for space and support peddling credit cards for major banks on campus.[34] Used in place of more traditional fund-raisers such as bake sales and walk-a-thons, Campus Dimensions' reach of more than one thousand campuses is evidence of its increasing presence on campus.

At Louisiana Tech, however, administrators abided by a student government resolution calling for a ban on credit card sales on campus.[35] While this was reported in *Business Week* as a defensive move against corporations on campus, it is worth noting that the university's foundation did not stop marketing and sales of its own credit card for alums and other campus supporters. Clearly, extricating educational institutions from corporations cannot be done overnight. Banning the profiteers from the physical campus is a first step, but enforcing a more complete and consistent division between education and profit requires another set of steps.

In answer to the basic question of why universities should have *any* relations with credit card companies, there are many who see the need for a significant retreat. Charging that the companies extend credit lines to students who often don't have the income to pay the bills, Georgetown University sociologist Robert Manning has stated that the marketing of credit cards on campuses "now poses a greater threat than alcohol or sexually transmitted diseases."[36] Regardless of the extent to which Manning's comments may be hyperbolic, the stress caused by credit card debt, particularly for income-poor students, is identified by some as an important motivating factor in at least two recent suicides.[37]

CONSTRUCTIVE PURCHASES AND NONPURCHASES

"Your consumption is complicity" is a phrase often used to exhort people to boycott Company X or Product W. One would think, though, that the phrase could be used for the exact opposite end. In other words, sometimes complicity is a valued trait.

Coffee, for example, presents itself as an interesting industry where dominant brands are part of concentrated and powerful multinational conglomerates, but also where there are a growing number of independent companies attempting to compete using a different model of business. A dominant coffee in the market is Maxwell House, a subsidiary of the nicotine-centered Philip Morris Companies. A coffee of choice among people actively concerned with the labor and environmental conditions of coffee growers is distributed by Equal Exchange, a firm founded in the 1980s on the principle of fair trade. Equal Exchange prides itself on dealing with small-scale, democratic farming cooperatives (which sometimes practice organic agriculture) in a way that contrasts sharply with many of its competitors. For these reasons, community members at a host of university and college campuses in North America have pushed for the on-campus sale of Equal Exchange coffee. Among the schools now offering the coffee are Evergreen State College in Washington, Brown University, and SUNY Binghamton.

The problem for university administrators with a case such as this is the fear that once the university aligns itself with any company that is explicit about its labor and environmental practices, then the university will be more easily pressed to make such matters an important consideration in other consumption patterns. Campus groups, however, are increasingly demanding such relations be made explicit. Once this is done, it is a rare person who will stand up for sweatshops or actively endorse union-busting corporate thugs.

While this essay addresses some of the items presently being handled by concerned parties, it could very easily be expanded to include other items of debate, including (in no particular order): recycled paper and recycling practices; computer software giveaways and contracts; computer hardware purchases; energy efficiency, sources, and costs; research grants from private corporations and/or the Department of Defense; food items (such as table grapes or vegetable burgers) that either are or have been the object of boycotts; trash-hauling arrangements; corporate advertisements on classroom and hallway bulletin boards; transportation arrangements; water quality and cost; and pesticides on campus lawns and campus food. All of these issues are being analyzed by students and other researchers, aware of the basic tendency for managers of profit to pervert goods unless kept under close watch.

Recent cases of doctors being paid to administer clinical trials for experimental drugs pays testimony to the facts that (1) the university as intended does not serve as a research and development branch for industry and (2) the influence of coercive temptations on research practices can lead to ill-based findings. As Kurt Eichenwald and Gina Kolata point out, drug companies, increasingly tired of the regulations that bind the university research community, are pushing clinical trials toward doctors' private practices.[38] Eichenwald and Kolata report that at least one case of extensive fraud paid doctors up to five thousand dollars for each patient they introducted into the trials.[39]

It is in a similar spirit that people object to corporations extending their reaches onto university campuses. A handful of major conglomerates already own most major news agencies in the United States, and they are anxiously pressing to grab pieces of the only institution even dreamed to be a place of independent and free thinking: the university. This grab is appearing (and sometimes disappearing) on many fronts.

Daniel Noah Moses has written about the encroachment of commercial enterprises on the university, noting some resemblance between today's campuses and airport shopping malls.[40] Indeed, the university-as-real-estate-broker metaphor does appear increasingly valid given the norm that corporations such as Sodexho Marriott, Barnes and Noble, and others are typically charged "rent" for use of the campus premises. Unfortunately, the university-as-curriculum-broker also carries increasing weight. Based on current practices, it is not too difficult to imagine an educational institution where Unocal donates teachers and books about geology, McDonald's handles nutrition and anthropology, and General Motors presents its treatment of transportation systems. Indeed, students in this "company town" could purchase food, books, and official university apparel through the "universityX.com" Web site using their university-sponsored credit cards. Interested nonstudents will be able to trade the stocks they own in various for-profit university chains, some of which have already popped up (for example, the so-called University of Phoenix). Whether these pressures will be stemmed or turned is a question and challenge open to people who find them ill-conceived and socially disastrous. The imagination of such a situation is most definitely idealistic—and not realistic. The question of whether these ideals—or others—will motivate our educational institutions in the future is being answered today.

NOTES

1. Daniel Noah Moses, "Distinguishing a University from a Shopping Mall," *Thought and Action* (spring 1999): p. 95

2. Jeff Ballinger, personal communication, 1998.

3. John C. Ryan and Alan Thein Durning, "The Story of a Shoe," *Worldwatch* (1998): 29; Christian Aid [online] http://www.oneworld.org/christian_aid/global_shoe.html.

4. Bernard Sanders, "Congressman Bernie Sanders Responds to a Letter from Nike CEO Phil Knight," press release, November 19, 1997.

5. Steven Greenhouse, "Nike Shoe Plant in Vietnam is Called Unsafe for Workers," *New York Times*, November 11, 1997, p. A1.

6. Bob Herbert, "In America: Brutality in Vietnam," *New York Times*, March 28, 1997.

7. "Campus Fight Leads Reebok to Modify Shoe Contract," *New York Times*, June 28, 1996.

8. Vince Sweeny, personal communication, 1997.

9. Lowell Reese, "University of Kentucky Embraces Nike Despite Human Rights Record." *Kentucky Gazette* 2, no. 14 (1998): 1.

10. Julia Fox, "Leasing the Ivory Tower: What are the implications of financial constraints at the University of Oregon?" presented at the Race, Work, and Economic Justice Conference, University of Oregon, April 4, 1998.

11. James O. Clifford, "Chain Store Booksellers Face Antitrust Lawsuit," *Press and Sun Bulletin*, March 19, 1998.

12. Jeanne I. Dugan, "The Baron of Books," *Business Week*, June 29, 1998, pp. 109–15.

13. Steven Frank, personal communication, 1998.

14. Stephan Salisbury, "Penn Book Center Prepared to Close," *Philadelphia Inquirer*, June 6, 1998.

15. Judith Evans, "Sodexho, Marriott: Together; They Hope to Run the Show," *Washington Post*, July 9, 1998, p. E1.

16. "Higher Education—Summary: 1970–1995," *Statistical Abstract of the United States* (1997), table 287, p. 183.

17. Kathy Boyle, personal communication, 1998.

18. Max B. Sawicki and Alex Molnar, "The Hidden Costs of Channel One: Estimates for the Fifty States," report, Center for Commercial-Free Public Education, 1998.

19. Online at http://sodexhomarriott.com/education/campusdine.html; emphasis mine.

20. Russell Mokhiber and Robert Weissman, "Marriott: Corporate School-yard Bully," *Focus on the Corporation*, March 1999.

21. Constance L. Hays, "Be True to Your Cola, Rah Rah: Battle for Soft-Drink Loyalties Moves to Public Schools," *New York Times*, March 10, 1998, p. D1.

22. Ibid.

23. "Punished for Preferring Pepsi," *Dollars and Sense*, July/August 1998, p. 4.

24. "U-E Board Votes Pepsi Plan Down," *Press and Sun Bulletin*, November 17, 1998, p. B1.

25. Jim Naughton, "Colleges Eye Restrictions on Promotions by Brewing Companies," *Chronicle of Higher Education*, January 9, 1998, p. A57.

26. Sawicki and Molnar, "The Hidden Costs of Channel One."

27. State University of New York, "SUNY Joins Forces with Channel One Network to Prep 4 Million High School Students for College," press release, October 29, 1998.

28. Center for Commercial Free Public Education, "Here Comes ZapMe, the Computer Version of Channel One," *Not For Sale* (summer 1999): 1.

29. State University of New York, "Sloan Foundation Awards SUNY Learning Network Unprecedented Fourth Major Grant," press release, June 24, 1999.

30. NetAction, "Questions Delay Corporate Takeover of Cal State University Tech," *Microsoft Monitor* 21 (January 8, 1998).

31. Carolina Wolohan Jr., "CETI Sets Off Protest," *Golden Gater Online* http://www.journalism.sfsu.edu/www/pubs/gater/fall97/dec11/PROTEST.html [December 11, 1998].

32. "Education or Corporate Marketing," *Nader Letter* 2, no. 5 (1997): 3.

33. Dean Stojkovic, "The Citibank Trap," *Ticker*, December 11, 1996.

34. Dennis Berman and Douglas Harbrecht, "Campus Revolt—Against Credit-Card Companies," *Business Week*, January 12, 1998.

35. Ibid.

36. "Credit Cards on Campus Get Bad Marks by Some," *CNN International*, June 9, 1999.

37. Ibid.

38. Kurt Eichenwald and Gina Kolata, "Drug Trials Hide Conflicts for Doctors," *New York Times*, May 16, 1999, p. A1

39. Kurt Eichenwald and Gina Kolata, "Doctor's Drug Studies Turn into Fraud," *New York Times*, May 17, 1999, p. A1.

40. Moses, "Distinguishing a University from a Shopping Mall," pp. 85–96.

3

MONEY CHANGERS IN THE TEMPLE

David F. Noble

Imagine sitting in a Catholic church, looking up at the crucifix, and discovering that Christ is wearing Calvin Klein underwear. Or in an evangelical church and hearing a prepackaged Microsoft-sponsored sermon: "Where do you want to go today?" Or in a synagogue, passing by the ark that holds the Torah and noticing that it bears the Apple logo and the inscription "Think Different." Or in a mosque, detecting the unmistakable flowing lines of Pepsi and Nike subtly woven into the calligraphic tapestry. People would be outraged by such sacrilege, whatever the economic advantages offered for such arrangements, because it is generally understood that these houses of worship are not intended to be vehicles for commercial enterprise; that they are about something else, something other than commerce. It is understood that such misuse of these sacred spaces, however much it might generate needed revenue, would destroy them; they would no longer be what they were.

Yet this is precisely what is happening to that other kind of sacred space in our society—the universities—without much sign of outrage. The universities are the only institutions we have that are dedicated to independent inquiry and learning, and which serve as a reliable repository of disinterested expertise, reflecting a wide diversity of viewpoints. This is not a romantic notion. To be sure, the universities are significantly compromised. But still, they fulfill a unique and invaluable function.

51

Whether or not we acknowledge it, we routinely depend upon the presumed independence of academia. Professors are called to give expert testimony in courtrooms, legislative hearings, and public forums of all kinds, because it is assumed that they can provide an informed and objective perspective. Every reporter has the numbers of scores of academics in their Rolodexes, whom they regularly call upon to lend legitimacy and an aura of objectivity to their stories. Parents—like my own, who had no experience with higher education—send their children to the universities expecting that they will be educated according to high standards of scholarship and pedagogy by people who have a calling, people who have forgone commercial enticements to do something higher. Yes, of course, parents hope an education will help their children get better jobs, but that is not the whole of it. They are not quite so cynical as some imagine. They want their children to be educated people so that they can have not only more prosperous but fuller lives. Why else would they sacrifice as much as they do for education? This all sounds romantic, I know, but we are a society of romantics (in Canada as well as in the United States), especially when it comes to higher education, which is remarkably well supported. And this is because there is something to it. Universities are indeed a place apart, outside the cash nexus. What is done there can be done no place else, a realm of relative freedom, independence, and integrity—a sort of knowledge commons dedicated to providing education and open inquiry as public goods for the public good.

And now this precious and precarious space is disappearing before our eyes. All across North America the divide between the campus and the commercial world is dissolving. Campuses increasingly resemble shopping malls. On my campus there actually *is* a shopping mall. Pepsi has the franchise for all vending machines. Over the sinks and above the urinals (or on the doors of the stalls) in the washrooms hang permanent plexiglass fixtures for advertisements of the latest movie, CD, or jeans. The tabletops in the cafeteria are fitted with similar fixtures. Above the areas where students congregate, TV monitors play nonstop commercials. Two years ago, the university solicited donations from corporations for the development of online courses, giving the companies the right to place their logos on course materials for as long as the course is offered. This unique space, the university, is being sold, bit by bit, to advertisers. But this is only the most apparent sign of academic commercialization. The real story lies beneath the surface, in the corporatization of academic administration and the wholesale commodification of the research and instructional functions of higher education.

Over the last two decades, the upper managements of academia and corporate America have become inextricably bound through a thickening

web of interlocking directorates. Corporate executives have long dominated university boards; now top academic administrators routinely sit on
Fortune 500 boards, sometimes earning more in fees and retainers associated with these directorships than they do from their academic positions. In addition to serious conflicts of interest, this network of relationships generates a corporate ethos and managerialist regime in academia
indistinguishable from that of private industry. Most important, it encourages academic administrators to view higher education in much the same
way as do their boardroom brethren; namely, as a site of employee
training, commodity production, and capital accumulation.

In the last two decades, both research and instruction have been recast
in this image. Since the '70s, the focus has been on knowledge production
and intellectual capital. In the wake of the Bayh-Dole amendments to the
Patent Act, which gave universities automatic ownership of patents
resulting from federally funded research, universities have become patent-
holding companies. Research, an activity formerly pursued in service to
scholarship and education, as a contribution to human knowledge and
learning, is now directed toward the production of products—marketable
inventions—which can be patented and licensed to the highest bidder.
Academic research agendas are now determined through myriad proprietary arrangements with industrial partners who seek to socialize the costs
and risks of research and privatize the benefits, while faculty are compelled to surrender their patent rights to their employer as a condition of
employment. Meanwhile, as the knowledge commons is enclosed for private gain, a harsh new research regime emerges, marked by secrecy,
nondisclosure agreements, prepublication censorship, fraud, theft, and
conflict of interest; eroding the community of scholars and compromising
the university as a source of reliably independent expertise. And now the
same ruinous regime is emerging in the heretofore neglected realm of
instruction, which has now become a new profit center with online courses
and distance learning. Here the primary agents are the vendors of hardware, software, and content, who envision a multibillion-dollar market for
their wares, and their academic partners, who imagine new revenue
streams and more cost-effective "delivery" of education. In this area of
campus commercialization, the interpersonal human process of education
is transformed into products—courseware, CD-ROMs, Web sites—and
then into copyrighted commodities that can be owned and bought and sold
on the commercial market. With no real evidence of pedagogical value,
economic viability, or even market demand, the new computer-based technologies of instruction are being deployed at a manic pace.

Teachers are being redeployed as content providers and producers of
instructional products who often surrender the copyrights to their own

course materials as a condition of employment. This arrangement enables universities to become vendors of courseware in their own right or to grant marketing and distribution licenses to their private partners. Here, too, the commercial ethos of secrecy and competition erodes the campus community, while the content of education is ultimately determined less by experienced educators than by the dictates of the commercial market, by Bill Gates and Walt Disney. Is this why parents send their kids to college, to watch more TV? Under this new (old) regime of commodity production, painfully familiar to skilled workers in all industries for over a century, faculty face an unprecedented threat to their autonomy, academic freedom, independence, control over curriculum, job security, and working conditions. Administrators argue reassuringly that all this is necessary for the preservation of the universities, much like the priest in the Catholic church who might have said of Christ's Calvin Klein briefs, "Don't worry, logos comes and go, but the Logos is eternal." Or the rabbi who might have said, "Look, with the Apple money we'll follow tradition and build an addition." Or the minister who might have said, "Sure, Jesus threw the money changers out of the temple, but that was a long time ago." But such arguments would ring hollow, and so do the arguments of the administrators. The commercialization of the universities cannot ensure their survival if it sacrifices their essential independence and integrity, what they are about. Happily, people are finally waking up to this challenge with the realization that it is indeed high noon for higher education. Throughout North America, students and faculty have begun to mobilize effectively against the corporate hijacking of higher education, and the struggle has only just begun.

4

SUCCEED WITH CAUTION
Rethinking Academic Culture
at RPI, PSU, and CSU

Donald W. Bray and
Marjorie Woodford Bray

A *Business Week* article reports that universities are "rethinking" academic culture.[1] Such fixtures as tenure and separate academic departments based upon disciplines are being abandoned and curriculum is becoming tailored to meet the requirements of business. The article credits Rensselaer Polytechnic Institute (RPI) and Portland State University (PSU) with being "years ahead" in making needed changes.

This kind of talk has gone far enough!

It was even taken seriously—with disastrous consequences—by Barry Munitz, the erstwhile chancellor of the California State University (CSU) system. Munitz succumbed to the ideology supporting the unfettered global sweep of transnational corporations. Indeed, he introduced aspects of that ideology to the CSU campuses, giving presidents corporate-like power to determine professors' remuneration. The resultant cronyism and unprofessional personnel judgements left the faculties demoralized. This was a dose of poison for the well of learning. Munitz's successor, Charles Reed, proceeded with the Munitz ideology, compounded by a trade-school mentality. Reed's undisguised contempt for faculty and his time-clock attitude toward faculty work produced unprecedented resistance throughout the system. Particularly galling has been his effort to divide the faculty by continuing the Munitz policy of undermining professional review procedures with corporate-like rewards in the form of "merit" salary increases. Universities are not businesses, and even if they were, there are many things better than good business.

Today, few institutions stand in the way of the corporate juggernaut rummaging for profit through every country in the world.[2] This juggernaut of unregulated greed carries a threat to the very life-sustaining capacity of the planet. For humankind it brings greater social inequality, laceration of culture, loss of community, alienation, and debasement of civil life; its ultimate result: "McWorld."[3]

What Rennsselaer and Portland State are "years ahead" in is movement toward McWorld. The university is a crucial institution for questioning the neoliberal madness of the day. When the university's leadership capitulates to that madness faculties are duty-bound to resist. Primary faculty accountability is to the tradition of liberal learning, not to neoliberal authority. The accountability resides in the individual scholar and in separate academic departments. It is the department and its members who guard the integrity of the disciplines and the whole intellectual enterprise. Departments dissolved into multidepartmental stews facilitate administrative and political manipulation. Interdisciplinary learning has always been productive, but that is not an acceptable argument for ending departments.

Of course neoliberal administrators would like to break up departments. Departments are run by faculty. They are democratic venues for intellectual difference and discussion. They are the spaces for resistance to the monolithic imposition of reduction of resources leading to virtual education, speed up, overuse of part-time instructors, and other aspects of the degradation of the education we are able to provide for our students. Another historic instrument of faculty influence, the academic senate, has seen its role reduced in the CSU system and is fighting for survival as a significant representative of faculty interests. A favored device of neoliberal managers, following the lead of their foundation mentors, is to stack committees that make university-wide internal curricular and other decisions with more representatives from units of the institution that represent applied disciplines such as business, engineering, education, and social services rather than the arts, humanities, social sciences, and science. This leads to policies imposed upon all the departments in the institution that are more suitable for a professional rather than a liberal arts education.

Do the universities that follow the lead of Rensselaer and Portland know what awaits them when they are fully modernized? Rensselaer and Portland were part of a pilot program promoted by funding foundations and the American Association for Higher Education (AAHE). These foundations—notably the Carnegie Endowment, the Pew Charitable Trust, and the Ford Foundation—the AAHE, and other external agencies such as regional accrediting bodies and state education commissions have usurped inordinate control of the future direction of higher education in the United States.

Many of their supposed innovations are cloaked in the language of an earlier radicalism. Multiculturalism has become the rage. A harmless kind of community-based research called *service learning* is favored. In the past, genuine faculty initiatives such as participatory research meant to engage the universities in the real social problems of the time—rampant racism and popular powerlessness—have been sanitized into concepts designed to palliate challenges to the social order, not to change it. The ideas and methods of Brazilian educator Paulo Freire are supposedly employed, but their utilization is devoid of his revolutionary implications. Documentation of multicultural and community-related teaching and research are to become part of a professional portfolio used for evaluating faculty performance. What kind of social agitation is that?

More than the noses of the foundations and their corporate donors are in our tents. These agencies attempt to design undergraduate and graduate curriculum, to determine the content of teacher and other professional education, to set research directions in all disciplines, to specify instructional techniques, to determine the overall purpose and outcome of the educational system. They misguidedly apply K–12 teaching concepts to higher education. They also tend to impose models and methodologies appropriate for professional schools such as medicine and business to evaluate liberal arts educational institutions. They promote this agenda by funding the kind of innovations introduced at Portland and Rensselaer. And their access to money talks in other ways. Professors are increasingly selected and promoted on the basis of whether or not they can get grant money.

We must keep a watchful eye on tenure. The corporate model abhors tenure. Tenure fosters independent minds and academic freedom. Although streamlined business management claims no longer to rely upon yes-men, it cannot tolerate fundamental challenge. Alternative models to neoliberalism will need to be conceptualized in the university. This will require the protection provided by tenure.

Consider the implications of the vocationalization of higher education. Our mission will no longer be the asking of profound questions. Our classes will be evaluated on their cash value. Potential employers of our students will become our masters. In the interest of scholarship in general, leave the strictly vocational responsibilities to Phoenix and other "drive thru" institutions.[4] McScience, anyone?

The neoliberal assertion that we can't afford liberal education in nonelite universities is balderdash, akin to the "globaloney" notion that international competition precludes good wages at home. These are *political* questions, not just economic ones. These are our choices to make.

CEOs are paid more and more to cut back jobs and pay, leaving economic justice unserved: a formula for social breakdown. Similarly, university management is disproportionately rewarded for downsizing education.

In California, increasing numbers of state legislators were educated in the CSU system. Will they want to have a liberal education unavailable to their children in their alma maters? Will citizens in general?

The information age in its early stages has given rise to illusions about learning and living. One illusion is that computers can replace instructors. There is enough experience now to debunk that notion. Computer instruction by itself produces unimaginative underliterates. Computer-instructed students receive "knowledge" popping up on a screen, information lacking context, a sustained line of reasoning, nuance, intonation, and human feeling. Compared to teacher-instructed students, unguided computer learners suffer loss of vocabulary and the ability to learn and to imagine. No one would deny that computers have their utility, but who wants virtual graduates?

Virtual education is not being prescribed for the elite institutions—the Ivy League; Stanford; the University of California, Berkeley; Pomona College; and so forth—which train the stratum of society that is upper class or those who are socialized to believe they are part of the elite and often become its ideological servants. Virtual education is being offered as a solution for the "problem" of funding the so-called comprehensive institutions—the places where lower-level management and technical personnel receive their training. What will they lose when "distance learning" means they no longer need to be on a campus to receive the instruction leading to a bachelor's degree? They will no longer have direct contact with their professors, in or out of the classroom. They will not engage in bull sessions with their fellow students, hashing out the meanings of what they have been exposed to in the classroom and in their reading. When they leave, who will write their letters of recommendation—who will know them? They will not have formed the networks with their peers; they will not be cohorts, available for the myriad social contacts that elite-school graduates enjoy as they make their way up the professional ladder. This deliberate construction of a second-class system would be a blatant case of institutional classism. Society should not tolerate it any more than it tolerates racism.

Virtual graduates will not be up to the challenges of the coming century, even if their immediate skills make them employable. Moreover, job skills change so rapidly that any given set is soon obsolete. Intellectual depth is what counts in the long run. Having masses of vocationally oriented college graduates is not a wise goal to offer the coming generation; it is not even good for business.

It is the responsibility of the university to save economic life from its own profit-driven logic. It is the responsibility of the university to civilize—not to please—corporate personnel officers. Faculty members, now pressured more and more to get grants and contracts from foundations and corporations must be careful or they will be playing the game on the donors' terms. As you conform to the needs of transnational corporations, you *participate* in the social injustice (the polarization of income) they wreak. They are not *our* employers. However, we, like all coming under their sway, suffer the declining living conditions (material, environmental, and social) spawned by their "structural adjustments" (SAPs).[5]

Under the current world governance by transnational corporations answerable to no one, more than one hundred countries have been SAPped by the World Bank and the International Monetary Fund—that is, forced to reduce social spending in favor of international debt repayment and profit remittance to foreign investors. Now, in the United States, we are being SAPped to make the management of public education contribute more directly to private profit. All of this is not divinely ordained. It is the politics of overly concentrated corporate power. The future equality of life on earth is at stake. Domestic and international awareness of the importance of resistance is spreading. The opposition to the World Trade Organization meetings in Seattle in November 1999 was perhaps the defining event of the late twentieth century.

The apparent triumph of the logic of capitalism over the logic of democratic politics is not inevitable or permanent. Workers made redundant by globalization and automation will demand meaningful work. It will be the role of the universities to participate in confronting this challenge. It is no coincidence that Chancellor Reed's trade-school model would be ill equipped for the task.

The growth of technology will increase the need for education. The accelerating demand for research will require that it continue to be done through higher education. There is more than enough ignorance for everyone.

Students and other citizens will eventually see through the neoliberal haze and seek higher education offering a good, sound liberal education. That means institutions where discovery is prized for its own sake, where critical imagination is rewarded, where faculties recruit and promote faculties, where community values outweigh material ones, where the arts are nurtured, where history and science are learned, where ethics are relevant, where students interact with each other and their professors, where the faculty teaches from the heart to students who are regarded as citizens, not future employees. This is not a business. This is a calling.

Faculty recognition of the threat to their profession is stirring. In the

California State University system, the Munitz-Reed regime has aroused a tempest of anger and organized opposition. Membership in the California Faculty Association (CFA) burgeoned. Some campuses voted for work suspension and/or contract rejection. Faculty senates passed resolutions affirming that a visit by the chancellor would be unwelcome. Meanwhile, a sweep by the Democratic Party in the 1988 elections strengthened the CFA's hand in Sacramento. When an impasse occurred in 1999 contract negotiations, pressure from Sacramento induced the chancellor to make concessions including the weakening of merit pay provisions. Later, a law was passed by the legislature requiring nonunion faculty to contribute "fair share" payments to the CFA. In the spring of 2000 the faculty senate at San Jose passed a proposed revision of the whole system that would sharply curtail the budget of the chancellor's office while granting expanded administrative autonomy to the campuses. The CFA organized public hearings starting with the San Jose and Los Angeles branches to explore with the community what the future role of the CSU should be. Recurrent themes in the fight against virtualization and corporatization were that corporate notions of efficiency hobble faculty teaching effectiveness; that encountering real persons, not machines, is what changes lives; and that corporate and university cultures are not the same. The CSU struggle demonstrates that with requisite strength and conviction faculty can resist being "corporatized," "HMOized," or "casualized." The struggle continues.

NOTES

1. Keith H. Hammonds and Susan Jackson, "The New U: A Tough Market is Reshaping Colleges," *Business Week*, December 22, 1997, pp. 96–102.

2. This phenomenon is usually called *globalization*, a term connoting negative effects. We have coined the term *transperialism* to better convey the full and devastating dimensions of the phenomenon. See Donald W. Bray and Marjorie Woodford Bray, "Scholarship in the Age of Transperialism," *Latin American Perspectives* 25, no. 5 (1998): 32–37. The word *globalism* is now being applied to constructive international cooperation.

3. Benjamin Barber is the elaborator of this concept.

4. James Traub, "Drive-Thru U.: Higher Education for People Who Mean Business," *New Yorker*, October 20 & 27, 1997, pp. 114–23.

5. Structural Adjustment Programs (SAPs) are the conditions imposed upon Third World borrowing nations by the World Bank and the International Monetary Fund in order to receive loans. The Department of State usually requires SAPs in place for countries to receive U.S. financial support.

5

RESISTING CORPORATIZATION OF THE UNIVERSITY

Richard Daniels, with Lisa Blasch and Peter Caster

Today you're looking at a highly personal human-mediated environ-
ment. The potential to remove the human mediation in some areas and
replace it with automation—smart, computer-based, network-based
systems—is tremendous.

> —Robert Heterich, president of Educom, Inc.,
> the academic-corporate consortium[1]

Behind ivied walls and on leafy quadrangles, administrators and pro-
fessors acknowledge this new reality. Higher education is changing pro-
foundly, retreating from the ideals of liberal arts and the leading-edge
research it always has cherished. Instead, it is behaving more like the
$250-billion business it has become.

> —*Business Week*[2]

At a recent conference on labor, Manning Marable opened his
keynote address by saying, "Today, the struggle is between the people and
the corporations."[3] I want to use that statement to frame the remarks that
follow, as well as the whole problem of corporatization, because it suggests that universities are part of the larger society and the larger struggle
for human liberation, not somehow separate from or above them, and that
concerned faculty, students, and staff have to join with other working
people in their fight for democracy, equality, and the transformation of

property relations to resist the corporatization of American higher education and its dehumanizing, authoritarian consequences.[4] Faculty and students need to engage in an ongoing critique of universities, their own and the national system, as producers of ideology that seem always to have served corporate interests; and to work to stop the dismantling of higher education—indeed, of public education at *all* levels—for the working class, especially for students of color, single mothers, and the poor.[5]

The word "corporatization" refers to the increasing presence of private businesses, especially the internationalizing ones, the multinational corporations and their emblems, in campus dining rooms and dormitories, classrooms and libraries, athletic fields and laboratories.[6] The word also refers to the increasing control that business corporations exercise over academic culture and governance, partly because as federal and state governments have grown more conservative and revanchist, intent on eradicating the social welfare or New Deal state, and government funding of public education in general continues to be both cut and redirected (to build the new prisons and new weapons systems, and to pay for "Big Science" efforts like the human genome project, for instance, or the savings and loan bailout or other cost-shifting financial rip-offs), academic administrators, departments, institutes, and researchers increasingly seek funding from the private sector.[7]

The signs of corporatization are everywhere, and any observant person can fill in the blanks from her own experience: the Coke and Pepsi logos (and campuswide concession monopolies); the ubiquitous Nike swoosh (inscribed in the backs of Indonesian workers as well as on college athletic jerseys); Westinghouse's sponsorship of nuclear engineering programs and the consequent ideological and ethical deformations within academic administrative bureaucracies and departments;[8] Barnes and Noble's efforts to take over campus bookstores (many of which were once cooperatives or nonprofits);[9] Hewlett-Packard and Apple supplying cheap computers for students' use and used office furniture to strapped humanities departments; Burger King and Taco Bell replacing nutritious (if bland) food in student union dining halls with their own infarctious and superprofitable fare; the balloon-and-pony shows on the campus quads that use the NCAA logo, the latest PR techniques, and students' love of sports and rock music to hawk corporate wares (Chevy pickups, computers, anything) and draw needy students into signing up for credit cards with usurious rates of interest; the efforts to turn Earth Week each April into a series of academic whitewashes of corporate practices like clear-cutting and failed nuclear cleanups, such as the one at Hanford; and on and on. Faculty and students should all keep lists of such examples of the increasingly pervasive efforts to privatize, commercialize, and commodify, and of the university's willing and even eager complicity in them, and draw these to people's attention.

In addition to these are the huge, often corruption-ridden building programs, as private hotels, apartment complexes, and shopping malls pop up on campuses everywhere, increasing the corporate presence, as now perhaps most notoriously at the University of Pennsylvania; and the rapidly growing endowments of the richest universities, which clearly have major economic stakes in preserving the multinational corporation–dominated status quo with its famously widening gap between rich and poor.[10] In fact, these rich universities *are* the status quo, or an essential part of it; Clyde W. Barrow, in his essential study *Universities and the Corporate State: Corporate Liberalism and the Reconstruction of American Higher Education, 1894–1928,* argues persuasively that modern research universities were rationalized and systematized in the 1890s and the opening decades of the twentieth century in the contradictory project of forming an "ideological state apparatus" to serve the changing needs of the capital-owning class.[11] This project's continuing contradiction lies in the clash between the profitability needs of corporate capital and the egalitarian demands of people who desire political and economic democracy—again, the corporations versus the people. It is within the space of this contradiction that the chances lie for effective resistance leading to fundamental change.

That there's more corporatization now than there used to be, that corporate control of universities is growing and changing, is indicated by the fact that corporate spending on university research blossomed from $235 million in 1980 to $1.2 billion by 1991. "[T]he driving force at universities today," a recent book notes, is "raising money from, and doing work for corporations. . . ."[12] Or, as Barrow argues in his study of the relations of universities to corporate America and the state: "Colleges and universities are once again in the midst of a continuing cycle of integrative policies designed to bring them and their personnel ever closer to the exploitative requirements of capital and the adventurism of state elites. The American college and university is continually pressured by business and state to adopt further modifications in its curriculum and research that emulate a corporate ideal first proposed more than three-quarters of a century ago."[13] That "corporate ideal"—based in the first instance on the great railroad companies—amounted to the higher education institution rationalized into a parodically corporate structure. *Parodic*, or a parody of a business corporation, because the overriding goal of a corporation is simply to maximize returns and profits, while such a goal is impossible to articulate in terms of educational institutions without significant and startling linguistic and institutional deformations—although even faculty have tried, a liberal-arts budget committee referring, for instance, to student credit-hours as "profits." More than one department chair refers to students who take his or her department's courses as "bodies," or more delicately as "customers" or "clients," the usual administrative terms. One hears and sees this kind of corporate lingo all the time. Specifically, the corporate ideal applied to universities meant (and means) following Carnegie Foundation for the Advancement of Teaching (CFAT) recommendations such as "line-itemized budgets for stronger administrative governance of teaching, curriculum, and research; functionally differentiated hierarchical administrative structures with clear lines of authority; centralized business and accounting offices; pre- and post-audits of expenditures; centralized allocation of classroom space, plant, and equipment; and administration by full-time professional managers who . . .utilize sound business procedures." ("Sound business procedures" aren't necessarily bad, of course; it depends on their definition and purpose and whose interests they serve.) Further, nationally and within the states, the "concept of a system was consciously applied to the problem of interinstitutional relations."[14] Ownership of a university belongs to whatever board of governors it has (mostly businessmen) and "the public" (generally a euphemism for corporate interests, and the state legislators and officials who mostly represent them). Major contemporary concerns at universities are efficiency and accountability, again in their corporate sense, as well as outsourcing and downsizing—everywhere, the percentage of full-time, tenure-track jobs is decreasing, their places taken by temporary teachers and researchers. Administration is understood to be management, faculty to be workers, and students to be customers or clients (although, interestingly, students are often also "products"). Universities have human resources departments now, just like corporations—and this is more than just a change of name—and they rely on modern marketing and public relations techniques to "sell themselves" and their "services."

These imitations of corporate structure, practice, and terminology result historically from the Fordist factory efficiencies furthered by Frederick Taylor, father of scientific management, and applied to universities with the counsel of Taylor himself, when asked by CFAT's first president Henry S. Pritchett (also president of MIT and eager to please Andrew Carnegie).[15] In the same time period, roughly the years around 1905, the large-scale commodification of basic university research began—commodification meaning the process of turning things into salable goods; and in capitalism anything at all, including intimate human qualities, can be commodified, made into something that can be bought and sold, owned and then taken to a market and exchanged—to this large-scale commodification of basic university research we can now add the rapidly growing commercialization of classroom teaching.[16] And to this we can add yet again the newly intensified desire to model universities ever more closely after private businesses. A case in point lies down the pike from me at the University of Oregon which, by admission and design of its own administration, grows ever closer to simply being a private corporation drifting in the global corporate sea. There, in the past decade, state funding has been halved (to 15 percent of the budget) while corporate funding has more than tripled (to 10 percent) and is now the main growth area. This effort to attract corporate funding, some University of Oregon officials say, "has muted discussion about the topic [corporate funding] . . . because people don't want to alienate potential donors." The university's administration tried in 1997 to erect what they called a "donor wall" in the student union, but this sychophantic PR project was stopped in its tracks by a timely student protest. The student newspaper stated that to "many students, the wall stands for the corporate buyout of the University system," a charge that is, of course, right on the money.[17] We need to note that the University of Oregon students' protest worked: The "donor wall" was never built. The protest's effect was limited, and symbolic rather than substantive, but the students should still be honored for having the vision and the courage to resist. Here I should also recognize the Oregon State University (OSU) students in the Vegetarian Resource Network, a recognized student group, who tried to protest in the student union at a corporate recruitment meeting against Proctor & Gamble's abuses of animal life in the production of cosmetics but were removed by police, and also the OSU Movimiento Estudiantil Chicano de Aztlan (MEChA) students who tried to protest Oregon U.S. Senator Ron Wyden's corporatist, antilabor, and anti-immigrant policies during his visit to the university and were kept from exercising their constitutional rights, again by the police, again in the student union.[18]

Where were the faculty, one wonders? What of their lack of vision and courage? Could it be that faculty are, in effect, being bought off by the funding system? Is this the example faculty are setting for their students: Go along to get along? What kind of education is that? An education very useful, of course, to those who are being programmed to take their places in the corporate ideal, for a future as obedient corporate drones.

A University of Oregon law school professor suggested to me in a confidential conversation that his school should be renamed the Phil Knight Law School (to honor gifts from the Nike chief, whose name already adorns the university's main library), and he worries often and rightly about the chilling effects of these gifts on both speech and academic work. He claims that some law professors no longer speak out about labor issues for fear of offending Nike, funder of a new building to house the law school, which, when finished, will be called the William Knight

Law Center (after Phil's father, an alumnus).[19] This in fact affected the Labor, Race, and Economic Justice Conference referred to at the start of this paper. A handbill written by Professor Julia Fox of the University of Oregon sociology department says that during a conference planning meeting on February 26, 1998, "Hiroko Nakamura proposed including Nike labor policies. . . . A director of the Labor Education Research Center (LERC) responded with concerns about including information about Nike and listing Nike on the flyers since President Dave Frohnmayer was providing the funding for the conference. If the information was to appear on the flyer, then it must be marginalized." Professor Fox goes on to ask "how can the Center provide information regarding labor issues if LERC must be silent about Nike's labor policies?" Good question. How many University of Oregon law professors now will speak out for the rights of labor in Indonesia, or against corporatization and its inequitable, dehumanizing consequences—such as temping, downsizing, and outsourcing—on which the house of Nike (like other corporate houses) is built? When exactly in academia did the search for money and the fear of not getting it replace the search for truth and the need for critical thought, one might ask?

Another example: In 1996 the faculty senate at my university voted not to seat a representative from the campus ROTC until the U.S. military stopped discriminating by policy against gay and lesbian service people (a tender issue with a troubled history at OSU). But then the College of Liberal Arts' chief fund-raiser (*not* someone from the business school) let it be known that a corporate donor threatened to withhold a large gift, asking the senate to overturn the vote (we peons were never told which donor or how much money, and thus do not know how cheap the sellout was; in academic life the price is often shockingly low), and indeed the faculty senate rescinded its principled vote in support of their gay and lesbian colleagues with unseemly haste at the first possible meeting in the winter of 1997. Another recent example from OSU of the speech-chilling effects of private sector funding: The OSU School of Forestry (called by some the School of Lumber) invited the distinguished American poet Gary Snyder to speak in the fall of 1998 on Buddhist forest practices, as part of a conference on forests. For that November election, however, there was an anti-clear-cutting measure on the ballot that was predicted to lose by a huge margin since it was opposed by practically everyone, including the labor unions. When big private donors expressed fear that Snyder's talk might prove inflammatory, causing rioting in the streets and sparking an anticorporate vote, the School of Lumber's dean at once disinvited the poet, who was fortunately reinvited immediately by the departments of philosophy and English. Gary Snyder spoke to a packed house, at the precise time and place originally scheduled, for intelligent, long-range stewardship of forests; and then, of course, the corporate side, including the fearful business interests that dominate the forestry school, won the election by the predicted huge margin. There were no riots. The faculty who reinvited the poet should be honored for negating this attempted censorship of an alternative perspective, as should the anonymous forestry professor who called on them, but they must not rest on their laurels. There is and will be much more to be done, most of it necessarily from the margins and outside official channels.

These foolish, cowardly actions occurred at major state universities in Oregon but could have happened anywhere in the country. No educational institution in America is exempt from such greed and intellectual cowardice, although they may take slightly different forms in different places.

That the leverage of a gift of money should be dangled to influence public policy is nothing new, of course, but it happens more and more often in universities as they are more thoroughly corporatized, according to recent studies such as Lawrence Soley's *Leasing the Ivory Tower: The Corporate Takeover of Academia*, so often that most university officials and privileged faculty never even seem to notice. But the fact that it is not new does not make it right. All units of universities should have an abiding interest beyond mere lip service in impartiality, critical thought, the pursuit of truth, and the free exercise of human reason and speech, difficult as that may seem to be in the face of intense financial pressure and temptation, this fevered grasping after dollars. If university faculty don't uphold such intellectual values in our pervasively commercial society, who will? David Noble notes that the "commercialization of academic research" has "ushered in a brash new regime of proprietary control, secrecy, fraud, theft, and commercial motives and preoccupations," all of which are now being extended to the heart of the university as even classroom teaching begins to be commercialized. "Some argue," Noble says, "that this new commercial ethos has irreversibly corrupted the university as a site of reliably independent thought and disinterested inquiry, placing in jeopardy a precious and irreplaceable public resource."[20] Not a bad statement of what's at stake from a societal as well as an institutional point of view. In this respect, corporate funding presents universities with different and even greater problems than has federal funding. As Noam Chomsky has said of the history of financing at MIT, "as you move away from government funding and toward corporate funding, then secrecy increases. Corporate funding is much more restricted and narrow than Pentagon funding, in general."[21]

Universities are neither new nor timeless, and they certainly are not free from the taints and constraints of class interest and ideology. The people who staff the ranks of universities, including the teaching and research faculties, are not necessarily purer or better, less self-interested or less desirous of material gain, than the general population (although they are often more privileged). Funding always comes with strings attached, at least potentially. All of these and other characteristics of universities have developed and changed over time in response to historical forces and events and to the conflicts and decisions of social classes, especially the dominant business class. The origins of the problem of the corporatization of American higher education stretch back at least to the 1890s, and to be effective any resistance and work for fundamental change in a democratic direction needs to be informed by this history.

In their influence on economic thought as well as government policy and action, several universities have become dangers to democratic and egalitarian possibilities in American society. In the vanguard of these at least in part reactionary academic institutions is the University of Chicago, formed out of a Baptist college by the Rockefeller fortune at the end of the nineteenth century and source in recent decades of the influential theories of Milton Friedman and the "Chicago School" of economic theory responsible for, among many other things, the economic makeover of Chile along thoroughly corporate, free-market lines after the CIA-aided overthrow of the Allende government in September of 1973. The Chicago School is now trying to remake the tattered American social safety net along the same debt-ridden lines, by privatizing social security for instance, which would be ruinous for many working people here as it has been in Chile. Universities and faculty must be responsible for the effects of their work in the world (and I'm not speaking here of the clichéd bureaucratic accounting term "accountability" that we all hear so much about and which is part of the corporate effort to control the university). All of this, in a sense, brings up the problem of Henry Kissinger, Jeffrey Sachs, and Harvard and its various associated think-tanks, institutes, and foundations, as well as the Harvard Management Company, which invests the university's huge endowment, at over $13 billion by far the largest such fund in the United States if not the world. Everyone who has read Seymour Hersh's book on Kissinger and Nixon and followed the news knows the leading role that Kissinger, in concert with the CIA and elements of the Harvard establishment—"the best and the brightest" as they were smugly called in the famous 1946 "redbook"—played in the murderous overthrow of the democratically elected Allende, as well as the secret bombing of Cambodia, the Phoenix Program, Operation Condor, and many another benighted and bloody affair.[22] Jeffrey Sachs, another Harvard luminary, was a leader of the free-market "reform"— they called it economic "shock therapy"—of the formerly socialist bloc countries, most notably Russia, persuading them to privatize practically everything helter-skelter, as quickly as possible, thus squandering Russia's national wealth, much of it pirated out of country with almost no return. The immiserating economic consequences (for all but the very rich, the justly so-called oligarchs) of this self-serving, historically ignorant Harvard-led free-market policy are evident throughout Russia today.[23] But like the oligarchs, Harvard officials and the Harvard Institute for International Development all made big profits. Although Chicago and Harvard led the reactionary charge, other prestigious universities are culpable in their ways, prominent among them the University of Michigan, Stanford University, the University of Pennsylvania, Yale University, the University of California at Berkeley, and the University of California at Los Angeles, as David Noble has indicated. One could easily list more such universities.[24]

In part the faculty problem arises from the fact that American intellectuals as a class in the first decades of the twentieth century—especially in the 1920s, as effects of the war hysteria that accompanied World War I, the Russian Revolution, and the "Red scare" that followed—compromised away any rights they had to an effectual role in university governance. At the same time they were, as a class, being institutionalized in universities. The organizational signs, and means, of this compromise between academic intellectuals, businessmen, and government officials were the AAUP and the American Council on Education (ACE), which emerged as ideological instruments of the state elites.[25]

Lawrence C. Soley, in *Leasing the Ivory Tower*—a book full of shocking examples of the venality of universities and many of the most distinguished members of their faculties—seems to assume, nostalgically, that American higher education had an edenic period of ivied innocence prior to World War II (or perhaps prior to the 1950s, when the GI Bill opened certain new possibilities) but that now we inhabit a fallen academic world: What "actually happened on college campuses during the 1980s and 1990s" was "the takeover of universities by corporations, tycoons, and foundations" rather than, he argues, by "tenured radicals," the conservative argument accepted by America's "uncritical media."[26]

But Clyde Barrow in *Universities and the Capitalist State* and David Noble in *America by Design* show that we would have to dig well back into the nineteenth century to find anything much resembling a period of innocence for American higher education, and then any such innocence would still be utterly class bound. During the late Populist and the Progressive Eras a new corporate order organizing itself to act in and dominate national and world markets also restructured American universities along the lines of corporate ideals and needs to (a) do their basic research; (b) satisfy their need for literate, well-trained manpower; and (c) help produce a business-supportive ideology.[27] In this process of reconstruction, the faculty (intellectuals) were ideologically remade (by social or class agreement, and through their increasing institutionalization in universities) as politically neutral producers of scientifically structured research and knowledge partly along the lines of the new, professionalized German model (the Ph.D., specialization, and so forth). Tenured faculty were allowed limited academic freedom only within the bounds of this agreement, which was specified in an American Council of Education report of 1925, and then by 1929 instituted practically everywhere in the United States by means of the American Association of University Professors.[28] As Barrow points out, "Most intellectuals have chosen to negotiate an opportunistic historical accommodation with business interests and the state by accepting the new organizational structure of university life in exchange for limited procedural guarantees of personal security, which . . . has not included academic freedom."[29]

University faculty were more generally remolded during the Progressive Era as one sector of what Barbara and John Ehrenreich in 1977 called the "Professional-Managerial Class," or PMC, which may include physicians, lawyers, and other "professionals" who are paid, often very well (except for the majority of faculty, who do not make what are called "professional salaries"), to provide support services to the owners of capital; the PMC is a class marked also by its developing code of professionalism, a social mask now being ripped away from the faces of most academics, and increasingly even of physicians, as they are proletarianized, turned into workers, by the very processes of corporatization.[30] And this shows progressivism's and the PMC's roots as in part evasions of socialism; as Barrow puts it, "The legitimation of progressivism as a democratic alternative to either populism or socialism thus partly hinged on the ability to expand access to higher education and the occupations to which it promised entry."[31]

Mainly because of sea-changes in national and global economies,[32] American society is now going through another major period of class restructuring, this one marked in part by the fragmentation and apparent disintegration of the PMC, and in part by the renegotiation of relations between the private and public sectors, perhaps including what Barrow refers to as the dynamic struggle in American history between the imperatives of profit maximization on the one hand, and of social equality on the other, [33] although the struggle is unbalanced because in our business civilization capital always has the upper hand economically and structurally, and thus, of course, officially. In the process of these changes occurring in our time, American universities are becoming more openly, crudely, and pervasively the servants of the corporate sector, the processes of commodification, and the unending quest to maximize returns—what is often called, perhaps not quite accurately, the corporatization of the university. As one student of the process notes, "The appropriation of the university by industry is now complete. Inside the university, on the other hand, uncertainty prevails."[34] It is important to recognize that these are also changes of degree and appearance, not only of substance, and that there never was an edenic period of purity and innocence for American higher education—nor for any other aspect of American life, which has been marked from its historical beginnings by the resource needs of capital, by racism and "ethnic cleansing" (for example, slavery and the genocide of Native Americans), and by the structural drives to privatize and to commodify.

Barrow points out that "higher education is required to assume a larger role in sustaining capital accumulation and the American ideology with each successive economic or legitimation crisis." He also notes that "the corporate ideal as a political program . . . can be opposed constructively with practical pedagogical and institutional alternatives, but only if intellectuals once again assume that responsibility,"[35] which is my particular interest and which I deal with specifically in the final part of this paper. He refers here to the years from the end of the Populist Era on, roughly 1894–1924, when there were instances of significant resistance to the imposition of the corporate model, and he refers also to the rebelliousness of the 1960s (arguably, 1954–1975), the era of the civil rights, antiwar, and cultural freedom movements that profoundly affected, and were affected by, universities and university students of the time. Unfortunately, up to this point "attempts to reject the corporate ideal through an alliance with the working class have failed to materialize except in scattered instances" because a majority of intellectuals "have chosen to negotiate an opportunistic historical accommodation with business interests and the state by accepting the new organizational structure of university life in exchange for limited procedural guarantees of personal security. . . ."[36]

What are the large historical factors that are leading to the renewed and increasing commercialization of American universities? What is the larger context in which it occurs? I would phrase the problem in the following manner: As a function of heightened competition, the globalizing economy, the overriding corporate goal of maximizing profits, the technologically revolutionary effects of computer chip innovations (carefully avoiding here the fallacy of technological determinism), the end of the Cold War, the relative powerlessness of labor, the dominance and harsh discipline of finance capital, and the mystifications of free-market ideology and of academic economics fixated on computer modeling, the private sector proceeds apace in its makeover of cultural and social institutions, including the American academy, in its own image, a structural process that leads us ever further into being a corporatist society, authoritarian, racist, and increasingly inequitable, in which our (potentially) democratic institutions and practices, or tendencies, are increasingly weakened and debased. Corporations can produce wealth but they are also authoritarian, hierarchical bureaucracies that subordinate human values to the drive for profit maximization. If conditions are right, the further slide in the United States from the corporatist society in which we already live into some kind of Mussolini-style fascism could occur.[37] This is the very real danger, and for the hundreds of thousands, perhaps millions of African American males languishing in the new, privatized American prisons or trying to live unemployed with those who depend on them in the harsh American inner cities, that neofascist order has already arrived.[38]

It is within such an analytical and historical framework that I want to consider modes of resistance to the increasing corporatization and commercialization of the American university. For concerned faculty and students, the university should become a site of concerted, sustained resistance, but a resistance always alert to the fact that the university is just a part of the larger social problem. I don't pretend that my list is exhaustive; but since I have been reading and thinking about the problem of corporatization for some time now, trying with others to develop the needed critique of universities as ideology factories, and sometimes acting to resist the new corporate order and to try to effect change, these suggestions grow from both experience and knowledge. I invite readers to add suggestions of their own, to communicate them to others and to me, but most importantly to organize in their workplaces, classrooms, professional organizations, and communities for action to resist corporatization—and then to act. Organizing is the key.

Increase the presence of organized labor on campus. Barrow does say, as quoted above, that efforts to "reject the corporate ideal" by allying with the working class have not often been successful, but that's no reason to quit trying. Labor unions—warts and all—are the obvious institutional, organized opposition to corporate exploitation, and an active labor presence on campus, which can come in a variety of forms, will make an excellent base for long-term resistance and have the double function of connecting with the economic and political world beyond the university. Best is to organize and begin a faculty or graduate student union of one's own; those faculty lucky enough already to have a union can become more active in it, recruit new members and invigorate older ones, and, especially, work to sharpen their union as a tool of resistance. But faculty who have no union, as is the case where I teach, should do all they can to (1) prepare the ground for organizing and (2) connect with union people and to bring them to campus to interact with faculty, students, and staff—as public speakers, as organizers, to join in protests, and as sources of information about workers' struggles for labor and human rights here and throughout the world. Such speakers and such a labor presence can connect with faculty and students and arouse their interest in ways that academic lecturers often cannot. Among other moves, faculty and students can join with the local Jobs with Justice group in their quest to establish living-wage laws; get to know the local union organizers and volunteer to picket, observe picket lines, or help in other ways; and attend labor and labor history conferences whenever possible, in order both to learn and to network with organizers and workers. It's also possible, certainly, to organize a labor-oriented conference involving labor organizers at one's own campus and thus to connect with students, faculty in other departments and colleges, the local staff union, community activists, and workers, as well as those brought in to speak. Another move is to get in touch with local or regional branches of the AFL-CIO to see if faculty can join with them to bring a summer camp to train young organizers to their campus. Most university governing boards and state boards of higher education are made up primarily of business executives (what "the public" mainly means to state elites) and do not include representatives of organized labor—not to mention faculty or students—and it would be worthwhile to begin to agitate for their inclusion. Local union officials may have other ideas and resources one can use as well.

There are, of course, other possibilities I haven't mentioned or thought of for increasing the presence of organized labor on campus, but there clearly are many different ways to do this, and it is, in my opinion, the single most important thing faculty and students can do to resist corporatization of their own college or university. It is abundantly clear that corporate values and business interests and personnel are represented everywhere on campus. The university administration is modeled after a corporate management structure and to a large extent shares its values. The corporations basically own the place—and more and more act as if they do—and their increasingly pervasive presence seems like just plain common sense (the surest sign of an entrenched ideology) to most faculty and students, and certainly to administrators. Why not an increasing labor presence to counter them?

Organize with students, other faculty, and staff. Those who have tenure can use the security it still offers to speak their minds in department, college, and university meetings and in public forums. All faculty, all those involved in university teaching, can use the academic freedom they do have and encourage others to speak out, too—and no encouragement works as well as the example of one faculty member or student (or preferably both together) speaking her mind, standing in protest to resist the increasingly authoritarian, stratified, undemocratic institutional structure that accompanies the processes of corporatization. As university faculty we are, after all, supposed to be teaching critical thinking and humane values and the values and skills of effective citizenship in a society that still has democratic content. Why not live and act by such practices, bring them into the places where we work? One of the problems of corporatization is that it mediocritizes as it narrows both education and thought to serve the demands of profit maximization and promotes authoritarian rather than democratic practices, even as managers, or administrators, natter on about the cult of excellence;[39] thus—and it is tremendously important to recognize this point—*our concerns and our resistance are always relevant to our intellectual work and educational practice*. Remembering this, we can organize teach-ins with participants from across the campus, from organized labor, and from the community speaking about the effects and dangers of corporatization and ways to resist it. The next time there's a meeting or conference on campus to discuss "marketing the university" or "accountability," or new definitions of scholarship, especially such a meeting sponsored by a foundation like CFAT, Lilly, or Kellogg, we can show up with some of our students and colleagues to express a contrary point of view, and make the executives and administrators who sponsor such meetings, and the ambitious faculty who try to please their bosses by going along, at least stop and think about, and explain, what they are proposing and its implications.

Resist the corporatization of discourse. In our time there are few more prolific sources of corporatized discourse than university administrations, and their officialese is filtering into departments, and thus classrooms, by means of chairs, deans, the legions of directors and assistant vice presidents, and others, including, of course, faculty who have (or wish to have) administrative duties. It is time to begin calling them on this thoughtless practice. Why should we allow administrators or faculty who imitate them to refer to student credit hours as "profits" and students themselves as "bodies" or "customers"? Why should we sit and squirm while they drone on about "accountability" and "educational outcomes"? Why not insist that they recognize the corporate, Fordist background of the very concept of "student credit-hour" and the corporate administrative ideal it implies?[40] Even the proud old word "excellence" becomes mediocritized and then emptied of meaning through constant repetition and misapplication. The final sentence of Spinoza's *Ethics* reminds us that "all things excellent are as difficult as they are rare," but that's not what "excellent" means any more, as in "excellence in parking"; and indeed, in my experience, some university and corporate people, and, alas, students influenced by them, find the philosopher's sentence insulting.[41] Most of the talk about "accountability" and "productivity" and "serving the public" is also corporate lingo, the purpose of which is to control the institutions and bend them ever more firmly to corporate will and purposes, that is, to making money.

In the process, higher education is dehumanized as well as mediocritized. A university is not an industrial or financial corporation, not a factory.[42] We do not, or should not, manufacture commodities for sale; we do not, or should not, invent services for cash. Maximizing returns—making profits—is not the "bottom line" for higher education. We do basic research and scholarship that should serve the common good, not corporate greed. We educate students, who are human beings, to help them take their places in the larger social world. This world should be, for the sake of justice and human fulfillment, in its very fabric democratic and involve some real, material degree of equality of the conditions of life; and it needs people skilled in the arts of citizenship and the requisite scientific and technical knowledge, including clear and critical thinking and writing, as well as the ability to figure out how corporate and administrative people—advertisers, public relations specialists, "human resources" managers, executives, and university officials—are using and abusing language and why they manipulate words, and thus people, as they do. We are not (or should not be) training young people to spend their lives as corporate drones, although every life has its economy and some of the vocational aspects of education are necessary, too. We do basic research, scholarship, science, and creative work, and we teach based on the fruits of these; but once these activities are bent to serve merely corporate ends, that is, to commodify knowledge, to maximize returns, and to mystify these practices, then they are no longer scholarship or science but something else, no longer able even to pose as impartial or disinterested.[42]

All of us have read Orwell's famous old essay "Politics and the English Language"; it is time to update it, realizing that the greatest threats to democracy and knowledge today come from the private sector, from the corporations, from our entrenched business civilization, and not from the much diminished public sector.[43] Politics, John Dewey once noted, is the shadow business casts across society, and that shadow grows ever larger and darker now, as the increasing inequities of the education and healthcare systems, for example, show.[44]

Teach. We can bring the issues raised by corporatization into the classroom and have students read and discuss relevant texts, such as the books and articles by Noble, Soley, Barrow, Chomsky, Ohmann, Cockburn, and Readings, among many others. We can encourage students to use the library and the Internet to study the problem on their own, write about it, discuss it with other students, raise it in other classes. Corporatization is often relevant, or we can find quite legitimate ways to make it so. Some graduate students will want to do research and write their theses on aspects of the topic. Time and again I see the faces of students, undergraduate more often than graduate, and even of some faculty, light up with interest when the problem of corporatization is broached. Many students really are quite concerned about it and would like in some way to work to resist it. It is up to the teacher, of course, to be able to suggest at least some courses of action.

Speak against corporatization of the academy every chance we get. We can bring the subject up in class and in department and college meetings. People throughout the university, staff as well as students and even some administrators, are increasingly concerned about the issue. We can discuss it with friends and colleagues. We can participate in panel discussions related to corporatization, especially those that bring together some mix of faculty, students, staff members, labor organizers, workers, and government officials, even administrators and business executives. We can be creative and organize such panels ourselves; this is one way we can offer students and colleagues an event to volunteer help for. We can arrange to be interviewed for the campus paper or a local radio or TV station. In master's and doctoral committee oral meetings, especially in the sciences and professions, faculty (including liberal-arts faculty acting as graduate school representatives) can pose questions about the funding of research and its possible effects on impartiality, which is still a value of great importance to most scientists and other intellectuals. Such funding is far less in the liberal arts, but it is growing and there is increasing emphasis on it. Graduate oral exams are particularly sensitive, vulnerable moments, and such questions, based on the student's thesis and presentation, can cause a stir, promote discussion, and linger for years in the memory, results one hopes will lead to change.

Write articles and letters in campus, local, regional, professional, and national papers—*things that people might actually read.* Faculty can write op-eds for the local or campus paper, or contribute to the local alternative paper; often these papers are eager to have such pieces as long as they address a newsworthy topic, which corporatization is. Faculty and students (undergraduate as well as graduate) can make their research and academic writing part of the process of active resistance to corporatization. At any land grant university, for example, faculty and students in agriculture are very interested in what's happening to family farms (they are disappearing, gobbled up by agribusinesses, and those left are often reduced to being mere sharecroppers in hock to Archer Daniels Midland); and clear-cutting and water quality are hot issues among foresters and environmentalists as well as the general public. The corporatization of discourse is a subject students can gleefully research and write about in many classes, not only those in the humanities and social sciences, and thus students can prepare themselves for democratic action in the larger world.

Read and become informed in order to act. This is the last point, one that in a sense hardly needs to be mentioned; but becoming informed must, of course, underlie, or better yet accompany, all efforts to resist the further imposition of corporate ideals and practices on higher education. "Accompany" is the better word because action is necessary for resistance, not a quietist pursuit of just sitting and reading, of passively learning some interesting things about corporatization. Action to resist and becoming informed should go hand in hand. Faculty are in a privileged position to read and become informed in order to act, and to help others do the same. As Chomsky has said, "If they choose, privileged intellectuals in the universities and elsewhere can contribute to protecting and advancing democracy, freedom, and human rights. That is unlikely to win them many plaudits, but it brings rewards that are immeasurable."[45] *If they choose.*

I would like to close with a quotation from the German-Jewish critic and thinker Walter Benjamin, who committed suicide in France in 1940 rather than be taken by the Nazis: "Is it still possible to isolate from the process of the disagregation of democratic society the elements that—linked to its origins and to its dreams—do not deny a solidarity with a future society, with humanity itself? German scholars who have abandoned their country would not have saved much, and would have had little to lose, if the response to this question were not yes. The attempt to read it on the lips of history is not an academic attempt."[46] Efforts to resist the corporatization of universities are also work in solidarity with a better future and with humanity; they are part of the larger struggle of our time, that between the people and the corporate order for a democratic culture in which all people, not just the privileged few, have the material means and thus the chance to find fulfillment. And our resistance also has to be, finally, more than an "academic attempt," although, as students, teachers, researchers, and staff members (as well as the odd administrator?) we must begin from the places in which we find ourselves, the classrooms, laboratories, libraries, offices, and coffee shops that are still the heart and soul of American higher education.

NOTES

My deepest thanks to Peter Copek and the Oregon State University Center for the Humanities for a one-term fellowship that gave me time to finish this essay and to work on the larger project of which it is a part.

1. Quoted in David Noble, "Digital Diploma Mills, Part 1: The Automation of Higher Education," *October* 86 (fall 1998): 114.

2. *Business Week*, December 22, 1997, p. 96.

3. Keynote address of the Race, Work, and Economic Justice Conference, organized by the Labor Education & Research Center (LERC), University of Oregon, Eugene, Ore., April 3, 1998.

4. Many recent books argue for transforming property relations if we are to have a democratic rather than a corporatist or soft fascist society. William Greider, for instance, in *One World Ready or Not: The Manic Logic of Global Capitalism* (New York: Simon & Schuster, 1997); Doug Henwood, *Wall Street: How It Works and for Whom* (New York: Verso, 1997); Robert Kuttner, *Everything for Sale: The Virtues and Limits of Markets* (New York: Knopf, 1997); and Kim Moody, *Workers in a Lean World: Unions in the International Economy* (New York: Verso, 1997).

5. The "MLA [Modern Language Association] Radical Caucus Statement on CUNY" (1997) refers to the "racist implications of current developments in public higher education—the end to affirmative action in the University of California system and, most recently, the dismantling of open admissions at CUNY" and to "the ways in which racism is serving ideologically to rationalize the increasing inaccessibility of higher education to large numbers of working-class and middle-class students. . . . " This is part of a larger economic pattern, as indicated by Robert Brenner's statement that "the cyclical upturn of the 1990s has done little or nothing to improve the lot of the poor. In 1996 the poverty rate was 13.7 percent (36.5 million people), clearly higher than in 1989, and at the end of 1997, the extent of hunger and homelessness was actually rising" ("The Economics of Global Turbulence: A Special Report on the World Economy: 1950–98," *New Left Review* 229 [May/June 1998]: 5). Carol Stabile points out that "Given the routine exclusion of children from decent public education, and ever dwindling access to higher education, that we should defend the 'democratic mission' of the university was not merely an ineffectual defense: it was a hypocrisy of the first order," in "Another Brick in the Wall: (Re)contextualizing the Crisis," in *Higher Education Under Fire*, eds. Michael Berube and Cary Nelson (New York: Routledge, 1995), p. 117.

6. Uses of the term "global" to describe contemporary capitalism and its forms are often uncritical. See Paul Smith, *Millennial Dreams: Contemporary Culture and Capital in the North* (New York: Verso, 1997), pp. 1, 11, 264. In issues of the *Monthly Review* from June through November 1997, there is an ongoing debate over this issue and use of the term, involving Edward Herman, William Tabb, and Paul Sweezy, among others. See also Bill Readings, *The University in Ruins* (Cambridge: Harvard University Press, 1996), p. 2.

7. Ernst Benjamin elaborates the problem and shows that there has been a general decline in public-sector funding, of which the problem of university funding is a part, in "A Faculty Response to the Fiscal Crisis: From Defense to Offense," in *Higher Education Under Fire*, pp. 52–72. See also Masao Miyoshi, " 'Globalization,' Culture, and the University," in *The Cultures of Globalization*,

eds. Fredric Jameson and Masao Miyoshi (Durham, N.C.: Duke University Press, 1998), p. 263. David Harvey articulates the principle involved: "One of the principal tasks of the capitalist state is to locate power in the spaces which the bourgeoisie controls, and disempower those spaces which oppositional movements have the greatest potentiality to command" (*The Condition of Postmodernity: An Enquiry into the Origins of Cultural Change* [Cambridge, Mass.: Blackwell, 1990], p. 237). .

8. Just one example illustrates the problem. The *Corvallis* (Ore.) *Gazette-Times* of May 18, 1997 (pp. E1, 3), reported that Professor Jose Reyes of Oregon State University received $8 million in grants to test the Advanced Plant Experiment (APEX) Project, principally developed and funded by Westinghouse Electric Corp., with help from the Electric Power Research Institute, the U.S. Department of Energy (DOE), and the Advanced Light Water Reactor Program, with final testing by the Nuclear Regulatory Commission, for whom Reyes worked for ten years before coming to OSU to head its Radiation Center. Reyes says APEX "could win back public confidence in nuclear plant safety that was lost after the nuclear accident at . . . Chernobyl . . . 11 years ago." Chernobyl, the article notes, was the "greatest man-made environmental disaster in history " and "so chilled the world community that it brought new construction of nuclear power plants to a virtual standstill." With the APEX system, however, there would be "virtually no chance" of a meltdown, and it can "easily be taken apart and shipped across the country on rail cars" and "can bring power to parts of the world where candles and firelight flicker in the night and people deforest their hillsides for firewood." Claims such as these have been made often enough for nuclear power in the past and have proved time and again to be simply illusory, at best, as well as expensive, potentially deadly, and destructive of the environment.

9. This was tried several years ago at Oregon State, but complaints from students and faculty made the administration relent and leave the campus's bookstore, a cooperative, alone. At the University of Pennsylvania, however, as Matthew Rubin's article in this volume tells us, the campus bookstore was outsourced to Barnes & Noble, with the usual layoffs and reductions in benefits for workers.

10. Matthew Rubin's article in this volume analyzes the fiscal and moral problems of the construction at Penn, out of which administrators and private sector operators are making small fortunes while decimating the old urban scene. A whitewash of the building project, with amounts involved, appeared on the Real Estate page of the *New York Times* (p. Y39) of September 21, 1997.

11. Clyde W. Barrow, *Universities and the Corporate State: Corporate Liberalism and the Reconstruction of Higher Education, 1894–1928* (Madison: University of Wisconsin Press, 1990), pp. 7, passim.

12. Lawrence C. Soley, *Leasing the Ivory Tower: The Corporate Takeover of Academia* (Boston: South End Press, 1995), p. 19.

13. Barrow, *Universities and the Corporate State*, pp. 9–10.

14. Ibid., p. 118.

15. Ibid., pp. 66–75. It's hard to overestimate the degree to which Pritchett and the administrators of most other universities, including the most prestigious ones (Columbia's Nicholas Murray Butler, for another example), were eager to

please the captains of industry. They went the extra mile for their betters. In 1905, Pritchett published an article titled "Shall the University Become a Business Corporation?" in which he noted approvingly "that the American university was already tending 'more and more to conform in its administration to the methods of the business corporation.' He pointed to the analogy between university governing boards and corporate boards of directors, under whom there was a president and various departments, each with its own managerial head as an example of this claim. He noted, on the other hand, that the European university was a 'free association of scholars and teachers' " and that European professors thus "enjoyed a level of self-determination in politics and scholarship that one could not find in the United States." Pritchett's own evidence showed that the European universities were "economically more efficient and cost-effective" than were the American, but he nonetheless oddly concluded that the corporate model was educationally most efficient. Pritchett argued that "no type of man has been developed who is a wiser councilor than the businessman of large sympathy and of real interest in intellectual problems" (p. 66)—ideological determination that still operates today.

16. David Noble, "Digital Diploma Mills, Part 2: The Coming Battle over Online Instruction," *October* 86 (fall 1998), p. 118, passim.

17. As reported in an informative AP article on p. A5 of the *Corvallis* (Ore.) *Gazette-Times* of November 2, 1998.

18. The *Daily Barometer*, November 12, 1998, pp. 5–6. (The *Barometer* is the student newspaper at Oregon State University.)

19. As reported in the *Portland Oregonian*, November 1, 1998, p. A20.

20. Noble, "Digital Diploma Mills, Part 2" p. 119.

21. In André Schiffrin, ed., *The Cold War and the University: Toward an Intellectual History of the Postwar Years* (New York: New Press, 1997), p. 182.

22. Seymour Hersh, *The Price of Power: Kissinger in the Nixon White House* (New York: Summit Books, 1983), pp. 258–96. Harvard's "best and brightest," of course, gave us much of the Cold War, the Vietnam War, the dozens of efforts to assassinate Castro, and so on. The phrase "the best and the brightest" apparently originated in 1946 in the "so-called Harvard Redbook, 'General Education in a Free Society,' " which "defined higher education as a compensation for democracy. The "best and brightest" were "almost exclusively white, male, and privileged." (Berube and Nelson, *Higher Education Under Fire*, pp. 24, 32).

23. The outlines of the story of the economic ruin that Sachs and some of his Harvard and U.S. government and private sector cronies brought to the former USSR (and which enriched many of them) are set forth in Janine R. Wedel's recent *Nation* article, as well as in her book *Collision and Collusion: The Strange Case of Western Aid to Eastern Europe 1989–1998* (New York: 1998). In a September 1997 *New Republic* article titled "Heil Harvard," Jacob Heilbrunn informs us that Austrian neofascist leader Jorg Haider, an admirer of Hitler, has spent a fair amount of time at the Harvard Institute for International Development and is a favorite of Sachs. Haider has lauded Hitler's "orderly employment policies." He also told the author that "Jeffrey Sachs is excellent.

... He's not left-wing, and he knows how to sell himself well in Eastern Europe" (pp. 1, 2 of the digital copy).

24. Soley refers to the Olin Foundation's sponsorship of programs in the "academically questionable field of 'Law and Economics' " ("the application of extremist laissez-faire economic philosophy to law") at several prestigious universities: courses "in this ideology-cum-discipline are taught at numerous prestigious law schools, thanks to the Olin Foundation" which "funds Law and Economics programs at the University of Chicago, Yale, Stanford, Harvard, Columbia, George Mason, Georgetown, Duke, Penn, and the University of Virginia" (*Leasing the Ivory Tower*, p. 137).

25. In *Universities and the Capitalist State*, Barrow argues that World War I "generated an American ideology of national science that subsequently served as an ideological basis for reorienting the activities of intellectuals in two ways. The infusion of money, equipment, prestige, and political power which accompanied the intellectuals' participation in the war left them far more receptive to the principle of centrally administered, mission-oriented research. The principle of autonomy was therefore increasingly set aside for a concept of 'public service.' Public service, however, was understood to mean the application of expert knowledge of 'means' to achieving administrative goals—a national interest— that was defined by state executive elites" (p. 124).

26. Soley, *Leasing the Ivory Tower*, p. 1.

27. Martin J. Sklar puts it this way: "The transformation of the market and of the form of capitalist property [1890–1916] included changes in the organization and management of labor, production processes, finance, distribution, and administration. These changes generated new professional, technical, and managerial functions with their corresponding social strata and, in turn, their values, attitudes, and ideological dispositions. Along with these strata came provision for their training and for the propagation of forms of consciousness appropriate to their functions, provision especially lodged in newly established or reoriented university professional and graduate schools and professional associations" (*The Corporate Reconstruction of American Capitalism, 1890–1916: The Market, the Law, and Politics* [Cambridge: Cambridge University Press, 1988], p. 431).

28. Barrow, *Universities and the Capitalist State*, pp. 247–48.

29. Ibid., p. 11. "The scholar," says Nietzsche in "Schopenhauer as Educator," has the "impulse to discover *certain* 'truths,' which comes from his servility to certain powerful persons, classes, opinions, churches, and governments, since he feels that he profits by bringing 'truth' to their side" (in *Unmodern Observations*, ed. William Arrowsmith [New Haven: Yale University Press, 1990], p. 204).

30. Richard Ohmann uses the idea of the PMC in *Politics of Letters* (Middletown, Conn.: Weslyan University Press, 1987), where on p. 79 he characterizes the PMC by "its conflicted relation to the ruling class (intellectuals managed that class's affairs and many of its institutions, and they derived benefits from this position, but they also strove for autonomy and for a somewhat different vision of the future); by its equally mixed relation to the working class (it dominated, supervised, taught, and planned for them, but even in doing so it also

served and augmented capital); and by its own marginal position with respect to capital (its members didn't have the wealth to sit back and clip coupons, but had ready access to credit . . .)."

31. Barrow, *Universities and the Capitalist State*, p. 95.

32. I have mainly in mind here the recent books on the internationalizing economy by William Greider, Kim Moody, Robert Brenner, and Paul Smith already referred to in nn. 4, 5, and 6. To these I would add the theoretically conflicted, even naive, but nonetheless useful book by David C. Korten, *When Corporations Rule the World* (West Hartford, Conn.: Kumarian Press, 1996).

33. Barrow, *Universities and the Capitalist State*, pp. 7, 258–59.

34. Masao Miyoshi, " 'Globalization,' Culture, and the University," in *The Cultures of Globalization*, p. 265.

35. Barrow, *Universities and the Capitalist State*, p. 10.

36. Ibid., p. 11.

37. Max Horkheimer and Theodor Adorno suggest that fascism begins to occur in a society when the private sector permeates and dominates the public sector when they write, for example, that while "the growth of economic productivity furnishes the conditions for a world of greater justice; on the other hand it allows the technical apparatus and the social groups which administer it a disproportionate superiority to the rest of the population. The individual is wholly devalued in relation to the economic powers . . . " (*Dialectic of Enlightenment*, trans. John Cumming [1944; reprint, New York: Continuum, 1995], p. xiv). Edward S. Herman writes that "in the ideology of fascism (sometimes referred to as 'corporatism'), 'natural leaders'—including top businesspeople—served as stewards of society, entrusted to balance private and social interests." He also argues that given the "traditional economic assumptions of unrestricted competition and a goal of profit maximization, 'corporate initiatives' are clear and simple and the very idea of corporate 'responsiveness' is meaningless—corporate behavior will always be based on adapting available means to a profitability end" (*Corporate Control, Corporate Power* [Cambridge: Cambridge University Press, 1981], pp. 4, 254). R. Jeffrey Lustig argues that at "the same time we witness the extension of technical rationality and bureaucracy, we therefore also experience greater disorder in our personal lives, and economic instability, along with increasing uses of force in the society. This is to say that the impulse to rational administration is to be understood as both a symptom and a cause of deeper social *ir*rationalities. That impulse is rooted in our primary social institution [the private corporation], and it can be expected to become stronger." He goes on to say that "corporatist to its core, [American society] creates mechanistic rather than organic social relations. It forces agglomeration, but without community. It mandates corporatism, but without diversity. It imposes close interdependence, without trust" (*Corporate Liberalism: The Origins of Modern American Political Theory, 1890–1920* [Berkeley: University of California Press, 1982], p. 247). In the years since Lustig's book was published, of course, "diversity," along with "excellence," has become a key word in the "University prospectus" and "responds very well to the needs of technological capitalism"

(Readings, *The University in Ruins*, p. 32). Still, Lustig remains correct that this diversity is mechanical rather than organic in American soceity.

38. Jonathan Kozol, in his searing book *Savage Inequalities: Children in America's Schools* (New York: Crown Publishers, 1991) details how the free market and corporate culture have impoverished and segregated inner-city schools in four American cities, schools that are by any standard savagely unequal to those in the mostly white and prosperous suburbs, and the cruel effects of this on students, families, and teachers, all of whom nonetheless keep trying to make their schools work.

39. Bill Readings argues throughout *The University in Ruins* that a denatured "Excellence" is to the contemporary university what "Culture" was to the modern university and "Reason" to the Kantian one before that, and there is a certain bite to his argument. The idea of excellence is "meaningless," "non-referential"; it has "no content to call its own" (p. 22).

40. In 1911, CFAT published the influential study *Academic and Industrial Efficiency* by Morris L. Cooke—engineer, corporate reformer, and friend of Frederick Taylor—who was "an advocate of social engineering based on the use of scientific data and technical processes in political and government decision-making. His ideal for the American nation was that it would . . . be organized as one vast 'socially efficient' production unit in which all aspects of social life— industry, government, family, and culture—would be coordinated toward the singular goal of national prosperity." Cooke argues for a "standardized statistical concept by which departments and universities could be compared for efficiency relative to an empirically derived average. A social average of efficiency could be established as the norm for making organizational and administrative judgments" throughout the nation. "The key unit of measurement in this new calculus was called the 'student hour,' " which he defines as " 'one hour of lectures, of laboratory work, or recitation room work, for a single pupil.' " This is our student credit-hour (SCH) with which, he notes, management can figure "relative faculty workloads, the cost of instruction per student-hour, and . . . the rate of educational efficiency for individual professors, courses, fields, departments, and universities." Cooke argues further that "the industrial world is coming more and more to feel that all work is done under certain broad principles, and that the application of these principles to one industry is little different from their application to any other." He also contends that professors "must be governed and measured by the same general standards that generally obtain in other occupations" (Barrow, *Universities and the Capitalist State*, pp. 67, 69–70).

41. Readings, *The University in Ruins*, pp. 21–43.

42. In his essay on "The Cold War and the University," Noam Chomsky observes that "the respectable intellectuals, those who will be recognized as serious intellectuals, will overwhelmingly tend to be those who are subordinated to power. Those who are not subordinated to power are not recognized as intellectuals, or are marginalized as dissidents, maybe 'ideological' " (Schiffrin, *The Cold War and the University,* p. 189).

43. Soley's *Leasing the Ivory Tower* gives plenty of evidence to support this.

44. I find Dewey's words in Chomsky, "The Cold War and the University," p. 190.

45. Chomsky, "The Cold War and the University," p. 194.

46. Quoted in Antonio Negri, *The Savage Anomaly: The Power of Spinoza's Metaphysics and Politics*, trans. Michael Hardt (Minneapolis: University of Minnesota Press, 1991), p. 229.

6

THE MYTH OF THE LIBERAL CAMPUS

Michael Parenti

For some time we have been asked to believe that the quality of higher education is being devalued by the "politically correct" tyrannies of feminists, African-American nationalists, gays, lesbians, and Marxists. The truth is something else. In fact, most college professors and students are drearily conventional in their ideological proclivities. And the system of rule within the average university or college, be it private or public, owes more to Sparta than to Athens.

The university is a chartered corporation ruled, like any other corporation, by a self-appointed, self-perpetuating board of trustees composed overwhelmingly of affluent and conservative businesspeople. The trustees retain final say over all matters of capital funding, investment, budget, scholarships, tuition, student campus organizations, school sports, and the hiring, firing, and promotion of administration and faculty personnel. And a fact less well known: Trustees also have final say over the academic curriculum. They can cancel any courses they do not like and mandate other course offerings they do like. They have final say regarding the existence and structure of course-distribution requirements, studies programs, and whole departments and entire schools within the university.

At no time do these affluent businesspeople have to explain how, upon appointment to the board, they were able to emerge as instant experts of higher education. At no time during their tenure as trustees are they troubled by anything that might be called democracy. They face no free and independent campus press, no elections, no opposing political slates, and no accountability regarding policy and performance. Conservative critics who rant about "politically correct" coercions appear to be perfectly untroubled by this oligarchic rule.

On these same campuses can be found faculty members who do "risk analysis" to help private corporations make safe investments in the Third World, or who work on marketing techniques and union busting, or who devise new methods for controlling rebellious peoples at home and abroad, new weapons systems and technologies for surveillance and counterinsurgency. (Napalm was invented at Harvard.) For handsome fees these faculty offer bright and often ruthless ideas on how to make the world safe for those who own it.

On these same campuses one can find recruiters from various corporations, the armed forces, and the CIA. In 1993, an advertisement appeared in campus newspapers promoting "student programs and career opportunities" with the CIA. Students "could be eligible for a CIA internship and tuition assistance" and would get "hands-on experience" working with CIA "professionals" while attending school. The advertisement did not explain how full-time students could get experience as undercover agents. Would it be by reporting on professors and fellow students who voiced iconoclastic views?

Without any apparent sense of irony, many of the faculty engaged in these worldly activities argue that a university should be a place apart from immediate worldly interests. In reality, most universities have direct investments in corporate America in the form of substantial stock portfolios. By purchase and persuasion, our institutions of higher learning are wedded to institutions of higher earning.

A MATTER OF SOME HISTORY

Ideological repression in academia is as old as the nation itself. Through the eighteenth and nineteenth centuries, most colleges were controlled by religiously devout trustees, who believed it their duty to ensure faculty acceptance of the prevailing theological preachments. In the early 1800s, trustees at northern colleges prohibited their faculties from engaging in critical discussions of slavery; abolitionism was a taboo subject. At colleges in the South, faculty actively devoted much of their intellectual energies to justifying slavery and injecting white supremacist notions into the overall curriculum. In the 1870s and 1880s, Darwinism was the great bugaboo. Presidents of nine prominent eastern colleges went on record as prohibiting the teaching of evolutionary theory. What is called "creationism" today was the only acceptable viewpoint on most of the nation's campuses of that day.

By the 1880s, rich businessmen came to dominate the boards of trustees of most institutions of learning. They seldom hesitated to impose ideological controls. They fired faculty members who expressed heretical ideas on and off campus, who attended Populist Party conventions, championed antimonopoly views, supported free silver, opposed U.S. imperialism in the Philippines, or defended the rights of labor leaders and socialists.

During World War I, university officials such as Nicholas Murray Butler, president of Columbia University, explicitly forbade faculty from criticizing the war, arguing that in times of war such heresy was seditious. A leading historian, Charles Beard, was grilled by the Columbia trustees, who were concerned that his views might "inculcate disrespect for American institutions." In disgust, Beard resigned from his teaching position, declaring that the trustees and Nicholas Murray Butler sought "to drive out or humiliate or terrorize every man who held progressive, liberal, or unconventional views on political matters."

Academia never has been receptive to persons of anticapitalist persuasion. Even during the radical days of the 1930s there were relatively few communists on college teaching staffs. Repression reached a heightened intensity with the McCarthyite witch-hunts of the late 1940s and early 1950s. The rooting out of communists and other assorted radicals was done by congressional and state legislative committees, and, in many instances, university administrations. Administrators across the land developed an impressively uniform set of practices to carry out their purges.

Almost any criticism of the existing politico-economic order invited suspicion that one might be harboring "communist tendencies." The relatively few academics who denounced the anticommunist witch-hunts usually did so from an anticommunist premise, arguing that "innocent" (noncommunist) people were being hounded out of their jobs and silenced in their professions. The implication was that the inquisition was not wrong, just overdone, that it was quite all right to deny Americans their constitutional rights if they were really "guilty" of harboring communist beliefs.

THE OPEN AND CLOSED UNIVERSITY

The campus uprisings of the Vietnam era presented an entirely new threat to campus orthodoxy. University authorities responded with a combination of liberalizing and repressive measures. They dropped course-distribution requirements and abolished parietal rules and other paternalistic restrictions on student dormitory life. Courses in black studies and women's studies were set up, along with a number of other experimental programs that attempted to deal with contemporary and community-oriented issues.

Along with the grudging concessions, university authorities launched a repressive counteroffensive. Student activists were disciplined, expelled, drafted into a war they opposed, and—at places like Kent State and Jackson State—shot and killed. Radicalized faculty lost their jobs and some, including myself, were attacked and badly beaten by police during campus demonstrations.

The repression continued through the 1970s and 1980s. Angela Davis, a Communist, was let go at UCLA. Marlene Dixon, a Marxist-feminist sociologist, was fired from the University of Chicago and then from McGill University for her political activism. Bruce Franklin, a tenured associate professor at Stanford, author of eleven books and one hundred articles and an outstanding teacher, was fired for "inciting" students to demonstrate. Franklin later received an offer from the University of Colorado that was quashed by its board of regents, who based their decision on a packet of information supplied by the FBI. The packet included false rumors, bogus letters, and unfavorable news articles.

During the 1970s, eight of nine antiwar professors who tried to democratize the philosophy department at the University of Vermont were denied contract renewals in swift succession. Within a three-year period in the early seventies, at Dartmouth College, all but one of a dozen progressive faculty, who used to lunch together, were dismissed. In 1987, four professors at the New England School of Law were fired, despite solid endorsements by their colleagues. All four were involved in the Critical Legal Studies movement, a left-oriented group that viewed much of the law as an instrument of the corporate rich and powerful.

One could add hundreds of cases involving political scientists, economists, historians, sociologists, psychologists and even chemists, physicists, mathematicians, and musicologists. Whole departments and even whole schools and colleges have been eradicated for taking the road less traveled. At Berkeley, the trustees abolished the entire school of criminology because many of its faculty had developed a class analysis of crime and criminal enforcement. Those among them who taught a more orthodox mainstream criminology were given appointments in other departments. Only the radicals were jettisoned.

One prominent Communist Party member, Herbert Aptheker, a stimulating teacher and productive scholar, was unable to get a regular academic appointment for over fifty years. In 1976, he was invited to teach a course at Yale University for one semester, but the administration refused to honor the appointment. Only after eighteen months of protests by students and faculty did the Yale oligarchs give in. Even then, precautions were taken to ensure that Aptheker not subvert too many Yalies. His course was limited to fifteen students and situated in the attic of a dingy building at a remote end of the campus. Aptheker had to travel from New York to New Haven for his once-a-week appearance. He was given no travel funds and was paid the grand sum of $2000 for the entire semester. Yale survived the presence of a bona fide Communist, but not without institutional officials trembling a bit. They were not afraid that Aptheker by himself would undermine the university but that his appointment might be the first step in an opening to anticapitalist viewpoints.

LEFTIES NEED NOT APPLY

The purging of dissidence within the universities continues to this day. More frequent but less visible than the firings are the nonhirings. Highly qualified social scientists, who were also known progressives, applied for positions at places too numerous to mention, only to be turned down in favor of candidates who—as measured by their training, publications, and teaching experience—appeared far less qualified.

Scholars of a dissident bent are regularly discriminated against in the distribution of research grants and scholarships. After writing *The Power Elite*, C. Wright Mills was abruptly cut off from foundation funding. To this day, radical academics are rarely considered for appointments within their professional associations and are regularly passed over for prestigious lecture invitations and appointments to editorial boards of the more influential professional journals.

Faculty usually think twice about introducing a controversial politico-economic perspective into their classrooms. On some campuses, administrative officials have monitored classes, questioned the political content of books and films, and screened the lists of campus guest speakers. While turning down leftist speakers, trustees and administrators have paid out huge sums for guest lectures by such right-wing ideologues as William Buckley and George Will, war criminals Henry Kissinger and Alexander Haig, and convicted felons G. Gordon Liddy and Oliver North.

PRESUMPTIONS OF OBJECTIVITY

The guardians of academic orthodoxy try to find seemingly professional and apolitical grounds for the exercise of their political repression. They will say the candidate has not published enough articles. Or if enough, the articles are not in conventionally acceptable academic journals. Or if in acceptable journals, they are still wanting in quality and originality, or show too narrow or too diffuse a development.

Seemingly objective criteria can be applied in endlessly subjective ways. John Womack, one of the very few Marxists ever to obtain tenure at an elite university and who became chair of the history department at Harvard, ascribes his survival to the fact that he was dealing with relatively obscure topics: "Had I been a bright young student in Russian history and taken positions perpendicular to American policy . . . I think my [academic] elders would have thought that I had a second-rate mind. Which is what you say when you disagree with somebody. You can't say, 'I disagree with the person politically.' You say, 'It's clear he has a second-rate mind' " (*Washington Post*, January 1, 1983).

Politically orthodox academics maintain that only their brand of teaching and research qualifies as scholarship. They seem unaware that this view might itself be an ideological one, a manifestation of their own self-serving, unexamined political biases. Having judged Marxist or feminist scholars as incapable of disinterested or detached scholarship, the guardians of orthodoxy can refuse to hire them under the guise of protecting rather than violating academic standards.

In fact, much of the best scholarship comes from politically committed investigators. Thus, it is female and African-American researchers who, in their partisan urgency, have produced new and rich critiques of the unexamined sexist and racist presumptions of conventional research. They have ventured into fruitful areas that most of their white male colleagues never imagined were fit subjects for study.

Likewise, it is leftist intellectuals (including some who are female or nonwhite) who have produced the challenging scholarship about popular struggles and often the only revealing work on political economy and class power, subjects remaining largely untouched by "objective" centrists and conservatives. In sum, partisan concerns and a dissenting ideology can actually free us from long-established blind spots and awaken us to things overlooked by the established orthodoxy.

Orthodox ideological strictures are applied not only to scholarship but to a teacher's outside political activity. At the University of Wisconsin, Milwaukee, an instructor of political science, Ted Hayes, an anticapitalist, was denied reappointment because he was judged to have "outside political commitments" that made it impossible for him to be an objective, unbiased teacher. Two of the senior faculty who voted against him were state committeemen of the Republican Party in Wisconsin. There was no question as to whether *their* outside political commitments interfered with their objectivity as teachers or with the judgments they made about colleagues.

In a speech in Washington, D.C., Evron Kirkpatrick, who served as director of the American Political Science Association for more than twenty-five years, proudly enumerated the many political scientists who occupied public office, worked in electoral campaigns or in other ways served officialdom in various capacities. His remarks evoked no outcry from his mainstream colleagues on behalf of scientific detachment. It seemed there was nothing wrong with political activism as long as one played a "sound role in government" (Kirkpatrick's words) rather than a dissenting role against it. Establishment academics like Kirkpatrick never explain how they supposedly avoid injecting politics into their science while so assiduously injecting their science into politics.

How neutral in their writings and teachings were academics such as Zbigniew Brzezinski, Henry Kissinger, and Daniel Patrick Moynihan? Despite being blatant proponents of American industrial-military policies at home and abroad—or because of it—they enjoyed meteoric academic careers and subsequently were selected to serve as prominent acolytes to the circles of power. Outspoken political advocacy is not a hindrance to one's career as long as one advocates the right things.

THE MYTH OF THE RADICAL CAMPUS

To repeat, at the average university or college, the opportunities to study, express, and support (or reject) iconoclastic, antiestablishment views are severely limited. Conservatives believe otherwise. They see academia as permeated with leftism. They brand campus protests against racism, sexism, and U.S. interventionism abroad as "politically correct McCarthyism." Thus the attempts to fight reactionism are themselves labeled as reactionary and the roles of oppressor and oppressed are reversed. So is fostered the myth of a university dominated by feminists, gays, Marxists, and black militants.

In dozens of TV opinion shows and numerous large-circulation publications across the nation, without any sense of irony, scores of conservative writers complain of being silenced by the "politically correct." Their diatribes usually are little more than attacks upon sociopolitical views they find intolerable and want eradicated from college curricula. Through all this, one never actually hears from the "politically correct" people who supposedly dominate the universe of discourse.

Today, a national network of well-financed, right-wing campus groups coordinates most conservative activities at schools around the nation and funds over one hundred conservative campus publications, reaching more than a million students. These undertakings receive millions of dollars from the Sciafe Foundation, the Olin Foundation, and other wealthy donors. The nearly complete lack of alternative funding for progressive campus groups belies the charge that political communication in academia is dominated by left-wingers.

Accusations of partisanship are leveled against those who challenge, but rarely against those who reinforce, the prevailing orthodoxies. By implicitly accepting the existing power structure on its own terms, then denying its existence and all the difficult questions it raises, many academics believe they have achieved a scholarly detachment from the turmoil of reality—and in a way they have.

Part Two

A SCHOOL OF FISH
Students, Faculty, and Administrators
Take the Corporate Bait

7

DEAD SOULS
The Aftermath of Bayh-Dole

Leonard Minsky

The passage of the Bayh-Dole Act in 1980 altered the nature of the university in a shorter space of time and more radically than at any other time in history. In the years leading up to its passage, proponents of the act, mainly CEOs of major multinational corporations and presidents of the elite universities, were joined in common efforts to persuade President Carter and the Congress to find ways to subsidize corporate research and development through the universities.[1] Corporate control of new patents and inventions created through university-based research was said to be essential to the "competitiveness" that would give American multinationals the technological edge needed to dominate global markets, and the military technology to protect its interests.

The control of new inventions and patents given to the corporations through Bayh-Dole would be dubbed "technology transfer," the "transfer of research results to the commercial sector" as one recent commentator defined it. This would facilitate the corporate takeover of the entire public investment in university research infrastructure and personnel. It would include the researchers, their labs, and their graduate students, together with the lion's share of the annual federal funding of research, which by 1995 exceeded $15 billion. All this in the service of American multinational imperial ambition.

Publicly claiming only a narrow target, corporate and academic CEOs privately understood that the entire culture of the university as it then existed

needed to be changed to serve their interests. These changes included traditions of academic freedom and the openness and common ownership of
intellectual property that had been the basis of scholarship and scientific
advances for centuries. This unfriendly takeover—now nearly twenty years
down the road—essentially altered the "nonprofit" nature of teaching and
research in higher education and produced problems for the academic community never understood to originate with Bayh-Dole.

The architects of Bayh-Dole, however, fully understood that subversion of the academic ethic was necessary to make university-based
researchers more amenable to serving corporate interests. Some university presidents professed to believe that this takeover could be friendly or
at least not actively inimical to the nonprofit, disinterested ethic of the
academy, but others knew better. The crafters of the act fully intended to
bend the university and its research capacity to corporate purposes, and if
some ethical commandments had to be broken to achieve this end, then,
as one cynic put it, "you cannot make an omelet without breaking eggs."

An early opponent of the act was Admiral Hyman Rickover. Rickover
had spent more than sixty years preventing corrupt contractors from ripping off the government through unethical and fraudulent practices, had
built a nuclear fleet of 161 ships without a single accident, and through
constant skirmishes with large corporations and defense contractors had
become acutely aware of the threat posed to democratic government by
unchecked corporate power.

In 1980, Rickover testified against the act and warned that its implementation would be disastrous for the universities and basic research. In
1982, as he was about to retire, he testified for the last time before the Joint
Economic Committee of the United States Congress, reminding them of a
long-standing policy of the government "to preserve for the American taxpayer title to the inventions developed by government contractors at the
public's expense."[2] He then issued this warning: "In 1980 the Congress
reversed this long-standing government policy by giving universities and
small businesses title to inventions developed at government expense. I testified against that because I recognized what would happen and it has happened. Now patent lobbyists are pressing Congress to extend that giveaway
practice to large contractors. This would generate more business for patent
lawyers but, in the process, will promote even greater concentration of economic power in the hands of the large corporations which already get the
lion's share of the governments research and development budget."[3]

In 1984, Ralph Nader, who had also testified against the act, spelled
out the salient implications of the intrusion of corporate power into higher
education. "Pressing the corporate model onto the university world," he
says in an article reprinted in this book, "jeopardizes the preservation of

precious academic values as well as broader democratic rights. The corporate model concentrates power, restricts the production and application of knowledge, and increases uniform behavior, self-censorship and—when needed—outright suppression."[4]

What follows is a brief analytical and historical description of the forces that gave rise to Bayh-Dole, and the consequent pressing of the "corporate model" onto higher education. While it is my belief that much can be done to minimize or reverse its effects, I do not believe that anything can be done without understanding the people and forces behind it.

Before Bayh-Dole, American universities were trusted institutions. But scientific fraud, athletic huckstering, and a nearly twenty-year history of inexplicable raises in tuition for which no satisfactory explanations are forthcoming have eroded that trust.

The problems of higher education—the fraud, the tuition increases, the falsified research, the transformation of teachers into workers, the scramble to steal intellectual property by administrators from faculty and students, and by colleagues from one another—are all new problems. They are symptoms of a profound alteration of culture in institutions of higher learning that was deliberately engineered by transnational corporations in a successful effort to get control of the federal investment in university research. As a result, university administrators gradually abandoned their support for the traditional academic goals of improving education and giving people the ability to think critically, and adopted instead the corporate goal of making a profit. While academics still value that tradition, intact in many places, they are nevertheless under pressure from administrators, newly recruited from the world of business, who have little tolerance for or understanding of academic goals and values. What is important to grasp, and grasp clearly, is that a relative handful of identifiable men collaborated to change the purposes and goals of higher education to suit themselves and the global multinational corporations they served. They needed the universities to be more like themselves, interested in money and profits, and oriented toward building a world focused on wasteful consumerism. They wanted the universities to act as handmaidens to the multinational corporations that dominate the global economy. In so doing, they changed the way teaching was done and who would do it; chose the materials to be taught, the research that would be undertaken, and the students that would be recruited to corporate-sponsored programs; and trained for jobs in a society constructed to suit corporate purposes.

Passed in 1980, the Bayh-Dole Act was the means through which the corporations achieved these goals. Its main purpose was to transfer effective ownership of new inventions and technologies generated in university-owned facilities to corporations through licensing. Prior to Bayh-Dole, inventions paid for by taxpayer dollars were considered to belong to the public. A license to manufacture the invention could be issued to a corporation, but only on a nonexclusive basis. What this meant in practice was that manufacturers of inventions would have to compete with other companies that could also secure licenses. In this manner, it was thought, the costs to the public would be minimized because market competition protected the public from monopolistic control and pricing.

Under Bayh-Dole, however, universities were designated as the owners of inventions rather than mere agents of the federal government protecting the public interest. No longer acting as agents of the taxpayers who had paid for the invention, the universities were simply given ownership by the legislation. They, in turn, pass the invention on to the corporations for a price, a price that never reflects the true cost of the development of the invention, already paid for up-front by the public. This sleight-of-hand dimension of "technology transfer," whereby public assets are basically handed over to transnational corporations for pennies on the dollar, remains invisible to the public because the mechanics of patenting and licensing are ill understood and, unfortunately, boring. In this way, corporations are able to walk away with exclusive license to manufacture, and are given a new license to bilk the public through monopolistic pricing.

Universities have now become major players in the marketplace, offering corporations risk-free investment in research outcomes by paying the up-front operational costs of research (building, labs, and the like) at taxpayer expense, and shielding them from the very expensive costs of failure by producing favorable or auspicious results before cutting a deal. Further, and most important, thanks to monopolistic pricing, corporations are assured of large profit margins while providing universities—and especially their administrators—with a share of the action.

This one change in the political economy of the university, hitherto shielded from market forces, has cataclysmic effects that change the kind of service higher education offered to American students and determine the kinds of issues, research, and policies nurtured in university labs and classrooms. Bayh-Dole leads to the displacement and subordination of the humanistic tradition and collegial society integral to the university, and will never be identified as the source of the problem. The public knows very little about it and the university community most affected was—carefully—not consulted. To this day, the public knows nothing about the act or its effects, and most faculty have never heard of it.

Originally called the Small-Business Universities Patenting Act, Bayh-Dole was an amendment to the Patent Act ostensibly designed to help small businesses. But "small business" was already a deliberately misleading misnomer: The first business recipients of federal largesse were venture capital firms initially capitalized in millions of dollars, and were small only by comparison to Dow Chemical, Monsanto, Hitachi, and the biggest of the multinationals, scheduled to participate later in the game.

The act was a gift of public money to private investors using the universities to launder the money. The money came from taxpayers to corporations in the form of the facilities, personnel, and operating costs for doing research for venture capital firms. University/industry partnerships, as these deals would come to be called, were offered by the universities for a nominal fee that never exceeded 15 percent of the cost of the research, and most often hovered around 7 percent. Thus, the cost of the research to the corporation never exceeded fifteen cents on the dollar, and was often as low as seven cents. Corporations had always feared that the open culture of university science would not protect their proprietary interest in inventions. Now, through Bayh-Dole, this fear was overcome. As part of the job of reassuring corporations of control, universities now forced faculty and students to sign contracts requiring secrecy, publication safeguards and acknowledgements of university ownership. Universities have since attempted to go much further by claiming ownership of *all* the intellectual property produced by faculty and students, including e-mail exchanges between students and their professors and faculty lecture notes. (Cf. David Noble's article in this volume.) The successful resistance of faculty at York University in Toronto and at California State University (CSU) to this demand suggests that universities may be vulnerable on this issue. In 1983, the provisions of Bayh-Dole were quietly extended by executive order[5] to the multinationals, thus completing the capture of higher educational facilities on behalf of global capital.

Why was Bayh-Dole necessary, and what were the economic circumstances and conditions that made American multinationals press for this legislation? While stealing public resources through well-crafted backdoor legislation was (and still is) normal operating procedure for corporations, the seventies had put American multinationals in greater need of a larger-than-usual corporate handout. When the profits from the Vietnam War disappeared, it turned out that the domestic market preferred the cheaper and more sophisticated goods manufactured by the Germans and Japanese. American corporations were unable to compete because they were unwilling to plough profits back into research and development (R&D), as was the normal practice. Since R&D was needed and the corporations were unwilling to pay for it themselves, they hit on the idea of annexing the huge public investment in the universities as an instant fix for their problems.

The multinationals initially persuaded the Carter administration to legislate Bayh-Dole by promising to protect American industry and jobs from foreign competition. The policy of carving technology from the body of university-based research, they claimed, would provide a healthy economy and jobs for the unemployed, and would justify the extreme step of taking control of the universities' research capacity. They called this industrial policy "competitiveness."

Carter bought it, in part because the promise of jobs and a healthy economy always has potent appeal, but also because of heavy lobbying by elite university presidents through their Washington-based organizations, the American Council on Education and the American Association of Universities. These organizations joined, or were joined by, CEOs of almost every major American-based multinational corporation to create the Business–Higher Education Forum (BHEF), in which both groups were represented. The BHEF, created in 1978, would act as the "umbrella" for planning and coordinating the necessary legislation to "restructure" higher education.

Housed at One Dupont Circle, in the offices of the American Council on Education, the Business-Higher Education Forum was "formed with the express purpose of promoting discourse and acting on issues shared jointly by American business and the nation's higher education institutions."[6] What their common issues turned out to be were shared hostilities to government regulation, health and safety standards, environmental restrictions on developing new plants, and protectionist trade policies. Why these policies concerned higher education's spokesmen has yet to be explained, but the fact that they signed on exposes the subordination of these "leaders" of higher education to the corporations, and foreshadows the way that corporations would use the universities to advance their agenda.

Support from BHEF members was critical to the passage of Bayh-Dole in 1980. One of its first publications was titled "America's Competitive Challenge,"[7] a relatively unknown but extremely influential document created at the direct request of President Reagan. Published in 1982, it summed up the positions and policies its members had developed and supported through the seventies, leading up to the passage of the act, and foreshadowed future developments. Specifically, it laid out the action agenda for the corporate restructuring of higher education as an enterprise. In this slick pamphlet, the Executive Committee of BHEF thanks Mr. Reagan for inviting its advice on the problem of economic decline, and tells him to "strengthen . . . the transfer to U.S. industry of technology developed by American universities."[8] It observes in a cheerful, self-interested way that "U.S. universities . . . are being asked to conduct pioneering research with obsolete equipment in run-down facilities. The severity of this problem has already caused the productivity of university research to decline."[9]

Later, in a section ostensibly recommending more support for "basic" research, the authors complain that although "more than half of the nation's research is performed in universities, . . . obsolete equipment and facilities, caused by many years of underinvestment, is a major problem. . . . A program of maintenance, replacement, and additions is necessary to keep American basic research at the cutting edge of scientific advance. The Forum welcomes the President's proposed increase in funds to upgrade scientific instrumentation. . . ."[10]

The BHEF's most brilliant stroke, however, the seed it planted that would grow to engulf the universities, was the idea that the American economy was in decline and had lost "competitiveness." This was due, it claimed, to federal, environmental, regulatory, and trade policies, rather than corporate failure to reinvest in R&D. Its own solution was to persuade Americans that in order to regain the productivity lost in the seventies—and hence jobs and economic security—university R&D should be turned over to America's major corporations.

This lobbying effort succeeded by deploying a gang of heavyweights drawn from both industries, corporate and educational, that made them hard to ignore. The BHEF's membership, revealed by the signatories to its most influential report, "America's Competitive Challenge" (1983), included R. Anderson, chairman and CEO, Rockwell International; Phillip Caldwell, chairman, Ford Motor Co.; Edward Donley, chairman, Air Products and Chemicals; John Burlingame, vice chairman of the board, General Electric Co.; and Gerald D. Lauback, president, Pfizer Inc. The universities were represented by the then-presidents Derke Bok of Harvard, Theodore Hesburgh of Notre Dame, Wesley Posvar of Pittsburgh, Richard Cyert of Carnegie Mellon, and Clifton Wharton Jr. of the State University of New York.

The influence of these prestigious and powerful university leaders alone would have guaranteed support for their recommendations, but in combination with the largest and most powerful corporate CEOs in the U.S. and purporting to represent the solution to America's most pressing economic problems of the late twentieth century, the enactment of their program became inevitable.

Bayh-Dole achieved all these powerful men wished without significant public scrutiny. It annexed billions of dollars in public investment in the universities, silenced corporate and military critics on campus by defunding their departments and programs, replaced students with a more docile group intent on securing corporate jobs and benefits, and altered the culture of higher education by focusing it on the needs of corporate sponsors for marketable products instead of basic research. It also rewarded the higher educators who had supported the corporate interest with salaries and fringe benefits far beyond their modest rewards as representatives of the academic community.

In the wake of the passage of Bayh-Dole, universities ceased to be primarily educational institutions and became "sites of production," knowledge factories that play a central role in developing profitable technologies. The mission of the newly corporatized colleges and universities, in effect, became the production of profits from marketable products. But the introduction of the profit motive into the research itself eventually meant that profits would be generated from environmentally damaging pesticides and seeds (Monsanto); from genetically engineered animals and, eventually, maybe human beings (Dow Chemical and companions); and from pharmaceuticals with unrevealed side-effects (Hoecht, Ciba-Geigy, and others). Topping it all off, corporate sponsorship developed phony "studies" emanating from the university to provide arguments for the damage being done.

GETTING OUT

This transformation has not been easy and has not yet been completed. That's the good news. The bad news is that too much of what the corporations wanted, they got. The story as told here is not generally known. The fantasy of a funding shortage drifted like snow on each campus, concealing the corporate story behind the changes. University presidents were themselves part of the snow job, while the unions, unused to dealing with problems of this nature, were distracted by immediate problems raised by the restructuring. Faculty ran to defensive positions in their departments and complained, but never aimed their guns higher than their own administrations, or at most the regents, all of whom were in on the game.

Also confusing was the fact that the restructuring raised different issues on each campus, depending on which programs or departments were under attack. Each campus thought it had a separate and different problem. In the end, each university administration blamed the crisis on the reduction of federal funds (later state funds), as part of a larger domestic policy that had no particular relevance to the campus. This policy, faculty were sometimes given to understand, had something to do with keeping the American economy afloat, and providing employment. Up against such a benign economic policy, faculty thought they had no alternative but to accept the diminution of funds as inevitable and, in any case, not directly aimed at them.

Following are some actual examples of how the artificially crafted funding shortage concealed how research and personnel choices were manipulated. President Reagan, for example, decided to dry up funds to the humanities and the "nonproductive" departments of the university, shifting those funds to the "Star Wars" program. The research money was not lost to the university, but it was reallocated to those departments that could contribute to the weapons system and the defense contractors involved. Instead of exposing the shell game, the university presidents told the deprived departments that there was no more federal money, and they must seek corporate support for their work. Alternatively, the dean of arts of a well-known midwestern university told the math department it had too many theoretical mathematicians, and that due to a shortage of funds, the department needed to divest itself of theoreticians and replace them with those who could teach applied mathematics. Or another variant: My university had to deny tenure to the Marxist economist not because we disapproved of her political perspective, but because we were unable to attract a corporate partner while she was in the department.

These goals and tactics were subsequently adopted by state legislators who had little sympathy or understanding for the needs of higher education, but who liked the idea of research parks, technology corridor, and silicon valleys in their own neighborhoods. They adopted the idea of the university as technology incubator, and have attempted, not always successfully, to create new research parks or industrial partnerships by providing funds—selectively withdrawn from the university budget—to industry. This practice has frequently resulted in genuine cutbacks, with university faculty in a real quandary about how to fight back, given the weight of public and legislative opinion supporting the supposed economic benefits.

The corporate raiders correctly believed that this approach would help to disarm the faculty. But while Bayh-Dole has taken care of some of the intellectual property issues, the faculty tradition concerning the ownership and exchange of research ideas and results has proved troublesome. The competition for ownership of intellectual property has expressed itself in lawsuits and in struggles led by faculty unions, senates, and associations as organizations fight to retain job security protection, but each fight on each campus is treated as a separate issue rather than as a particular illustration of the broader changes wrought by Bayh-Dole.

Thus, traditional ideas about research and knowledge remain a problem for the corporations, and in many places have left a residue of bitterness as individual faculty members, disturbed by the changes in the nature and conditions of their work, feel compelled to fight back.

To the chagrin of the corporatizers, the alienation of their intellectual property is still an unacceptable idea to researchers. It remains an ethical problem and continues to produce friction between faculty and administrators—sometimes in the form of lawsuits. Faculty members continue to believe that the advancement of knowledge is a common enterprise, and continue to pass this view on to their students. Faculty still believe that advancing the frontiers of the knowable requires the sharing of information, as well as the prompt sharing of their discoveries with their col-

leagues. In this ancient and enduring tradition, information is not proprietary but is held to be common property. Secrecy, what the corporate
world needs to protect its stake in intellectual property, is inimical to the
free exchange of information, and the advancement of science and knowledge is still believed to depend on openness.

In the 1970s, when the multinationals conceived the idea of inte-
grating university labs and scientists into the productive machine they
envisioned, they knew these "ivory tower" values would be a major
obstacle. They could not make a profit on property held in common. To
properly incorporate higher education, they had to turn ideas into intellectual property that could be bought and sold; they had to "own" the
products produced in the "plant"—inventions, scientific breakthroughs,
and the like. Knowledge had to become intellectual property, a concept
nearly antithetic to the notion of shared knowledge that is the core tradition of the university. It is this ancient core tradition of knowledge and
research that remains incompatible with the notion of the corporatized
university. It is this tradition that crops up again and again as individual
faculty file lawsuits, or try to fight back through their unions and senates.
It was this tradition that Bayh-Dole aimed to eradicate, or at least undermine. Its corollary idea, that the intellectual property of the academic
cannot in any fundamental way be alienated, aroused faculty at York University to strike with the support of 90 percent of the faculty—a strike the
faculty won. And the recent attempt by CSU to sell the lecture notes and
e-mail exchanges of faculty with students has evoked similar rage and a
vow from the California Faculty Association (CFA) to fight back.

Thus, over time, the universities are being made into accomplices of
corporate conservatism, and are turning away from their most important
mission—the preservation of a democratic form of education without
which democracy itself cannot survive. In the years since Bayh-Dole, the
universities have declined as defenders of academic freedom and critical
thought and have indeed become the new cradle of corporate invention.
They have reconciled with the military and the CIA. They are aiding and
abetting the corporations to maintain profits from uncompensated labor
via student loans, tuition, fees, and unremunerated student work on corporate research. They are conspiring to permit dangerous drugs into the
market by protecting them from critical review.

Bayh-Dole was passed because powerful interests—the multinationals—successfully concealed their eagerness for its passage by hiding
behind the very willing and very much more respectable university presidents who lobbied on their behalf. The Congress that passed the act scarcely
understood its implications and few congressmen or senators had knowledgeable staff to explain it to them. One senator, a longtime opponent of this

kind of giveaway, was asked why he finally voted for the act. He explained that he got a phone call from the president of the University of Wisconsin, who followed up by meeting for him for lunch and pressing him to vote for the act. And so it went. University presidents acted as respectable fronts for the multinationals that lurked behind them, while the congressmen and senators were in the dark or, if suspicious, permitted themselves to be soothed by the fact that university presidents were asking for the act's passage.

And, since the passage of the act, the darkness has continued. There has been no resistance to the effects of the act from the academic community, no demonstrations against Bayh-Dole by students, no demand from disappointed parents who can no longer afford the tuition that rises steadily and inexplicably at 4 percent per annum ahead of the rate of inflation, and no explanations or articles in the popular press explaining the issue—because nobody knows the history.

So perhaps what we need is a little sunshine. What was done in the dark should not be able survive the light of day. Bayh-Dole infringes on and damages too many communities—parents, students, academics, people of color, and poor people who can't pay the price of admission—to survive a serious debate, or indeed serious resistance from the campuses. The most powerful voices on campus belong to the faculty unions, and these voices, once informed and raised in unison, have the interest, commitment, and resources to lead a strong coalition that should be able to restore much of what has been lost of academic freedom and independent thought.

NOTES

1. Business Higher Education Forum, *America's Competitive Challenge: The Need for a National Response*, Washington, D.C., April 1983.

2. Note on Sen. Russell Long, during whose tenure most government-funded inventions were preserved in public ownership.

3. Admiral Hyman Rickover, *No Holds Barred: The Final Congressional Testimony of Admiral Hyman Rickover* (Washington, D.C.: Center for the Study of Responsive Law, 1982), p. 10.

4. Ralph Nader, "Greed in the Groves: Part One," in *Thought and Action: The NEA Higher Education Journal* 1, no. 1 (fall 1984): 41–42.

5. Cite of Ronald Reagan's executive order extending Bayh-Dole to "large" corporations.

6. Business Higher Education Forum, *America's Competitive Challenge*, p. 51.

7. Ibid., p. 20.

8. Ibid.

9. Ibid., p. 10.

10. Ibid., p. vi.

8

TOUGH CUSTOMERS
Business' Plan to Corner
the Student Market

Sonya Huber

"It is business' best interest to get themselves . . . directly involved with funding for universities, but also with a direct involvement in setting the curricula, so that they will get the kind of student they want."
— A former president of the Royal Bank of Canada, in a fund-raising video for Queen's University[1]

Our mothers always told us not to look a gift horse in the mouth. If state and federal governments are cutting educational budgets and student aid, wouldn't a university be foolish—or even downright irresponsible—to refuse a new Reebok field house, an Olin Foundation honorary business faculty position, or a new Microsoft computer system and online teaching center? Isn't this "partnership" between business and the university ultimately in the best interests of our students? The problem is, students today are learning through experience as much about the negative results of corporate control as they are learning about biology and English.

A President's Report to Harvard University's board of overseers states: "The commercialization of universities is perhaps the most severe threat facing higher education. . . . Universities appear less and less as charitable institutions seeking truth and serving students, and more and more as a huge commercial operation that differs from corporations only because there are no shareholders and no dividends."[2]

The university, for all the ideals we may invest in it, has always been controlled by the monied class. However, our era is seeing three new developments: (1) Most importantly, the corporate world has determined that higher education is a multibillion-dollar industry; (2) heavily influenced by the attention from the corporate world and increasingly cut off from public-sector funding, the university is running itself like a corporation, seeking profit through formal and informal close relationships with other corporations; and (3) students organizing to reclaim higher education are exploring how these trends affect their quality of life and quality of education in both superficial and deeper ways. The corporatization and monopolization of the campus creates superficial changes, such as a lack of choice about soft drinks on campus. But the same problem runs deeper, from a lack of choice about majors and courses to the future of accessible, quality higher education in this country.

CHEAP RESEARCH, DONE JUST THE WAY YOU LIKE IT

According to a report from the Association of University Technology Managers, universities in the United States and Canada made $592 million in 1996 from licenses and royalties from research sold to corporations. Profit from products born out of academic research generated about $25 billion for the U.S. and Canadian economies during the same year. The problem? "Money is a pretty strong driver, and as the money gets bigger, the push to get more involved in things that have a potential for making big money gets stronger and stronger," said Jules LaPidus, president of the Council of Graduate Schools.[3] Students are seeing connections between corporate control of the campus and the university's shifting research priorities. As one student wrote in the October 1996 edition of the Iowa State University alternative newspaper, the *Drummer*: "The commercialization of university research is the dirty little secret behind tuition increases. . . . When universities shift priorities from basic research to research with foreseeable commercial application, they need a huge amount of up-front investment. They need to set up state-of-the-art industrial labs."[4] Some students see themselves as providing a backdoor version of corporate welfare, as their tuition dollars go to fund projects they have no voice in and will never benefit from. Finally, the nature, and possibly even the results, of academic research are being tainted by corporate influence. A study conducted by researchers at Harvard University and the University of Minnesota concluded that "more than half of all university scientists who received gifts from drug or biotech companies admitted that the donors expected to exert influence over their work, ranging from prior review of published academic papers to patent rights for commercial discoveries."[5]

What goes on behind closed corporate doors on campus can even lead to physical harm and death of students. Activist Ali Zaidi was harassed by the University of Rochester (UR) as he attempted to expose the corporate-funding links at the university. After Energy Secretary Hazel O'Leary issued an official apology to human test subjects injected with plutonium in the UR labs, Zaidi began investigating the university's role. The UR administration has consistently denied responsibility for the plutonium medical experiments because they were, according to UR Medical Center spokesman Robert Loeb, "government-created and government-funded." As Zaidi says, "This attribution of sole responsibility to the government ignores the circulation of elites between government, corporations, and universities, particularly at UR, which was built in the shadow of Kodak and the national-security state." Zaidi investigated the negotiations that took place between faculty and Eastman Kodak staff to initiate the experiments. In his investigation, Zaidi encountered a UR whitewash regarding this and other experiments, from which UR has consistently profited:

> UR's moral crisis in medicine continues to this day. Last spring, UR sophomore Nicole Wan died in a university medical experiment. Just months prior to Wan's death, the Food and Drug Administration had warned that UR's failure to follow proper experiment procedures placed human subjects at risk. Around the same time, UR's parentage of the Westfall Health Facility, where a comatose woman was raped and impregnated, became public knowledge. A Gannett newspaper investigation suggests that UR distanced itself from the facility in order to avoid liability.[6]

FREE FACILITIES AND CAPTIVE MARKETS

In some cases, universities that have embarked on the corporate method of "fund-raising" have begun to place the profit motive above concern for their students or their educational mission. The University of Pennsylvania made a deal with bookstore giant Barnes and Noble: In exchange for a university-funded $4-million bookstore, the university would receive a share of Barnes and Noble's profits. But "the bookstore deal may well represent a net loss in the money available to fulfill Penn's academic mission," reported a student investigative journalist. The profits that Barnes and Noble promised "will be used almost exclusively to subsidize the construction of the Inn at Penn," as well as other private ventures.[7]

A captive university market means big profits. Marriott, the largest campus food service contractor in the United States, presently serves over five hundred college campuses. At the State University of New York at

Binghamton, Marriott is allowed to take 4 percent profit on its base expense budget of approximately $10 million, which means that Marriott makes at least $400,000 each year at this school alone.[8] Students have also witnessed the corporation-university connection as their administrators become entangled in corporate agendas and drag their universities along behind them. Thomas Kean, president of Drew University since 1990, also sat on the Board of Directors for Aramark, a major food service provider with many college contracts. Aramark began a multimillion-dollar contract with Drew in May 1997.[9]

Coke and Pepsi have negotiated exclusive "pouring rights" contracts at universities across the United States and Canada, as well as advertising contracts at primary and secondary schools. A deal between Coca-Cola and York University in Toronto was estimated to be worth around $10 million, though "contracts with the corporation prevent the disclosure of all financial figures."[10] According to Pepsi, the first "pouring rights" arrangement was a ten-year deal between the soft-drink giant and Pennsylvania State University for $14 million in 1992, and other universities lined up soon after.[11] In January 1997, students in Canada used their schools' exclusive vending agreements with Pepsi to force the company out of Burma, and students around the country have revealed similar corporate connections.

DOWNSIZING THE CLASSROOM

As universities accept the corporate mandate of the market, students have watched departments such as anthropology, French, Spanish, comparative literature, cultural studies, and a variety of history, art, and social science courses cut because administrators would rather use the resources to expand the business school. Using "supply and demand" as a justification, administrators who make sweeping staffing and curricular changes claim that they are acting in accordance with what the job market requires, and that their responsibility is to prepare students for the job market. In the process, the idea that every student is more than just a worker-to-be is lost.

The corporate university rejects the notion of quality public education for all. New technology such as the Microsoft Online network, which might be very useful as a supplement to in-class interaction with an instructor, is being proposed in some cases as a replacement for class attendance. York University has required all nontenured faculty to develop electronic versions of their courses, and the administration has created a for-profit subsidiary for the "commercial development and exploitation of online education."[12] UCLA, in conjunction with its own for-profit Home Education Network and other private corporations, launched an "Instructional Enhancement Initiative," which required online versions of all arts and science courses. Canadian students' analysis of this trend reveals the profit motive:

> Course materials, converted into educational products, become the property of the university. The subsidiaries are then able to sell knowledge for a profit and the university decreases its teaching cost. Administration may then dismiss the non-tenured teacher, and the student receives a low-quality education delivered in a teacherless classroom.[13]

James L. Wood, a sociologist at San Diego State University, stated that elite colleges will not be bearing the brunt of these teacherless classrooms. "Down the ladder, when you get to community colleges, where there are poorer students of ethnic minority backgrounds, this is the group ticketed for distance education because it is [perceived to be] good enough for them," he said.[14]

The few faculty that are left in such classrooms are too overworked to have time to connect with their students. As they have for many years, administrators are overloading faculty and increasing class sizes in order to cut down on labor costs. Frazzled instructors may be more intent on searching for their next job than on their lesson plans because of reduced job security and attacks on tenure: "At the University of Toronto, a $15-million donation by businessman J. Rotman bought him the ability to withhold funding if he becomes unhappy with the faculty's performance."[15]

Students today are fighting the assault on their freedom of speech and privacy, the lack of choice in education, and the lack of access by developing a multi-issue analysis of the problem. Access to higher education for working- and middle-class people is in jeopardy, and to a large extent, corporate agendas have shaped this specific crisis, as well as the larger economic context. In the coming years, fewer students will attend post-secondary programs, and those that do will leave with larger debt loads. Nontraditional students, including many students of color, will find the university unwilling to adapt to their educational needs. Two-thirds of students say they are concerned they won't have enough money to finish college. In the face of these large obstacles, students are developing new ways to fight back, and learning from past struggles.

STUDENTS FOR SALE

Corporations today—from McDonald's to MasterCard to Reebok to Wall Street investment firms—view students as a gold mine, a captive and naive audience. Students are a young and relatively poor group in society, one which the mushrooming "poverty industry" can use to make a sizable profit.[16] From check-cashing services to lottery tickets to secured credit cards, the poverty industry is counting on the fact that students may not think about the long-term effects of debt. And corporations with products to sell view students as potential lifetime customers and vie to win their "product allegiances." "For as little as $10,000, a corporation can put its name on a course at York University. Students' consumption habits, values and political views are being influenced by business interests from within the walls of academia."[17] A national study done by MasterCard and *Careers and Colleges Magazine* found that 32 percent of high school students and 82 percent of college students in the United States have at least one credit card. The student credit card problem has gotten so severe that Iowa State University has set up a Financial Counseling Clinic. Says Brian Johnson of the independent newspaper the *Drummer*: "A single seminar may offer some advice, but it can hardly compete with the constant avalanche of promotions and slick advertising targeted at college students by the credit card companies."[18] At Louisiana Tech, this barrage of marketing flyers caused the student government, with the administration's consent, to ban credit card marketers from campus.[19]

Some credit card campaigns are less visible and more insidious. Banks and campus administrators have recently attempted to launch cooperative campaigns, combining a school identification card with an ATM card, the school's meal card, library card, and phone card, all in one. Banks receive a mandatory group of new consumers, and administrators receive a share of the profits. The Alumni Association at Iowa State University issues an ISU credit card featuring the school's mascot, and the university recently introduced the ISU card, which serves as both a bank card and a student ID card.[20]

Inevitably, treating students as raw material to be sold and traded results in abridgment of their rights to freedom of speech and privacy. At the City University of New York (CUNY), student activists protested the CUNYCard, a CUNY-wide ID card that administrators are attempting to implement throughout this system of 206,000 undergraduate and graduate students. The CUNYCard was produced by Citibank and its subcontractors (MCI, Diebold Inc., and Digital Equipment Corp.), and at one point was made mandatory at some CUNY campuses, including Baruch College, LaGuardia, Queensboro, and New York Tech.

Student organizers contended that the card would give corporations, and CUNY, open access to students' personal information. Students stated that in the negotiations for the card system, CUNY gave MCI information about students' social security numbers and home addresses, all without students' consent, and that MCI created a common database that would allow Citibank, MCI, and CUNY to share information about students. Activists at CUNY, as well as at the University of Florida, have reported that they were harassed as a result of political activities, and that campus security used information that could only have been taken from such ID cards.[21] At Baruch College, the CUNYCard "is required for entrance to the buildings, the libraries, the washrooms and the offices. Each use is instantly recorded on a computer and appears in real time on a screen in the security room. This means that anyone can be tracked in, out, and around a building complex by administration," according to Chris Day of the *Hunter Envoy*.[22]

Students argue that the card will shift the burden of paying for CUNY onto working-class students through the card's hefty fees. Students were also alarmed at the fact that they had no choice but to become customers of Citibank; the institution's history of racist redlining and antistudent biases with regard to lending was brought to light by students (as reported in the *New York Times*). As a result of heated protests throughout CUNY campuses and coverage in the local media, the administration declared a one-year moratorium on the implementation of the card. This may have been a temporary victory, or a stall tactic designed to wait out student organizers.

Students can be manipulated and spied on by corporations, and they can also be silenced outright by giants such as Reebok and McDonald's. At the University of Wisconsin–Madison, Reebok negotiated a $7.9 million contract to become the sole supplier of equipment to the school's athletic teams. In an attempt to shield itself from potential criticism from University of Wisconsin employees, Reebok International included a "nondisparagement" clause in a 1996 sports product contract with the school. In other words, in exchange for this contract, administrators promised that no one employed by the university would publicly criticize Reebok. Many community members interpreted this move as an attempt to deflect criticism from Reebok's record of labor exploitation in the Asia-based factories that produce the company's wares. After vocal protests on campus, Reebok was forced to remove the clause and claimed that its intent was never to "abridge anyone's First Amendment rights." The school's chancellor expressed shock at the suggestion that the university would abandon its "historic commitment to freedom of expression" by being involved in such a contract.[23]

In 1997, activist members of the Progressive Student Alliance at the University of New Mexico (UNM) were charged with "amplification" after a protest in which a march was diverted through a McDonald's restaurant in the UNM Student Union Building. McDonald's had previously barred students from handing out flyers in the restaurant. Student activists realized that if the entire student union was privatized, the right to disseminate information would be effectively erased. Student activists made a connection in this case to the free speech movement at Berkeley, which began around similar issues. Students saw it as a fundamental contradiction, and asserted that their union should belong to them, and not to corporations.

In England, the National Union of Students stopped distributing McDonald's discount coupons when the student body "voted to bow out of the arrangement, citing the company's 'anti-union practices, exploitation of employees, its contribution to the destruction of the environment, animal cruelty and the promotion of unhealthy food products.' "[24] Students at Iowa State University united with alumni, faculty, and staff in 1996 and successfully prevented McDonald's from building a restaurant on the central campus. This struggle mirrors many other local campaigns around the country to keep students' public space from becoming a glaring shopping mall filled with national chains, all of which lack a basic commitment to the students.

THE CAMPUS IN THE GLOBAL ECONOMY

"The desperate desire to imprint brand loyalty on the young is being used as a moral lever by those very same young people to pressure corporations on everything from unfair labor conditions to trading with dictators."[25]

University endowments, built from alumni contributions and student tuition payments, are often invested in morally bankrupt schemes. Students have fought to convince universities to invest these endowments in a socially responsible manner, during, for example, the 1980s movement against apartheid in South Africa, as well as more recently. Of the University of Pennsylvania's $3.2-billion endowment, $14.3 million is invested in Lockheed Martin, the world's largest defense contractor; $10.8 million in Royal Dutch Petroleum (Shell Oil), "which has perpetrated massive abuses of the Ogoni people in Nigeria"; and over $8.7 million in tobacco company RJR Nabisco. Students demanded that the university divest from UNOCAL Inc., ARCO, and Hyundai, all corporations with ties to the military dictatorship in Burma.[26] A coalition of students and members of the Oil, Chemical, and Atomic Workers Union is calling for Donald Jacobs, dean of the School of Management at Northwestern

University, and University of Michigan professor Marina Whitman "to resign from their university positions if they care to keep their positions on the board of UNOCAL, the oil giant providing crucial financial support to the Burmese dictatorship."[27] Six students undertook a hunger strike at Occidental College in California and successfully persuaded President John Slaughter, an Arco board member, to issue a public statement denouncing Arco's involvement with Burma.[28]

The "End Corporate Dominance" campaign, organized by Earth First! in October 1997, saw a wide range of student participation. More than one hundred anticorporate teach-ins were conducted across the United States, as well as in Great Britain, Canada, India, South Africa, and beyond, and organizers provided activists with information about trends in global capitalism, including popular analyses of international trade agreements like the North American Free Trade Agreement (NAFTA) and the Multilateral Agreement on Investment (MAI).

The Canadian Federation of Students, in a campaign to educate young people about these complex economic trends, has produced fact sheets to educate students about the MAI. Such tools make organizing and outreach a reality. Students in Vancouver held a five-thousand-person rally to protest the University of British Columbia's decision to host the Asia-Pacific Economic Cooperation (APEC) Leaders' Summit on November 15, 1997. Students spoke out against the fact that Canada and UBC gave such a warm welcome to repressive leaders of Indonesia and China. In addition, students drew connections between this meeting of eighteen world economic leaders and their own educational problems. APEC leaders state that "decisions must be taken by a school system for good business reasons with maximum business intervention."[29] Larry Kuehn, director of research and technology at the British Columbia Teachers' Federation, said in a commentary paper that APEC supports the economic globalization agenda, and this agenda is driving the massive downsizing of education.

In Eugene, Oregon, students and community groups formed a coalition called VOICES to organize against the MAI, organizing an "End Corporate Greed" rally against Nike on April 18, 1998, and marking an international day of protest against Nike. Local organizers used the day to speak out about corporate greed across the globe, from Nike's influence at the University of Oregon and its sweatshops internationally, to "Norpac's (a popular 'veggie burger' manufacturer) gruesome labor record and how their connection with Nike prevented the University from removing Norpac Gardenburgers from campus cafeterias," to the MAI.[30] From Duke University's "no-sweatshop" licensing agreement to Students Stop Sweatshops campaigns, student-labor activism is on the rise around the country, protesting labor practices of transnational corporations and supporting local union struggles.

HIGHER EDUCATION FOR SOME

Tuition is rising more rapidly than the rate of inflation, so students and their families have to take out more loans to afford either a public or a private education. Two-thirds of students today receive loans to attend college. Students ten years ago received 40 percent of their school funds from loans, and that figure has increased to 60 percent today. Not surprisingly, the loan industry, intent on exploiting students' desire for an education, is making a profit on students' financial need. U.S. college students and their parents took out $36 billion in federally guaranteed educational loans. The servicing and collection of these loans makes a great profit for companies like the USA Group, an agency that tracks and collects student loans. United for a Fair Economy, a Boston-based economic justice organization, revealed that the USA Group paid its CEO $1 million in 1996 alone.[31]

The United States Student Association (USSA) has been on the forefront of the battle for access to higher education, and mobilized its members to fend off a proposed increase in the interest rate for student loans. During USSA's spring 1997 organizing work, a member of the Oregon Student Association received a letter sent by a political action committee called "The Friends of Higher Education." The "Friends" were members of the loan industry, soliciting funds for the purpose of making campaign contributions to members of Congress who supported the interest rate hike.[32] The PAC hoped to raise $100,000 by the end of 1997, according to the letter, which described its purpose as "promoting a continuing healthy private-sector role in financing higher education," and fighting potential changes to student loan interest rates, through "high-level forums" and "personal contacts," rather than any sort of public debate.

The Canadian Federation of Students (CFS), a national organization with over four hundred thousand members, played a pivotal role in crushing an "income-contingent loan repayment scheme," which would have divided students into two categories: the "deserving" and "undeserving" of financial aid. Under the scheme, the government would no longer fund institutions of higher education. It would slash budgets, and instead fund a handful of individuals who were hardest hit by the cuts, while neglecting need across the board. Students, including CFS members, responded to the government–banking industry plans with a series of student strikes across the country in January 1998. One week after the national action, the government backed down from the scheme.

A CFS pamphlet explains the bottom line of corporate handouts and their effect on education: "No longer able to afford needed supplies or technical equipment, college and university administrators are entering into partnerships with technology, communication, and publishing corporations." Jennifer Storey, national deputy chair of the CFS, said, "Corporate donations are filling in [funding] gaps, therefore being used as a justification by governments to further decrease federal and provincial funding."[33] From primary to secondary to higher education, we are seeing similar developments in the United States. As government abandons higher education, schools are forced to choose between closing their doors and selling their students and their educational mission to the highest bidder. The government then uses this "new" source of funding as an excuse to make new cuts.

As many social commentators have observed, it should come as no surprise that corporations cut costs and attempt to generate profits. That is what they are set up to do. However, allowing educational institutions to behave in this manner defies every educational mandate. Public education was won not by accident, but by long struggles on the part of social reformers and radicals. They envisioned a better life, including a life of the mind, for children and other working people—rather than simply a job generating profit for someone else. Now it seems we are slipping back to an era where job training is the central mission of education, where corporations determine what will be studied and by whom. As in the past, the mandate for a just education must come from those affected by and involved in the system: parents, teachers, and potential students. With thoughtful and thorough organizing, these people will be able to rally around an inspiring vision of what education can be.

Infusion *and the Center for Campus Organizing can be reached at 165 Friend St., Boston, MA 02114; (617) 725-2886; www.cco.org.*

NOTES

1. Andrew MacDonald, "Corporate Universities, Corporate Student Unions: Are Students Selling Students?" *Student Activist* 2, no. 1 (May 1998): 14.

2. Report by Derek Bok, as quoted in the *Drummer* (Iowa State University), October 1996, pp. 1–16.

3. "Universities Reap Windfall from Research," AP Wire, February 18, 1998.

4. Reported in the *Drummer,* October 1996, pp. 1–16.

5. Sheryl Gay Stolberg, "Gifts to Science Researchers Have Strings, Study Finds," *New York Times,* April 1, 1998, p. A17.

6. An edited version of Zaidi's article appeared as "University of Rochester, Radiation, and Repression," *Infusion* 2, no. 3 (spring 1997): 4.

7. Paul Lukasiak, "Outsourcing and the Cost of Dining: A Fiscal Analysis of the Little Potential Savings from Outsourcing," *PANic* (University of Pennsylvania), May 1998, p. 15.

8. Kevin Kniffin, writer for *Multinational Monitor*, in an e-mail to the Center for Campus Organizing, 1997.

9. Ibid.

10. Angela Pacienza, "Hard Cash for Soft Drinks," *York University Excalibur,* May 6, 1998, p. 1.

11. Anne Barnard and Robert F. O'Neill, "School Districts See Green in Potential Ad Spaces," *Philadelphia Inquirer*, June 14, 1998, via e-mail.

12. "Multilateral Agreement on Investment," Canadian Federation of Students 1998 fact sheet, February 1998, p. 2.

13. Ibid.

14. "A Wary Academia on Edge of Cyberspace," *Los Angeles Times,* March 31, 1998, p. A-1.

15. "Multilateral Agreement on Investment," p. 2.

16. For an excellent explanation of this industry, see Michael Hudson, ed., *Merchants of Misery* (Monroe, Maine: Common Courage Press, 1996).

17. "Multilateral Agreement on Investment," p. 1.

18. Brian Johnson, "Giving Credit Where Credit is Due," *Drummer* (Iowa State University), September 1997, p. 3.

19. Dennis Berman, "A Campus Revolt—Against Credit Card Companies," *Business Week Online,* www.businessweek.com [January 12, 1998].

20. Johnson, "Giving Credit Where Credit is Due."

21. Robert Wallace, "The Pawnbroker," self-published paper. Wallace is editor and publisher of *Leftward Ho!* (City University of New York). See also "CUNY Activists Hold Corporations at Bay," *Infusion* 3, no. 2 (January–February 1998): 9.

22. "CUNY Activists Hold Corporations at Bay," p. 9.

23. "Reebok U.," *Infusion* 2, no. 2 (winter 1997): 6. Source was the *National Campaign for Freedom of Expression Quarterly* (autumn 1996).

24. Naomi Klein, "Campus Brand Deals Backfire," e-mail from student organizers in Great Britain to the Center for Campus Organizing and "corporations" listserv.

25. Ibid.

26. Peter Chowla, "The Ethics of Investment: Students Demand that Administrators Take Action," *PANic* (University of Pennsylvania), March 1998, p. 4.

27. Kevin Kniffin, excerpts from "Serving Two Masters," *Infusion* 3, no. 3 (March–April 1998): 14. Originally appeared in *Multinational Monitor* (November 1997).

28. Ibid.

29. Larry Kuehn, "Schools for Globalized Business," commentary paper distributed via e-mail in response to a May 1997 paper published by the Ministry of Labor of the Republic of Korea. Kuehn is Director of Research and Tech-

nology, British Columbia Teachers' Federation. See *Infusion* 3, no. 2 (January–February 1998): 13.

30. Agatha Schmaedick, "Local Activists Challenge Neoliberal Agenda," *Student Insurgent* (University of Oregon), May 1998, p. 15.

31. *Too Much*, the newsletter of United for a Fair Economy (1997).

32. http://www.tray.com is an excellent online source of PAC funding information. "The Friends of Higher Education," FEC ID #C00324467. Public Disclosure, Inc. (updated regularly).

33. Pacienza, "Hard Cash for Soft Drinks."

9

FACULTY WORKERS
Tenure of the Corporate Assembly Line

Sonya Huber

If education is being turned into a commodity, are faculty members
the workers on the assembly line? And if the stuff they're told to pass
along to students is unfit or dangerous, if they're told to speed up their
output for less pay, could they be the force to grind production in this factory to a halt until conditions are improved?

In the hallowed halls of the university, the words used to describe
working conditions for faculty and staff and learning conditions for students sound suspiciously similar to those at a factory or a nursing home
or other sites of labor unrest: "downsizing," "speed-ups," and "total
quality management." Yet, strangely enough, many instructors in higher
education resist seeing themselves as workers who are capable of acting
collectively to change their places of work. The causes are many: the
dream of a tenure position, the prestige of an intellectual job, the weeding
out of "overly vocal" employees, or a general middle-class resistance to
labor unions. Many faculty are held enthralled by their hope that the university is a special place where ideas of all types are respected and no
one's agenda, including the corporate agenda, is favored.

In contrast, wealthy investors, administrators, and politicians have no
problem portraying higher education as just another industry. Students are
defined in business studies as "product."[1] Powerful institutions, including
the World Bank, advise investors and policy makers to introduce "user

119

fees" in higher education to make a profit on this market.[2] Making themselves market-friendly, universities have engaged in bidding wars over big-name business faculty, wooing them with starting salaries of over $100,000, even as they recommend cutting less profitable departments. Universities accept funding from conservative front organizations with deep ties to corporate interests, such as the Olin Foundation and the Intercollegiate Studies Institute, and allow their faculty positions, curricula, and research priorities to be transformed.[3] Today, a large piece of the funding for research comes from conservative companies that want to purchase research or legitimacy, such as the Olin Foundation's $40 million in awards to conservative faculty.

For some reason, major Wall Street speculators care what happens in our universities. Lehman Brothers, Inc., an investment firm, declared in a 1996 internal report that "[t]he health care sector 20 years ago and the education industry today have similarities that indicate strong growth potential for education in the next decade."[4] A careful, hundred-plus-page report details the many ways that the educational system, considered a massive service provider like the health-care industry, can be revamped in order to generate billions of dollars in profit.

The impact of these trends will increasingly affect access to education for the next generation of working people, says union activist and professor Michael Zweig of the State University of New York (SUNY) at Stony Brook.[5] The change in higher education is occurring as education becomes "privatized" and "corporatized." Zweig defines privatization as the transfer of services at public schools into the private sector, which includes outsourcing of union jobs to nonunion private contractors. Corporatization is the overall trend toward viewing the educational system as a profit-making industry and changing education to conform to a corporate model, including the replacement of full-time, secure union jobs with part-time positions.

Frequently, faculty must compete with colleagues in other departments for funding. They may have to worry about obtaining one of a shrinking number of tenure positions, and often have to conform to the expectations of administrators to ensure job security. In November 1997, Massachusetts State Board of Higher Education chairperson James F. Carlin called for a sweeping reduction of professors' influence, an elimination of tenure, and an increase in the workloads of professors because, in his eyes, colleges are "managerially dysfunctional." He said of his efforts to shape the roles of faculty: "We are making their lives a little uncomfortable. We are pushing them. We are challenging them."[6]

The corporate world sees whole universities as captive markets and sites for producing research at bargain-basement rates. Faculty are manipulated by the corporate agenda because, in recent years, corporate sponsors often write their paychecks and fund their research. Kim Moody of *Labor Notes* articulates a grim scenario: "Most academics are content to stay within the often unwritten guidelines of the corporations and wealthy families who fund universities and underwrite big research grants."[7]

Administrators and investors, in their attempt to weaken and destroy faculty unions, have repeatedly questioned whether faculty are actually workers. This question proved to be the linchpin in legislation that drastically weakened faculty union organizing. In addition, this question has continued to be an effective tool for dividing faculty because it plays on the contradictory class position that they inhabit. This question is a common smoke screen, an attempt to disempower workers by telling them that they already have all the privileges that they are fighting for and that their number one enemies are their coworkers.

If the corporate world has its way, the broad goal of a liberal arts education, meant to prepare all young people to be thinking members of society, will never be reached. Instead, schools will become merely sites for job training and preparation to make profits for someone else. Faculty have a choice: They can either help the corporate world to destroy this essential function of higher education and many of their jobs, or they can unite with other members of their communities to make education work as it should in a democratic culture. Because of the momentum and power of the corporate grab for higher education, building this united response is the single most effective way that faculty can act in their own interests and in the interests of the majority in this country.

The corporate takeover of higher education has been sounding the alarm bells for faculty and students for decades. Thirty years ago, faculty and students saw higher education as being in a state of crisis and organized to respond. Between 125 and 150 formal contracts existed between institutions of higher education and professional staff in 1971. At that time, Gus Tyler wrote that "[t]he push of the National Education Association and the American Federation of Teachers has bestirred even the staid American Association of University Professors to behave like a union."[8] From 1965–1971, membership in the American Federation of Teachers (AFT) rose from 60,000 to 250,000.

Since the 1970s, the situation for faculty and for higher education in general has only gotten worse. As tuition has increased for students and federal financial aid has plummeted, faculty salaries have not increased to keep pace with inflation. Work conditions and job security have diminished, from the attack on tenure to the continued exploitation of part-time instructors. The AFT drafted a first statement on part-time faculty in 1979, and recently revised it because of the continuing problem: Between

1971 and 1986, the number of part-time faculty positions increased 133 percent. AFT literature states that "the welfare and professionalism of all faculty depend upon recognizing the status of part-time faculty and their use and abuse as colleagues."[9] Corporate concerns have come to determine ever more of the mission and product of many U.S. universities.

Despite the fact that many private school faculty had been organizing in the workplace against these attacks and acting like workers for two decades, the courts essentially told these faculty in 1980 that they already had the privileges they had been "mistakenly" fighting so hard to get. The 1980 decision in *National Labor Relations Board* v. *Yeshiva University* described eighteen different ways in which private school faculty (and public school faculty in Puerto Rico) are supposedly managerial. This decision meant that that "people on campus end up being at the mercy of their employers," says Jennifer Berkshire of the Massachusetts Jobs with Justice Higher Education Project, because private universities are not accountable to anyone but the trustees, and can't be influenced in the way that regular corporations can be pressured by shareholders. The Yeshiva decision's implication that faculty are in full control of their work lives, despite evidence to the contrary, also problematized the legitimacy of faculty union concerns at public universities. Mark Blum, consultant to the Communication Workers of America's (CWA) Higher Education Project and a former faculty and Association of American University Professors (AAUP) staff member, explained that faculty's participation in hiring decisions, and the ability to give recommendations about administrative matters, curriculum, and hiring and tenure, were framed in the decision as managerial functions.[10] In the eyes of the courts, even if a university governance structure does not allow faculty members to have final say on any decision, the mere ability to give input to the administration makes them managerial. Using a common tactic, conservatives took the steam and the feet out from under faculty by arguing that they already had the rights they seemed desperate to gain.

Despite the *Yeshiva* decision, faculty organizing has continued on private school campuses since 1980, according to Blum. These faculty are able to organize bargaining units and sit down as a group with the administration to present demands, but faculty do not have legal recourse to seek assistance from the National Labor Relations Board (NLRB) in the case of a dispute. The administration in these situations always has recourse to the *Yeshiva* decision like a "nuclear bomb in their back pocket," says Blum.

In public universities, which make up two-thirds of U.S. institutions of higher education, union organizing is still an option, although some faculty are covered by state laws that prevent them from striking because they are state employees. Blum explained that only about half of the states have "enabling legislation" that sets up a legal framework for organizing faculty and that requires university administration to sit down at the bargaining table. In Arizona, Texas, Indiana, Mississippi, and other states, there is no enabling legislation, so faculty unions don't have legal recourse if their rights to organize are violated. Despite *Yeshiva*'s assumption that faculty are not supposed to want or need unions, faculty are still attempting to organize. When the University of Minnesota administration tried to eliminate tenure in 1996, faculty organized to have a union election and narrowly missed—by only twenty votes— unionizing one of the largest systems in the country.

THE CORPORATE ADMINISTRATION

Julie Andrzejewski, a professor and former union president at St. Cloud State University (SCSU) in Minnesota, has observed a staunch ally of corporate concerns infiltrating the leadership of universities over the past few decades: a new breed of administrators. These administrators arrive on campus for a few years to "revamp" a college and make it run more like a for-profit corporation. They are attempting to climb the corporate ladder and build their resumes, says Andrzejewski, so they cannot leave a campus without making their mark. They identify—or create—a problem and then solve it with a grand initiative, which usually involves more surveillance of and demands on faculty and more numeric tabulation of student performance, all in the interest of "quality control." These administrators are adept at diffusing labor conflict by dividing and conquering the workforce in small pieces and interest groups. At SCSU, Andrzjeweski observed members of the administration working through personal deal cutting as opposed to open negotiation. For example, the business college at SCSU was given extra allowances, such as a five-thousand-dollar summer teaching contract, that the rest of the faculty did not have access to. Often, these administrators play on the imagined "partnership" between administrators and faculty to emotionally manipulate faculty into conforming to a business plan. At the University of New Hampshire, an administrator warned that a 1994 faculty strike for higher pay would "fundamentally destroy the quality of interaction at the campus" and would create a wound that "doesn't heal quickly."[11] Andrzejewski described the ironic administrator stance: Faculty are supposed managers and decision makers, yet they are penalized for being involved in faculty governance. "Your department can be harassed if you're too vocal." In recent years at SCSU, when a vocal union president was elected, the person was labeled "adversarial" and "not willing to work with the administration."

Faculty are especially vulnerable to being manipulated with the unwritten rules of "professionalism." They often have a difficult time developing a sense of themselves as a group separate from their managers. Lured by individual privileges that the highest echelons of academia promise, many faculty see traditional unions as irrelevant, and even as a hindrance.[12] At the same time, lower-paid instructors, graduate students, and adjunct faculty struggle to bring the reality of their working conditions closer to the dream of this privilege.

Corporate administrators, to diffuse the potential of labor unrest, tell faculty that they are in control of the university. This works to undermine faculty organizing because some faculty are, in fact, almost in control at their jobs. Faculty constitute a range of privilege: some direct the labor of others, while others don't even control their own work situation.[13] Thomas Meisenhelder, a professor and longtime union activist in the California State University (CSU) system who was involved with an attempt to unionize under the American Federation of Teachers, argues that the potential for privileged working conditions holds many faculty enthralled: "Faculty are in a sense seduced by status into forgetting their quite ordinary income and organizational position."[14] A few prizes, like department chairs and tenure positions with extreme job autonomy and freedom to research and think, keep a whole class of employees on their best behavior. This potential combines with the fact that for many, intellectual work brings concrete rewards. According to Meisenhelder, faculty do all have some access to means of "cultural production and social reproduction," which is a privilege compared to the mind-numbing quality of many other jobs available to workers today. Jennifer Berkshire, who received a Ph.D. in English and knows the system from the inside, says that although exploited adjunct instructors are "perfectly positioned to see themselves as oppressed," many feel privileged because they are able to work in a profession they enjoy, even if it means working for a low salary and without any benefits or job security.[15]

Meisenhelder has struggled to show faculty at CSU that they truly "are subordinate salaried employees in educational bureaucracies. They neither own nor independently control the university as a workplace. Indeed, as workers, faculty are exploited in indirect service to the profits of the dominant capitalist class." He argues that faculty do sometimes direct the work of others, but "the managerial qualities of faculty work are largely a result of delegated political authority rather than a product of original power."[16] And although administrators hearken back to a supposedly golden past, where a collegial partnership of faculty ran a chummy, democratic university, the reality is that "professors have never been individual practitioners but have nearly always been tied to clerical or secular corporate systems of training or employment."[17]

Meisenhelder points out that even in the category of elite faculty, if resources are cut, their status may be limited or withdrawn. "By teaching more students for less pay, lower faculty produce a surplus of work-time units, some of which are then granted by the campus administration to tenured senior faculty in the form of fewer courses and more leaves. . . ."[18] In effect, the privileges offered to a few elite faculty are made possible by the work of many exploited among their ranks. In addition, the presence of this reserve force of part-time and temporary faculty, which Meisenhelder calls an "academic proletariat," in effect "intimidate[s] lower and middle faculty into acquiescing in their own subordination."

The ideology of professionalism, in the end, is very good for managers. It allows faculty to see themselves, writes Meisenhelder, "as a self-governing community of independent intellectuals and thereby masks the very real internal differentiation of professors. . . ."[19] Professionalism also leads faculty to think that they don't need alliances with other workers because they are scholars and their situation is so different, thereby passively inhibiting them from forming labor alliances. Meisenhelder wrote that "the biggest hurdle for the pro-unionization forces was overcoming many/most [faculty members'] identification with an ideology of professionalism that prevented them from seeing themselves as workers employed by a huge public bureaucracy."[20]

Gus Tyler predicted in 1971 that if university resources were to become more scarce, and if faculty were to continue viewing themselves as specialized individuals instead of a group, faculty might turn against each other, fighting for a limited pool of resources defined by the university rather than questioning the entire allocation of resources for higher education. "It is even possible . . . that academe may repeat the history of the earlier aristocrats of labor by opting for 'craft unions' speaking for special interests, rather than 'industrial unions' representing the whole campus."[21] This prediction has in many cases come true, as faculty fail to see that they have anything to gain by supporting other workers. During the 1996 strike of Yale University graduate employees and service staff, faculty (including a labor historian self-identified as "progressive") issued public statements condemning the strike and threatening individual students. During a strike at the University of Toronto in 1996, laid-off clerical workers existed on "meager" pensions because faculty had previously voted to pull out of a pension pool and had taken the vast majority of pension funds for themselves.[22] It is vital to unite faculty with other workers, or administrators can use their position of intermediate power in the universities can be used as a tool to further corporatize the universities.

RAISING THE CHALLENGE

Faculty options for higher education organizing currently include the AFT, the NEA, the CWA Higher Education Project, and the AAUP, many of which have been around since the 1940s or 1950s and have presented conservative to progressive political positions.

The AAUP's membership has decreased by 50 percent in the last twenty years.[23] The decentralized nature of the organization means that in some states, progressive and aggressive wings of the organization have represented faculty bargaining units.[24] The AAUP also has a censure list of universities that violate academic freedom, with around 50 schools currently censured, although the organization has no mechanism for enforcement of censure.[25]

The NEA has responded to requests from the rank-and-file for negotiations and stronger sanctions, and also represents faculty in union struggles. The NEA claims that "higher education faculty and staff are a highly unionized workforce," stating that public institutions of higher education employ 71 percent of roughly 741,000 faculty, and 60 percent of these institutions are unionized.[26] But this is an inflated indicator of faculty unionization, because many of these schools have staff unions but not faculty unions.

The AFT has undertaken proactive initiatives and lobbying around "distance learning," or the use of new technologies to make in-class teaching hours less central to education. The AFT won a model contract that binds administration at a community college to keep a stable number of full-time faculty. The contract also preserves all recorded classes as faculty's intellectual property.[27] The AFT's "First Principles Campaign," launching its vision of higher education, includes such statements as "all citizens have a right to a high-quality education that carries them as far as their ambitions, talents, and hard work will permit" and "public higher education should be affordable for everyone."[28] These large organizations represent an important unifying point for faculty to come together to talk about common concerns.

A PARTNERSHIP WITH MANAGEMENT?

The leaders of these unions, however, have recently been unwilling to develop a fundamental critique of trends in higher education. The NEA in particular has criticized "traditional trade unionism" for being too confrontational. In the latest of many failed merger negotiations between the AFT and the NEA, one of the major fears cited by NEA members was that the merger, and subsequent national affiliation with the AFL-CIO, would lead the new organization to adopt blue-collar styles of labor organizing.[29]

Labor Notes reported that NEA leadership, at least in some cases, has attempted to make itself into more of a professional association than a union:

National Education Association President Bob Chase and other NEA officials spent a couple days with officials from Saturn [automobile manufacturer] and the United Auto Workers discussing how the labor-management collaboration practiced at Saturn can be transplanted to the classroom. At the same time, the NEA is working with its long-time rival, the American Federation of Teachers. AFT President Sandra Feldman says she and NEA leaders are "trying to lead our unions down a new path, . . . seeking partnerships instead of conflicts with management."[30]

Seeking to avoid inevitable "conflicts with management" preempts the development of a structural critique of the state of education in this country. Instead, such efforts in effect encourage faculty to do the work of management without having any of the final say that management has.

NEA president Bob Chase has called for a "quality revolution in America's public schools. . . . After all, the economic security of our members is linked inextricably to the quality of public education as an institution." By linking the economic security of union members to the quality of public schools, Chase implies that teachers bear the responsibility for fixing public education—or else. In other words, if the schools are failing, it is the teachers that are to blame, instead of larger factors like resources available for public education. It remains to be seen whether collaboration with management will reproduce the erosion of workers' rights that has been experienced in other fields.

Chase accepts the concept of professionalism and holds faculty to be separate from other workers. He writes: "The industrial-era assumption that teachers are 'essentially manual workers, pouring curriculum into passive minds' no longer fits. In the 1990s . . . teachers are becoming elite 'knowledge-era workers. . . .' " In addition, Chase vaguely implies that teachers already have power, without explaining what comanagement means for teachers or how it was won: "22% of teachers are 'fully' involved in decision-making, and another 56% are partially involved. These teachers are effectively co-managing their schools."[31]

The NEA, based on this evidence, seems to hope that if they conform to corporate expectations, teachers will be hit less hard in future rounds of cuts to education. According to *Labor Notes*, "Union leaders hope that such [partnership] programs will improve delivery of government services and avoid contracting out of members' jobs. . . . [T]he NEA sees this as a defense against those who want to gut public education through proposals like voucher programs and charter schools."[32] The NEA may see these cooperative ventures with management as an attempt to position the union at a time when it is vulnerable. Although the NEA's Chase describes this scheme as the "new unionism," Meisenhelder wrote twelve years ago that this moderate approach is widespread and that it "exchanges progress for in-group economic security."

SCSU's Julie Andrzejewski saw firsthand the effects that the "quality" argument can have on faculty unity.[33] She argues that because of the power of this management trend a traditional faculty union working on narrow faculty bread-and-butter issues is insufficient. Faculty need political education and organization in order to learn about their situation and formulate a response.

Andrzejewski challenged the use of "Total Quality Management" on her campus by providing information to faculty on the deleterious effects of work speed-up fostered under the euphemism "continuous improvement." She saw that many faculty members are attracted to the corporate model and feel that being asked to participate in "Total Quality Management" studies represents a continuation of the idealized collegial cooperation between administration and faculty. In reality, they may be participating in downsizing themselves: "Once deconstructed, tasks can be redesigned and reassigned, new deskilled jobs can be created, and nonperforming components can be replaced."[34]

Faith in the collegial nature of the campus and in management leads faculty to participate in faculty-administrator committees. Andrzejewski says that many faculty on her campus don't understand that if they state their opinions in a committee of administrators who will be evaluating them later, they can be putting themselves and their jobs in jeopardy. In her work with the campus union, she has explained to faculty that such tools as faculty-only committees exist to protect faculty, to present a group opinion to the administration so no one is targeted individually as a rabble-rouser.

Even having a union, of course, does not guarantee that the faculty act in solidarity with one another. Andrzejewski said that her union supports whatever benefits the majority of faculty members. "As long as the predominant group in higher education is white males, oftentimes of a certain class background," faculty will support the status quo at the university rather than defending the marginalized within their ranks. Although she has seen the union majority support a woman or a person of color if her issue applies to the majority's self-interest, if narrow self-interest is conflicted, they'll be staunchly against it. According to Andrzejewski, until there are more progressive people on campuses, the baseline issues in the unions will stay the same, which necessitates trying to convert faculty to more progressive political views.

After fifteen years of business-as-usual leadership, her union launched this agenda. Four progressive union presidents were elected in succession: a white man with radical politics, then a feminist lesbian, then an African American man, then another feminist woman. The first progressive president organized faculty to look beyond pocketbook issues to really study their contract, and subsequent radical presidents began the process of educating faculty about the broad, political uses of a union. With this leadership, the progressive section of the union successfully organized in the mideighties to bring more women and people of color into the faculty. Andrzejewski filed a sex discrimination lawsuit, which resulted in stronger enforcement of affirmative action policies.

After these moves forward, a backlash occurred, and many departments did not support these new faculty when they were reviewed for tenure. Departments and faculty resistant to change "began to manufacture bizarre and illegal reasons for why these people shouldn't get tenure." Andrzejewski feels that the majority of faculty did not want these new faces to be a part of the community where they lived and worked. The progressive union trained a group of grievance officers to challenge these practices, but many faculty were not committed to union issues beyond those that affected their paychecks.

Andrzejewski argues that it is necessary to conduct simultaneous political education and union organizing, to emphasize the gains that can be made through solidarity in the workplace but also to move the discussion beyond bread-and-butter issues to talk about the political importance of a union in today's economic and political environment. A union can bargain effectively as a group to fight for academic freedom—for example, by demanding no individual layoffs of faculty to protect those who might be targeted politically—and for open forums in all hiring and firing decisions. Through her extensive organizing experience, Andrzejewski has found that unionizing faculty is half of the battle, and struggling with faculty over political questions is the other half.

UNION POLITICS AND POLITICAL UNIONS

Many factors contribute to the depressed "political" content of today's faculty unions. Mainstream labor has not been forcing faculty unions leftward. Since 1935, when the National Labor Relations Board (NLRB) and associated labor laws were created, conservative forces have attacked the basic right to collective bargaining and democratic unionism. Activists within the labor movement as a whole, like Andrzejewski, have had to struggle for broad political perspectives to be adopted, with varying degrees of success.

Kim Moody describes a rift between labor and academia, formed by "the increased bureaucratization of the unions after World War Two, the deadening atmosphere of McCarthyism and the Cold War, the deep split in opinion during the Vietnam War," and other class-based rifts.[35] As an attempt to reunite progressive thinkers with unions, the AFL-CIO has been involved in a series of "teach-ins" between academia and labor.

In October 1996 the AFL-CIO sponsored "The Fight For America's Future: A Teach-In With the Labor Movement," a labor-academia meeting of the minds at Columbia University in New York City. Speakers including John Sweeney, Betty Friedan, Cornel West, and Patricia Williams addressed overflow crowds and spoke about tensions between labor and academia that have been festering since the 1960s. Sweeney urged faculty to consider themselves part of the "bottom" in the struggle of the bottom against the top of the economic structure. This effort has been described as " . . . on the one hand, progressive intellectuals in significant numbers . . . once again looking to organized labor as a force for social change. On the other, labor leaders are willing to broaden the range of thinkers as they look for fresh ideas or expertise."

Although this is a promising development, as long as moderate labor and academia see this as a partnership between thinkers and workers, it will not be truly productive for higher education workers or for activists who want to change higher education. This moderate perspective treats the rift between academia and labor as an intellectual problem, a tension or a misunderstanding, rather than addressing the structural conditions in higher education and in labor in general that produced this rift. Sweeney urged faculty to consider themselves workers, as if this concept were the whole battle instead of just the first step to getting organized. In addition, it accepts the managerial assumption that intellectuals are separate from workers. Although the AFL-CIO seems willing to take fresh ideas, legitimacy, and relevance from individual progressive scholars, there was little mention in this forum of grassroots organizing in higher education, which is crucial for progress in addressing this rift.

As Andrzejewski argues, a faculty union will not function to represent faculty rights as a group unless faculty members simultaneously get politically educated. The converse is also true. Many union activists argue that a political message is essential as a rallying point for organizing the many faculty who cannot seek representation through legal means such as the NLRB. Blum argues that faculty are up against tough odds, so they need to be urged to organize, and to see collective bargaining as a long-term political method for achieving change based on strength in numbers rather than strength in court. And this strength in numbers requires a message and a vision to give activists sustenance when legislative avenues remain closed and faculty seem to have few bargaining chips. Union organizers at the 1997 Massachusetts Jobs with Justice Conference on Higher Education pointed out that legal limitations such as the *Yeshiva* decision and no-strike legislation at many public universities, while an obstacle, should not be seen as an excuse not to organize. The National Labor Relations Board did not exist before 1935, and it was the strength of "illegal" organizing that resulted in gains for many workers, including the public pressure that led to the creation of the NLRB.

Elaine Bernard, director of Harvard University's Trade Union Program, argues that it is important to battle for better labor law, and for things like enabling legislation and the repeal of the *Yeshiva* decision, but that even the 1935-style pristine U.S. labor laws did not confer true rights upon workers in the United States. She argues that "...even the much-touted right to collectively bargain is a very limited right. Like a hunting license, it does not guarantee anything but an opportunity which may or may not yield results. It should not be confused with actually conferring rights on workers, though it does help workers create a power which can win them rights."[36]

FACULTY UNITY IN ACTION: FULL-TIME AND PART-TIME WORKERS

Organizing of all sorts that incorporates political arguments for faculty solidarity is resulting in new approaches at the local and state level. Employing an interesting pro-labor twist on the official NEA language, activists at Lane Community College in Eugene, Oregon, recently succeeded in winning rights and protections for part-time faculty at a statewide level with the rallying cry, "Quality and Justice." In October of 1996, part-time and full-time faculty formed the Lane Community College Education Association and issued a white paper entitled, "Reliance on Part-Time Faculty is a Matter of Quality and Justice." The white paper enumerated twenty-eight ways that reliance on part-time faculty wastes money on "work that is not adding value to education, but is aimed at allowing us to work people cheap," and negatively affects the faculty, the educational mission of the school, the students, and the long-term goals of the institution. The committee called for a transition plan to a substantially full-time faculty and claimed the issue not just as a concern for part-timers themselves, but for everyone at the school.

As of spring 1999, more than fifty Oregon adjunct faculty from union-affiliated AFT and NEA campuses as well as nonunion campuses met to discuss concerns and to form strategies to prevent full-time and part-time faculty from being pitted against one another. Attendees announced that they would develop the discussion points into legislative campaigns, bargaining points, and organizing campaigns.[37] The concepts enumerated in the Lane Community College white paper have taken hold with many national unions and their locals. Columbia College in Chicago won recognition in spring 1999 for the Part-Time Faculty Association, which subsequently earned a pay increase of at least 30 percent for its members.[40]

Alliances among educators seem to have potential for practical gains. Graduate student organizing has made significant gains in the last few years, depending on on-campus alliances for key organizing support.[39] And NEA organizers in California reported in May 1999 on the formation of an educational initiative in that state, bringing together a combined membership force of 275,000 from K–12 through the university level to impact state educational policy.[40]

FACULTY UNITY IN ACTION: TEACHERS AND COMMUNITY

Michael Zweig, union activist and professor of sociology at SUNY Stony Brook, argues that one of the major ways that faculty can gain negotiating power is to build bonds with community members who are affected daily by higher education and to rally around the ways that higher education intersects with wider social justice issues.[41]

Zweig's union, the United University Professions (UUP), emerged from an extended conflict with the SUNY administration and trustees in which union members worked without a contract for twenty-five months. The state lawmakers illegally cut off vision and dental benefits for SUNY workers in a move to pressure them to settle. In response, union members reached out to community members and local businesses. The university is a major employer in many towns in New York, and the salaries for SUNY employees affect local businesses that serve primarily university employees. After the university cut staff dental benefits, local dentists were organized to pressure the school directly, and dental associations lobbied legislators. In addition, the UUP enlisted the support of mayors throughout the state, the University Faculty Senate, the New York Public Interest Research Group (NYPIRG, a student multi-issue group), other student organizations, and many local businesses.[42] This multipronged strategy paid off. As part of the fall 1997 contract, members were reimbursed for all dental, prescription, and vision expenses incurred during the struggle. This contract lasted until summer 1999, and the UUP started negotiating again in summer 1998 to prepare for the next contract.[43]

In a related struggle surrounding academic freedom throughout the SUNY system, the UUP is making a political argument to protect academic freedom for the good of everyone in New York State, as opposed to surrendering control of the SUNY system to a corporate-controlled board of trustees and the governor.[44] Zweig stated a concern about a broad trend of reactionary trustees organizing to eliminate progressive faculty.

Zweig said that in his experience, unorganized faculty traditionally think of themselves as "have vitae, will travel." His challenge has been to help them understand what the issue of collective interest means in the largest sense. Because collective bargaining has as much or more to do with mass political power than legislated negotiation, he states that faculty need to reach out to community allies for support, and the political vision has to include the well-being of the entire community.

FACULTY UNITY IN ACTION: POLITICAL GAINS

One practical and inspiring example of community-faculty organizing comes from the CWA, the self-described "community-minded union." Stephen Schlossberg, author of *Organizing and the Law* and consultant to the CWA Higher Education Project, spoke to a gathering of CWA organizers about the "historic importance of community coalitions of educators and labor." Schlossberg's message also illustrated the perspective that community-labor organizing is about a long struggle as opposed to short-term, narrow gains, although those are also important.[45]

Addressing the social benefits of higher education, Schlossberg described the now-endangered federal financial aid to students as "the best investment this country ever made." Schlossberg states his political perspective in a CWA newsletter: "If the enemies of public higher education and student aid make college the exclusive province of the rich, this country will have the most stratified, rigid class system in the developed world."[46]

In practice, CWA is struggling to build a record of success around this political perspective. After affiliating with the CWA in 1996, the Maricopa County Community Colleges District (MCCCD) United Crafts Association in Arizona started on a plan of getting the attention of the administration by "developing an independent and direct line of communication to state legislators and the public." The union planned the "Faculty and Staff Leadership Summit on Political Action and Legislative Relations" in April 1996, in conjunction with Arizona AAUP and the faculty association. Attendees decided on three objectives: form a faculty, staff, and community coalition; get involved in the upcoming MCCCD Governing Board elections; and develop a common lobbying agenda. The

CWA agenda mirrors the vision that CSU's Thomas Meisenhelder advocated in the mideighties, of a faculty union movement that would draw power and support from a larger coalition oriented toward socially just, useful, and accessible education.

University union organizing can capitalize on long-standing resentment from a community over poor treatment and fight for higher wages for the entire community. In Indiana, the CWA Local 4730 and the Indiana Conference of the AAUP formed a state coalition, the Indiana Alliance for Higher Education Advocacy and Defense (AHEAD), to create a unified voice for university workers. The AHEAD mission statement includes the formation of "a broad and effective alliance of Indiana citizen organizations, enterprises, and groups that share a common belief in preserving the importance of high quality, affordable higher education opportunities for all Hoosiers."[47] The coalition does outreach to unions, citizens, and industrial leaders and explains the necessity of broadening access to higher education. Part of its approach is that students learn in the classroom, but they also learn by observing working relationships. The coalition asks what a nonunion school that exploits workers is teaching young people, and asserts that because of its nature as a place of learning, the university system should be a model for workplace relations. This strategy also brings in another potential coalition partner: students.

FACULTY UNITY IN ACTION: TEACHERS AND STUDENTS

Community support for faculty can come from many constituencies, including alliances with students, but outreach to students leaves faculty open to the accusation that they are using the lecture hall as a soapbox. But if the link between faculty concerns and broader issues of education and justice for students isn't made, faculty are still vulnerable. Some students at University of New Hampshire did not support a faculty strike, saying that the faculty protests "sucked" and that faculty were "using us and our education for leverage."[48] In some cases, faculty in this situation had not explained to students the reasons for their labor actions.

Students who are allied with faculty because of shared concerns for a just education have often turned out to be very supportive of campus workers. During a strike at the University of Toronto, active students worked in a coalition with faculty and were instrumental in mobilizing wider support for a strike.[49] Because students currently pay to attend a university, organizing them (and their parents and alumni who donate money to the school) can prove a powerful tool. During the 1996 Yale strike of staff and graduate students, undergraduates protesting the administration's stand in negotiations walked out of commencement, providing high visibility to the strike. Under the increasing financial burden of attending college, decreasing financial aid, and in keeping with the university's trend to hire part-time workers, students are serving as on-campus workers in ever-increasing numbers, providing a bridge between the experiences of campus employees and students. Students around the country are drawing connections between their labor solidarity work and conditions in their own lives. Student activists at the University of Wisconsin completed a successful campaign in 1998 to raise the minimum wage for six hundred on-campus workers, the first step in a campuswide living-wage campaign.[50] Because of labor situations of students, the Campaign on Contingent Work in Boston, Massachusetts, launched the "Campus Temp Organizing" campaign in 1999.[51] In this type of situation, where student interest in labor and consciousness of economic issues continues to grow, outreach to students is vital.

CONCLUSION: FACULTY AS WORKERS IN COMMUNITY

Elaine Bernard writes that it is important that workers realize that they have few rights on the job, that democracy does not extend to the place where we spend most of our waking hours. "Fighting for democracy in the workplace, and not simply the right to form unions, is vital to restore the social mission of labor and to return unions to their social movement heritage . . . it is important for unions to lead the charge on the whole anti-democratic workplace regime."[52] I have argued above that this a double battle for faculty in higher education. who must fight for workplace democracy even as they fight their profession's tendency toward individualization and resistance to collective action.

Because of their relatively unorganized and contradictory position, faculty organizing can most profitably be waged simultaneously from within and beyond faculty unions. Progressive activists should support and encourage faculty unionization and support the formation of an explicitly pro-labor faculty organization to provide the political education that faculty need in order to break away from enervating coalitions with management.

To make higher education better and more accessible, not dismantle it, we need a base of power within the academy. Counting on individual professors is not enough, as these "tenured radicals" can be isolated in a number of ways. Counting on the ever-renewing presence of student activism to reclaim the campus for the Left is insufficient. It overlooks the fact that student activists rely on a base of progressive faculty who transmit history and serve as institutional support and mentors.

An isolationist, bread-and-butter union approach will most likely split faculty from other workers, as faculty become more and more attached to their meager privileges at the expense of community alliances. Even with a few examples of successful mainstream faculty unions, Bernard writes that "the sad lesson for labor is that by failing to extend the gains made by unions to the rest of working people, these gains have come to be threatened."

Faculty have a choice: They can either help the corporate world pervert higher education and destroy many of their jobs, or they can unite with other community members around an explicitly social justice vision for higher education. Because of the momentum and power of the corporate grab for higher education, building this united response is the single most effective way that faculty can act in their own interests and in the interests of other working people in the United States.

Infusion *and the Center for Campus Organizing can be reached at 165 Friend St., Boston, MA 02114; (617) 725-2886; www.cco.org.*

NOTES

1. Lehman Brothers., Inc., "Investment Opportunities in the Education Industry," an internal report for investors, February 9, 1996, p. 5. Thanks to Elaine Bernard of Harvard University for sharing this fascinating report.

2. Diane Meaghan, "Academic Labor and the Corporate Agenda," *Socialist Studies Bulletin* (July–September 1996): 24.

3. See *Uncovering the Right on Campus* (Boston: Center for Campus Organizing, 1997). The Center for Campus Organizing can be reached at 165 Friend St., Boston, MA 02114.

4. Lehman Brothers, "Investment Opportunities in the Education Industry," p. 41.

5. Presentation at the *Labor Notes* Biannual Conference, Detroit, April 29, 1997.

6. Richard Chacon, "Carlin Says Colleges Are Run Poorly, Hits Faculty," *Boston Globe,* November 5, 1997, p. 1.

7. Kim Moody, "Review: Audacious Democracy, the New Labor-Intellectual Alliance," *Labor Notes* (January 1998): 12; Steven Fraser and Joshua Freeman, ed., *Audacious Democracy: Labor, Intellectuals, and the Social Reconstruction of America* (Boston: Houghton Mifflin, 1997). There has been a wide range of writing on this subject. For more information, see the work of Leonard Minsky, Larry Soley, and others.

8. Gus Tyler, "The Faculty Joins the Proletariat," *Change* 26, no. 3 (May–June 1994): 75; originally in *Change* (1971). This is a far cry from 1954, when the AAUP supported McCarthy's agenda on campus, and decided that

Stanley Moore of Reed had failed in his "professional duty" by not responding when asked if he was a Communist.

9. American Federation of Teachers, "Statement on Part-Time Faculty Employment" [online], www.aft.org.

10. From a phone interview in March 1997. Blum also argues that the *Yeshiva* decision has dangerous implications: In any workplace where workers participate effectively in shaping their work environment, they can lose the right to organize because they become their own managers.

11. Mary Crystal Cage, "Professors at U of NH Vote to Strike Over Pay," *Chronicle of Higher Education,* September 14, 1994, p. A44.

12. Blum described cases in which a union tried to fight the *Yeshiva* decision by showing that faculty did not have control of their workplace and were not managerial, and the faculty in the campaign opposed this strategy, as they were more attached to an illusion of participating in management than in gaining a union.

13. Thomas Meisenhelder, "The Class Position of College and University Faculty," *Social Science Journal* 23, no. 4 (1986): 375.

14. Thomas Meisenhelder, "The Ideology of Professionalism in Higher Education," *Journal of Education* 165, no. 3 (summer 1983): 300.

15. From a personal interview in March 1997. Berkshire explained that in an attempt to organize adjunct faculty, a conference was scheduled at George Washington University in Washington, D.C., at the same time as the 1996 meeting of the Modern Language Association, a prime schmooze and résumé-distribution opportunity for hungry and overworked adjuncts, and saw firsthand the difficulty of attracting graduate students to a conference that discussed their working conditions.

16. Meisenhelder, "The Class Position of College and University Faculty," p. 376.

17. Meisenhelder, "Ideology," p. 298.

18. Meisenhelder, "The Class Position of College and University Faculty," p. 380.

19. Ibid., p. 382.

20. From an e-mail on the Center for Campus Organizing's faculty discussion list.

21. Tyler, "The Faculty Joins the Proletariat," p. 75.

22. Margot Francis, "Merger Politics: OISE Eaten by U of T," *Canadian Dimension* 30, no. 5 (September–October 1996): 41–42.

23. Cary Nelson, *Manifesto of a Tenured Radical* (New York: New York University Press, 1997), p. 7.

24. For example, at the University of New Hampshire, Wayne State University, and Oakland University. See Cage, "Professors at U of NH Vote to Strike Over Pay," p. A44.

25. Mary Crystal Cage, "Professors' Group Censures 3 Colleges," *Chronicle of Higher Education,* June 21, 1996, p. A13

26. National Education Association, "Unions," [online] www.nea.org; quoting Gary Rhoades in the *Journal of Higher Education* (May–June 1993).

27. "Contract Breaks More Ground on Distance Learning," *On Campus: American Federation of Teachers Newsletter* (October 1996) [online], www.aft.org.

28. "First Principles," AFT Web Page (www.aft.org).

29. Jeff Archer, "AFL-CIO Label Is Most Ticklish of Issues for NEA Members Deciding Union's Future," *Education Week*, June 24, 1998, pp. 16–17.

30. "News Watch," *Labor Notes* (January 1998): 4.

31. Bob Chase, "United Mind Workers" [online], www.nea.org [May 25, 1997].

32. Leah Samuel, "NEA Embraces Partnership," *Labor Notes* (September 1997): 8.

33. The union is currently called the Interfaculty Organization, made up of seven state universities (but separate from the four land-grant branches of the University of Minnesota). The initial contract in 1976 was excellent, but it's been slowly chipped away. At the time, the AAUP was more in support of women and people of color, but faculty chose not to affiliate because it was a weaker organization.

34. Tom Good, "The Trojan Horse: A New Factor in Collective Bargaining in Canadian Universities," *Socialist Studies Bulletin* 45 (July–September 1996): 64.

35. Moody, "Review," p.12.

36. Elaine Bernard, "Why Unions Matter" [online], www.nea.org.

37. "NEA Affiliates in Action," *Higher Education's Advocate Online* (January 1999) [online] www.nea.org/he.

38. "Windy City Part-Timers Win," *NEA Today* 17, no. 7 (April 1999): 10.

39. Graduate student organizing is a large, complex topic that has important connections to other campus work. The Web site of the Graduate Employee Organization at University of Michigan [www.umich.edu/~umgeo/index.html] listed fourteen active graduate unions nationwide (eight organized by AFT, six other organized by either United Auto Workers, United Electrical Workers, NEA, CWA, or AAUP) and 16 other current organizing campaigns being waged. For detailed analyses, please seek information from the National Association of Graduate/Professional Students, the Center for Campus Organizing, and unions organizing in this sector.

40. "NEA Affiliates in Action," *Higher Education's Advocate Online* [online], www.nea.org/he [May 1999].

41. Zweig serves on the state executive board of the United University Professors. UUP, the nation's largest higher education union, represents twenty-one thousand faculty and staff. Zweig has a long history of work within the UUP, working on a local level in the 1970s and statewide since 1981.

42. In a labor struggle at Cornell University in Ithaca, New York, in 1997, labor activists described Ithaca as Cornell's "company town," providing a pool of inexpensive labor to be exploited. Many workers reported receiving below a living wage and reported their benefits being cut. A worker with children stated during a speak-out that her children will never be able to attend Cornell because she doesn't make enough to save for their tuition.

43. In its battle with the union, SUNY "insourced" tenure-track union jobs, transferring them to a nonunion research facility set up as a separate entity but still under SUNY's control. Another example of privatization, seen at SUNY and across the country, is the "contracting out" of services and whole departments. The UUP's latest contract took the most serious teeth out of the clause that allowed contracting out to a nonunion SUNY internal organization, although organizers say that this is still an area for vigilance.

44. John Mather, "SUNY System Now Needs a Magna Carta," *Albany Times-Union,* February 11, 1998, "Commentary" section, via e-mail. Mather is president of the Preservation of the State University of New York Association. The recent controversy concerns a SUNY New Paltz women's studies conference. Governor Pataki, Chancellor Ryan, and trustees reportedly "savaged" and threatened the career of President Roger Bowen because Bowen permitted a conference that discussed a wide range of issues related to women's sexuality. In response, a writer and organizer from a SUNY support organization called for a law that would prevent the governor from interfering with SUNY personally or through proxies on the board of trustees, that trustees "may not usurp administrative responsibilities and interfere in the operation of SUNY campuses . . . ," making a public call to keep the SUNY schools in the service of the people of New York State instead of in the service of trustees' private interests.

45. Sue Hemphill, "CWA and Arizona AAUP Help Build Faculty/Staff Coalition in State Community Colleges," *CWA Campus Voice* (summer 1996) [online], www.cwa-union.org.

46. Steve Schlossberg, "Save Higher Education!" *CWA Campus Voice* (summer 1996) [online], www.cwa-union.org.

47. *CWA Campus Voice* (winter 1996–97): 7.

48. Cage, "Professors at U of NH Vote to Strike over Pay," p. A44.

49. Margot Francis, "Merger Politics," p. 42.

50. "Student Labor Updates," *Infusion* 3, no. 3 (March–April 1998): 4.

51. Jason Pramas, "Join the Campus Temp Organizing Movement," *Infusion* 4, no. 4 (May–June 1999): 4. The Campaign on Contingent Work can be reached at 33 Harrison Ave., 4th Floor, Boston, MA 02111.

52. Bernard, "Why Unions Matter."

10

PROFESSORS GOING PRO
*The Commercialization of Teaching,
Research, and Service*

Sheila Slaughter and Larry Leslie

Academic capitalism is a theory that explains how changes characteristic of "late capitalism"[1] affect higher education. In the past, economists saw land, labor, and capital as the elements that created wealth and profit. Recently they have added a new element (actually, an enhancement of labor): knowledge. High-technology knowledge is particularly valuable because it lends itself to being patented and copyrighted. Colleges and universities are the building blocks of a high-technology knowledge economy. Colleges and universities are the institutions that house faculty who perform high-technology research; produce scientists, engineers, and a variety of researchers who create high-technology products and processes for corporations; and educate knowledgeable consumers, able to use high-technology products. Taken together, these changes, which have occurred piecemeal over the past twenty-five years, constitute a new education/knowledge regime, which we call "academic capitalism."[2]

In this essay we analyze how academic capitalism manifests itself with regard to faculty.[3] First, we outline the broad changes that have occurred, concentrating on the ways that universities increasingly compete for external revenues in markets and quasi markets, and the consequent privatization and commercialization that results from such endeavor. Second, we examine the ways that the state and nonprofit sector interact with the profit-making or corporate sector, paying attention to who benefits. Finally, we look at countervailing trends, at sites and organizations through which people oppose academic capitalism.

FACULTY

As the changing nature of capital put pressure on universities to generate more revenue, faculty became involved in academic capitalism in every aspect of their tripartite role: teaching, research, and service. Research was the most obvious site of faculty involvement in academic capitalism. Faculty were pushed and pulled to win grants, to patent and, most recently, to copyright, and to share these revenues with the colleges and universities for which they worked. Many teaching activities began to be redesigned: packages specifically tailored for off-campus sites, training for corporations, distance education. Service, putting expert knowledge to use for the public good, began to disappear and was often replaced by joint economic development activities run through government-university-industry partnerships.

Research

Prior to World War II, academic research was a small-scale endeavor, supported primarily by corporations engaged in science-based research and by a small number of philanthropic foundations. After World War II, which resulted in the first far-reaching government-university-industry partnerships for research—in this case research to make weapons of mass destruction—academic and industrial research was supported primarily by government, with most research funds going to national defense, prompting Dwight D. Eisenhower's warning to "beware the military-industrial complex." At first only twenty or so elite universities were heavily involved in federally sponsored research, but over the years, as federal sponsorship broadened to include a wider array of research and to broaden political support, more and more colleges and universities became involved.

Grants

Faculty were drawn to research because of the funding that made complex projects possible, the "pleasures of analysis," the prestige, and, occasionally, the economic benefits that came with start-up companies. Universities encouraged faculty to pursue research because of the large overhead funding—ranging to as high as 50–85 percent of a project's cost—that came with grants. These overhead funds were not insignificant amounts of money, in particular because they represented the "extra" money for projects unsupported by state appropriations. By the mid-1980s, annual federal grants and contracts roughly equaled the amount spent on student aid, but was concentrated in roughly one hundred universities rather than distributed among the thirty-five-hundred-plus colleges and universities in the United States. As state funding for colleges and universities decreased proportionately, universities encouraged a generally willing faculty to devote more and more energy to capturing the external streams of revenue that came with grants and contracts. In other words, colleges and universities competed in research markets for external revenues, becoming more and more involved in academic capitalism. It was not so much that the dollar amounts were large as it was that the money had great marginal value and was associated with the most prestigious university activity–research.

Patents

In 1980, Congress passed the Bayh-Dole Act, which gave universities ownership of patents developed by their faculty under federal grants. This act reversed the position historically held by the federal government. After World War II, Congress debated hotly and at length who should benefit from the fruits of federal research, deciding that research results should remain in the public domain, available for anyone to use at no cost. By the mid-1970s, however, business leaders began to claim that technology stemming from federally funded research in universities was rarely transferred to the public because the risks associated with using unpatented research were too great and the "ownership" too uncertain. Government officials and university presidents joined business leaders in arguing that products and processes developed from federally funded research should be patentable. They made the case that the costs of product development was so great, far more than the cost of research itself, that no corporation would risk investment unless they were assured a patent. Otherwise, a competing company could simply copy the technology and garner all the profits without risking any of the investment.

In 1983, Bayh-Dole was amended to allow all businesses to patent any intellectual property they developed with federal research grants. Businesses, particularly large corporations with contracts from the Department of Defense, the Department of Energy, and the National Aeronautics and Space Agency, received about two-thirds of federal research and development (R&D) money, so their opportunities to patent increased even more than colleges and universities.

Before Bayh-Dole, universities had sometimes patented discoveries made by their faculty and some even had patent programs, for example, the University of Wisconsin's WHARF foundation, but the practice was not common. If they patented, universities often awarded nonexclusive licenses, which meant that more than one company could manufacture the product or use the technology. After Bayh-Dole, many research universities started intellectual-property offices and began developing patent programs. States began to see patents as a way of "sharing" the costs of higher education with their public research universities. They passed laws that required faculty to disclose all their patentable research to university intellectual-property offices, and sometimes even determined how income from royalties on licenses would be distributed within the university. By the mid-1990s, the top ten or fifteen research universities had developed considerable revenue streams from patents, while virtually all the remainder hoped to become major players.

Patent law requires that the name of the individual who reduces an invention to practice must have his name on the patent. Given the nature of academic discovery, faculty and/or graduate students usually hold the patent, but the university owns it. When it comes to patenting, graduate students, who are almost always research assistants in the sciences and engineering—where the highest incidence of patenting occurs—are considered employees rather than learners and the university lays claim to its share of the invention, although the faculty and/or students invariably receive some share of profits. Faculty members and graduate students are entitled to own patents only if they are able to demonstrate that they made a discovery without using university time or resources. Because patenting is a costly procedure, universities often pursue only those patents for which a corporation will pay the costs. If the university decides, after the faculty discloses an invention, that it does not want to pursue the patent, faculty who wish to pursue a patent in their own name are often allowed to do so. If the university does not pursue a patentable disclosure, there is sometimes the opportunity for faculty and graduate students to develop spin-off companies.

Universities, then, have come to follow much the same practices as corporations with regard to patents. An employee makes a discovery that leads to a patent and gets a bonus or, in the case of faculty, a share of any royalties. The organization owns the invention and disposes of it as it will, without any consultation with the employee/faculty. The patent is licensed to a corporation and the university, acting as academic capitalist, reaps the royalties. Unlike corporations, universities to do not pay taxes on revenues from intellectual property if such revenues are reinvested in research, a claim easily made by research universities.

The state has created a series of laws and rules that offers incentives to universities to engage in academic capitalism in the patent arena. After Bayh-Dole allowed universities to own patents, many of the states made disclosure of patentable research mandatory. Research universities have become more and more involved in the pursuit of patents and, concomitantly, more deeply involved in academic capitalism.

Research universities and corporations benefit greatly—some would say unfairly—from this new education/knowledge regime. The public pays for the federal research grants, which support scientists' work; universities then patent this research and license it to corporations that no longer have to pay for their own research laboratories because they are able to get exclusive rights to universities' patents. The public, who already have paid for the initial research, have to pay again when they purchase the products the corporations have developed using their licenses to the universities' patents. Every time a sale occurs, both university and corporation benefit. To illustrate, among the very successful products developed with university patents licensed to corporations are genetically engineered human insulin and human growth hormone, both initially patented by the University of California.

There has not been a great deal of opposition to university ownership of patents. When biotechnology first developed, scientists at the Asilomar Conference pledged to license their work only through nonexclusive contracts, making their discoveries available to any company that wanted to commercialize. This public-spirited approach rapidly changed, however, under the onslaught of commercialization. By the mid-1980s, almost every full professor of molecular biology sat on the board of at least one biotechnology company.[4]

Copyrights

In important ways, copyrights are quite different than patents. Faculty have always written books and articles and assigned their copyrights to publishers who produced and marketed the books and articles for them, giving them a royalty or fixed percentage for each copy sold. This was a form of academic capitalism, but the professor rather than the university benefited. Most faculty do not make a great deal of money from copyrights because the audiences for specialized material are very small; however, textbooks and, occasionally, encyclopedias and general reference books often generate a significant amount of money for the faculty member. Historically, these works have not been valued highly by scholarly communities because they are not at the cutting edge of research.

Journals put out by learned societies were the exceptions to publishing for profit—for example, the journals of the American Sociological

Association or the Modern Language Association. These journals were usually produced and distributed by the learned associations, and often were included in the price of association membership. But during the past twenty years, this has changed. Many learned associations have attempted to make their journals profit centers by turning them over to commercial publishers, who are able to make profits through economies of scale and through access to mailing lists and advertising. Commercial journal publishers also use practices that "tax" universities. Their rates for college and university subscriptions are sometimes three or four times the cost of subscriptions to individuals.

Legally, colleges and universities could probably lay claim to faculty copyrights under the work-for-hire doctrine. This legal doctrine says that if an employee is hired to do a specific creative or artistic job, clearly articulated in the job description, the results belong to the employer who supplied the materials and paid for the labor. Since faculty are hired to do research, work that depends on university time or resources and is in the faculty member's area of expertise could probably be deemed work-for-hire. Other writing, for example, a romantic novel written by a physicist on his/her vacation, would not fall under the work-for-hire doctrine. Some appellate court cases have suggested that universities have a stake in faculty copyrights but note that universities thus far have not chosen to exercise such rights. This may be changing. Stanford University, for example, now requires faculty to sign preemployment contracts that turn over 50 percent of all their copyright and their patent income to the university.

Recent Supreme Court rulings involving copyright cases and the Eleventh Amendment have given public universities a great incentive to pursue academic capitalism in the publishing arena. In *Chavez v. Arte Publico Press and the University of Houston* (1998), Denise Chavez, a playwright who lived in New Mexico and was a dramatist with strong reputation as a spokesperson for Hispanic women, had a book contract with Arte Publico Press. Arte Publico Press is a component of the University of Houston "and legally indistinguishable from the University. The University is owned and operated by the State of Texas." Chavez wanted Arte Publico to stop publishing one of her books because the press did not correct errors she brought to their attention. Chavez also objected to the press' identification of her as a judge of plays chosen for an anthology, saying this identification was "a misrepresentation of sponsorship in violation of her right to publicity." In 1998, the Supreme Court ruled that Congress could not abrogate states' rights to immunity under the Eleventh Amendment, suggesting that Chavez could not sue because of sovereign immunity, and remanded the case to the appellate court for a rehearing. The appellate court reheard the case, and found for the University of Houston.

At first glance this case seemed concerned with rather abstruse issues of constitutional law that bear on states' rights. Yet the decision effectively encourages universities to act as state-subsidized entrepreneurial publishers. Although the Supreme Court decision noted that publishing for profit was not part of the "core mission" of the university, it nonetheless extended Eleventh Amendment protection to this activity. In other words, the Supreme Court gave public universities special protection to engage in for-profit activity. The effect is that because public universities are not legally liable in the same way that private university presses or private publishing companies are, the former are granted a competitive advantage. By affirming the university as state-subsidized entrepreneur, the Supreme Court opened the way to universities broader engagement in academic capitalism in the copyright arena.

In terms of ownership of research, administrators as well as faculty and graduate students have become academic capitalists. Administrators, often at the behest of research-active professors and graduate students, encourage faculty to compete in external research markets for grants and contracts that bring in external revenues. Colleges and universities, often mandated by the state, encourage and provide infrastructure and opportunity for faculty to patent the results of research, which is owned by the university and licenced competitively in the market to companies who pay the university a royalty or a share of their profit, thus contributing to university revenue generation. Copyright has always been a tool that faculty use to pursue academic capitalism. Some universities are beginning to claim a share of these profits and more may attempt to have faculty to sign over copyright in preemployment agreements. University presses, formerly required only to "break even" financially, are beginning to use copyright to generate revenues.

Neither faculty nor graduate students at research universities have attempted in any sustained or organized way to protest against or alter the emerging research/academic capitalist regime, whereas unionized faculty at four-year, comprehensive, and even community colleges have collectively bargained contracts that sometimes allow them full ownership of intellectual property and give them a voice in how the college or university disposes of intellectual property. Collective bargaining is a way of forestalling preemployment agreements that force faculty to sign over their rights in patents and copyrights to the university; however, research universities, as a sector, are the least unionized, even though they generate the most intellectual property income for universities.

Teaching

Teaching generates university revenues through tuition that students pay to attend classes and get degrees. For public institutions—and many private ones as well—teaching usually costs an institution more than the tuition paid by the students. In the public sector, tuition may cover as much as one-third to one-half of the cost of education, and in some cases more. Some private colleges and universities charge tuition high enough to cover the cost of a student's education and perhaps even generate excess revenues.

Another important source of teaching-related revenue for some institutions is the high tuition charged to out-of-state students. Within college and universities of all types, some programs are relatively low cost—for example, education, business, and law—and these sometimes serve as profit centers, with the revenues used to defray other institutional costs or cost-subsidize other programs. Indeed, it is these programs—relatively cheap professional degrees—that for-profit educational corporations, such as the University of Phoenix, offer precisely because they are inexpensive to operate. Their classes are quite large, creating economies of scale; part-time faculty are readily available at low cost; almost no specialized equipment or materials are required; and content is somewhat routinized.

The nonresident students aside, the vast majority of colleges and universities generate teaching revenue externally in three ways: from packages specifically tailored to off-campus sites, from training for corporations, and from distance education. These activities differ from on-campus education in that they are usually conducted off-site; are often off-load for faculty or, even more commonly, use adjunct faculty; fully recover costs or generate revenue in excess of costs; and are often tailored to student niche markets that on-campus programs would have difficulty meeting. Such teaching activity is a form of academic capitalism because it generates external revenue in competitive markets for the college or university. Often all these activities are housed in a single office for greater efficiency, and the office is free from much of the close faculty oversight of curriculum that typifies on-campus programs.

Like for-profit colleges and universities, nonprofit colleges and universities externally market inexpensive programs such as education and business. Sometimes public colleges and universities compete with other institutions of higher education within the state for these student markets. At other times state colleges and universities market these degree programs to students in other states, trying to capitalize on what they see as underserved markets.

Corporate training most often occurs in the community college sector. Sometimes corporations pay for the full cost of training, but usually the training is subsidized at the state and/or local level. Often corporations are willing to pay because community colleges organize the training; provide instructors, space, and screening; and recruit students at a cost substantially less than the corporation's costs for such activities because many of the infrastructure and start-up costs are subsumed under the general operating costs of the community college. Sometimes community colleges pay for training as an incentive to attract corporations to an area and students to the college. This is discussed more fully in the next section.

Currently, technologically based distance education is viewed as a profit center for many colleges and universities. College and university administrators are planning to require faculty to make their courses available on the Web so that the institution can offer the courses to distance learners who are willing to pay for them. In some cases, corporations are participating in using faculty cyberproducts to create virtual universities. The faculty member who creates the course may be responsible for interacting with students electronically, but more likely less-expensive adjuncts are used. Faculty course materials can be used again and again, and presumably altered by university-appointed course supervisors to better meet the needs of the market toward which they are directed.

In the long run, distance education may meet university management's desire to reduce costs, but in the present this is rarely, if ever, the case. Nevertheless, teaching is a labor-intensive activity, making it difficult to reduce the number of high-cost professional workers. Just as business leaders have always envisioned a "factory of the future" that is fully automated, reducing labor costs, rasing productivity, ending labor problems, and increasing profits; so postsecondary leaders think of distance education as the solution to problems faced by the university of the twenty-first century–a university without walls and without faculty. Distance education is automation of teaching.

Colleges and universities exploit the teacher-student learning relationship to extract profit from nontraditional, external sources through distance learning. The teaching-learning relationship, however, can also be used by external entities to extract profits. As late capitalism accelerated, corporations increased their press for profits and began to see the faculty-student relationship in traditional colleges and universities as a possible profit center for themselves. Several recent appellate court cases involving universities and copyright suggest that competition between universities and corporations for profits from intellectual property related to teaching may become intense.

A-Plus Notes is a company that produces commercial study guides for courses taught by University of Florida faculty by hiring students attending the university to take lecture notes, which A-Plus Notes then markets to the student body as a whole. In 1996 the university sued KPB, the parent company of A-Plus Notes, for copyright infringement and trademark violations. The court ruled against the University of Florida on both grounds. In taking this position, the court cited the Copyright Act (17 U.S.C. 107, 1976), which states: "The fair use of a copyrighted work, including such use by reproduction in copies . . . for purposes such as criticism, comment, news reporting, teaching (including multiple copies for classroom use), scholarship, or research, is not an infringement of copyright."

The ruling implies that the content of courses at public universities, delivered in public settings, are not protected by copyright nor is it owned by the university. External companies—in this case, A-Plus Notes—can send paid representatives, such as students, into classrooms, to mine professors course content, which the company may then repackage and sell. Similar issues arise when dealing with the content and structure of distance education courses, over which professors, institutions, and ancillary companies are currently struggling. Very often the institution, while not owning the material, stands to benefit from arrangements with ancillary companies that repackage professors' work, as is the case in the current struggle at UCLA over distance education. While making course content accessible may increase the circulation of ideas, the content is not free; indeed, external entities are interested in packaging these ideas for circulation only at a profit. Such a ruling deprives faculty of control over the content of their courses, and may create situations in which the external entity rather than the university or faculty member has final say over what is included or excluded in the package.

In *Princeton University Press, Macmillan, and St. Martin's Press* v. *Michigan Document Services* (1996), the presses sued Michigan Document Services (MDS), a company that used photocopied materials to produce course packs tailored to meet University of Michigan professors' requirements for specific classes. MDS took a principled position on fair use, arguing that the doctrine protected educational use, and even advertised that it did not require permissions and could therefore get course packs to professors quickly. MDS claimed that it was covered by fair use because the course packs were educational, not commercial. The court disagreed, basing its argument on the Supreme Court's ruling that market value is the most important of the four tests of fair use. The court was convinced by the three publishers that MDS's refusal to seek and pay permission fees for use of material to which they held copyright deprived them of over $500,000 annually. Given that profitability of scholarly books is often marginal, the court reasoned that the publishers needed the fees, stating, "The fact that a liberal photocopying policy may be favored by many academics who are not themselves in the publishing business has little relevance in this connection."[5]

Chief Judge Martin, voicing the dissent, argued that the majority offered a too-strict interpretation of fair use. "The fair use doctrine, which requires unlimited public access to published work in educational settings, is one of the essential checks on the otherwise exclusive property rights given to copyright holders under the Copyright Act."[6] He continued,

> [t]he majority's strict reading of the fair use doctrine promises to hinder scholastic progress nationwide. By charging permission fees of this kind of job, publishers will pass on expenses to colleges and universities that will, of course, pass such fees on to students. . . . The fair use doctrine contemplates the creation and free flow of information; the unhindered flow of such information, through . . . education in turn spawns the creation and free flow of new information.[7]

As in the previous case, the for-profit corporations external to the university benefited from the majority decision. (Although Princeton University Press is legally part of the university, its mission is publishing for profit and not part of the core mission of the university.) Again, university communities were considered intellectual commons, and profit-making corporations were able to "enclose" (appropriate for private use) sections of it almost at will. Such enclosures may well destroy the intellectual commons, just as the sixteenth-century British enclosures of common land in Scotland destroyed the clan system and the identity of that country.

Like research, teaching is no longer valued primarily for its contributions to student learning, but is being reconceptualized as a profit center. Teaching as a profit center has been concentrated at the periphery of universities and colleges and marketed to clusters of students not usually served by traditional four-year institutions. Such efforts usually have been organized into administrative offices with names like Extended University. They are full-fledged academic capitalism endeavors that often compete directly with for-profit educational institutions for student markets.

Because the possibility of profits from educational endeavors are increasingly obvious, for-profit institutions are growing in size and number. No longer are colleges and universities secure in their ability to make profits from faculty-student relations within their traditional purview. Private corporations are beginning to compete with colleges and universities for these profits.

Profit is to be had from the teacher-learner relationship primarily because the state subsidizes education. Without payments to faculty and aid to help students pay tuition, none of these ancillary activities would result in profits. Student aid, whether in the form of grants or loans, sustains increased institutional revenues as well as private profit.

There have been some attempts to challenge increased costs for and/or profits from education. Students have regularly protested tuition increases and have occasionally been able to reduce them. Public and nonprofit educational institutions have lobbied vigorously against granting student aid to commercial education endeavors, righteously pointing to the very high default rate on student loans in that sector. Unions are trying to control off-site teaching and distance education through collectively bargained contracts. However, these contracts focus more on protecting the rights of senior, full-time, tenure-track faculty than on controlling the expansion of this form of academic capitalism that relies on the use of adjuncts to teach nontraditional student populations.

Service

Historically, service meant putting expert knowledge to public use, much like a lawyer's practice of doing a certain amount of free, or pro bono, work for the community. Over time, the concept of service was refined: It came to be thought of as service to a faculty member's department, college, or university, a service that consisted primarily of committee work; service to the profession, which covered a variety of activities that included serving in national learned associations, editing scholarly journals, reviewing other faculty for promotion and tenure; and service to the public or community, the original meaning of service, and the one on which we focus here.

Currently, service is in the process of being redefined, changing from a gift of knowledge or expertise given freely to the community that supports the university, to a means of generating revenue for the university. "Practice plans" in medical schools are perhaps the most obvious examples. As nonprofit teaching hospitals, university medical schools historically served the community, particularly the poor and indigent, and especially those with interesting diseases. However, in the 1980s, university medical schools began to hire increasing numbers of clinical faculty who provided medical service for a fee and sometimes even organized health maintenance organizations (HMOs). Given the increasing costs of health care, the fees from practice plans quickly became necessary to maintain the annual operating budgets of medical schools. In some medical schools, tenured physicians who have failed to cover their own salaries, whether through revenue generated through grants or clinical practice fees, have been fired.

Practice plans are not widely developed for faculty in fields other than medicine in the United States. In some other countries, Australia, for example, faculty outside the medical field routinely form consulting groups run through the university. The most common fee split is one-third to the university, one-third to the department or college and one-third to the professor. The benefit to the university is obvious as is the benefit to the department or college. Faculty join because the income is held in tax-free accounts, ostensibly for their professional use, and the university covers any liability they may incur.

In the United States, faculty are still far more likely to consult independently than to join a practice plan. This activity cannot be considered directly as academic capitalism because the income accrues to the individual faculty member rather than the institution. In the future, universities may move more aggressively to capture this income, as they have done with patents and spin-offs. For the time being, the contribution to academic capitalism is more indirect. Professors may indirectly contribute to academic capitalism when they act as independent consultants because they very often create ties to the corporate community, ties that stimulate lucrative government-university-industry relations (GUIRs), which bring relatively long-term income streams to universities. Further, permitting faculty to earn consulting fees indirectly improves the competitive position of the university in labor markets.

GUIRs are now the form by which the greatest amount of private grant and contract dollars reach universities.[8] These research arrangements were pioneered through the National Science Foundation's (NSF) engineering/manufacturing programs in the 1970s and 1980s. All the partners contribute in one form or another; although the government usually supplies the greatest share of the money, corporations usually have the most powerful voice in defining the project and universities often contribute most of the knowledge or expertise, sometimes contributing money as well.

Universities present GUIRs as service to the public. University officials argue that these partnerships contribute to economic development and hence to the well-being of the community through job creation. They make the case that the jobs created are high-technology, highly paid positions, although they offer little evidence for the number of jobs created and rarely address the question of whether the jobs go to citizens who have lost their jobs due to downsizing or outsourcing or whether they go to residents from other states who are attracted to these new jobs.

Generally, service has shifted from being service for free to service for a fee; that is, it generates revenue for colleges and universities. In short, service has become a site for academic capitalism. Universities and colleges label research that concentrates federal and state dollars on projects that articulate with corporate development plans as service. By pursing such research, universities and faculty devote their intellectual effort to commercial endeavors. GUIRs often become important vehicles for deciding the economic future for the regions in which colleges and universities are located, removing planning from the citizenry as a whole. Because these alliances are quite stable and long term, they are highly favored by faculty and university leaders; that is, they provide sources of revenue that allow universities and colleges to plan for their futures as well. GUIRs are yet another example of academic capitalism because they are awards for which faculty and universities compete in research markets.

Radical grassroots organizations sometimes oppose GUIR activity, as do antistate conservative groups. The latter have been more effective at the national level, however, holding back President Clinton's competitiveness legislation, which envisioned commercial research on a very broad scale, than they have at the regional and local level. Universities, federal research agencies, and corporations continue to successfully create GUIRs despite lack of firm congressional commitment. Unless faculty and graduate students are part of such partnerships, they tend, for the most part, to be unaware of them, and even when they are part of these consortia, faculty and graduate students often do not recognize how widespread they are. Although GUIRs are relatively unobserved and understudied phenomenon, they contribute to academic capitalism by funding research with commercial potential.

CONCLUSION

The idea of academic capitalism brings together and explains many of the piecemeal changes that have occurred over the past twenty-five years, changes that have pushed and pulled faculty and their universities and colleges in the direction of the market. If faculty and students are unhappy with the reformulated faculty roles, they need to do at least four things. First, they need to understand more about how activities in science and engineering influence other disciplines and colleges. Second, they need to understand how activities at the periphery of universities and colleges are increasingly shaping the academic core. Third, they need to develop an analysis of the university as a whole, not just look at their own fields or at what is happening to undergraduates. This means paying attention to service activities far away from the classroom. Fourth, they need to organize to change the way faculty roles are being reformulated.

In many ways, research funding for science, mathematics, and engineering (SME) initially drove academic capitalism. Most federal funding for research is in these fields. The SME share of higher education research dollars has increased while the funding for most other fields has decreased. In addition to bringing grant and contract revenues to colleges and universities, SME fields are most likely to yield intellectual property. The possibility of a "big hit" with patents, generating an endless, major stream of royalties from patent licenses has pushed colleges and universities to expand opportunities for academic capitalism. Every research university hoped to be able to patent something like the Cohen-Boyer patents Stanford held on rDNA technology.

Because most patents do not yield a great deal of income and because there are not large numbers of undergraduate students in SME fields, the wisdom of reformulating all faculty roles based on what occurs in SME fields is dubious. Faculty and students outside SME have to keep track of what goes in SME and work to deflect role reformulation that fits these fields but not others.

Most faculty and students who are likely to be opposed to academic capitalism are focused in the liberal arts, which give much of their attention to undergraduates. Because liberal arts faculty and students' attention is concentrated on the experience of traditional students, they do not see the buildup of activity at the periphery of the university, activity that reformulates faculty roles in the teaching area. Faculty and students who want to reform the reformulated faculty role need to work to include off-campus students in curriculum deliberations. Such programs should not be excluded from the university, because they do in fact serve students who often are unable or unwilling to take advantage of on-campus programs, including poor students, working students, older students, and students of color. Students and faculty on campus need to develop common cause with these students to ensure they get the same quality education as the relatively privileged students in residence at four-year campuses.

Professors and students who want to change the reformulation of the faculty members' tripartite role have to focus on the way service is being reformulated as service for fees rather than service for free. They will have to attend faculty senate meetings, regents and trustees meetings, and especially department meetings to make a case for using expertise in ways that transcend economic development. This should not be a terribly difficult case to make, since using expertise for the common good is laudable and there are usually many community groups eager for such service. Moreover, building such relations with the community builds a base of support for higher education.

Generally, faculty and students who do like the direction academic capitalism is taking the university need to broaden and deepen their analysis of what is causing these changes and begin to understand the breadth and the degree of those changes. Faculty and students will not be able simply to turn back the clock and return to a time when academic capitalism was less well developed. They would probably do well to figure out what aspects of academic capitalism are worth saving—for example, the idea of student as consumer has many merits because it gives students some leverage over faculty authority; however, focusing only on consumption is too limiting, allowing students only to "buy" education or withhold their tuition dollars. The concept needs to broadened to let students become partners in a dialogue with faculty about their education and the careers for which they are being prepared. To counter academic capitalism effectively, students and faculty will have to develop different ideas about higher education, ideas that raise revenues for colleges and universities. Simply expecting the state to supply more money is unrealistic.

Finally, students and professors will have to organize to bring their critique of academic capitalism, as well as their counterproposal and ideas, to the university community and the public. To be effective, they will probably have to move beyond student government, unions, and single-issue protests. They will have to build a social movement able to garner support and new organizational structures will have to be developed for what will be a long-term enterprise. The task is difficult, but not impossible. Professors and students can draw on the knowledge and expertise of the university community to begin making these changes.

Students in particular can draw upon and exploit their knowledge of academic capitalism. They can deploy the leverage they possess. They are, after all, the fastest growing sector among all resource providers for higher education, public and private, two-year and four-year.

NOTES

1. George Soros, *The Crisis of Global Capitalism: Open Society Endangered* (New York: Public Affairs, 1998.

2. For a detailed account of how and why these changes have occurred, see Sheila Slaughter, *The Higher Learning and High Technology: Dynamics of Higher Education Policy Formation* (Albany: State University of New York Press, 1990); "Academic Capitalism As a Middle Range Theory," Center for the Study of Higher Education, University of Arizona, 1993; "Federal Policy and Supply-Side Institutional Resource Allocation at Public Research Universities," *Revise of Higher Education* 21, no. 3 (1998): 209–44; Sheila Slaughter and Gary Rhoades, "The Emergence of a Competitiveness Research and Development Policy Coalition and the Commercialization of Academic Science and Technology," *Science, Technology and Human Values* 21, no. 3 (1996): 303–39; Sheila Slaughter and Larry L. Leslie, *Academic Capitalism: Politics, Policies and the Entrepreneurial University* (Baltimore: Johns Hopkins, 1997); Larry L. Leslie and Sheila Slaughter, "The Development and Current Status of Market Mechanism in U.S. Postsecondary Education," *Higher Education Policy* (June

1997): 1–14; Gary Rhoades and Sheila Slaughter, "Academic Capitalism, Managed Professions and Supply-Side Higher Education," *Social Text* (summer 1998); Ben Baez and Sheila Slaughter, "Academic Freedom and the Corporate, Christian, Entrepreneurial State," in *Higher Education: Handbook of Theory and Research*, vol. 15, ed. John C. Smart (New York: Agathon Press, 2000). The references in these articles will lead interested readers to an array of empirical evidence that supports the arguments made in this paper.

   3. For a broader analysis, see Sheila A. Slaughter and Larry L. Leslie, "Beyond Basic Science: Research University Presidents' Narratives of Science Policy," *Science, Technology and Human Values* 18 (summer 2000): 278–302.

   4. Sheldon Krimsky, *Biotechnics and Society: The Rise of Industrial Genetics* (New York: Praeger, 1991).

   5. *Princeton University Press, Macmillan, and St. Martin's Press v. Michigan Document Service* (1996), p. 11.

   6. Ibid., p. 13.

   7. Ibid., p. 14.

   8. Irwin Feller, "Technology Transfer," in *Higher Education: Handbook of Theory and Research*, vol. 14, ed. John C. Smart (New York: Agathon Press, 1998).

11

GIVE ME AN $
Moonlighting in the Company Boardroom¹

Kevin Kniffin

INDICATORS AND EFFECTS OF "CORPORATIZATION"

"Corporatization" is a word that can sometimes be confusing. To answer the question, "What officials are selling out my university?" however, there should be little mystery. By far, it is the university trustees—and the presidents who serve them—who should be held most accountable. Increasingly, we find presidents and trustees openly walking to the same corporate drum, attempting to set up enclosures throughout the campus, drawing "profits" with no shame or dignity.

The goal of this essay is to present the reader with cases involving these two sets of people and their corporate relations while simultaneously drawing out some of the basic ways in which these relations impact the university and its educational mission. While it is the case that educational institutions are supposed to serve the interests of society at large (hence their nonprofit status), this essay will show a number of cases in which various people appear to be corrupting the supposed autonomy of the university in the process of serving themselves as individuals or corporate executives. The effects of these relationships are discussed so that the reader may be able to appreciate the gravity of the facts of the relationship. Attempts that have been taken to mitigate these effects are also discussed.

THE HANDS THAT PICK THE PRESIDENT
ARE THE HANDS THAT RULE THE TOWER

The roles and responsibilities of university presidents are typically not clear to most people. Those mildly familiar with such boards know that they select presidents and vote on issues such as the construction of new buildings. They may also not be surprised to know that the largest occupational group represented on university boards is that of corporate executive: Instead of educators, alumni, and local community stakeholders, it is big business that dominates university boards. It is fair to infer from this, then, that corporate executives are guiding our educational institutions. Commenting on how at least one institution is being directed by its trustees, Barbara Ehrenreich has tagged Yale as a place that "teaches the humanities while ignoring the humanity of its employees and part of its teaching staff."[1] Yale's active and open battles against unions make it the subject of such special attention; however, many adjunct professors in fields such as English may well argue that the tag has more universal application.

The corporation-based trustees are increasingly open about using their model of commercial enterprise to describe the university and guide their presidential selection processes. In fact, Glenn Burkins reported that business school deans are increasingly being tapped for the job of university president.[2] In this context, it is unsurprising that some time in the last decade or so students have regularly become "clients" and "consumers," while university presidents became "CEOs of large conglomerates." Judith Rodin of the University of Pennsylvania has been so encouraged by her trustees to work for industry that she has placed a link on her university Web page that leads to the Aetna Corporation—one of the companies on whose board she sits. Rodin has said that the trustees expect that "what I do, I do for Penn."[3]

The boards of universities may also vote on tuition rates and salary changes. At the University of New Mexico (UNM), the board has voted for a tuition increase for each of the last twenty-one years. Further, the rate of this increase has outpaced inflation by an unbelievable margin. Tuition and fees in 1998–1999 were 390 percent greater than tuition and fees twenty-one years previous. This is a clear (and all-too-common) case of public resources being drained. At UNM, however, there is a similarly clear reason why such raises, in recent years at least, are problematic. Larry Willard, the president of the UNM board of regents (appointed by the governor) is also the CEO and chairman of the board of Norwest Banks New Mexico/El Paso. Willard's bank just happened to be the nation's fourth largest lender of federally sponsored student loans in the period between fiscal years 1994 and 1996 and undoubtedly makes loans to many UNM "customers." In a recent article tagging Willard as Albuquerque's "most influential person," he remarks that "I sincerely believe in giving back to the community. There is no greater satisfaction."[4] One wonders, however, why Willard is allowed to "serve" UNM not only as a codeterminer of tuition but also as supervisor of a bank that many would think must be making some money off of the students' increased tuition needs.[5]

In New York, the board of the State University of New York (SUNY) has been labeled "embarrassing" by the president of the United University Professions (AFT Local 2190), William Scheuerman.[6] Testifying before the state legislature, Scheuerman identified SUNY as "the only public higher education system not to request a budget increase in 1997." Appointed by Governors Pataki and, to a much lesser extent, Cuomo, the board has complied with and sometimes abetted cuts in the state university system that eliminated over sixteen hundred professorial positions during the mid-1990s. It has also gone from receiving 74 percent of its budget from aid from the state in 1988–1989 to approximately 40 percent state support in 1997. At the same time, corporate taxes have been slashed. Under the budget passed for 1998, corporate taxes were cut—without any substantive debate—from 9 percent to 7.5 percent over a three-year period. With a $2-billion surplus to use for the 1998 budget, Pataki and the legislature shaped a budget that cuts corporate taxes, shifts the burden of future deficits away from corporations, and provides no major improvements in the state's teaching forces.

As Ali Zaidi notes, after Cuomo and state Republicrats cut corporate taxes in the mid-1980s, SUNY tuition increased from $675 per semester in the fall of 1990 to $1,700 per semester in 1998.[7] That means that a 250 percent tuition increase coincided with the loss of more than sixteen hundred professorial positions—and a big decrease in taxes for corporations. The cuts in corporate taxes will inevitably manufacture deficits in the future, since it is impossible to expect growth to continue strongly enough to cover the cost of the cut, but it is not surprising that machine politicians remain mute on subjects such as this.

Similarly, it is not surprising that members of the boards of trustees—at SUNY or other schools—remain quiet, since they are important parts of the communities benefiting from moves such as cuts in corporate taxes. One indication of the SUNY board's priorities can be found among the other roles of the board's chairman, Tom Egan. Egan's current occupation as president of Baltimore Financial Analysis and his former position with Smith Barney make it clear that his interests lie in the private, for-profit sector. Indeed, fourteen businesspeople and no active educators serve on the sixteen-member SUNY board.

Specific to the budgeting process, the decision to build or not to build is another power typically assumed by the board of trustees. Having decided to go ahead with building, it is a common practice for the board to encourage and invite philanthropic and foundation support for the construction. And while sponsors are permitted and encouraged to do this in the form of tax-deductible contributions that are often only a small portion of the total building costs (but that give them long-lasting status on the campus), the rest of the costs are often paid by unmemorialized students, taxpayers, and alumni.

Investments by universities are another arena that has periodically made trustees the subject of attention. When divestment campaigns were successful in pressuring universities to withdraw their partial ownership of companies involved in South Africa's apartheid government, it was the board of trustees at most universities that needed to make the decisions. More recently, students have succeeded in gaining divestment from companies involved with Burma (because of its military dictatorship), but a recent decision by the Yale University board is not as encouraging. The Yale board formally adopted "ethical investment guidelines," but in practice they have not been as respected as many see fit. In late April 1998, with opposition from the author of the guidelines and from David Kessler, former Food and Drug Administration chief and current dean of the Yale School of Medicine, the Yale board voted to remain holders of more than $16.9 million worth of shares in companies that promote and sell carcinogenic nicotine products.[8] Because the vote count was not made public—and therefore left the trustees unaccountable—we are left only with secondhand reports, including the claim that many administrators fear that "[a move to divest of nicotine companies] could send Yale down a slippery slope toward divesting from other lucrative industries." We are also left with the observation that policy enforcement requires a degree of activity comparable to policy enactment.

One board that came under public scrutiny during the mid-1980s for abusing some of the privileges of office as trustees was the Adelphi University board and president. Eventually removed by the New York State Board of Regents, the Adelphi "trustees" did many inappropriate things—and were caught.[9] George Lois was an Adelphi trustee who was also the owner of a company hired by the board for Adelphi's advertising campaigns. The chair of the board, Ernesta Procope, gave insurance contracts to a company of which she was a director, even though alternatives existed that would have saved large sums. Without accountability, this is the kind of recklessness that entrepreneurs are able to wreak on our educational institutions.

UNIVERSITY PRESIDENTS ON THE DOLE

One of the ways in which university presidents interact with their trustees off campus is on the boards of directors of for-profit (and nonprofit) corporations. For the most part, the president only receives such jobs because of the office he or she holds and because of the prestige and trust typically endowed to universities.

Richard Cyert, former president of Carnegie Mellon, is frank in stating that presidents "have to recognize they probably wouldn't have the job if it wasn't for their university affiliation."[10] As a result, Cyert says that he made it a practice to donate some of his stock option profits back to the university. At Georgetown, Leo O'Donovan donates all of his directorship fees from the Walt Disney Company into a student scholarship fund. O'Donovan is exceptional among his professional peers, however: His vows as a Jesuit priest force him to forgo the personal financial benefits of his offices. Few, if any, others appear bound to such standards.

In contrast, Manuel Pacheco, current president of the University of Missouri, has claimed that he serves on the board of ASARCO, Inc. as a private citizen, not as a representative of the university.[11] Acceptance of these identity games from a university president, however, requires a generous interpretation—one that was unwelcome by a Sierra Club officer who initiated public calls for Pacheco to resign from the ASARCO board because of its infamous pollution record. Just as a rose is a rose is a rose, so it is that Manuel Pacheco is President Pacheco is Director Pacheco.[12]

Even if all presidents donated all of their directorship "earnings" back to the university and acknowledged the inextricable ties they have with the university, there would still be important problems with their service to the corporation. Once someone accepts a position as director of a for-profit corporation, she does much more than accept a big paycheck for attendance at meetings—often less than ten each year. She also adopts legally binding duties of loyalty and care to shareholders of the corporation on whose board she serves. In short, she becomes beholden to the interests of the corporation and its shareholders.

Because of this, it is not always a matter of personal privilege for university presidents to accept such positions. Indeed, some form of "permission" from supervisors certainly appears to be the norm. The procedures for university presidents to gain permission for "service" on corporate boards range from pro forma approval by the university trustees to somewhat rigorous processes involving outside parties. At most private universities, the president only needs permission from the board. This appears to be typically easy to get—especially given statements by some that service on corporate boards is exactly what is expected of university board members.

At public universities, there are clearer reasons why the process should be more stringent. Only in New York State, however, does any kind of effective regulation appear to exist. There, the State Ethics Commission, established by law in 1987, must give prior approval for all outside posts with potential earnings of $4,000 or more. In three recent cases, SUNY presidents were not allowed to serve on the boards of banks with which the university did business. In another case, stock options were not allowed for one president-director because the company did some business with the university. New York's ethical codes are exceptional; in contrast, the University of New Mexico only needed permission of the board of regents to serve as a director of a bank that serviced the campus.

The direct relationship of university presidents to their boards of trustees is often fuzzy. Robert Weissman writes that the role of the university president and board of trustees is ambiguous enough so that, in practice, the trustees allow the president to act with a degree of freedom dependent upon the degree to which the trustees' will is being executed.[13] More generally, it appears to be the case that high-level administrators are co-opted with differential raises, bought to execute the will of the trustees, and replaced if they step too far out of line.

To help explain why businesses would seek university presidents for their boards, it is instructive to consider the general trend that presidents of liberal arts colleges do not typically appear on big-business boards. One can speculate that this difference is influenced by the fact that colleges lack the potential research advantages sought by corporations. But this hypothesis that liberal arts colleges are relatively ignored by corporate headhunters because they lack control over research facilities deserves systematic testing to confirm or disprove it.

RELATED ASPECTS OF CORPORATIZATION

In my earlier study, I found twenty-four of fifty presidents serving on corporate boards, using *U.S. News and World Report*'s top fifty national universities as my arbitrary sample. Four points must be added to provide context for the statistics. First, some of those not included among the twenty-four were on boards of companies that had recently been taken over. As a result, they had no connections at the time of my study. Second, several university presidents in my sample act as consultants for various industries, even though they are not directors. Third, and most directly important, some schools try to protect their image of autonomy by placing very special restrictions on their chief executives, allowing more freedom for less visible officials. For example, Stanford University's current president does not belong to a for-profit board, but the provost belongs to the boards of Chevron, Transamerica, and Rand; just as many professors and deans belong to the boards of other multinational corporations.

A fourth point must be added with regard to the more innocent-sounding nonprofit board positions. Most would agree that university presidents should be involved in noncampus community activities, but the same problems involving university-industry relations also exist when corporate directors join nonprofit nonuniversity boards. In other words, a corporate director is a corporate director and, in some sense, it does not matter if the person's day job is that of university president. A case in point: Not only are there problems with Harold Shapiro serving as president of Princeton University while simultaneously serving on the board of Dow Chemical, but there are multiplied problems when one notices that Shapiro also maintains other "nonprofit" roles as trustee of the University of Pennsylvania Medical Center and chair of the National Bioethics Advisory Commission. Since Shapiro's service relationship to Dow requires him to act in the interests of the company, one can see how this not only affects his presidential position, but also how he is pressed to serve other nonprofit groups.

Simply put, university officials "serving" on corporate boards violate the fiduciary trust typically given to leaders of educational institutions. Second, this service often promotes a conflict of commitment. A president's attendance at forty corporate board meetings will no doubt impede his ability to fully understand his campus environment. Third, service on corporate boards involves a conflict of priorities, at least, and a conflict of interests, at worst.

CURRICULAR EFFECTS OF CORPORATE ENCROACHMENT

The domination of university governing boards by people whose worldviews are dictated by profit inevitably pressures universities to resemble the models familiar to their governors. The result is often what Robert Kuttner would identify as a "boundary violation"—his name for the invasion of market principles into enterprises (for example, health care, blood donations, and educational settings) where markets arguably do not result in socially beneficial outcomes.[14] Effects of this violation are found in both research and teaching.

Karen Heller and Lily Eng's study of the University of Pennsylvania provides an excellent starting point.[15] Counting the number of full-time undergraduate students between 1980 and 1996, they found an increase of twenty-nine students. Over the same time period, during which the cost of attendance increased by more than $13,000, there was a simultaneous increase of 1,820 administrators and nonteaching staff members. Nationally, Eng and Heller reported that the student population increased 28 percent between 1975 and 1993, while nonteaching administration increased in personnel by 83 percent. Some argue that the need for administrators is spurred by more careful overview mandated by federal regulations, but it seems just as likely that commercial impulses to develop and market research and curricula are also factors in the administration boom.[16]

Granted ownership rights over all discoveries made by university employees by the 1980 Bayh-Dole Act, universities were given the green light to compete in markets with for-profit corporations. Typically, however, universities contract corporations into licensing agreements whereby the company is allowed to rent the ownership rights for a period of time for a given price. To gain some idea of the scale of these agreements, a recent Associated Press article stated that U.S. and Canadian university patents and licensing agreements generated close to $500 million in 1996. Jules LaPidius, president of the Council of Graduate Schools, said of that figure, "There's nothing wrong with capitalizing on the results of research, but we have to be careful that the university doesn't turn into the development arm [for industry]. These figures are one indication that there's been a movement in that direction."[17]

A look at the Massachusetts Institute of Technology (MIT)—one of the nation's leading research universities—provides a case study in understanding this movement. In 1984, the federal government supported approximately 86 percent of the university's research funds.[18] In 1996–1997, however, industry replaced the Department of Energy and Department of Defense to become the number one sponsor of research, as total federal government support fell to 73 percent.[19] Monies from the federal government were not falling in an absolute sense, but were simply being outpaced by industry "investments." This trend will do nothing but continue if officials like Senator Jeff Bingaman (D–NM) have their way. In 1998, Bingaman introduced a bill (S.2268) that would permanently extend tax credits for corporations sponsoring university-based research.[20]

The transformation of universities into research and development centers for profiteering corporations presents a variety of ethical problems. In a general sense, the privately-sponsored research is not only owned but too often controlled by its patrons. This control presents itself most clearly in the increasing number of cases involving the suppression of results when researchers find a company's product to be failing in some regard. David Shenk writes about Knoll Pharmaceuticals' attempts to suppress and discredit work done by a client scientist who found that its brand-name thyroid drug did not yield significantly different effects than the much cheaper generic competitor.[21] One could infer from this that Knoll's executives do not have unconditional faith in "free-market" education.

Elina Hemminki, David Hailey, and Merio Koivusalo recount a similar case in which Bristol-Myers Squibb (BMS) attempted to suppress results from the Canadian Coordinating Office for Health Technology Assessment that, while not critical of any of its products, simultaneously described a BMS product in the same class as (and not significantly better than) one of its competitors.[22] BMS filed a lawsuit with the Canadian agency, lost the case, then filed an appeal and lost that as well. As the authors note, this kind of action helps to create a culture of fear that can inhibit research directions.[23] The authors propose publication of such cases as the best and most available way of redressing such wrongs, in conjunction with some kind of institution to provide defense for scientists made the subject of attack by industrial representatives.

The indirect effect of this kind of privatized research is that the scientific community's progress on various puzzles is impeded at the cost of providing material incentives for corporations to move things forward in competition with each other. As Lawrence Soley notes, progress in arenas such as cancer research is being slowed because university contracts with drug companies can leave scientists bound to maintain the proprietary nature of results, both positive and negative.[24] Irving Lerch, a physicist leading the American Association for the Advancement of Science (AAAS) against these kinds of encroachments, has stated that "the commercialization of science has led to a new regimen of secrecy that is of great concern to the scientific community . . . secrecy of an entirely new scope and scale."[25]

A more subtle effect of corporate-sponsored research is found in the publication of results that are positive and encouraging of a specific drug, product, or service. A recent study published in the *Journal of the American Medical Association* finds that researchers (anonymously) admit that "gifts" affected their publicized evaluation of various drugs or other objects of research.[26] Because of this, an increasing number of researchers, such as Sheldon Krimsky and L. S. Rothenberg, have called for journals to request and publish any financial ties a scientist has with industries relevant to her research topic.[27] *Nature*'s editors have addressed the issue, but their ruling has so far been that "research as we publish it is indeed research, not business."[28]

This view of science as somehow isolated from industry seems sheltered and unjustifiably hopeful. Indeed, in a recent *American Scientist* column, zoologist Steven Vogel wrote about the "pernicious implications" of a "growing institutional preference for expensive science."[29] Vogel contends that importing commercial principles into the research enterprise results in the subversion of the "historically proper and useful role of universities as institutions in which the creation of knowledge is insulated from cries for immediately tangible yield." An example of Vogel's point can be found in David Ehrenfeld's observation that people studying fields such as earthworm taxonomy can no longer find jobs in advanced research.[30] This is despite the fact that even the great Charles Darwin made much of his reputation studying earthworms, finding that "[i]t may be doubted whether there are many other animals which have played so important a part in the history of the world, as have these lowly creatures."[31] Ehrenfeld argues that this is a result of the fact that research dollars cannot be gained (and capitalized upon by administrators) from studies of earthworms. Both Vogel and Ehrenfeld, however, share the same motivation for caring about this situation. They both believe that the scientific community must be free from commercialism if it is going to be able, as it is expected, to deal with unanticipated social or environmental problems posed to humans in the coming centuries.

Under the watch of the trustees, and under the institutional leadership of their presidents, the law of survival in today's universities is "profit or perish." The survival of the academic researcher is not what is solely at stake, of course. Nor is this matter simply about whether or not a certain company's products are advertised or given monopoly rights on college campuses. Instead, analyses of "corporatization" can provide important background for understanding why medical research may not be making optimal progress, or why less-than-spectacular agribusiness-sponsored research might unnecessarily jeopardize the food supply we and our descendants will rely upon.

RESISTANCE TO CORPORATIZATION, AND CONSTRUCTION OF DEMOCRACY

A wide range of possible actions are available to those seeking to stem and attack "corporatization" of the university. Advancing legislative reforms, creating public pressure, and organizing direct actions such as hunger strikes have all resulted in gains in one campaign or another. Targets for these campaigns also can change from trustees and their electors to the campus presidents themselves.

The State Legislature of New York attempted to stem the corporatization of SUNY in 1997 with a measure calling for the SUNY board to include at least four SUNY graduates at all times. Governor Pataki, however, vetoed the bill, calling it an infringement on his authority. Pataki aides also noted that there presently were several alums on the board. It is important to add, though, that one of the two graduates on the board is E.

E. Kailbourne, the vice chair of the board and the CEO of Fleet Bank, the nation's twelfth largest creditor of federally sponsored student loans. A more aggressive legislative attempt is found in the Preservation of SUNY Association hope to see a successful bill that would require all SUNY trustees to take an oath of office as part of their installation onto the board.

At the University of Wisconsin–Madison, students have created trading cards for their university's board members, with such statistics on the back as the amount of money donated by the trustee to the governor in the last election. At the same school, the "Buy A Regent" campaign was aimed at drawing attention to the lack of adequate representation on the board.[32] In states where university board positions are elected, the prospect of "buying" the election is unfortunately common, but that has not stopped a Green Party run in 1998 for a spot on the board of trustees for the University of Colorado. These efforts are important in keeping some space open for debate while working at the same time to win positions in the future, retrieving them from the monied elite.

Regarding the issue of presidents "serving" on corporate boards, the most fundamental exercises include monitoring all publications about or involving your university, investigating any unseemly connections, and educating others about your perspective on such relationships.[33] When J. B. Neilands discovered that the chancellor of the University of California, Berkeley ignored an engineering firm's recommendation to use federal power instead of energy from Pacific Gas and Electric (PG&E), the local power monopoly, he did his best to make public—via media such as the *San Francisco Bay Guardian*—the fact that the chancellor served as a director of PG&E.

Organizations of students and labor unionists have targeted directors of the Los Angeles–based oil company Unocal for their "service" to a corporation that serves as an important prop for the military dictators in Burma, who have run the country since imprisoning the rightfully elected Nobel Peace Prize winner Aung Sun Suu Kyi in 1989. Two directors of Unocal also enjoy the trust and respect given to university officials. Don Jacobs from Northwestern University's Kellogg Graduate School of Business and Marina Whitman from the University of Michigan are the two moonlighters. They have been called on by members of the student-organized Free Burma Coalition, who recognize the two roles to be wholly incommensurate, to either resign from Unocal or resign from their university positions.[34]

Likewise, the Oil, Chemical, and Atomic Workers Union (OCAW) has called on all directors of Unocal (except employees of Unocal) to take a public stance against the company's participation with the Burmese dictatorship. Special Projects Director Joe Drexler wrote that "[t]he letters were written to specific Unocal board members who are particularly vulnerable to being associated with slave and forced child labor, heroin trafficking, brutal police suppression, murder and rape of the civilian population, and other crimes in Burma."[35]

Citizens at Occidental College staged a weeklong hunger strike outside their president's office to get Mr. John Slaughter—a director of ARCO—to dissent publicly about the company's position in Burma. Slaughter did make a statement claiming disagreement with ARCO's profit-blindness; but, of course, he is still a director of ARCO (as well as Northrop Grumman, IBM, Monsanto, and Avery Denison). Indeed, several months later, ARCO announced it was terminating business in Burma, leaving Unocal as the most prominent U.S. firm actively involved with the nation's rulers.[36]

CONCLUSION

The transformation of American universities is by no means unique. Not only are the same pressures making their presence felt across the globe in centers of higher education, but it is also the case that higher education is not the only target of the entrepreneurs. To gain some insight into this, one can look at Ehrenfeld's report that a recent New Jersey Board of Higher Education ruling has allowed public school boards to hire principals who lack any teaching experience, so long as they possess management degrees.[37] The idea that managers of capital are somehow especially capable of being managers of education is the thread that ties these trends together. Many people, however, recognize this tie as either loose or untied altogether.

As for how people express their opinions, the means of governance in universities are not usually transparent to the passer-by. When students or other campus stakeholders think about voicing their opinions, they're sometimes stopped by the traditionally unpublicized structure that constitutes university governance. John Steinbeck's *The Grapes of Wrath* contains one scene especially representative of the way students and other citizens of the campus can be made to feel about their ability to fight back. When approached by foreclosure officers from the bank, the farmers desperately want to convince someone to stop the eviction. The bank agents make clear, however, that they are simply following orders of manager X, who is following orders from supervisor Y, who is following orders from vice president Z, and so on and so on. In this scheme, there is no accountability. The system is used to muffle all cries and move toward further concentration of power and wealth. The response to this situation can be, as Tom Joad says, "Lot a the folks jus' got tired out lookin for someone to be mad at. . . ." One purpose of volumes such as this is to demand accountability from the supposed stewards of our educational institutions, while at the same time providing some of the tools needed to produce results.

NOTES

1. Barbara Ehrenreich, "Foreword: What Yale is Teaching Us," in *Will Teach for Food,* ed. C. Nelson (Minneapolis: University of Minnesota, 1997), p. xi.
2. Glenn Burkins, "Work Week," *Wall Street Journal,* May 19, 1998, p. A1.
3. Kevin Kniffin, "Serving Two Masters," *Multinational Monitor* (November 1997): 10.
4. Rebecca Murphy, "The Influential Larry Willard," *New Mexico Business Journal* [online], www.nmbiz.com [November 1997].
5. Ehrenreich, "What Yale is Teaching Us."
6. William Scheuerman, "UUP Lays Legislative Groundwork," *Voice* (March 1998): 4.
7. Ali S. Zaidi, "SUNY in Crisis," *Dollars and Sense* (July/August 1998), p. 8.
8. Isaiah Wilner, "Corporation Votes No on Divestment," *Yale Daily News* [online], www.yaledailynews.com [April 22, 1998].
9. Ali S. Zaidi, "At Adelphi," *Thought and Action* (spring 1998): 109–18.
10. Kniffin, "Serving Two Masters," p. 10.
11. Karen Strosnider, "U. Of Missouri President Urged to Quit Board," *Chronicle of Higher Education,* August 15, 1997, p. A32.
12. Kniffin, "Serving Two Masters."
13. Robert Weissman, "How Harvard Is Ruled," in *How Harvard Rules,* ed. J. Trumpbour (Boston: South End Press, 1989), p. 36.
14. Robert Kuttner, *Everything for Sale* (New York: Alfred A. Knopf, 1997).
15. Karen Heller and Lily Eng, *Philadelphia Inquirer* series on higher education, March 1996.
16. Scheuerman, "UUP Lays Legislative Groundwork."
17. "Universities Reap Windfall from Research," Associated Press, February 18, 1998.
18. Martin Tolchin and Susan J. Tolchin, *Selling our Security* (New York: Penguin Books, 1992), p. 229.
19. MIT Report of the Treasurer, 1997, p. 6.
20. Zaidi, "SUNY in Crisis."
21. David Shenk, "Money + Science = Ethical Problems on Campus," *Nation,* March 22, 1999.
22. Elina Hemminki, David Hailey, and Merio Koivusalo, "The Courts—A Challenge to Health Technology Assessment," *Science,* July 9, 1999, pp. 203–204.

23. Wilner, "Corporation Votes No on Divestment."

24. Lawrence Soley, "Phi Beta Capitalism," *Covert Action Quarterly* 60 (1997): 40–45.

25. American Association of University Professors, "University Professors Protest Corporate Influence in Medical Research," press release, June 1999.

26. Sheryl Gay Stolberg, "Gifts to Science Researchers Have Strings, Study Says," *New York Times,* April 1, 1998, p. A17.

27. Sheldon Krimsky and L. S. Rothenberg, "Financial Interest and Its Disclosure in Scientific Publications," *Journal of the American Medical Association* 280, no. 3 (July 15, 1998): 225–26.

28. Cited by Shenk, "Money + Science = Ethical Problems on Campus," p. 18.

29. Steven Vogel, "Academically Correct Biological Science," *American Scientist* (November–December 1998): p. 504–506.

30. David Ehrenfeld, *Beginning Again* (Oxford: Oxford University Press, 1993).

31. Zaidi, "At Adelphi."

32. Kniffin, "Serving Two Masters."

33. Weissman, "How Harvard is Ruled."

34. Boyer, personal communication.

35. Joe Drexler, "President of Oil Workers' Union Tells Unocal 'Outside' Board Members to Take Stand Against Burma's Dictatorship," press release, July 10, 1997.

36. Oil, Chemical, and Atomic Workers International Union, "ARCO to end Burma Project: A Victory for Burma's Democracy Movement," press release, August 12, 1998.

37. David Ehrenfeld, "The Management Explosion and the Next Environmental Crisis," in *People, Land, and Community,* ed. H. Hanum (New Haven, Conn.: Yale University Press, 1997).

Part Three

BUSINESS MAKES THE GRADE
Case Studies of Campus Incorporation

12

HOW FREE IS
HIGHER EDUCATION?

Howard Zinn

I n early 1950, Congressman Harold Velde of Illinois, rising in the House of Representatives to oppose mobile library service to rural areas, told his colleagues: "The basis of communism and socialistic influence is education of the people."

That warning was uttered in the special climate of the Cold War, but education has always inspired fear among those who want to keep the existing distributions of power and wealth as they are.

In my thirty years of teaching—in a small southern college, in a large northeastern university—I have often observed that fear. And I think I understand what it is based on. The educational environment is unique in our society: It is the only situation where an adult, looked up to as a mentor, is alone with a group of young people for a protracted and officially sanctioned period of time and can assign whatever reading he or she chooses and discuss with these young people any subject under the sun. The subject may be defined by the curriculum, by the catalog course description, but this is a minor impediment to a bold and imaginative teacher, especially in literature, philosophy, and the social sciences, where there are unlimited possibilities for free discussion of social and political issues.

That would seem to be an educational ideal—an arena for free discussion, assuming a diversity of viewpoints from a variety of teachers, of the most important issues of our time. Yet it is precisely that situation, in the classrooms of higher education, that frightens the guardians of the status quo.

They declare their admiration for such freedom in principle, and suggest that radicals are insufficiently grateful for its existence. But when teachers actually *use* this freedom—introducing new subjects, new readings, outrageous ideas, challenging authority, criticizing "Western civilization," amending the "canon" of great books as listed by certain educational authorities of the past—then the self-appointed guardians of "high culture" become enraged.

Early in my teaching career I decided that I would make the most of the special freedom that is possible in a classroom. I would introduce what I felt to be the most important, and therefore the most controversial, questions in my classes.

When, as a young professor at Spelman College, a college for black women in Atlanta, I was assigned a course called "Constitutional Law," I changed the course title to "Civil Liberties" and departed from the canonized recital of Supreme Court cases. I did not ignore the most important of these cases, but I also talked with the students about social movements for justice and asked what role these movements played in changing the environment within which Supreme Court decisions were made.

When I taught American history, I ignored the canon of the traditional textbook, in which the heroic figures were mostly presidents, generals, and industrialists. In those texts, wars were treated as problems in military strategy, not morality; Christopher Columbus, Andrew Jackson, and Theodore Roosevelt were treated as heroes in the march of democracy, with not a word from the objects of their violence.

I suggested that we approach Columbus and Jackson from the perspective of their victims, that we look at the magnificent feat of the transcontinental railroad from the viewpoint of the Irish and Chinese laborers who, in building it, died by the thousands.

Was I committing that terrible sin that is arousing the anger of today's fundamentalists—"politicizing the curriculum"? Is there any rendition of constitutional law, any recounting of American history that can escape being *political*—that is, expressing a political point of view? To treat Theodore Roosevelt as a hero (which is usually not done overtly, but in an expression of quiet admiration)—is that less "political" than pointing to his role as an early imperialist, an enthusiastic supporter of a long string of crude U.S. interventions in the Caribbean?

I have no doubt that I was taking a political stand when, in the early 1960s, I expressed respect for my students who missed classes to demonstrate in downtown Atlanta against racial segregation. In doing that, was

I being more political than the fundamentalist Allan Bloom, at Cornell, who pointed with pride to the fact that the students in his seminar on Plato and Aristotle stuck to their studies and refused to participate in the social conflict outside the seminar room?

In my teaching I never concealed my political views: my detestation of war and militarism; my anger at racial inequality; my belief in a democratic socialism, in a rational and just distribution of the world's wealth. To pretend to an objectivity that was neither possible nor desirable seemed to me dishonest.

I made it clear to my students at the start of each course that they would be getting *my* point of view on the subjects under discussion, that I would try to be fair to other points of view, and that I would scrupulously uphold their right to disagree with me. (I understand that radicals too can become dogmatic and intolerant, or—and I'm not sure which is worse—recondite in their pretentious theorizing, but these are traits one finds at all points on the political spectrum.)

My students had a long experience of political indoctrination before they arrived in my class—in the family, in high school, in movies and television. They would hear viewpoints other than mine in other courses, and for the rest of their lives. I insisted on my right to enter my opinions in the marketplace of ideas, so long dominated by orthodoxy.

Surely the expression of "political views" (What is just, or unjust? What can citizens do?) is inevitable in education. It may be done overtly, honestly, or it may be there subtly. But it is always there, however the textbook, by its very bulk and dullness, pretends to neutrality, however noncommittal the teacher.

It is inevitably there because all education involves *selection*—of events, of voices, of books—and any insistence on one list of great books or great figures or great events is a partial (in both senses of that term) rendering of our cultural heritage.

Therefore it seems to me that the existence of free expression in higher education must mean the opportunity for many points of view, many political biases, to be presented to students. This requires a true pluralism of readings, ideas, and viewpoints—a genuinely free marketplace of thought and culture. Let Shakespeare and Wole Soyinka, Bach and Leonard Bernstein, Dickens and W. E. B. Du Bois, John Stuart Mill and Zora Neale Hurston, Rembrandt and Picasso, Plato and Lao-tzu, Locke and Marx, Aeschylus and August Wilson, Jane Austen and Gabriel García Marquez be available to students.

Such a free marketplace of ideas does not depend essentially on "the curriculum." How many words have been wasted moving those empty shells around the debating table! What is crucial is the content of those shells, which depends on who the teachers are and who the students are. A thoughtful teacher can take a course labeled "Western Civilization" and enlarge its content with an exciting global perspective. Another teacher can be given a course grandly called "World Civilization" and give the student an eclectic, limp recounting of dull events and meaningless dates.

That pluralism in thought that is required for truly free expression in higher education has never been realized. Its crucial elements—an ideologically diverse faculty, a heterogeneous student body (in class, race, sex—those words that bring moans from the keepers of the "higher culture")—have always been under attack from outside and from inside the colleges and universities.

McCarthyism—in which the corporate nature of academic institutions revealed itself in the surrender of university administrators to government inquisitors (see Ellen Schrecker's book *No Ivory Tower: McCarthyism in the Universities* for the details)—was only the most flagrant of the attacks on freedom of expression. More subtle, more persistent, has been the control of faculty appointments, contract renewals, and tenure (inevitably with political considerations) by colleagues, but especially by administrators, who are the universities' links with the dominant forces of American society—the government, the corporations, the military.

Boston University, where I taught for many years, is not too far from typical, with its panoply of military and government connections—ROTC chapters for every military service, former government officials given special faculty posts, the board of trustees dominated by corporate executives, a president eager to curry favor with powerful politicos. Almost all colleges and universities are organized as administrative hierarchies in which a president and trustees, usually well connected to wealthy and important people in the outside world, make the critical decisions regarding who may enjoy the freedom of the classroom to speak to the young people of the new generation.

Higher education, while enjoying some special privileges, is still part of the American system, which is an ingenious, sophisticated system of control. It is not totalitarian; what permits it to be called a democracy is that it allows apertures of liberty on the supposition that this will not endanger the basic contours of wealth and power in the society. It trusts that the very flexibility of a partially free system will assure its survival, even contribute to its strength.

Our government is so confident of its power that it can risk allowing some political choice to the people, who can vote for Democrats or Republicans but find huge obstacles of money and bureaucracy if they want an alternative. Our corporations are so wealthy that they can afford some distribution of wealth to a supportive middle class, but not to the thirty or forty million people who live in the cellars of society.

The system can allow special space for free expression in its cultural institutions—the theater, the arts, the media. But the size of that space is controlled by money and power, the profit motive limits what is put on stage or screen, and government officials dominate the informational role of the news media.

Yes, there is, indeed, a special freedom of expression in the academy. How can I at Boston University, or Noam Chomsky at MIT, or David Montgomery at Yale, deny that we have had more freedom in the university than we would have in business or other professions? But those who tolerate us know that our numbers are few; that our students, however excited by new ideas, go out into a world of economic pressures and exhortations to caution. And they know, too, that they can point to us as examples of the academy's openness to all ideas.

True, there is a tradition of academic freedom, but it is based on a peculiar unspoken contract. The student, in return for the economic security of a career and several years with some degree of free intellectual play, is expected upon graduation to become an obedient citizen, participating happily in the nation's limited pluralism (be a Republican or Democrat—but, please, nothing else).

The boundaries for free expression in the university, though broader than in the larger society, are still watched carefully. When that freedom is used, even by a small minority, to support social change considered dangerous by the guardians of the status quo, the alarm goes out: "The Communists are infiltrating our institutions"; "Marxists have taken over the curriculum"; "Feminists and black militants are destroying classical education."

Their reaction approaches hysteria: "With a few notable exceptions, our most prestigious liberal arts colleges and universities have installed the entire radical menu at the center of their humanities curriculum," says Roger Kimball in his book *Tenured Radicals*. The shrillness of such alarms is never proportionate to the size of the radical threat. But the Establishment takes no chances. Thus J. Edgar Hoover and Joseph McCarthy saw imminent danger of communist control of the U.S. government; protectors of "the canon" see "tenured radicals" taking over higher education. The axes then get sharpened.

Yes, some of us radicals have somehow managed to get tenure. But far from dominating higher education, we remain a carefully watched minority. Some of us may continue to speak and write and teach as we like, but we have seen the ax fall countless times on colleagues less lucky. And who can deny the chilling effect this has had on other faculty, with or without tenure, who have censored themselves rather than risk a loss of promotion, a lower salary, a nonrenewal of contract, or a denial of tenure?

Perhaps, after all, Boston University cannot be considered typical, having had for twenty years probably the most authoritarian, the most politically watchful university president in the country. But although it is hard to match John Silber as an educational tyrant, he can be considered (and I base this on spending some time at other universities) not a departure from the norm, but an exaggeration of it.

Have we had freedom of expression at Boston University?

A handful of radical teachers, in a faculty of over a thousand, was enough to have John Silber go into fits over our presence on campus, just as certain observers of higher education are now getting apoplectic over what they see as radical dominance nationwide. These are ludicrous fantasies, but they lead to attacks on the freedom of expression of those faculty who manage to overcome that prudent self-control so prominent among academics. At Boston it must have been such fantasies that led Silber to determinedly destroy the faculty union, which was a minor threat to his control over faculty. He handled appointments and tenure with the very political criteria that his conservative educational companions so loudly decry. In at least seven cases that I know of, in which the candidates were politically undesirable by Silber's standards, he ignored overwhelming faculty recommendations and refused them tenure.

Did I have freedom of expression in my classroom? I did, because I followed Aldous Huxley's advice: "Liberties are not given; they are taken." But it was obviously infuriating to John Silber that every semester four hundred students signed up to take my courses, whether it was "Law and Justice in America" or "An Introduction to Political Theory." And so he did what is often done in the academy; he engaged in petty harassments—withholding salary raises, denying teaching assistants. He also threatened to fire me (and four other members of the union) when we held our classes on the street rather than cross the picket lines of striking secretaries.

The fundamentalists of politics—the Reagans and Bushes and Helmses—want to pull the strings of control tighter on the distribution of wealth and power and civil liberties. The fundamentalists of law—the Borks and Rehnquists—want to interpret the Constitution so as to put strict limits on the legal possibilities for social reform. The fundamentalists of education fear the possibilities inherent in the unique freedom of discussion that we find in higher education.

And so, under the guise of defending "the common culture" or "disinterested scholarship" or "Western civilization," they attack that freedom. They fear exactly what some of us hope for, that if students are given wider political choices in the classroom than they get in the polling booth or the workplace, they may become social rebels. They may join movements for racial or sexual equality, or against war, or, even more dangerous, work for what James Madison feared as he argued for a conservative Constitution, "an equal division of property."

We have some freedom, but it needs to be guarded and expanded. As Bertolt Brecht was prevented from saying to his inquisitors of the House Committee on Un-American Activities: "We are living in a dangerous world. Our state or civilization is such that mankind already is capable of becoming enormously wealthy but as a whole is still poverty-ridden. Great wars have been suffered. Greater wars are imminent, we are told. Do you not think that in such a predicament every new idea should be examined carefully and freely?"

13

SPOOK SCHOOL
The CIA at RIT

Ali S. Zaidi

"RIT should stand for 'really in touch' with the real world," said Carl Kohrt, executive vice president of Kodak, in his keynote address during the November 14, 1996, installation of the cornerstone for the 157,000-square-foot Center for Integrated Manufacturing Studies (CIMS). The building was financed at a cost of $21 million, $11.25 million of which was provided by the federal government and $9.25 million by the state of New York.[1]

The Rochester Institute of Technology (RIT) has also earned the appreciation of the Central Intelligence Agency, which designated the institution as a "strategic national resource worthy of explicit development and support." In a 1985 Memorandum of Agreement, RIT agreed that its curriculum would be "responsive to certain defined specialties of the CIA."[2]

RIT's responsiveness to those specialties may well explain its recent attempt to cut art programs, and the ensuing student unrest. In late April 1996, four weeks before the end of the final academic quarter, RIT professors leaked word to students that several art programs—including painting, printmaking, glass, textiles, ceramics, art education, medical illustration, and interior design—were about to be discontinued or placed on "probationary continuation."

The cuts would have devastated RIT's prestigious School of Art and

180

Design (SAD) and the School for American Crafts (SAC). On a Monday, a couple of days after learning about the cuts, students gathered at RIT's Bevier Art Gallery to organize. When they heard that the trustees were meeting at that very moment on campus in Building 1, they moved to its lobby to get their attention.

Soon President Albert Simone and Provost Stanley McKenzie came down from the trustee meeting to hear the concerns of the students. Simone might have calmed the students, right there and then, with some vague words of reassurance. Instead, one of his gaffes, caught on video-tape by a film student, propelled the students into action.

When a student asked Simone where the art schools fit into his vision of RIT's future, Simone replied that while RIT was primarily known for its engineering and computer science, there was a danger that graduates could be too "narrowly focused." What the schools of American crafts, photography, and interior and graphic design did for engineers, said Simone, was to provide them with "breadth of experience." "As they walk on campus they see, uh . . . somebody . . . there are not too many engineers with, uh . . . long hair, for example," he said, pointing to Kurt Perschke, a grad student in ceramics.[3]

There was a moment of stupefied silence. Troy Liston, writing for the student publication *GDT*, describes what followed:

> I think I heard a cricket at this point. The silence in the room was actually tangible as everyone had to stop and take a mental step back. I know that I was whispering inside my skull, "Please dear lord, let this be a metaphor for something. Please don't let him mean what I know he's saying." Of course, he had to keep talking. I, and everyone else in the room who had been repeating that silent plea, could no longer block it out: he was indeed saying what we thought he was saying. In the wake of that aftershock, the room's ambient animosity level grew ten fold and threatened to precipitate out of solution. Simone eventually realized his folly and made a feeble attempt to save his floundering position by saying, "Well I guess there are a lot of people here with short hair." All was lost.[4]

The next day, students rallied in a breezeway, packed tightly together. A new activist group, Save Our School (SOS), had been born of panic and anger. "The art programs are world-renowned," said engineering student Jesse Lenney to the crowd. "Who runs this place? Who are they trying to please by booting the art students?"[5]

Later, at a RIT community meeting, students expressed their concerns to Margaret Lucas, the dean of the College of Imaging Arts and Sciences (CIAS). On Thursday, students formed committees for speakers, alumni and parent contacts, rally organizers, and research, as well as media and community outreach. Using donated office space, SOS set up a "war room," complete with committee charts and maps of Rochester.

At a mass rally at Webb Auditorium attended by hundreds, students viewed the videotape in which Simone made his infamous hair remark. "That's what we're here for, to run around so the engineering students can have some diversity, " said Kurt Perschke, unappeased by Simone's apology to him a couple of days earlier. "I want an apology for cutting my school. I don't give a damn about my hair."[6]

That day, the faculty voted unanimously to support the efforts of the SOS students to save the art programs. Professors who had previously limited themselves to slipping information under the door of the new SOS office at night now openly criticized the process that had led to the cuts.

RIT professors had been given an "Academic Program Review Criteria" form to numerically evaluate their programs according to their centrality, financial viability, marketability, and quality. Administrators were to recommend programs for consolidation or discontinuance based on the raw data provided.

The professors do not appear to have understood the purpose of the valuative "tools," which were meant to give the appearance of "scientific objectivity" to corporate downsizing. Not surprisingly, the programs that won out in the valuative process were those dear to the corporate interests on the RIT trustee board, including accounting, business administration, management, finance, information systems, and marketing.

In a memo to RIT administrators, written during the first week of student protests, Thomas Lightfoot, an associate professor in CIAS, said:

> Numerous proposals have been put forth . . . which have not been seriously considered or even responded to. Is the faculty the driver of the curriculum or the administration? Is the faculty even a partner in the process? Or are we just employees, to do what we're told, as the President has suggested? . . . I must add that the faculty, of at least the SAD/SAC component of the college, also pointed out its judgment that the review instrument was seriously flawed. . . . It is also notable that the reasons for discontinuance keep changing. The President wanted to identify a pot of money that could be saved through this process. He was convinced that there was lot of waste and money being lost by our programs. When it was discovered that there was no money to be found, the reasons shifted to a resource reallocation rationale."[7]

That week, SOS obtained donations from parents, student groups, and alumni. They passed out flyers to students and asked alumni to write to the trustees, some of whom professed to be unaware of the proposed cuts. Local television stations covered their actions.

The rallies were followed by image-oriented protests. With the permission of Albert Paley, an RIT artist-in-residence, SOS students symbolically shrouded his sculptures outside the Strong Museum and the Eastman School of Music. They also wrapped the Main Street Bridge railings that Paley had designed.

At the Memorial Art Gallery, ceramics grad students Molly Hamblin and Kurt Perschke used gauze and string to cover works by Paley and Richard Hirsch, an RIT ceramics professor who attended the event in support of the arts. "We intend to keep the heat on," said Perschke. "Today's demonstrations are about showing the fundamental connection between the school and the art community."[8]

The media images of a Rochester without art succeeded in embarrassing the trustees, and the RIT administration quickly backed away from its intention to cut the arts. In under two weeks, SOS had proved that students, alumni, faculty, and even much of the business community strongly supported the arts. Through efficacious aesthetic persuasion, the students had saved their programs, at least for the time being, while alerting the RIT community to the implications of the Strategic Plan.

It was impossible, however, to sustain this activism, which began to wane as finals drew near. "A lot of students have shown how dedicated they are, but their work suffers," explained glass grad student Luis Crespo. "Come 'crunch time,' people will feel torn. In the end it boils down to the fact that they are students and have to get a grade."[9]

In a series of informational meetings, Simone tried to promote the Strategic Plan, but the authoritarian character of the plan made it a hard sell. In addition to downsizing programs, the plan called for outsourcing RIT's physical plant services. At one meeting, Anthony Burda, an editor of the student weekly, the *Reporter*, witnessed Simone's response to a woman who had asked him about the outsourcing:

> "As an alternative to out-sourcing . . . we might move towards student help . . . like 50 percent, something like that. . . ." He points to catering, where the student staff comprises about 90 percent. He also points to savings in pensions, health insurance, etc., by having student janitors. Not to mention the saving in flat pay, resulting from paying students only around $5.25 an hour. "By the time they're ready for a pay increase, they graduate." He starts laughing before he can finish his sentence. Everyone laughs. Well, the professors laugh. The lady in the audience, and the janitorial staff of about thirty, sit in the back quietly. For some reason, it appears they really don't find getting replaced by student workers too funny.[10]

At another meeting, an undergraduate asked Simone what role students played in the decision-making process at RIT. Christopher Hewitt, writing for the *Reporter*, described Simone's response:

> He responded by telling the student that "in my opinion, the 18–22-year-old age group is not qualified in making decisions. You're a customer . . . and if you don't like it, you can vote with your feet." When asked about Simone's comment, the student replied, "We can vote with our feet by stamping them down in protest. Why should we run away from a place that we belong to when we can stay and make it a place that others will come to, not run away from. I think that these old men who are making the decisions don't realize how qualified the 18–22 age group is in making change and solid, competent decisions."[11]

Thus did Simone squander the trust and goodwill that had come to him as RIT's new president—soon after the CIA controversy.

Cut to 1991. As it edged toward Bush's reelection campaign and the Gulf War, the United States laid to rest the much-anticipated windfall from the peace dividend soon after the Soviet Union's collapse. In this climate, Richard Rose, then president of RIT and a former Marine, announced that he was taking a four-month sabbatical to work on "national policy and procedures" in Washington. It occurred to someone to try to reach Rose at the CIA. When Rose answered the phone, the RIT-CIA scandal began to unfold.

Although most documents pertaining to CIA activities at RIT were shredded, some were leaked to the press, including a 1985 Memorandum of Agreement which stated: "The objectives of the relationship between RIT and CIA are to encourage the interchange of knowledge between organizations, to provide useful research employment, to establish/enhance the RIT curriculum to be responsive to certain defined technical specialties of CIA, as well as the general fields of imaging science and graphic arts, and to encourage and stimulate the appropriate faculty and students to interact with CIA on information exchange, project support and potential employment." The Center for Imaging Science was designated the "lead organization" in the CIA-RIT relationship. RIT would add new courses in artificial intelligence, integrated electro-optics and digital image processing, while the CIA would "offset the salary and benefits of specific faculty members whose assignments provide measurable direct benefit to CIA."[12] The Memorandum of Agreement between RIT and CIA was drawn up at a time when an executive order already prohibited the CIA from secretly influencing the activities of domestic institutions and organizations.

In 1985, the year that RIT formalized its CIA ties, Rose consulted with

CIA agents over the choice of a new director for the imaging science center. One agent, Robert Kohler, became an RIT trustee in 1988. Another, Keith Hazard, joined RIT's advisory board for imaging science. In 1989, the administration tried to remove the center from the College of Graphic Arts and Photography and place it under the RIT Research Corporation (RITRC), which administered most of the CIA training, recruitment, and research at RIT. Edward McIrvine, dean of RIT's College of Graphic Arts and Photography resisted the move at the time. "It made no sense educationally," he recalled. "Only later did I realize that this strange proposal made sense if the purpose was to position the Center of Imaging Science to serve the CIA."[13]

The Federal Programs Training Center was created in 1988 as part of the RITRC to give technological support to the CIA. There, students forged documents for eight to ten dollars an hour, paying special attention to bar codes, laminates, and holograms.[14] The crafts were also put to CIA use. Woodworking majors designed furniture with secret drawers and picture frames with cavities for listening devices. In one course, students identified only by their first names designed wax molds for keyholes.

The CIA's interest in RIT student projects goes back decades. One alumnus, a 1975 photography major, recalled how during the seventies the CIA wrote $1,500 checks to undergraduates who forwarded their senior projects to the agency.[15]

When the press and a fact-finding commission began to investigate CIA involvement at RIT, professors and administrators described their experiences with the agency. Some had declined to cooperate with the intelligence agency, including Edward McIrvine, who twice refused CIA security clearance requests. Nonetheless, the CIA conducted a check on McIrvine without his permission and asked to see his medical records when it found that he had seen a psychiatrist a few years earlier.

Malcolm Spaull, head of the Film and Video Department, was asked to train CIA agents in video surveillance. Spaull declined because he is a friend of the family of Charles Horman, the journalist who was kidnapped and murdered in Chile during the 1973 coup. Spaull said that there was "some evidence that the CIA knew he was in captivity and acquiesced in his execution." Another professor, John Ciampa, head of RIT's American Video Institute, refused to work for the CIA by pointing to a clause in his contract that says that the institute would only engage in life-enhancing activities.[16]

Others defended the CIA relationship. "As a corporate citizen if we have something to contribute to our nation we ought to do it," said President Rose. "If we're going to have a leading program in imaging science, we ought to have a relationship with the leading practitioner."[17] John Schott, an imaging science professor, claimed that the criticism of the RIT administration was, in effect, a demand that RIT be "politically correct." Since 1987, Schott had received $200,000 a year to engage in satellite image analysis for the CIA. As a result of the controversy, Schott's CIA contract was not renewed, which appears to have greatly displeased him.[18]

Andrew Dougherty, Rose's executive assistant and a member of the Association of Former Intelligence Officers, supervised CIA activities at RIT. He authored the 1985 memorandum and two controversial consulting reports for the CIA.

The first report, "Changemasters," resulted from discussions among six panelists, including Robert McFarlane (of Iran-Contra fame) and former vice presidents of Xerox and AT&T. "Changemasters" advocated economic espionage against "adversarial" U.S. trading partners, the transfer of government-funded technology to the private sector, and the repeal of antitrust legislation. The report also recommended new legislation to allow the CIA to sell its intelligence.[19] "Not for nothing," wrote Jack Bradigan Spula in the Rochester weekly *City*, "do insiders refer to the CIA as 'The Company.'"[20]

The second report, "Japan 2000," was an outgrowth of discussions with such experts on Japanese culture as McFarlane; Tim Stone, a former CIA agent and director of corporate intelligence for Motorola; and Frank Pipp, a retired Xerox executive. It warns our nation's decision makers: "Mainstream Japanese, the vast majority of whom absolutely embrace the national vision, have strange precedents. They are creatures of an ageless, amoral, manipulative and controlling culture—not to be emulated—suited only to this race, in this place." The report concluded, " 'Japan 2000' should provide notice that 'the rising sun' is coming—the attack has begun."[21]

RIT historian Richard Lunt observed, "It is the height of hypocrisy to solicit gifts from leading Japanese corporations to finance the imaging science building while at the same time preparing a confidential document for the CIA which claims the Japanese government and Japanese corporations are conspiring to attack and destroy the United States."[22] Rose tried to distance himself from "Japan 2000" by claiming that the report was only a working draft. Doughtery immediately released a revised version but the report continued to arouse widespread indignation since it claimed, for example, that "the values that shape the Japanese paradigm do not seem designed to benefit the rest of the world."[23]

As the RIT scandal drew attention to CIA involvement at other universities, Dougherty advised his CIA superiors that time was of the essence if the agency's activities at RIT were to be preserved. "Every day that the Federal Programs Training Center can be identified with RIT compounds our problem."[24] Dougherty proposed replacing the RITRC with a nonprofit university foundation that would include the University of Rochester.

Rose and Dougherty hastened to reassure the RIT community that the CIA was not unduly influencing the curriculum or threatening academic freedom. Claiming that "morality is built into every fiber of my being," Dougherty said that the CIA would never do anything morally objectionable. "They are really gun-shy about doing anything improper with an academic institution," he maintained.[25]

Monroe Freedman, the senior fact finder of the commission that investigated the RIT-CIA ties, disagreed. In his report he wrote,

[i]ntimidation and fear are recurring themes in comments about matters relating to the CIA at RIT and, specifically, about Mr. Dougherty. One Dean called him "authoritarian," "harsh," and a "threatening individual." Another Dean said that Mr. Dougherty "had the power to make you or break you." "To clash with him meant that you were going to be fired," the Dean said, giving the name of one person who, he alleged, was fired because he had said that Mr. Dougherty did not understand what a university is. One Vice President expressed resentment that he had been compelled to accept the appointment of an unwanted subordinate for an administrative position, noting that the subordinate also had responsibilities at the RITRC. "Things were done," said the same Vice President, "and I had to go along."[26]

The graduation ceremonies in May 1991 were marked by protests. Visitors to RIT found the outlines of bodies drawn in chalk on sidewalks and parking lots. That June, the administration announced that a blue-ribbon trustee committee would investigate CIA activities at RIT. Somehow, a committee containing the likes of Colby Chandler, then chairman of Kodak, and Kent Damon, a former vice president of Xerox, did little to reassure critics of RIT-CIA ties that its inquiry would be impartial. After all, Kodak and Xerox benefit from the "dual-use" projects that develop the components of high-tech military weaponry and enhance the corporate bottom line. The administration later added two students, five professors, and an alumnus, who happened to be a Kodak vice president, to the committee. It also brought in Freedman, a former law school dean at Hofstra University, to serve as its senior fact finder.

In June, Rose announced that he would sever all personal ties with the CIA, and Dougherty resigned as his assistant. That month, another resignation followed, that of Dennis Nystrom, the RIT development officer who recruited students for projects at the Federal Programs Training Center. Nystrom denied that his resignation had to do with the CIA scandal. Upon leaving RIT, Nystrom took a job with Ektron Applied Imaging, part of Kodak's Government Systems Division, which engages in classified research for U. S. intelligence agencies.[27]

That summer, RIT hired the lobbying firm Hill and Knowlton to improve its public image, which was tarnished by articles in the *New York Times*, the *Chronicle of Higher Education,* and the foreign press. Hill and Knowlton had CIA ties of its own: Its overseas offices were used to provide cover for CIA agents.[28]

In September, Rose announced that he would step down as president the following year. The CIA ended a $20,000 support fund for imaging science students that dated back to the midsixties.[29] It also ended its controversial officer-in-residence program, which had been used to recruit RIT students for the agency.

In November 1991, Monroe Freedman concluded his four-month investigation at RIT. In his final report, Freedman recommended banning classified research at RIT and closing the Federal Programs Training Center. He also pointed to problems with unclassified research involving the CIA: "Despite the fact that a contract is called unclassified," wrote Freedman in his final report, "the fact that the CIA is sponsoring it may be classified, the identity of one or more of the people involved may be classified, the problem or purpose for which a solution is sought may be classified, or the end product may be classified." He noted that CIA research was creating two classes of faculty: those willing and able to obtain security clearances and those who were not.[30]

Freedman concluded that the ideals of the academic community were "inherently inconsistent" with those of the CIA. "The ideal of the academic institution is the pursuit of knowledge and the free and open exploration of ideas," he said. "The nature of the CIA is covert, secretive and sometimes deceptive."[31]

Freedman noted that RIT had a corporate model of university governance, "with a strong chief executive officer answerable to a Board of Trustees that is assumed to be informed and responsible." RIT's corporate trustees, Freedman found, had been neither informed nor responsible.[32] He called the RITRC "a wholly owned legal fiction," whose purpose was "to allow the institution to do something 'off-campus' that almost everyone agrees the institution itself should not be doing 'on campus.'"[33] According to Freedman, RITRC president Robert Desmond had "deliberately distanced himself from knowledge about the CIA contracts."[34]

Despite Freedman's recommendations, RIT's trustees continue to allow classified CIA research at RIT. As a result of the CIA controversy, however, a committee was created to oversee research contracts at RIT. In October 1996, the committee informed the administration that it was not receiving the information it needed to independently verify grants or enforce research policy. Provost McKenzie called local news reports regarding the oversight committee's complaint "unfortunate and perplexing."[35] In fall 1996, RIT trustees unanimously voted to designate President Rose as RIT President Emeritus.

RIT's current president, Albert Simone, took office in 1992. At first, the RIT community welcomed Simone's accessibility and his involvement in university affairs. He was quoted in the October 10, 1994, *Henrietta Post* as saying, "If you're not an open person, a sensitive person, a person who genuinely likes others, you can't be an effective decision-maker."[36]

Compared to his predecessor, Simone appeared forthright and in touch with students and faculty. In an early speech, he expressed his commitment to the liberal arts. "He's a breath of fresh air," said philosophy professor Wade Robison.[37]

About six months after his inauguration as president, Simone began to craft a ten-year Strategic Plan for RIT, calling it "the most participatory plan in all of academia."[38] He then embarked the university on a path of managed attrition, and began to make plans to expand partnerships with industry and to revamp the curriculum. Having slashed $6 million from the annual budget, Simone announced his intention of cutting $10 to 20 million more, citing the need for "teamwork" if the RIT community was to benefit from the plan.

"If we have the sense of community I've talked about . . . I believe that we'll be able to find ways to—if we have to—downsize, restructure, reorient, reprioritize, reallocate," Simone said, adding reassuringly, "I think we're going to have to do all of those things, but that doesn't mean we have to do them and have a lot of hurt and bloodshed and despair and destruction."[39]

Had the RIT community been more familiar with Simone's tenure as president of the University of Hawaii (UH) from 1984 to 1992, it might have been wary of the changes in store for RIT. David Yount, who served as vice president under Simone at UH, says in *Who Runs the University?* that it was widely rumored that Simone had been brought in as a "hit man" and that approximately one-third of the twenty-four deans left office early in his administration.[40]

According to Yount, Simone's brash personality did not endear him to the UH community:

Many of his listeners echoed the sentiments of former Manoa Chancellor Marvin Anderson when he confided privately to his staff that "Al Simone has no class." Especially embarrassing were the sexist comments and ethnic slurs that sporadically popped out—his golfing double entendre about the hooker or his careless pronunciation of local names. . . . Although he was coached for years by female staffers who managed most of the time to put the right words in his mouth and the right thoughts in his head, the wrong words and thoughts continued to emerge. He habitually said "woman" when he meant "women," introduced professional couples as "Dr. and Mrs.," instead of "Dr. and Dr." and betrayed genuine surprise whenever the career of a married woman surpassed that of her husband.[41]

Several student groups, including Students Against Discrimination and Hawaii Women of Color, held a mock trial of Simone. Their mentor, Haunani-Kay Trask, professor of Hawaiian studies, charged Simone with incompetence, racism, sexism, and ignorance of Hawaiian history. The jury found him guilty on all counts, and the judge pronounced him "an embarrassment to the entire university community and to the human race."[42]

The origins of RIT's crisis in the arts do not lie, however, in the colorful personality of Albert Simone, but in the convergence of the interests of large corporations with those of the national security state. The development of Kodak and Xerox products depends in large part on the advances made in the imaging sciences. Simone, who is both RIT president and chair of the Greater Rochester Chamber of Commerce, has built up the well-connected CIMS at the expense of the arts.

Speaking of connections, CIMS was built by the Pike Company, a construction firm which tops the list of a dozen Monroe County companies that last year exceeded the legal limit on corporate campaign contributions. Tom Judson, Pike Company president, claiming to be ignorant of the New York State statute that limits such contributions to $5,000, said, "Maybe I can get some money back."

Indeed. No corporation has ever been fined for violating the statute, which was enacted in 1974.[43]

Thus are connections made. The first off-campus RIT trustee meeting convened in Washington, D.C., in April 1997. President Simone explained, "We want Washington to know us better. We have had a lot of support from the federal government. We need more."

During their three-day stay in Washington, the trustees met with members of Congress and federal officials to discuss such matters as technology transfer and research, and were briefed by a Department of Defense (DOD) undersecretary on U.S. technology policy.[44] Anita Jones, the director of DOD's Defense Research and Engineering, observing that she didn't know of any other university board coming to Washington, said of the RIT trustees visit, "I thought it showed a lot of forward thinking."[45]

In March 1997, I interviewed Kurt Perschke and fellow ceramics student and SOS organizer Molly Hamblin. They related to me the history of the School of American Crafts, which owes its existence to Aileen Osborn Webb, founder of the American Craft Council. SAC opened at Dartmouth in 1944 and moved to RIT in 1950. As the first school in this country exclusively devoted to crafts, SAC was inspired by the crafts movement, which has been a counterweight to the values of the Industrial Revolution for over a century.[46]

To hear Hamblin describe the material with which she works is to come to feel that it has a life of its own, giving new meaning to Keats's "strife between damnation and impassioned clay." Hamblin believes that RIT students are too engrossed in the information highway, too dazzled by the prospect of being able to purchase groceries by computer, to bother to express themselves. She described to me the eeriness of RIT buildings that "are full of people and silent except for the clicking of computer keyboards."

While Perschke and Hamblin were elated that the art schools have earned a reprieve, they knew that their existence remained precarious. Hamblin said that the art schools had been given a three to five year "umbrella," during which they have to successfully market their programs. While advertising had increased student enrollment in the art schools for fall 1998, the RIT administration remained uncommitted to the art programs. "I personally don't doubt for a second," said Perschke, "that three or four years from now, when everybody who's here now is gone, the administration wouldn't think of doing this again."

Perschke recalled the administration's shift from one rationale to another to justify the elimination of the art programs. "I think what was most indicative of the strategy of the administration," said Perschke, "was that there was a rotating organizational chart of reasonings, and that it didn't really matter which one it was in the end—they all led toward the same goal."

Hamblin noted that positions were being left unfulfilled as professors retired, and that the increased number of art students had not led to an increase in available work space or to significant improvements in their facilities. SAC may eventually have to leave RIT and become independent again in order to survive, said Hamblin, who did not relish the idea of being in an institution where she was not wanted.

Perschke lamented the absence of institutional memory at RIT. Most SOS activists only dimly remembered that activists had forced a past RIT president to resign. Few had considered the implications of the continuing CIA presence at RIT.

Unless the disjunction between past and present is overcome, the arts and crafts may go the way of the dodo and the carrier pigeon. RIT activists need to discover their own "strategic national resource worthy of explicit development and support," the national student movement that is organizing annual Democracy Teach-Ins. Its time has come. For as Jonathan Worthen, an RIT undergraduate ceramics major said, "When the voices of the messengers, the artists, the poets, the teachers, when they cannot be heard, there will be no future for any of us."[47]

NOTES

1. "Cornerstone Ceremony: CIMS 'Making a Difference to Industry,' " *News and Events* (RIT Administration Newsletter), December 1, 1996.

2. Jean Douthwright, "Rochester Institute of Technology: A CIA Subsidiary?" *Covert Action Information Bulletin* 38 (fall 1991): 6

3. SOS Video Transcript.

4. Troy Liston, "Martyr of the Week," *GDT,* April 28, 1996, p. 5

5. Donna Jackel, "Art Students Rally," *Democrat and Chronicle,* April 1996.

6. Greg Livadas, "Cuts at RIT Protested," *Democrat and Chronicle,* April 26, 1996, p. B1.

7. Thomas Lightfoot, memo to RIT administrators, April 26, 1996, pp. 1–2.

8. Donna Jackel, "A Shroud of Visual Silence," *Democrat and Chronicle,* May 1, 1996, p. A1.

9. Christopher Robin Hewitt, "Don't Tread On Us," *Reporter,* May 3, 1996, p. 18.

10. Anthony Burda, "Wolf at the Door," *Reporter,* April 26, 1996, p. 17.

11. Hewitt, "Don't Tread on Us," p. 17.

12. Jennifer Hyman, "Memo Established Formal Relationship," *Democrat and Chronicle,* June 2, 1991.

13. Jennifer Hyman, "CIA Vein Runs Deep Inside RIT," *Democrat and Chronicle,* June 2, 1991, p. A4.

14. Jennifer Hyman, "Millions In CIA Funds Enriched RIT Coffers," *Democrat and Chronicle*, May 16, 1991, p. A4.

15. Jennifer Hyman, "CIA Ends Student Fund, Research Contract At RIT," *Democrat and Chronicle,* September 6, 1991.

16. Jennifer Hyman, "Faculty Member Recalls CIA Offer to Train Spies," *Democrat and Chronicle,* May 16, 1991, p. A4.

17. Denise K. Magner, "At Rochester Institute, a Spectrum of Opinions on Links with the CIA," *Chronicle of Higher Education,* July 10, 1991, p. A14.

18. William Glaberson, "College's C.I.A. Ties Cause Furor, and Soul-Searching," *New York Times,* June 20, 1991, p. B6.

19. Jennifer Hyman, "RIT Advises CIA To Plan For Future," *Democrat and Chronicle,* May 19, 1991.

20. Jack Bradigan Spula, "RIT And The CIA: The Company They Keep," *City,* December 4–10, 1996, p. 6.

21. Jennifer Hyman, "Secret RIT Study Bashes the Japanese," *Democrat and Chronicle,* May 24, 1991, p. A12.

22. Jennifer Hyman, "RIT Took With One Hand, Skewered With The Other," *Democrat and Chronicle,* May 24, 1991, p. A12.

23. Jennifer Hyman, "Revised RIT Report Softer On Japanese," *Democrat and Chronicle*, May 25, 1991, p. A12.

24. Jennifer Hyman, "Stolen Papers Suggest Plan 'To Cut Losses,' " *Democrat and Chronicle*, June 8, 1991, p. A1.

25. Jennifer Hyman. "Millions in CIA Funding Pumped into RIT Coffers," *Democrat and Chronicle*, May 16, 1991, p. A4.

26. Monroe K. Freedman. "Deficiencies of Leadership," fact-finding report, November 14, 1991, p. 6.

27. Jennifer Hyman, "Pair Tied to CIA Resign," *Democrat and Chronicle*, June 27, 1991, p. A1.

28. Jennifer Hyman, "PR Firm Also Tied To CIA," *Democrat and Chronicle*, July 22, 1991, p. A8.

29. Jennifer Hyman, "CIA Ends Student Fund, Research Contract at RIT," *Democrat and Chronicle*, September 6, 1991.

30. Jennifer Hyman, "RIT Panel Criticizes Classified Research," *Democrat and Chronicle*, November 17, 1991, 8A.

31. Jennifer Hyman, "RIT Investigator Says CIA Ties Hurt Integrity," *Democrat and Chronicle*, September 25, 1991.

32. Jennifer Hyman, "College's Leaders Blamed," *Democrat and Chronicle*, November 17, 1991, p. 8A.

33. Jennifer Hyman, "RIT Panel Criticizes Classified Research," *Democrat and Chronicle*, November 17, 1991, p. 8A.

34. Jennifer Hyman, "6 Officials At RIT Urged To Resign," *Democrat and Chronicle*, November 16, 1991, p. A1.

35. Michael Wentzel. "RIT Plans Research Oversight," *Democrat and Chronicle*, November 5, 1996, p. 1.

36. Derek Murphy, "He Plans to Make a Difference at RIT," *Henrietta Post*, October 10, 1994.

37. Kathleen M. Wagner, "New President Still Charms RIT," *Democrat and Chronicle*, April 14, 1993, p. 8A.

38. Murphy, "He Plans to Make a Difference at RIT."

39. Wagner, "New President Still Charms RIT," p. 8A.

40. David Yount, *Who Runs The University?* (Honolulu: University of Hawaii Press, 1996), pp. 32–33.

41. Ibid., p. 25.

42. Ibid., p. 26–27.

43. David McKay Wilson and Gary Craig, "200 Firms Exceed N.Y. Campaign Gift Limit," *Times-Union*, May 8, 1997, p. 1.

44. Michael Wentzel, "RIT Trustees To Wine and Dine Washington," *Democrat and Chronicle*, April 10, 1997, pp. B1, B4.

45. "Trustees Hold Historic Board Meeting in Nation's Capitol," *News and Events*, May 1, 1997.

46. Jack Bradigan Spula. "PrioRITies: How Go the Arts at the Institute?" *City*, May 16, 1996, p. 4.

47. Hewitt, "Don't Tread on Us," p. 19.

14

PENN AND INC.
Incorporating the
University of Pennsylvania[1]

Matthew Ruben

[Q]uality is not the ultimate issue, but excellence soon will be, because it is the recognition that the University is not just like *a corporation; it* is *a corporation. Students in the University of Excellence are not* like *customers; they* are *customers.*[2]

In April 1998, the Philadelphia City Council held hearings on a bill to regulate the century-old practice of street and sidewalk vending in the neighborhood where the University of Pennsylvania is located. The ordinance prohibited vending on most of the area's major thoroughfares and created vending spaces that required city licenses. It also imposed regulations ranging from a ban on gasoline-powered generators to constitutionally suspect limits on the content of signs posted on vending trucks and carts. The bill had been introduced by the local Councilwoman at the behest of the university. More than 150 people came to testify—more than double the typical turnout for a controversial bill[3]—and the hearings ran for more than nine hours. At the end of the first hour, however, it became clear that the council intended to pass the ordinance without making any of the locational or operational amendments that vendors and their allies demanded. After a few hours, city council president John Street—himself a former vendor and the city's future mayor—declared, exasperated, "We *don't care* if you don't like the bill. You're not *supposed* to like the bill."[4]

"We have an obligation to the second largest employer in the city of Philadelphia," Street continued, referring to Penn. "If you don't think that I and the other members of council are conscious of all the economic benefits that flow from that, you're wrong." Later he opined that in any event the council could do nothing to alter the ordinance without Penn's approval because "[t]he university has rights as a property owner and I think that's often forgotten." According to Street those "rights" included ownership of the sidewalks and the streets out to the center line. "In fact," he added, "I suspect that many of the regulations we pass in this chamber are illegal."

This last, seemingly total abdication of governmental power left the already dispirited crowd in stunned silence. Dean Varvoutis, a vendor leader, gamely began to read his prepared testimony, which focused precisely on the idea that the university should not be able to assert blanket control over what everyone had thought could be called public space. He stopped abruptly, looked up at Street, and gestured toward his young son sitting in the gallery. "I brought my son here today," he said. "I want him to see this. I want him to learn how this works. This country is supposed to be for the little guy. It seems like there's no room for the little guy anymore. If there's no room for the little guy," he said, shaking his head, "I don't know what it's all for."

Street's expression changed from boredom to annoyance. "You can't think doing what you're doing is a stable way to make a living. . . . There's no law that gives you the right to conduct business on a public right-of-way. . . . You've got to grow up. Twenty years ago I was sitting exactly where you are today. . . . I knew if I wanted to take care of myself and my family I needed to find something else. . . . I went to law school. What you've got to do is make a plan, decide what you're going to do with your life."

This exchange, and the council's unanimous vote in favor of the ordinance the next day, represented the final act of a bitter, divisive drama that had been unfolding on the Penn campus, in the local media, and at city hall for an entire year. On one side was the university administration, backed by its trustees and a handful of local businesspeople. On the other were the vendors, students, staff, faculty, and members of certain neighborhood groups.

There are, of course, a variety of factors that help explain how the council, led by a former community activist whose electoral base is rooted in working-class, African American North Philadelphia, came to carry the water of the University of Pennsylvania. The most striking of these developments is the process by which the university—a nonprofit entity widely perceived by the general public as a genteel, elitist bastion of political correctness—came to be perceived as the kind of corporate entity the council felt compelled to defend.

In most scholarship on universities, the process of corporatization is seen in terms of the infusion of corporate money into universities through the funding of proprietary research, endowed chairs and ideologically slanted programs. Lawrence Soley's *Leasing the Ivory Tower* is the best-known example and has proven an invaluable resource for researchers and organizers. Yet discussions of university incorporation often miss the full scope of what is happening on and around the campuses of private research universities in the United States. Universities are not "corporatized" only because for-profit firms are providing funds for research and endowed chairs. Modern research universities are not simply becoming more influenced or "tainted" by corporations. More fundamentally, they are becoming for-profit corporations themselves, key players in neoliberal modes of governance and economic development that have taken hold in cities throughout the nation during the past twenty-five years. This shift may be seen most clearly in two major developments:

- universities' embrace of corporate models of downsizing and outsourcing; and
- universities' increasing involvement in for-profit schemes to develop real estate and gentrify the areas around their campuses.

Taken together, these two developments indicate the extent to which the educational mission of universities is becoming subordinated to financial concerns, and is playing a sharply decreased role in shaping the priorities, activities, and cultures of universities.

The following sections of this paper examine several instances of each of these two developments at the University of Pennsylvania (where the author was a Ph.D, student in the School of Arts and Sciences from 1992 to 1999) with an eye toward analyzing their execution, their ideological underpinnings, and their effects on the campus and surrounding communities. The focus on Penn is meant to highlight phenomena generalizable to private research universities, and to a lesser extent to all universities across the United States.

THE NEUTRON BOMB THEORY OF EXCELLENCE: DOWNSIZING AND OUTSOURCING

Many CEOs work with great people under them. . . . The best a CEO can hope for is to have really talented people around her, and I am blessed.
—University of Pennsylvania president Judith Rodin,
September 1998[5]

To call someone in and then suddenly the next day you're not working—
I think it's inhumane. . . . They always say, "You make the difference at
Penn, we're all a community here." Then they say, "Turn in your ID
and keys by tomorrow or you won't get your [final] paycheck." That
kind of stuff hurts. It's like a slap in the face. I'm wondering what kind
of people are making these decisions.
    —downsized University of Pennsylvania employee, March 1997[6]

Some might find it surprising that a university president refers to herself as a CEO and breezily compares herself to chief executives in the corporate world. In fact, Judith Rodin has good reason to think of herself as a CEO, as that is precisely the role she was hired to play. In the wake of a flurry of disastrous press coverage during the administration of Sheldon Hackney in the early 1990s,[7] the University of Pennsylvania's trustees, dominated by corporate CEOs, determined to hire a new president who would improve Penn's image and manage the university in a more businesslike manner.[8] They chose Rodin, a Philadelphia native, a Penn alumna, and the first woman to hold the position on a permanent basis.

Since Rodin took over the administration in July 1994, the university's operations have indeed shifted toward a corporate model. This model may be referred to as the Neutron Bomb Theory of Excellence. Like the infamous weapon that gets rid of people and preserves buildings, Penn's management practices entail the liquidation of labor in order to stockpile funds for ambitious capital projects. As of this writing, Rodin's administration has laid off more than thirty-five hundred of Penn's thirty-one thousand employees, contributing to a reported $12 million in annual savings in the general budget.[9] The coming years will no doubt see more firings as the university attempts to reach its cost-cutting target of $50 million. Eventually Penn may lose its status as the largest private employer in Philadelphia and the fourth largest in Pennsylvania.

The shrinking of the labor force began with the announcement of a major restructuring initiative and the publication of a comprehensive administrative evaluation prepared by the Big Eight accounting firm of Coopers and Lybrand. A week before the Coopers report was released, a letter signed by Rodin was sent to every student, staffer, and faculty member. The letter exemplified the new administration's corporate sensibility. "Penn is a great institution for many reasons," it began, "but one of the most important is that, throughout its history, Penn has been able to change with the times. Often Penn has led the way." From the outset, nonmarket narratives of Ivy League gentility, academic tradition, and the like were discarded in favor of a market-based model of competition and innovation. The letter continued:

Just as we must continue to change in the academic sphere to ensure excellence, we must also change in administrative and fiscal areas. The brightness of our future depends on how we meet these changing times. Global competition, new information technologies, limited economic growth, political change, the uncertainties of Federal and Commonwealth support for private higher education and for research, the limited abilities of families to sustain large tuition increases—all these are combining to force upon us a new set of economic realities. . . .

The drive for better service and higher quality at the lowest possible cost will increasingly dominate the higher education environment, just as it has for business and government. Only by striving for fiscal, administrative and academic excellence will Penn, and Penn's people, achieve their full potential in such a climate. . . .

Our goal is to reduce costs, improve services, make strategic investments and enhance our competitive position. . . . [10]

The private sector logic of competition, introduced at the letter's outset, was reinforced by the use of market terms like "mak[ing] strategic investments" and "enhanc[ing] our competitive position." Any hint of an ideological or political slant—explicit advocacy of business models of outsourcing or downsizing, for example—was countered by the letter's fatalistic invocation of "global competition," "new information technologies," and "political change" to describe a "new set of economic realities." One cannot argue against realities; one can only respond to them or ignore them. In this manner, Rodin adopted the pragmatic, flexible, "postideological" feeling of neoliberal policy discourse to justify activities whose adherence to market ideology would become clear in the months and years to follow. The letter ended with a declaration that "[w]e can and will realize Penn's extraordinary potential for academic excellence and leadership, as long as we are willing to change." This statement neatly mimicked Bill Clinton's vacuous, neoliberal campaign rhetoric, in which he repeatedly declared, "We can do much, much better if we have the courage to change."[11]

When the Coopers report itself was published in the faculty/staff newspaper, it was prefaced by a letter entitled "The Case for Administrative Restructuring at Penn," which began:

For some time now, American business has been learning how to adjust to rapidly changing market conditions in order to remain competitive in a global economy. That effort is evident in the commitment of leading American corporations to total quality management, reengineering of key business processes and the exploration of customer-supplied alliances. The focus of those efforts is to improve the quality of products and services, enhance ability to meet customer needs, lower costs,

increase productivity and improve efficiency by eliminating administrative tasks that do not add value.[12]

Signed not only by the acting executive vice president but also by the
provost, the statement made it clear that the standards, practices, and
jargon of the business sector were to become the benchmark for achieving
"excellence" at the university.[13] The report itself contained a variety of
restructuring suggestions, but the main effect was to frighten the staff
without being specific enough to allow units or employees to know who
was going to be laid off, or under what terms.

Most significantly, John Fry, the Coopers and Lybrand executive
whose division wrote the report, was hired the following summer as executive vice president to implement it, thus placing a management consultant from the heart of corporate America in the de facto number-two position at the university.

With the Coopers report as the blueprint and Fry in place to carry it
out, restructuring activities began in earnest, focused on three main areas:
campus services, health provision and benefits, and facilities management.

- In 1996, the campus bookstore was outsourced to the academic
  division of Barnes and Noble, which manages more than 340
  campus bookstores nationwide. More than two-thirds of the
  employees fell off the payroll in the process, losing the child and
  spousal tuition remission benefits that are the main reason many
  Penn employees accept below-market salaries.[14]
- In 1997, the office of the vice provost for university life (VPUL),
  which is responsible for all student services, lost fifteen workers, a
  significant portion of its core administrative staff.[15] While "The
  Case for Administrative Restructuring at Penn" spoke of "freeing
  up" staff salaries for "strategic reinvestment,"[16] VPUL saw its programming budget cut as well.
- In 1998, university catering services were outsourced to a California
  firm, which was granted monopoly control of all food concessions
  in a new $82-million student center called the Perelman Quad.[17]
- In January 1999, the administration effectively broke the Penn Faculty Club employees' union, moving the club's facilities to a new
  Penn hotel and outsourcing management and staffing to the DoubleTree chain. In an open letter to the campus, Fry stated that since
  "DoubleTree, not Penn, will be the employer at the Inn at Penn. . . .
  We simply cannot, indeed it's improper, for the University to force
  terms and conditions of employment and a pre-determined staff on
  DoubleTree and its many other employees."[18] Two months later the

hotel's manager committed to hiring 70 percent of the laid-off workers, if they were willing to re-apply individually, on Double-Tree's terms, as nonunion employees.[19]

- Later in 1999, the College of Arts and Sciences attempted to entice department heads into laying off support staff by offering discretionary funds equal to half the annual salary of anyone who was fired.[20]

- In the fall of 1996, as the University of Pennsylvania Medical System paid a $30-million Medicaid fraud fine to the federal government, its workers faced a new contract that combined increased out-of-pocket benefits costs with pay raises totaling only 2 percent over two years. Meanwhile, the medical system's CEO earned a seven-figure salary and the five highest-paid doctors earned salaries one-and-a-half to three times the Northeastern United States average—a figure itself way above the national average.[21]

- The next year, university staff health benefits were restructured, with the low-cost fee-for-service option discontinued and HMO premiums for families increasing by as much as $104 per month.[22] While two existing plans were dropped, one new one was added: Aetna/U.S. Healthcare, from whom Rodin earned nearly $120,000 in cash, stock, and dividends in 1997 as a member of the board of directors.[23] The next year, Aetna also became the university's student health insurance provider.[24]

- Two years later the medical system, which supplies 56 percent of the university's annual revenue,[25] announced the elimination of 2,800 positions between May 1999 and June 2000 in order to stanch a $288-million flow of red ink during the previous two years, and to compete more effectively with a for-profit firm that had bought up several Philadelphia hospitals.[26]

- In 1996, management of the university's for-profit real estate arm was outsourced to the Dallas-based Trammell Crow Corporation. Trammell Crow, in turn, outsourced the real estate security force to the Spectra Guard Company. The university also hired Spectra Guard to provide campus security.[27]

- Over the next two years the administration did something no university had ever done before: It outsourced management of all its buildings and facilities. Perhaps not surprisingly, the contract went to Trammell Crow.[28] Approximately one-third of the 175 affected employees failed to secure positions with Crow.[29] An additional 600 unionized facilities employees faced layoffs or reduced pay in the near future, when their union contracts with Penn would expire.[30] At that point, Crow would be under no legal obligation to deal with the unions or rehire any of the employees. The deal was announced and publicized just as Crow was preparing an initial public offering (IPO) of stock. In exchange for helping the company create a whole new area of the real estate management industry and thereby increase the value of the IPO, Penn was to receive two lump payments totaling $32 million, or nearly half the revenue generated by the offering. In this manner Penn effectively issued its own IPO, financed on the backs of its workers.[31]

In addition to these cases, many smaller administrative departments were quietly downsized, outsourced, or simply eliminated, and their employees received little assistance in putting their lives back together.

The other side of the Neutron Bomb Theory—the stockpiling of capital—may be seen most clearly in the university's behavior toward its endowment. The endowment is a university's most powerful asset. It constitutes a gigantic tax-exempt investment portfolio, a storehouse of wealth running into the billions. Officially a university endowment functions much like that of a bank's (or nation's) cash reserves: It exists to safeguard the institution's existence in the event of an extreme fiscal crisis such as the precipitous loss of an entire year's operating funds. In reality, the endowment is used to supplement the annual operating budget and to help fund capital projects (either directly or as collateral for loans and bond issues).

In the past two decades, Penn has built its endowment at breakneck pace, even compared with its Ivy League peers. In 1976 its endowment totaled $164 million; by 1998 it had grown to more than eighteen times that size, surpassing $3 billion. In 1976, Penn's endowment was just over one-fourth the size of Yale's and one-ninth the size of Harvard's; by 1997 it was nearly half as large as Yale's and closing in on one-fourth the size of Harvard's. This represented a rate of growth two to three times that of the other institutions.[32]

Some of this growth spurt is attributable to the university's increased willingness to invest in high-risk ventures.[33] But the more telling factor concerns the way the university's trustees understand their roles as Penn's fiscal custodians. Even as the endowment's value has skyrocketed, growing as much as 20 percent year-to-year, the trustees have dictated that less and less of it be used to make the university run. In the early 1980s, they established guidelines limiting the percentage of the endowment that could be used to fund the general operating budget. Officially a hedge against inflation,[34] the policy has reduced the allowable percentage every year, with the result that less than 2.5 percent of endowment funds get released into the budget.[35] In this manner, Penn prioritizes endowment growth the way a corporation seeks to maximize profits and shareholder dividends. Of course, the "shareholders" are trustees, and the "profits" and "dividends" get retained in the endowment; but the underlying sensibility is identical—not surprising when one considers the extent to which the board of trustees is dominated by CEOs. For the trustees, capital growth, facilities expansion, and the cutting of labor costs are not merely as means to an end. They are *social values in and of themselves*—values that signal to the financial world, the media, and the public that Penn is sufficiently possessed of that elusive quality, "excellence," to compete with the nation's most elite universities.

While this mode of trustee behavior enriches the university as a fiscal entity, it squeezes the general operating budget, increasing the already disproportionate burdens placed on certain groups within the university by outsourcing and downsizing. Shrinking central support for schools and departments exacerbates differentials among them, increasing the extent to which they must depend on outside funding—a situation clearly less feasible for some disciplines than others. One visible sign of this situation is that the facilities of the Wharton School (the beneficiary of choice for many corporate donors and wealthy alumni) and the Annenberg School for Communication (bankrolled largely by Walter Annenberg) increasingly look like those of another university when compared to the buildings that house the Schools of Arts and Sciences, Education, and Social Work.[36] As one graduate student wrote, "The policy of the University seems to be if you want to build something or improve, then you need to find the money yourself. For some reason, I don't think the Psychology Department, [the] School of Social Work, or the School of Education is going to get a $10 million donation from one of their 'rich' alumni anytime soon."[37] In 1996, the well-funded law school closed access to its library to non-law students.[38] And while Wharton students may take advantage of the university's broad range of programs, education students cannot easily take classes in Wharton or the law school because the School of Education cannot afford the tuition transfers.

Inequalities impact Penn's labor environment as well, undermining job security and stratifying wages. As one staff group stated, "Each of us has been told to 'do more with less.' We all feel we are doing just that, but how do we weigh whether our efforts will save our jobs or not?"[39] Similarly, recent faculty salary increases have been distributed unevenly by rank and among schools: Pay raises allotted to many faculty in the School of Arts and Sciences, for example, did not keep pace with inflation.[40] While the endowment, adjusted for inflation, increased nearly 400 percent from 1976 to 1996, tuition doubled and salaries for low- and mid-level staff actually decreased slightly. At the other end of the scale, Rodin's salary increased from $350,000 to more than

$500,000 in four years, and Fry's $300,000 annual compensation exceeds that of most university presidents.[41]

In this environment it should not come as a surprise that conflict and resentment flourish. The outsourcing of facilities management saw a fairly united front of staff, students, and faculty organizing demonstrations against the arrangement, detailing the destructive effect on campus morale and community in letters to campus media, and passing numerous resolutions condemning the administration's handling of the process.[42] The Trammell Crow deal, along with a handful of similar moves, became a lighting rod for the pent-up frustrations of staff, students, and faculty who had spent years languishing on moribund administrative advisory committees while Rodin and Fry got raises for overseeing the wholesale transformation of the university. The administration retained corporate consulting firms to write reports recommending outsourcing and layoffs as it endured withering criticism for not involving the campus community in key decisions. It also hired top administrators *as if* they were consultants: brought in to perform specific tasks, paid historically high salaries to take the heat, and then transferred within the administrative bureaucracy afterwards. At a public meeting, one worker stated:

> Employees with twenty-five or more years of hard, dedicated, extremely effective service to the University are being told that the understandings under which they came to work here, on the basis of which they have planned their futures and the education of their children, are vapor, and that they were naive to believe that those understandings actually represented commitments by the University. Not only that—they are being given this message by people who have been at the University for three years or less, who don't know the staff or their work.[43]

Others observed that "certain very highly paid members of the administration whose job it is to provide leadership and management [are instead] selling off parts of [the university] once problems have been identified."[44] Entirely new positions were created in economic development and government and community relations to expand retail speculation and economic development activities. "Administrators used to come to this University because they wanted to build a legacy," commented one senior faculty member. "They would work very hard, and you would end up having the Goddard Building, the Harnwell House, and the Provost Smith Statue. But now, in the last ten to fifteen years, you have people who are just careerists coming in . . ."[45] Penn hired a new vice president for human resources to oversee the benefits redesign. After the redesign was completed, but before it took effect, he left for a better position at Duke.[46] A *Philadelphia* magazine profile found even Fry publicly musing about his plan to parlay his current position into the presidency of a second-tier university or a "small liberal arts college in a hotly competitive market where there's a lot of other schools just like them," and in turn to use such a post as a stepping stone to the head job at a place like Penn.[47]

Just as *Philadelphia* was gearing up to interview Fry on his bright future, Penn facilities employees who had survived outsourcing began working for Trammell Crow, with an additional hour tacked onto the workday.[48] One manager told the student newspaper, "I'm just working for another company. I haven't felt as though my legs have been cut out." His subordinate, however, described the new situation as "strange" and unsettling: "You come to Penn and find a family at Penn and all of a sudden something comes along and threatens that family tie." A lower-level employee who had been forced to search for another position within the university said, "[Trammell Crow] messed up my whole world." The feelings of most of the workers were never to be known, however, because they "declined to comment on the transition, citing fears of being fired for talking."[49]

COMMUNITY AND CONTROL: GENTRIFICATION AND THE WAR ON VENDING

Critically important to our environment . . . is the condition of the neighborhoods surrounding the University. Understanding this, Penn has made an extensive and long-term commitment to its host community in West Philadelphia—and at the heart of this commitment are community partnerships.

—Judith Rodin, 1997[50]

When we went here the whole city was our community. You can't do that anymore. The city's not safe. We have to make the campus the city. It would be crazy not to build everything we need right here in University City. . . . That's the long-term goal. . . . Also, we have to get rid of those food trucks.

—University of Pennsylvania trustee, June 1997[51]

During Rodin's tenure, the university has embarked upon its first major economic development initiative in thirty years, arguably the most ambitious set of projects in its history. The crown jewel in this endeavor is called Sansom Common. Sansom Common is a three-hundred-thousand-square-foot, $120-million complex featuring a two-story campus "super-bookstore" run by Barnes and Noble, a $73-million hotel managed by DoubleTree, and ninety-thousand square feet of cafés, restaurants, and retail shops. Described by the administration and its contracted real estate agents as "upscale" and "funky," the project makes explicit the for-profit model the university has adopted in the past several years. Sansom Common has been designed to make University City a "destination," drawing in visitors and consumers from throughout the metropolitan area, and helping to stem the exodus of faculty and graduate students from West Philadelphia (home to the city's second largest African American population) to Center City (the gentrified downtown business and tourist district). Rodin told the *Philadelphia Inquirer* that the project would "bring new life to our community, provide new places to shop, and provide many new jobs." And the project's close proximity to campus residences would allow people "to shop and dine where they live, as in the great cities of Europe."[52]

These kinds of statements are most often heard in the context of developers' efforts to market gentrification projects. In fact, gentrification is an apt model for understanding the effects of Penn's economic development agenda, but with a twist. There is a slippage in Rodin's language, and in other Penn officials' incessant vacillation between using the terms "University City" and "West Philadelphia" to specify the geographic bounds of "our community." The root of this slippage lies in the history of Penn's economic development activities.

University City, consisting mainly of about three hundred acres of Penn-owned property,[53] did not exist until the 1960s, although Penn had been located there since 1872. In the early sixties Penn and nearby Drexel University took advantage of a city declaration of a cluster of neighborhoods in working-class, African American West Philadelphia as a "redevelopment zone." The two universities bought up acres of land on the cheap, demolished row homes and owner-run businesses, and christened the area University City.[54] The land grab lacked a coherent redevelopment plan, so many of the blockfaces were turned into parking lots and never redeveloped. This process is known as land banking, and it earned Penn lasting contempt in the surrounding community.

In the current phase, the university is doing things differently. It has made a point of hiring local, minority-owned firms to participate in the construction of Sansom Common. The rather candid statement made by a trustee in the epigraph to this section notwithstanding, the university has artfully avoided giving the impression that the new development represents the creation of an enclave, or a city within a city. Nevertheless, an ambitious mortgage incentive program is targeted at stabilizing the western boundary of University City and drawing in Penn faculty and administrators who will increase the local base of consumers with disposable income.[55] And a luxury apartment complex set to be constructed in the next few years is meant to solidify the eastern boundary. These efforts have been supplemented with initiatives such as UC Brite, which provides neighborhoods near the campus with streetlights, to bolster the university's image and counter lingering suspicions among many West Philadel- phians. It has earned Penn kudos in the local media for participating in community development in a more thought-out, democratic manner than it did when University City was first created.[56] It has gone unremarked, however, that the university's current projects are being built on the land it acquired in the "bad old days" of the sixties. In fact, one of Penn's most powerful ideological assets lies in the stark visual contrast between the buildings it is erecting and the parking lots those buildings are replacing. The irony of this situation—that Penn is obtaining political and economic power by improving a bad situation of its own making—seems to have been lost in the uncritical boosterism of the university and the local media.

Yet the fact remains that this round of kindler, gentler development is actually the dropping of the other shoe, thirty years later. In the sixties Penn bought short, and in the 1990s it has sold dear, by developing large-scale retail complexes whose storefronts it can lease at above-market rents, and whose concessions it can auction off in exchange for lucrative profit-sharing arrangements.[57] The current projects are not displacing poor and working-class residents, because they have already been displaced. They were moved out decades ago, and the slippage in administrators' state- ments between "University City" and "West Philadelphia"—between upper-middle-class faculty and students, and poor and working-class resi- dents—constitutes the mark of that process, and an attempt to paper over it. In short, the current Penn-driven redevelopment of University City con- stitutes part of a *historically discontinuous* process of gentrification.

In this context it seems clear what the University City Vending Ordi- nance (described at the outset of this paper) was meant to accomplish. A wide-ranging ordinance was not necessary simply to enable the vendors to coexist peacefully with the new retail projects. There is, after all, little overlap between a Vietnamese food truck that charges $3.25 for a full-size portion of lemon grass chicken in a styrofoam container, and a café that charges the same price for a tall mochachino in a fancy glass. Nor does a clothing store have much to fear from a vendor who sells cheap scarves and sunglasses from a foldaway table two blocks away. The problem for the university was that, consistent with the trustees' emphasis on stock- piling capital, Sansom Common was to be built without any endowment funds. Instead, the university tried soliciting private investors, and then took out tens of millions of dollars in loans via bond issues, loans collat- eralized by anticipated future revenues from the retail concessions.[58] This revenue is to come in the form of rent and profit-sharing arrangements. As a result, rents in Sansom Common have been set well above the market rate for University City, and according to anecdotal information even higher than much of the prime space in Center City, the downtown business district. The only way to get away with such high rents is to guarantee a tightly controlled commercial *and aesthetic* environment, attuned to an affluent consumer demographic—hence gentrification.[59]

Of course, the university did not seek to justify the vending ordinance on those terms. Instead, administrators first attempted to mobilize concerns about safety, sanitation, and blocked hospital entrances. They repeatedly referred to the vending situation as "anarchic" and "chaotic."[60] Vendors were harassed and allegedly told by an administrator that they would be "picked off one by one."[61]

This situation created an obvious, imminent threat to vendors' livelihoods. Opposition was therefore swift and widespread. After an e-mail went out in May 1997 warning of the ordinance's imminent introduction by the councilwoman, her office was paralyzed by hundreds of phone calls from outraged students, faculty, and staff.[62] The bill's introduction was delayed, during which time the vendors organized themselves into the University City Vendors Alliance and a coalition of students, staff, and faculty created the Penn Consumers Alliance (PCA). Together these two organizations succeeded in delaying the ordinance's introduction further.

The vendors and their supporters constituted an extremely diverse group of different classes, ethnicities, races, genders, family status, and native languages. While vendors usually are politically marginalized because of their position in the informal economy,[63] Penn's vending operations were established businesses offering full menus of hot, prepared foods from trucks complete with refrigeration, generators, coolers, and stoves. Their tenure at Penn dated back as many as three decades. As a result, the vendors adopted relatively entitled identities of merchants and small-business owners, angered by what they saw as the university's attempt to control a free market that seemed to be working fine on its own. In complimentary fashion, the Penn Consumers Alliance, as its name implies, united as the vendors' customers, who required the convenience, variety, and affordability of the vendors' wares.[64]

From the outset, then, the struggle against the ordinance consisted of people who represented themselves as small-business owners and their customers. This formation produced a number of initial successes. In addition to the delays, vendors and consumers collected more than ten thousand petition signatures supporting their position, and embarrassed university officials at a community meeting convened by the councilwoman. Finally, they upstaged the Sansom Common ground breaking with a public protest, helping to kill the first version of the ordinance altogether after it finally was introduced.[65]

Over time, however, the university developed strategies to counter the opposition. It toned down its rhetoric on safety and cleanliness, and redirected its efforts toward themes of beautification and community economic development. Several weeks before the city council hearing a glossy, full-color trifold pamphlet was sent out to every student, staffer, and faculty member. The pamphlet cleverly juxtaposed recent increases in the number of vendors in University City with an increase in retail vacancies. It stated that while "vending should and will remain part of the way of life at Penn . . . it must be done in a way that enhances the aesthetics and image of the campus; allows for the healthy co-existence of retail shopping; instills consumer confidence in food safety and hygiene; and minimally impacts traffic safety and parking conditions. . . ."[66]

At the same time, the administration apologized for "not involving the public enough," and promised to consult all the relevant parties before getting a revised version reintroduced in council. [67] The administration proposed "fresh-air food plazas" located on Penn property. The plazas were used to deflect attention from the ordinance, as administrators went around the campus making colorful presentations on the plazas and counting them as consultative meetings on the ordinance. Locating vendors on the campus helped enable Penn to obtain even greater control over the commercial environment while lessening the wrath of the affected vendors and consumers. In short, the administration discovered that it did not need to eradicate the vendors entirely. While it did need to reduce their numbers,[68] what it really needed was to reorganize them physically, economically, and aesthetically to correspond to the rigidly segmented market environment of the "new" University City—not unlike the reorganization of campus labor as part of what the staff termed "the new Penn world."[69] The vendors were to be converted from autonomous economic entities into "local color." The unsophisticated look of food carts and merchandise tables, along with the racially diverse faces of the vendors themselves, help blunt the rather contrived new urbanism of Penn's projects with their color-coordinated awnings, upscale merchants, neotraditionalist nomenclature, and neoclassical architecture.

Faced with these emergent subtleties and apparent concessions, the vendor and consumer groups began losing ground. Vendor leaders found it difficult to communicate the increasingly complex situation to their membership—especially those who did not speak fluent English—and to articulate the correspondingly complex critique of gentrification the situation required. The consumers, hobbled from the beginning by the lack of a consensus position on Penn's development agenda, found it similarly difficult to rally their constituents on a consistent basis. Many students looked forward to the opening of the new bookstore and shops in Sansom Common and saw no reason to rain on the parade; and many faculty became positively disposed toward the ordinance as a result of the administration's emphasis on urban beautification.[70] By the time Dean Varvoutis threw up his hands at city council, he knew the vendors' position as free-market heroes had been evacuated of its ideological power, and he knew there was nothing he could do about it. In the end the basic structural conditions had soundly trumped the political agency of the vendors and their allies. In a city hemorrhaging hundreds of jobs every week, no city council member was going to go against a university that was promising to create jobs and draw in the elusive suburban consumer with the gentrified Sansom Common. Moreover, while the vendors gained limited support from certain neighborhood and civic groups, the nature, size and composition of the University City community had been changed and denuded significantly three decades prior in the precursor to the current round of Penn redevelopment.

In its focus on real estate speculation and retail development, Penn is exemplary of the manner in which universities located in metropolitan areas have become major players in the new finance-dominated economy. Recent scholarship has shown that major urban centers feature the geographical juxtaposition of highly stratified job categories, exemplified by the florists, dry cleaners, restaurants, and messenger services that locate near banks, investment houses, law firms, and insurance companies in downtown areas.[71] In the case of Penn the obverse situation obtains: a *structural* rather than geographical linkage of far-flung finance capital and localized merchant capital. The *Wall Street Journal*, commenting on the Trammell Crow deal, noted that at a time when universities "are stepping up their cost cutting efforts . . . real estate could be one of the most promising areas for cost savings."[72] In this scenario, the university "cuts costs"—which in this case is just another way of saying that a nonprofit firm finds ways to make profit—by mobilizing finance capital to bring in merchant capital that will create revenue for the university and, of course, profits for the financiers and merchants.[73]

CONCLUSION

Free choices academic or otherwise
Will certainly face a demise
If corporations make decisions
With economic precision
Of whether profit margins are the right size.

Consider Barnes and Noble, Trammell Crow
Whose main ambitions are to grow.

Cappuccinos awash, great books in short supply,
Frightened employees passing by
Who gets the benefit while Penn loses its soul?
          —Penn employee, November 1997[74]

Penn is dead. It's nothing like it used to be intellectually [or] culturally.
          —Penn administrator, May 1998[75]

To speak of the "corporatization of the university" is not to speak narrowly or metaphorically. It is to speak broadly and literally. While the university will never look or work exactly like a for-profit firm, it will continue to transform itself into something that does not resemble what most scholars and citizens think of as a nonprofit educational institution.

As universities make this transition, they react to national and international shifts toward privatization and "market discipline." Large-scale economic restructuring, intensifying inter-city and intra-city competition for middle-class residents and consumers, and a brutal private health-care market exert tremendous pressures on universities to reinvent themselves. At the same time, it is clear that Penn and its peer institutions are responding to these pressures by abandoning important practices and ideals long associated with educational and nonprofit institutions. Trustees have appointed administrators who will happily seize control of urban space and local commerce, downsize workforces, roll back employee benefits, fight graduate student unionization, exploit adjunct instructors, and initiate distance learning programs. They also have adopted ideologies that justify these measures in the name of promoting "excellence." When Judith Rodin attempts to insulate outsourcing, retail speculation, and the vending issue from criticism by saying, "We are taking these measures because we need to concentrate on our core academic mission,"[76] it is clear that we must understand the university's activities in a broad context of incorporation, in which neoliberal economic discourses colonize all realms of political discourse and social life.

All struggles over the corporate university are influenced by this shift away from the political discourses of equality characteristic of reform liberalism, and toward the economic discourses of the market endemic to neoliberalism. In defending the administration's handling of the Trammell Crow outsourcing, for example, Fry noted administration measures taken to ease the transition, declaring that Penn wanted to be "a little bit different" than Westinghouse and the Allegheny Health System, each of which had just announced massive layoffs.[77] Soaring glass walls, multicolored awnings, and chain-store windows aside, "a little bit different" fairly encapsulates the extent to which the Penn's administrators are prepared to attend to the human dimension of corporatization.[78] Similarly, in reference to employee benefits, Fry told *Time*, "We want to be market competitive, but at the same time, we shouldn't be excessive."[79] (By Fry's reasoning, the sole criterion is competitiveness: It is purely a matter of what benefits other institutions offer. Of course, for this logic to work, the other institutions must cast the same sideward glances to determine the extent of their own benefits. In this scenario, freestanding ethical considerations of employees' actual needs go the way of the dodo, replaced by "résumé-writing workshops," "job interview training sessions," and tacky "news" headlines in the administration's newsletter declaring, "Fry Backs Staff Growth."[80] These empty gestures, ostensibly aimed at "bringing the campus together" and promoting "reasoned and reasonable discourse,"[81] are in fact indicators that the brutal class hierarchies of the market have been grafted onto the university at the economic, political, and cultural levels.

In this context, the neoliberal, corporatist university administration thrives on the co-optation of "difference" and "diversity" even as it turns a blind eye to economic difference and material inequality. It welcomes dissent because the assimilation of dissenters into a broad hegemony only makes the administration stronger. It will take all comers, so long as opposition is domesticated within the fetishized realm of "reasoned discussion among equals" in the standard committee meetings, public forums, and the like. The only way to combat the neoliberal corporate university is to form cross-class alliances that extend beyond the boundaries of the campus, by developing communities of interest that do not depend entirely on the university for their existence, resources, and sense of purpose. In this respect, community organizations and staff unions represent essential parts of the equation, for their relationship to the university is much more explicitly dominated by coercive, economic relations than that of students and faculty.[82] The Penn administration's weakest moments came when broad cross-sections of the campus community rallied around images of loyal, longtime staff breaking the bad news to their families, and of hardworking street vendors being pushed around by the corporate university.

It is the job of those who wish to oppose the corporatization of the university to engage in a full-time effort to demonstrate, as one Penn employee wrote, that "the values of big business are no more the values of a university than they are the values of a family, a church or any other institution for whom making money is a means rather than an end."[83] This sort of awareness, backed by broad, cross-class alliances, may yet slow down the freight train of university incorporation, and perhaps make it jump its tracks.

ACKNOWLEDGMENTS

The author wishes to thank Ananth Aiyer, Judith Goode, Jeff Maskovsky, and Elayne Tobin for helpful comments and feedback on earlier drafts of this paper. The author also wishes to acknowledge Penn students and staffers Donna Arthur, James Bean, Sean Crist, Christy Doran, Jason Eisner, Oiy Glaewketgarn, Scott Goldstein, James Gray, John Hogan, Paul Lukasiak, Maria Oyaski, Dean Varvoutis, Alex Welte, and others who cannot be named here for their solidarity in the struggles detailed herein.

NOTES

1. Many of the events and figures in this article have histories and contexts that are impossible to detail here due to space considerations. The author has established a Web page with updates and additional documentation at www.eserver.org/home/mruben. When relevant, the reader is referred to the Web page throughout the notes that follow.

2. Bill Readings, *The University in Ruins* (Cambridge: Harvard University Press, 1996), p. 22.

3. Telephone conversation with city council administrative staff, April 13, 1998.

4. Quotations from the hearing are drawn from the author's notes and from Cynthia Burton, "Proposal on Vendors Draws a Protest," *Philadelphia Inquirer*, April 15, 1998, p. B1; Seth Grossman, "City Shows Support for Vending Bill," *Daily Pennsylvanian* [online], dailypennsylvanian.com [April 15, 1998]; "Penn's Influence in the City Evident During Vending Hearings," *Daily Pennsylvanian* [online], dailypennsylvanian.com [April 20, 1998]; "Tales from the City's Vending Bill Hearings," *Daily Pennsylvanian* [online], dailypennsylvanian.com [April 22, 1998]; Mark McDonald, "Penn Vendors Protest Council's Relocation Bill," *Philadelphia Daily News*, April 15, 1998, p. 5.

5. Mark Cohen, "Ivory Power: How Penn's John Fry Turned the Battle for West Philadelphia into His Own Private Chain Store Massacre," *Philadelphia* (September 1998), p. 32.

6. "Maya," quoted in Matthew Ruben, "Downsizing at Penn," *Black and Blue* 2 [online], english.upenn.edu/~mruben/BBindex.html [April 1997].

7. The "water buffalo" incident of 1993 made Penn an object of national controversy and derision. Go to the author's Web page (address in n. 1) for a list of representative articles.

8. In the 1990s the board included the current or former CEOs of, among others, First Boston, Merck, the Reliance Group, Unysis, Charles Schwab, I. Magnin, Estee Lauder, Bristol-Meyers Squibb, Corestates/First Union, and General Electric.

9. Go to the author's Web page (address in n. 1) for details.

10. Judith Rodin, Letter to all university students, staff and faculty, January 10, 1995, pp. 1–2.

11. Bill Clinton, statements from the third presidential debate, October 19, 1992.

12. Stanley Chodorow and Jack Freeman, "The Case for Administrative Restructuring," *Almanac Supplement*, January 17, 1995, p. S3.

13. In fact, the restructuring initiative was part of the broader "Agenda for Excellence," a blueprint for all of Penn's future academic and nonacademic functions.

14. Ben Hammer, "Barnes and Noble to Manage New Campus Bookstore," *Daily Pennsylvanian* [online], dailypennsylvanian.com [June 30, 1996]; Maisie Wong, "Rehired Book Store Staff Will Not Lose U. Benefits," *Daily Pennsylvanian* [online], dailypennsylvanian.com [October 3, 1996]. In this and other outsourcing cases, Penn's reported staff retention percentages are higher than those cited in this article. The university derives its figures by dividing (1) the number of employees offered positions by the contracting firm by (2) the number of employees who seek positions with that firm. In contrast, this article simply compares the total number of employees in a given department prior to its being outsourced with the number of employees left in that department after outsourcing has taken place. Penn's figures are meant to indicate the good-faith effort of the university and the contracted firm to retain employees who wish to continue in their existing positions. The author's figures in this article are meant to illustrate the degree of disruption and displacement produced by outsourcing. An important assumption of this article is that "voluntary" attrition in these situations is not in fact voluntary in any meaningful sense of the term. Additionally, since some administrative units have had hiring freezes in place for some time prior to outsourcing, the actual displacement is often even greater than this article's figures would indicate.

15. Dina Bass, "U. May Be Cutting Too Close to the Bone," *Daily Pennsylvanian* [online], dailypennsylvanian.com [March 27, 1997].

16. Chodorow and Freeman, "The Case for Administrative Restructuring," p. S4.

17. Tammy Reiss and Edward Sherwin, "To Improve Dining, U. Taps Lacey as Food Czar," *Daily Pennsylvanian* [online], dailypennsylvanian.com [September 23, 1998]; Edward Sherwin, "U. Surpasses Its Fundraising Goals for Perelman Quad Project," *Daily Pennsylvanian* [online], dailypennsylvanian.com [November 10, 1998].

18. John Fry, "A New Faculty Club Offer," *Daily Pennsylvanian* [online], dailypennsylvanian.com [January 27, 1999].

19. Sharon Male, "U. Lays off 35 Faculty Club Employees," *Daily Pennsylvanian* [online], dailypennsylvanian.com [January 18, 1999]; "U., Faculty Club Union Make No Progress in Talks." *Daily Pennsylvanian* [online], dailypennsylvanian.com [February 16, 1999]; "Inn at Penn Says It Will Rehire Workers," *Daily Pennsylvanian* [online], dailypennsylvanian.com [March 17, 1999].

20. Samuel Preston, School of Arts and Sciences Dean's budget memo, 1999.

21. Andrea Gerlin, "Despite Tight Budgets, Schools Pay Top Dollar for Top Doctors," *Philadelphia Inquirer*, June 12, 1998, p. A1; University of Pennsylvania, *University of Pennsylvania Annual Report 1994–1995* (Philadelphia: University of Pennsylvania, 1995), p. 15.

22. Barbara Lowrey et al., "Benefits Programs of the University of Pennsylvania: Review and Recommendations," *Almanac* [online], upenn.edu/ almanac [February 11, 1997].

23. Aetna, Inc, "Proxy Statement Pursuant to Section 14(a) of the Securities Exchange Act of 1934," Securities and Exchange Commission [online], sec.gov [1998]. The $120,000 includes cash payments for director services, as well as stock and dividends. Go to the author's Web page (address in n. 1) for details.

24. In response to a threat by the graduate student government to self-insure, the administration re-signed with the old student insurance provider the year after, allowing students to choose between it and Aetna.

25. University of Pennsylvania, *University of Pennsylvania Annual Report 1997–1998* (Philadelphia: University of Pennsylvania, 1998), p. 33.

26. Karl Stark, "Layoffs of 450 at Health System," *Philadelphia Inquirer*, May 26, 1999, p. A1; Eric Tucker, "Health System Makes Major Layoffs," *Daily Pennsylvanian*, October 22, 1999, pp. 1, 5.

27. In addition to security guards, Penn also has its own detachment of Philadelphia police officers.

28. The actual contracted firm was Trammell Crow Higher Educational Services, a new division of Trammell Crow created to service the Penn contract.

29. The exact percentage is not clear. Go to the author's Web page (address in n. 1) for details.

30. The 600 figure was cited by Fry in Ralph Cipriano, "Penn to Lay Off 175 Managers in Maintenance," *Philadelphia Inquirer*, October 14, 1997, p. B2.

31. Scott Lanman, "Trammell Crow due for stock release." *Daily Pennsylvanian* [online], dailypennsylvanian.com [October 22, 1997]. Go to the author's Web page (address in n. 1) for more information.

32. Go to the author's Web page (address in n. 1) for details. See also Erik Larson, "Why Colleges Cost Too Much," *Time*, March 17, 1997, pp. 46–55; Harvard University, "The Harvard Guide: Finances: Harvard's Endowment Funds," [online] hno.harvard.edu/guide/finance/index.html [1998]; University of Pennsylvania, *University of Pennsylvania Annual Report 1996–1997*, (Philadelphia: University of Pennsylvania, 1997); Yale University, *Yale University Financial Report 1996–1997* [online], yale.edu [1997].

33. Go to the author's Web page (address in n. 1) for details.

34. *University of Pennsylvania Annual Report 1996–1997*, p. 28.

35. Go to the author's Web page (address in n. 1) for details.

36. As of this writing the Annenberg School's facilities have just undergone extensive renovation and expansion; and construction has begun on a new $120 million building for the Wharton School.

37. Amar Kosaraju, "And Justice For All: The University of Wharton," *Daily Pennsylvanian* [online], dailypennsylvanian.com [January 30, 1997].

38. Suzanne Albers, "Students Still Seeking Access to Law Library." *Daily Pennsylvanian* [online], dailypennsylvanian.com [October 8, 1996]; Maisie Wong, "Law Library Changes Policy for Undergrads," *Daily Pennsylvanian* [online], dailypennsylvanian.com [March 6, 1996]. Also go to the author's Web page (address in n. 1) for more details on the policy.

39. Penn Professional Staff Assembly, "Outsourcing and Its Consequences for Staff," *Almanac*, November 4, 1997, p. 4.

40. Faculty Senate Committee on the Economic Status of the Faculty, "Report of the Faculty Senate Committee on the Economic Status of the Faculty," *Almanac* [online], upenn.edu/almanac [May 13, 1997]. The rate of inflation here refers to the local Philadelphia consumer price index.

41. On tuition increases, see Larson, "Why Colleges Cost Too Much." On staff salaries, go to the author's Web page (address in n. 1). On Fry's and Rodin's salaries, see Andrea Ahles, "Rodin Earned $350,000 for First Year in Office," *Daily Pennsylvanian* [online], dailypennsylvanian.com [September 12, 1996]; Cohen, "Ivory Power," pp. 30, 42.

42. Go to the author's Web page (address in n. 1) for more information.

43. John Hogan, "Statement of John Hogan on Benefits Redesign to University Council," March 5, 1997.

44. Victoria Tredinnick, Comments at November 5 University Council special meeting (addendum), *Almanac*, November 18, 1997, p. 4.

45. Henry Teune, quoted in David Michael Kalstein, "A Conversation with Dr. Henry Teune: Undergraduate Chair of Political Science," *Red and Blue*, November 1997, p. 8.

46. "Leaving for Duke: V.P. Clint Davidson," *Almanac*, March 11, 1997, p. 3; Amy Lipman, "VP for Human Resources Named," *Daily Pennsylvanian* [online], dailypennsylvanian.com [August 3, 1995].

47. Cohen, "Ivory Power," p. 42.

48. A facilities management employee who was a plaintiff in a class action suit filed against Trammell Crow and Penn, and who had spoken against the outsourcing at the special meeting of the University Council, did not receive an offer from Trammell Crow, despite having applied for six different positions during the transition process.

49. Margie Fishman, "Employees Adjust to Trammell Crow." *Daily Pennsylvanian* [online], dailypennsylvanian.com [April 7, 1998]. Less than two years later, as this article went to press, Trammell Crow lost the facilities management contract because of poor performance. Go to the author's Web page (address in n. 1) for updated information.

50. Judith Rodin, "Message from the President," *University of Pennsylvania Annual Report 1996–1997* (Philadelphia: University of Pennsylvania, 1997), p. 10.

51. University of Pennsylvania trustee, June 1997 (author's notes).

52. Ralph Cipriano, "Penn Will Overhaul Campus Environs," *Philadelphia Inquirer*, June 8, 1997, p. A1.

53. The three-hundred-acre figure cited in this article is based on official figures for property containing academic buildings (University of Pennsylvania,

"Penn-at-a-Glance Fact Sheet," [online], upenn.edu/pennnews/pennglance.html [December 1996]), supplemented by the author's estimate for property containing the medical system and other Penn-owned buildings (residential units, commercial space) in the immediate area.

54. For a capsule history see Larry Fish, "Penn, Reexpanding, Hopes it Learned a Lesson," *Philadelphia Inquirer*, May 4, 1998, pp. A1, A12.

55. Go to the author's Web page (address in n. 1) for more information.

56. ". . . And Penn's Retail and Residential Complex Should Benefit the School, Residents and the City," *Philadelphia Inquirer*, June 13, 1997, p. A30; Fish, pp. A1, A12; "Penn's Plans for Its Neighborhood," *Philadelphia Daily News*, June 10, 1997, p. 8. The other major activity related to this history involves public schools. Go to the author's Web page (address in n. 1) for more information.

57. Most of the land for Sansom Common, for example, was purchased for only $2 million (Cipriano, "Penn Will Overhaul Campus Environs," p. A1).

58. Ibid.; Margie Fishman, "Renovations may Require Bond Issue," *Daily Pennsylvanian* [online], dailypennsylvanian.com [April 10, 1998].

59. A magazine article published after the vending ordinance went into effect revealed that Fry "[had thrown] his weight behind the banishment of Penn's most unique culinary tradition to a handful of out-of-the-way alleys and lots" because "a potential Sansom Commons [sic] tenant complained about an unsightly food truck blocking his view . . ." (Cohen, "Ivory Power," p. 36).

60. Cipriano, "Penn Will Overhaul Campus Environs," p. A1; Burton, "Proposal on Vendors Draws a Protest," p. B1.

61. This information is based on a series of conversations the author had with vendors in the spring of 1998.

62. The e-mail was sent by the author, who had received the information in a meeting with a Penn administrator.

63. See for example Roberta M. Spalter-Roth, "Vending on the Streets: City Policy, Gentrification, and Public Patriarchy," *Women and the Politics of Empowerment*, eds. Ann Bookman and Sandra Morgen (Philadelphia: Temple University Press, 1998), pp. 272-94.

64. Go to the author's Web page (address in n. 1) for background information on the vendors' organization and the Penn Consumers Alliance.

65. Shannon Burke, "Penn Consumer Alliance Demonstrates at Sansom Common Groundbreaking," *Daily Pennsylvanian* [online], dailypennsylvanian.com [June 26, 1997]; Stephanie Cooperman, "City Council Postpones Vote on Vending," *Daily Pennsylvanian* [online], dailypennsylvanian.com [August 29, 1997]; Paul Davies, "Truck-ulent Talk at Penn Event," *Philadelphia Daily News*, June 21, 1997, p. 6.

66. University of Pennsylvania, "Vending at Penn: What's Happening and Why," [online], upenn.edu/foodplaza/guide.html [1998].

67. Lindsay Faber, "U. Seeks Fresh Start with Public on Vending Law." *Daily Pennsylvanian* [online], dailypennsylvanian.com [September 3, 1997].

68. The administration stopped taking applications for the vending plazas after allocating less than two-thirds of the forty-five promised spaces. (Laura

McClure, "From Streets to Food Plazas, Ordinance Forces Vending Shift," *Daily Pennsylvanian* [online], dailypennsylvanian.com [September 4, 1998]). Go to the author's Web page (address in n. 1) for more information on the effects of the vending ordinance.

69. Penn Professional Staff Assembly, "Outsourcing and Its Consequences for Staff," p. 4.

70. In fact, the chairperson of Penn Faculty and Staff for Neighborhood Issues testified in favor of the ordinance at City Council, making the same reference to Paris and other "great cities of Europe" that was cited in the *Inquirer*'s article on Rodin and Sansom Common the year before (see Cipriano, "Penn Will Overhaul Campus Environs," p. A1; Burton, "Proposal on Vendors Draws a Protest," p. A1).

71. Saskia Sassen, *The Global City: New York, London, Tokyo* (Princeton: Princeton University Press, 1991); Neil Smith, *The New Urban Frontier: Gentrification and The Revanchist City* (London: Routledge, 1996); Sharon Zukin, *Landscapes of Power: from Detroit to Disney World* (Berkeley: University of California Press, 1991).

72. Neal Templin, "Trammell Crow Going Back to College," *Wall Street Journal*, October 15, 1997, p. 18.

73. Go to the author's Web page (address in n. 1) for an account of how the university also obtains increased revenue as a byproduct of this kind of gentrification.

74. Judith Bernstein-Baker, "Ode to the Corporate University," *Almanac*, November 11, 1997, p. 10.

75. Personal communication with the author. The administrator's identity is not revealed for obvious reasons.

76. Judith Rodin, comments at University of Pennsylvania Trustees Meetings, November 7, 1997 (author's notes).

77. John Fry, "Discussion on Outsourcing," *Almanac*, October 21, 1997, p. 5.

78. Ironically, as detailed above, Penn's own medical system eliminated a comparable number of positions two years later in the same manner—and for the same basic reasons—as Allegheny.

79. Larson, "Why Colleges Cost Too Much," p. 53.

80. Sandy Smith, Fry Backs Staff Growth," *Pennsylvania Current*, March 19, 1998, p. 1.

81. The latter phrase ("reasoned and reasonable discourse") is taken from the motto of the Penn National Commission on Society, Culture and Community, a sort of think tank Rodin formed in 1996 and continues to chair.

82. Of course students (and their parents) have their complaints about rising tuition, but the notion that students should get their money's worth from the university does not easily lend itself to a critique of corporatization. Faculty, for their part, are typically invested in the notion of tenure as a way to escape the capriciousness of the economic relation under which staff operate. Except at certain public universities where faculties have unions, most faculty members do not consider their primary relationship to the university to be an economic one.

83. John Hogan, "Penn's Values Misdirected," *Daily Pennsylvanian* [online], dailypennsylvanian.com [January 29, 1998].

15

WIRING THE WORLD
Ameritech's Monopoly on the Virtual Classroom

Todd A. Price

Ln the civics classes of the past we learned that government of the people, by the people, and for the people shall not perish from this earth. Later in life we learned that big business abhors government interference, and it abhors social services performed without a profit even more. Health care, public transportation, social security, and education are designed to meet basic human needs in a democracy. These institutions, therefore, are fair game for big business and its primary tool, the corporation.

BEFORE WE GIVE THE SCHOOL AWAY

Our cherished educational institution is on the auction block. I became increasingly concerned about education's relation to society, having studied in Cuba several years ago. In Cuba, I learned that students, workers, nurses, doctors, and others traveled to the farthest reaches of the island to teach peasants to read. Today this literacy campaign remains the most successful the world has ever known.

Upon my return, I was shocked to find education in the United States was increasingly up for sale. State-imposed revenue caps, experiments with private-school vouchers, and advertising in the schools was the norm, but a new corporate project was looming. This project seemed innocent enough; it was "wiring the schools."

I became concerned that behind "wiring the schools" lay a plan to reinvent not only the public education curriculum, but the management of the school itself. My specialty is analyzing the implications of private-sector, corporate control of one of the latest technologies, video distance learning (VDL). VDL allows for the transmission of voice, video, and data services. By using VDL, it is possible to teach a course in one place and transmit it to any number of locations. Some refer to video distance learning as the electronic field trip or the virtual classroom. As with all forms of technology, it can be used to serve or support the public interest.

Yet my story concerns a large telecommunications company, Ameritech, that built a monopoly around VDL technology in the Midwest. To be certain, there are many vendors, including GTE, Video Images, W2 Com, V-Tel, and Tektronix, that partner with the company. But Ameritech is the key network provider. With the help of state government officials, school administrators, and powerful business interests, Ameritech managed to reconstitute itself as one of the most powerful monopolies, and a leading contender for the edutainment market. Long-term concerns regarding Ameritech and other corporations' involvement in public education curriculum include: (1) students being fed a fast-food curriculum, (2) the public education budget effectively subsidizing commercial enterprise, and (3) total corporatization of the public education system.

OLD WINES IN A NEW BOTTLE

The irony is that Ameritech was born out of antitrust legislation. A monopoly concentrates power in a manner antithetical to democratic principles, so the federal government broke up Ma Bell, as was reported in the *New York Times* on January 1, 1984:

A new era for American telecommunications and for American business begins today as the once unified Bell System begins life as eight separate companies. It is a time of great expectations and great concern for both the telephone industry and the nation as a whole.[1]

Although the rules of the game have changed, the players remain the same and monopolistic structures still exist. Indeed, the "baby bells" mentioned in the news release were quickly reconstituted. Illinois Bell, Indiana Bell, Ohio Bell, Michigan Bell, and Wisconsin Telephone, along with other divisions, combined to form Ameritech.

Ameritech was the first U.S. company to offer commercial cellular service and, following massive sales, it set its sights on a new world market. Partially, the baby bells as public utilities were still bound to rate-of-return regulation. For much of the 1980s, Public Utility Commissions considered 12 to 14 percent return on investment to be a reasonable profit.[2] The old rules needed to be discarded, however, if local exchange telephone companies like Ameritech were to engender greater profits or, as they were quick to assert, if they were going to be able to compete in the emerging telecommunications field.

Thus, during the 1990s, local telephone companies pushed hard to change the rate-of-return rules, but none pushed harder than Ameritech for relaxed regulation. Not your average mom-and-pop company, Ameritech made the promise that in the regions it served it would wire every hospital, nonprofit agency, and public school to the information superhighway. Indeed, Ameritech Wisconsin promised to spend $750 million on broadband infrastructure deployment. Never mind that the Citizens Utility Board and the Public Service Commission placed the figure at a more accurate $150 million or that Ameritech's figures were not really above what they would have otherwise spent given their business-as-usual investment manner.[3] The point is that Ameritech made lofty promises and received the legislation it paid for. Many politicians in Ohio, Indiana, and Wisconsin were sold on the idea of an information superhighway with high-tech schools. These politicians rode the fast lane with Ameritech, and were rewarded for it.[4] Ameritech made several contributions to the campaigns of its many advocates and, through skillful public relations, won the coveted prize: sweeping telecommunications deregulation. In other words, the old "rate-of-return" system would be discarded in favor of "price regulation," which gave telephone companies "almost carte blanche to invest in new things, whether Internet services, or cable [just] as long as it's a compatible field."[5]

The lobbying paid off and telecommunications deregulation, Act 496 in Wisconsin, was passed in 1994, to be followed by the national model two years later. Telecommunications deregulation has served Ameritech, now a $33-billion firm, quite well, but what did the public get in exchange?[6] Despite the interactive technology offered, they received much less than what was promised.

What one finds in the pages that follow is that Ameritech reconstituted the monopoly using a clever showcase that was more virtual than real. This showcase was called "Ameritech Superschools." Behind the slogan lies the steady advance of corporatism into public education. To many, it is not difficult to make the case that advertising in the classrooms is wrong; when the classroom becomes a vehicle for posters, logos, and television commercials, students are treated as mere consumers of the products offered. But corporatism goes one step further. While a commercial (like those provided by Channel One) or a corporate logo in a classroom is a violation, it pales when compared to a blueprint for corporatism. Corporatism seeks to radically redesign the classroom, the role of teachers, the role of students, and the curriculum content toward corporate ends. This is the real threat that an Ameritech poses. Why? Because Ameritech owns the network, the virtual pipeline along which not only educational programs travel, but upon which the management of the school is being entrusted. What happens when the private sector largely determines who funds, owns, manages, participates, and benefits from that pipeline? For starters, teachers are deskilled, disempowered, and expendable to the new pipeline manager. Students are monitored like laboratory mice to test educational products, and they are screened for participation in the wired classroom. But worse of all, public education is up for sale, corporations are the vendors, and democracy is in jeopardy.

PUBLIC EDUCATION AT A DISTANCE

Hardly a day passed during the telecommunication deregulation of the 1990s without some politician, somewhere, promising "to wire every classroom to the information superhighway by the year 2000."[7] None stood out more prominently than Wisconsin's own governor, Tommy Thompson. Thompson was the point man for the Ameritech corporation and he did not shy away from his task. Time and time again, the governor would travel the state, vouching for the information superhighway and Ameritech, often while demonstrating one of its key products, a large-screen monitor connected to fiber-optic cables. This application is known as teleconferencing. In the educational setting it is known as interactive television or video distance learning (VDL).

Indeed, the information superhighway slogan served to mobilize disparate forces from across our narrow political spectrum under a banner of educational reform. Many common citizens bought into technology as a boon to the economy and the empowerment of children. Yet in their zeal to accept the wire, the primary mission of public education, to provide for the common good through equal access and equal opportunity, has been denied. Given that school districts have been told to tighten their budgetary belt, how did it come to pass that the public could so easily be sold on this expensive technology?

After all, distance education emerged largely out of the progressive tradition of the state of Wisconsin, the Wisconsin Idea, not out of the board rooms of Ameritech or AT&T![8] At the turn of the century, distance education, or "extension," was intended to supplement, enhance, and distribute the university's public education curriculum. However, contemporary distance education, through corporate enterprise, has sought to replace it. Indeed, the most outspoken free marketers claim that the purpose of today's distance education is to "reinvent" public education. Through several projects, Ameritech has sought to improve public education.[9] Yet if public education is to be improved according to the dictates of the market in which Ameritech thrives, what will public education in the next millennium look like?

CLASSROOMS WITHOUT WALLS?

Ameritech Superschools was the moniker given to a showcase, and the plan was to sell VDL to the public schools, staking Ameritech's claim on a new world market of profit and control. In essence what has developed since is the edutainment industry, and corporations such as IBM, Lotus, Microsoft, GTE, and others are hoping to capitalize on and corner this market. To several telecommunications regulators and prominent industry analysts (RAND), the edutainment industry has always been suspect: "There's no market in it" was the sentiment of one Public Service Commission employee.[10] Nonetheless, many companies think differently.

The roots of Ameritech Superschools go back to Ohio. Ohio Bell, in partnership with faculty at Ohio University in Athens, chose Appalachia, one of the poorest regions of the country, as the proving ground for their own edutainment experiment. This humble location, where generations have labored in poverty to mine the earth, was the site of the first video distance learning prototype for children. In other words, the sons and daughters of coal miners were used to advance the largess of a large utility company. Big business likes to find the cheapest and least accountable locations to jump-start their new products, and Appalachia was no exception to this golden rule. The VDL equipment, housed in a trailer for a third-grade elementary class, was slated to link up the rural and the urban, but despite the rhetoric, the VDL failed to extend curriculum to rural Appalachia in a manner that would truly aid the impoverished students.

The Appalachian Distance Learning Project (ADLP) was formed to manage VDL program(s). ADLP, which oversaw elementary schools in Athens, Deering, and Coal Grove, consisted of Ohio Bell (an Ameritech subsidiary), Ohio University at Athens, and the Appalachian Regional Commission (ARC), a federal aid agency that served this impoverished region. The ADLP entity served to create an overarching sense of credibility for the technology.

It's fascinating how technological products—computers, automation, video distance learning—bring with them an air of rarely challenged credibility. Unless these products are carefully tested, we can easily have yet another case of artificially created needs, which is, of course, the purpose of Madison Avenue advertising agencies.

In advertising, as in war, truth is the first casualty. A series of promotional videotapes[11] followed the early Superschool prototypes, replete with testimonials, unverified claims, and questionable contrivances. Politicians went to bat for Ohio Bell not only in Appalachia, but also in Findlay, Columbiana, and Columbus, Ohio. In one promotional video, holding out a strand of cable, one Ohio Bell salesman stumped for the technology, suggesting it was needed to better compete with the Japanese. In another, Representative Michael Oxley appeared in support of the Skill-link program, whose purpose was to save money and bring training to employees while working on-site at a corporate factory.

In the case of Ohio, none of the promotional videotapes of the early Superschools prototypes presented any hard evidence of the effectiveness, risks, or costs of VDL. Rather, Superschools was a carefully orchestrated and scripted political show from beginning to end. Ameritech would bring experts along to demonstrate the applications, as one teacher explained: "They flew me and six children to Chicago. I taught live back every day to a group of students here in Ironton."[12] Governor George Voinovich of Ohio noted how the technology would avail public schools of Sesame Street–type programming, while a prominent city official claimed that the technology was a perfect example of "how businesses can positively impact teaching and learning."[13]

In reality, there was plenty of student and teacher frustration, dismay, and confusion. Behind the seamless, virtual classroom lay the reality, as one teacher's comments explain: "They hooked up my classroom, put it [wire, switching hubs, equipment] in my building . . . the module wasn't even there yet, the technology wasn't in place, they ripped my classroom up."[14]

The Appalachian experiments with VDL were a parody of the Ameritech vision of the future. A lead teacher (and an early VDL proponent) in an interview described a macabre scene. A student teacher was sitting in front of a row of students. She was wearing a headset with an attached microphone. Each third grader had a microphone on the desk just in front of them. A curriculum expert from the University of Athens sat in the background, miles away, and transmitted corrective feedback to the student teacher.

From all accounts this was clearly an intimidating first experience.

Indeed, the same lead teacher acknowledged that the curriculum added little value. While outgoing students seemed to enjoy it, many of their more withdrawn peers pushed back into reclusive silence. The lead teacher summed it up for everyone when he remarked that VDL was an amusing show but hard to justify when used on a day-to-day basis in the schools.

While equal access and opportunity are hallmarks of public education, they mean little if an unaccountable, superwealthy corporation can sell untested products to one of the poorest school districts in the nation.

AMERITRICK

Despite the failure of the ADLP experiment, other VDL experiments would follow. Perhaps the most extravagant of the Ameritech Superschool demonstrations occurred in Madison, Wisconsin, with Governor Thompson leading the parade. Heavily themed with pictures of presidents adorning the walls, the exhibit, held in Dane County Coliseum, was the means by which Ameritech could be thrust into the public eye in order to win critical support for deregulating the Wisconsin telecommunications industry.

Of great importance was the need to create the look and feel of a twenty-first-century classroom. The "classrooms without walls" exhibit did just that, and was the focus of much attention. Highlighted prominently was a wall-length screen, several overhead and display cameras, and a number of tabletop microphones taped down on the rounded tables. The exhibit was replete with a smiling, professionally attired instructor. Seated in front of the instructor were several blue-and-white uniformed students. Noticeable was the size of this class: It was quite small, with less than fifteen students, an ideal size but hardly typical of the public school classroom. Behind the classroom was a technical engineer. He was seated in front of a number of panels with full vertical interval switching capabilities. In other words, this individual's job was to keep the images flowing. As such, he piped in different screens at the instructors request, along with tinny electronic music, for background and for the students to hum along to. Elected officials, teachers, parents, and other interested onlookers watched in rapt attention. Conspicuously, Hanna Rosenthal, chair of the Democratic Party, hovered around the scene. She was working as public relations consultant for Ameritech on that important day.[15]

Despite its best attempts, Ameritech's installation still reflected the "sage on the stage" pedagogy; the teacher mostly lectured, albeit in a remarkably cheerful manner. Banal attempts at interactivity included the following:

Teacher: How are you like this big bolt? What are your creative thoughts?

Of equally questionable worth was another lesson where students were asked to decode letters in order make an equation turn out correctly. The technology seemed to provide little curriculum value beyond turning the wall into an extremely sophisticated-looking blackboard.

Many of the attendees were nonetheless impressed and, coupled with a special legislative session paid for by Ameritech, Wisconsin's telecommunications deregulation became law. Ameritech Superschools explains it all, using students to advance their vision. In a promotional video, Hi-Mount elementary students sang an ode to the company:

> Communications highway, electronic highway,
> telecommunications highway, this is the information age!
> The data is written into the computer disk,
> the computer disk is put inside the disk drive,
> the disk drive is connected to the computer,
> the computer is connected to the network,
> the network is connected to the file server,
> the file server is connected to the fiber optics,
> the fiber optics are connected to the Ameritech,
> Ameritech is connected to the world,
> and that's the information highway, yay![16]

Following telecommunications deregulation, another Ameritech Wisconsin Superschool classroom, Appleton East High School, suggested VDL was not all it's cracked up to be. A teacher reflected on the difficulty of using the equipment: "Well, it's really stressful. The most negative thing about it is not being able to hear the students on the other side of town as well as the students here. It kind of depersonalizes the teaching. I don't feel like I really know those kids over there."[17] One of the Appleton East students pointed out that the challenge of being simultaneously in front of the class and on camera was particularly intrusive: "Once we had to go up here [in front of the room]. It zoomed in on you, you had to do a little conversation . . . it was really, really nerve racking."[18]

THE FREE ENTERPRISE NETWORK

Behind Ameritech Superschools is a blueprint for reinventing public education. Terry Forkner, a distinguished special operations engineer with Ameritech and an adjunct professor at Indiana University, claimed that the premiere VDL network design emerged from a group of engineers he worked with, known as "Skunk" operations. Forkner recalls that his supervisor Dick Noetbaert, president of Indiana Bell, directed him to come up with a marketing solution to "push" broadband technology by demonstrating what was possible in the educational setting. Forkner responded with a new idea: the free enterprise network. "This network is actually funded through private enterprise capital investment. We won't spend a lot of time on the philosophy or politics here, but Indiana is not likely to build a large infrastructure for telecommunications in the state via tax dollars."[19] Indiana Bell was playing hardball at the state level of government and sought to receive a new regulatory structure. According to commission documents they threatened to "hold hostage" the Indiana Utility Regulatory Commission (IURC) if they were not given favorable conditions.[20] The proceedings for changing the system of regulation were at an impasse, and several doubted Indiana Bell's intentions, especially in lieu of the suggestion by a telecommunications expert that Indiana customers were unlikely to get much in return if the entire industry was to be regulated in accordance with the terms the parent company Ameritech had won over the years.

Yet through the skills of one Marv Bailey, a chief Ameritech lobbyist for the Indiana and Ohio regions, a solution came along to break the impasse. Bailey characterized this breakthrough as a golden egg "a quantum price breakthrough; a thousand-dollar 'brick' [that] provides full motion video."[21] Forkner felt Ameritech could sell a cheap CODEC (the piece of software, which can perform millions of operations per second, coding and decoding information for video signal transmission). This piece would be available to schools for the price of one thousand dollars, and this turned out to be the winning formula.

On December 22, 1994, Bailey called an aide in the governor's office. They discussed the educational benefits and economic incentives of deploying this technology and, on December 23, Bailey penned a proposal, basically the critical element of "Opportunity Indiana," to allocate funds for wiring schools via the CODEC infrastructure solution. In an interview, Bailey remarked that "Opportunity Indiana is going on the proposal using the 'brick.' . . . "[22] Opportunity Indiana in essence became a quid pro quo for Indiana Bell and Ameritech. In exchange for its investment in broadband infrastructure, Ameritech would again receive widespread power to set prices and investment practices. The Corporation for Educational Communications (CEC) was created to manage the VDL networks and locate content providers to serve the schools connected. Ameritech had done its part and left others to work out the details. Ameritech set out on its next plan, to create (and thereby own) the entire higher education network in the state of Indiana. In the years ahead, Ameritech also guarded its markets jealously, keeping long-distance companies like AT&T out by dragging its feet in court. While AT&T and Ameritech squabbled, other fish were to be fried. Ameritech moved quickly, partnering with Disney and others to create the cable company Americast. Once again, the free-enterprise-loving Ameritech was looking at greener pastures ahead.

TELECOMMUNITY

With a great deal of fanfare, the first "telecommunity" project was unveiled in a lavish press event, as announced on the Ameritech Web site:

> COLUMBUS, Ohio—Ameritech, in conjunction with the Ohio Department of Education, presented a check today to the Columbus City Schools totaling $682,640, which will be used to establish a large "telecommunity" of schools linking Columbus, Ohio University, Athens, and schools in the Appalachian region of Ohio.[23]

Of course this was no mere philanthropic donation. Ameritech had "had its hands slapped" over a rate charge "discrepancy."[24] As part of the "Advantage Ohio Plan," Ameritech was required to return funds in this form so as to offset its practice of overcharging customers for basic telephone service. As in the case of telecommunications deregulation in Wisconsin and Indiana (where consumer advocacy groups advocated for returning excess profits to local exchange telephone customers), the legal slight in Ohio was turned into a fortunate chain of events which in no sense discouraged Ameritech's bottom-line plan. They stood to gain billions in relaxed telecommunications deregulation, and the investment of several million dollars in the telecommunity fund was great for business. This fact was not lost on people in the know. But it is often standard procedure for corporations to be found guilty of ripping off the consumer, of causing great havoc to the environment (as in the case of Exxon Valdez), or the like—and then turning the misfortune around, in effect "greenwashing" their blight and turning it into a public relations coup. Ameritech is no stranger to this practice.

To continue the charade, Ameritech Ohio president Jacqueline Woods announced her company's intention to ensure that educators get their fair share of the pie: "We feel it is crucial for educators to have access to technologies that will engage their students and help them prepare for the workplace of the twenty-first century."[25]

Initially, the Learning Community Link (LCL) was established to pick up where the old ADLP left off. LCL was intended to link the rural with the urban, and Ameritech brought in teachers from several different schools for a two-week training session. Each teacher received a personal computer, hundreds of dollars worth of free software, instruction on the V-Tel, and was "introduced to video distance learning" as one skeptical technician recounts.[26] It was all for naught, however, as the lines to many of the schools were late in coming, and the content even slower, if it arrived at all. The same technician notes that "we had one teacher who wanted to hook up with the Cleveland Metropolitan Zoo; Ameritech said: 'Can't do it.'"[27] Furthermore, he pointed out that "promises, promises" were made by Ameritech, but failure to follow through was the norm: "There was supposed to be a video bridge at OSU [Ohio State University]; it was never done."[28] Also fairly typical of Ameritech is the difficulty in locating technical support when the system doesn't work properly. The LCL network, which Ameritech claims was open, was extremely difficult to manage: "We don't have any control over it, we have to dial out. We have to call [the LCL coordinator]; she says we have to dial Ameritech."[29]

Even one of the two VDL coordinators of the network was incredulous of Ameritech's claims to have provided a seamless, easy-to-use product. LCL was servicing the same region as the former ADLP. One would think that by this time there would have been some carryover of knowledge in how to do video distance learning, and some continuation from Ohio Bell to Ameritech in helping to foment the development of content transmission. Yet this was clearly not the case. Ameritech was a major part of the reason the VDL failed to work. In the words of one VDL coordinator: "Ours was one of the biggest projects to come down the pike, and we were the prototype, and the governor had made all of these wonderful statements and then they didn't really come on board. And they've [Ameritech] kind of been a problem since day one."[30]

AMERITECH'S VIRTUAL CLASSROOM

Despite the failure of the Superschools in Ohio and the sham that was called Learning Community Link, Ameritech moved along as if nothing happened. In 1998, a unique partnership was established with Kent State University to develop the latest application out of the Ameritech bag of tricks: a virtual classroom.

The virtual classroom, the accompanying observation deck, and the "peanut butter room" are the subject of much pride at the Kent State University School of Education. Dean Joanne Whitmore, President Carol Cartwright, U.S. Representative Tom Sawyer, and Ameritech Ohio president

Jacqueline Woods dedicated what was dubbed the "Ameritech Electronic University School Classroom" at a press conference on April 7, 1998.

In the last month of 1998, a concerted push was made to secure further funding for the project. Initially the Ameritech Foundation provided $250,000 and the GAR Foundation provided $1 million for an endowed professorship, hiring Kent State faculty Dale Cook, a twenty-two-year technology enthusiast. In an interview, Cook pointed out that baseline data was acquired, videos have been used throughout, a conceptual framework has been established, and a check from AT&T for $100,000 to aid research has been accepted. But long-term support is needed to make the project sustainable. Toward that end, ten promotional videotapes were mailed to key legislators in the state of Ohio.

Initially, an important task in winning support for the Kent State University partnership with Ameritech was to orient the faculty to the new building, the Technology Center at Moulton Hall. The next task was to get them interested in putting their coursework online. Most faculty who attended were fairly skeptical about how this was supposed to work. One professor who belonged to the faculty union noted that these seminars, when the technology for the presentation even worked, were less invitational and open to discussion than most. The technology was presented as a fait accompli.

The Ameritech virtual classroom at Moulton Hall is quite an exhibit. It houses several monitors, cameras, and equipment available for students to use in performing a number of computer applications. Immediately outside the classroom, however, and behind a one-way mirror, is the area where researchers are able to peer in on the students in their lab setting. The researchers are able to zoom a camera in on any student merely by touching a point on the computer screen simulation of the classroom. With one touch, a camera overhead is activated to display this scene, of a student at a table, a student in the foreground, or a student in front of a monitor, for example, and the computer does the rest, rendering the scene in real time. The students and teachers, not much different than laboratory mice in this classroom, are subject to the type of scrutiny and invasiveness that would hardly be accepted if directed on the daily operations of the typical corporate manager or elected politician.

AUTOMATION

Ameritech's plans are better understood by our neighbors to the north. "Fighting Neoliberalism in Canadian Telecommunications," by Elaine Bernard and Sid Shniad, describes how the Telecommunications Workers

Union (TWU) has organized intensely with other consumer advocacy groups to fight the Ameritech strategy for telecommunications "reform." The strategy to which they refer included "de-averaging" rates and introducing "Local Measured Service," which leads to price hikes for rural customers—after the "price-cap" has been lifted.[31]

Yet the greatest threat to the public sector, one which has already taken it share of grief from NAFTA (the North American Free Trade Agreement), is the right to a job itself. Ameritech and other telecommunications companies play a critical role in downsizing the unionized workforce and replacing it with a nonunionized workforce. What would such a corporation ultimately do to teacher unions?

On August 2, 1999, at McDonald's Hamburger University in Oak Brook, Illinois, the chief executive officer of Ameritech, Dick Noetbaert, spoke to educators about the new digital economy, putting in a few plugs for his friend Governor Tommy Thompson (who spoke on an alternate day). This event, sponsored by Ameritech, GTE, and IBM, attracted over one hundred educators who were awarded "Pioneering Partner" grants. Noetbaert expressed a keen interest in the educators' use of new technology. He told the educators that the new digital economy is a boon to his business, suggesting that during the period from 1995 to 1998, information technology industries were responsible for more than one-third of real U.S. economic growth. Noetbaert coyly stated that he needed to fill five hundred jobs and was unable to do so because he was having trouble finding persons who were "qualified." He then lauded the teachers saying: "My hat is off to all of you, because its people like you who ensure the employability of the students who are in your charge."[32]

However, Ameritech isn't only interested in hiring more qualified employees. Noetbaert pointed out that in June of 1999, Ameritech, in partnership with the North Central Regional Educational Laboratory (NCREL), launched a $2.2-million program called "Parentech." The complimentary kits, complete with user guides and interactive CD-ROMs, are slated for every sixth, seventh, and eighth grade student living in Ameritech's five-state area. The book is free (only in the sense that those who receive it don't pay to purchase it) and, as Noetbaert mentions, "gives us, those who are adults, the kind of tools that we need to oversee children's use in a responsible way, and how to help them use the resources that are at their disposal."[33]

Ameritech's motives are suspect. At the same time they claimed to be helping parents and children, in August of 1999 Ameritech received more complaints by consumers than any other telephone company in the state of Wisconsin.[34] Customers, so valued by Ameritech, spend upward of three-quarters of an hour on the phone when problems with their service arise. In Ohio, as one customer points out, Ameritech representatives often don't know or even talk with one another across divisions. The frustration has been so great that, finally, a representative from the Public Service Commission has stated that the telecommunications deregulation needs to be rewritten.[35]

Poor phone service is only one problem since the ill-fated deregulation legislation has passed. Ameritech's attention is directed elsewhere, at expanding its partnerships, for example. In a recent news article in the *UWM Post*, Bryan G. Pfeifer wrote about and challenged the wisdom of one of these partnerships, in this case, between Ameritech and the University of Wisconsin–Milwaukee: " . . . on March 7, UWM announced the establishment of the Richard C. Noetbaert Distinguished Chair of Global Studies and International Business."[36]

Ameritech's involvement in privatization or, more accurately, corporatization of foreign world markets is real, not virtual. The article refers to how Noetbaert was an interested party in the North Atlantic Treaty Organization (NATO) campaign in the Balkans, as evidenced by Ameritch's willingness to spend $250,000 to have a seat at NATO's fiftieth anniversary celebration.[37] Apparently, Ameritech would like to be part of the restructuring of the Eastern European states, certainly at least to provide service for several of the countries whose infrastructures have been destroyed in bombing campaigns. Through the telecommunications business, cable television networks, home security monitoring, Internet access, and other forms of electronic commerce, Ameritech could be a major player in globalization. Having merged with the Southwestern Bell Company (SBC), perhaps it will take the superschools to the Balkans. Only SBC-Ameritech knows.

CONCLUSION

It's often been said that if you don't learn from history, you're destined to repeat it. History teaches that Ameritech reconstituted the monopoly and used Superschools and VDL as a justification for great profit. They collaborated with trusted elected officials who became salespersons for private enterprise. They preyed on a vulnerable population to sell new products. Big business pulled off another fancy scam. The only difference between this scam and those of old is that Ameritech used high-tech smoke and mirrors.

As I sit at my desk, I reflect on how far I've come in trying to tell this story. I am educated as a curriculum and instruction philosopher, a video producer, and a media activist. On returning from Cuba, I was faced with a choice: pursue what I loved (Cuban education) or expose the telecommunications scam that took my state and our nation by storm. In Wisconsin, the educators were too quiet, they were taken in by the information superhighway rhetoric, and at times my struggle felt like a lonely one. However, through WYOU community television, and with the help of producers Joe, Luciano, and Teresa, I documented telecommunications deregulation in the state of Wisconsin on video. I rendered the complicated legislative hearings, the state-sponsored propaganda, and the key interviews down to a thirty-minute program called *Enter Sandman*. I screened the video on public access television, at the university, and in a course I taught. I received incredibly mixed reviews—one of the most amazing comments was that I must have worked for a competitor, the TCI cable company! But one comment kept me going. A Korean student, speaking little English, replied that while she was unfamiliar with the content matter, the video was nonetheless very powerful. That served to allay my fears, because my point is that Ameritech represents power, as do all corporations, that few can truly imagine. But the corporations are legal fictions and are truly vulnerable. My work has been to deconstruct the corporate fiction. Truth is the only power on the side of the people, and the truth is that unless the people speak up now, the public education diet will soon be made up of junk-food curriculum. And our democracy will be lost.

Hamburger U. and Hamburger me? Or education for the people, by the people, with liberty and justice for all? Lets take back public education from those who distribute the junk-food curriculum! Its time for activists to get hungry for the truth.

NOTES

1. Reported in the *New York Times*, January 1, 1984, and listed on the Ameritech Web site, www.ameritech.com.

2. I spoke with several members of the Public Service Commission (PSC), the Indiana Utility Regulatory Commission (IURC), and the Public Utility Commission of Ohio (PUCO) to estimate this figure. PUCO documents show that Ohio Bell was making well over 9 percent during the late 1980s, which was considered a reasonable return for a public utility. Ameritech–Wisconsin, has easily made over 18 percent return on equity; probably far more.

3. Glen Unger, Public Service Commission, 1994.

4. For a very comprehensive analysis of Ameritech employee contributions, Team Ameritech contributions, and the officials who received funds, see the Wisconsin Democracy Campaign, Gail Shea, chairperson.

5. "Chic" Young, a longtime expert on broadband telecommunications regulation, expressed these sentiments.

6. See Ameritech's Web site, www.ameritech.com, or call the Public Utility Commission in the Ameritech service areas of Illinois, Indiana, Wisconsin, Ohio, and Michigan for the latest figures. The recent merger with Southwestern Bell Corporation dramatically expands Ameritech's reach, as does the Americast cable company, a partnership with the Disney corporation.

7. Wisconsin governor Tommy Thompson uttered this statement at the Ameritech Superschool Awards ceremony in Milwaukee, February 1994.

8. Barbara L. Watkins and Stephen J. Wright, *The Foundations of American Distance Education: A Century of Collegiate Correspondence Study* (Dubuque, Iowa: Kendall/Hunt, 1991).

9. Such as Ameritech Superschools, Project Homeroom, the Buddy Project, Ameritech Advanced Video Services (AAVS) and the Free Enterprise Network, Learning Community Link, the Ameritech Electronic University School Classroom, and Parentech.

10. Interview with Public Service Commission Employee, 1995.

11. Among them *Open Up Your World Ohio* and *Unlocking the Future*.

12. Annette Massie, interview with the author, 1998.

13. *Ohio Superschools* promotional videotape.

14. Annette Massie, interview with the author, 1998.

15. Hanna Rosenthal, interview with the author, 1994.

16. *SSN: The Student News Network*, presented during the Superschools Award Show between Hi-Mount Elementary and Washington High School in Milwaukee, Wisconsin, 1994.

17. German III teacher, Appleton East, interview with the author, 1994.

18. Ibid.

19. Ameritech Advanced Video Services report, 1994.

20. Indiana Utility Regulatory Commission, "Opportunity Indiana" proceedings, 1994.

21. Marv Bailey, interview with the author, 1998, 1999.

22. Ibid.

23. See Ameritech's Web site, www.ameritech.com.

24. Jennifer Moormeier, Marv Bailey, interview with the author 1997.

25. See Ameritech's Web site, www.ameritech.com.

26. Technician, interview with the author, 1998.

27. Ibid.

28. Ibid.

29. Ibid.

30. VDL Coordinator, interview with the author, 1998.

31. Elaine Bernard and Sid Shniad, "Fighting Neoliberalism in Canadian Telecommunications," in *Capitalism and the Information Age: The Political Economy of the Global Information Age*, eds. Robert W. McChesney, Ellen Meiksilos Wood, and John Bellamy Foster (New York: Monthly Review Press, 1998).

32. Pioneering Partners Awards, 1999.

33. Ibid.

34. *Wisconsin State Journal*, August 2, 1999.
35. Ibid.
36. Bryan Pfeiefer, *The UWM Post*, March 10, 2000.
37. Ibid.

Part Four

TAKE BACK THE NIKE!
*Campus Communities Battle
the Corporate Giants*

16

TOIL AND TROUBLE
Student Activism in the
Fight against Sweatshops

Medea Benjamin

Clothing emblazoned with college logos—a mainstay of student wardrobes—is a $2.5-billion business. With the explosion of media attention around sweatshops starting in 1996, students began questioning under what conditions the products sold in their campus stores were made. Receiving no satisfactory answers from their administrations, they began demanding that their universities pass codes of conduct prohibiting the purchase of goods made in sweatshops. By 1999, students throughout the country were staging militant sit-ins to demand not only strict codes, but also serious enforcement of the codes.

Coming together in 1998 to form United Students Against Sweatshops (USAS), students became the vanguard of the antisweatshop movement. They took on individual companies like Nike, pressured the U.S. Department of Labor to enforce standards, critiqued watered-down monitoring proposals, hosted garment workers on their campuses, and demanded that workers be paid a living wage. This essay explores the origin and growth of this student movement, and some of the dilemmas it faces as it confronts the apparel industry giants. But first, we'll take a look at the garment industry itself.

GLOBALIZATION AND THE
RESURGENCE OF SWEATSHOPS

Starting in the 1960s, U.S. garment and shoe companies fanned out all over the globe in search of cheaper and cheaper labor. Companies that owned factories in the United States and paid workers decent wages realized that they could move their factories overseas and pay a fraction of U.S. wages. Companies also discovered that it was cheaper and easier for them to contract out their orders to other factory owners than it was to produce the products themselves.

This system of contracting from overseas factories has now become the industry norm. So when U.S. garment workers ask for raises or better work conditions, companies threaten to close shop and move overseas. Pitting workers against workers has led to a proliferation of overseas sweatshops—workplaces where there are serious wage, hour, and health and safety violations. It has also led to the resurgence of abuses in the U.S. garment industry itself—abuses that had been largely eliminated by the mid-1900s due to hard-fought struggles for strict labor laws and government enforcement. In 1995, Secretary of Labor Robert Reich called the U.S. garment industry a "national disgrace" and claimed that half the nation's twenty-two thousand sewing shops fell within the definition of sweatshops.

Sweatshop workers tend to be young women. Factory owners say they prefer young women because they have "nimble hands" and work fast, but the owners also believe that young women make few demands and will not organize labor unions. Of course, they prefer single women with no children. In many countries—even right across the U.S.-Mexico border—women are forced to prove they're not pregnant to get a job. If they get pregnant while on the job, they are often fired so the owners don't have to pay the legally mandated maternity benefits. In some factories, women have to line up every day and take birth-control pills before leaving the factory!

Working hours can be grueling. Salvadoran workers making clothes for Liz Claiborne said they worked seven days a week, from 6:45 A.M. to 8 P.M., with obligatory overtime.[1] A report on Chinese factories producing Disney products found workers putting in eleven- to sixteen-hour days, six or seven days a week—a flagrant violation of Chinese law calling for a forty-four-hour week.[2]

In addition to extremely long hours, garment workers are often exposed to health risks such as toxic chemicals, improper ventilation and drainage systems, repetitive tasks that cause undue stress, high levels of noise, and excessive heat. Marilou Alvarado, a young garment worker from Honduras, came down with chronic bronchitis after working for two years in the ironing section of the factory. "I went to work in the factory thinking that my income would help our family move out of poverty," she told a visiting U.S. delegation. "Now I can't work anymore and will be a burden to my family for the rest of my life." Carmencita Adad, a garment worker from Saipain who made clothing for the Gap, contracted tuberculosis. "We lived in crowded, unsanitary dorms and worked in hot factories with dust in the air. It's no wonder so many of us get sick," she told us.

Workers are also subjected to physical and verbal abuse. Managers in Asian footwear factories are known to hit workers with the sole of the shoe for working too slowly. In some Central American factories, women are prohibited from talking to their coworkers during the day, can only use the restroom twice a day, and are cursed at for being slow or making a mistake.

Perhaps the most common complaint from workers, however, is low pay. With countries vying for foreign investment, government officials push the legal minimum wage level lower and lower to improve their "comparative advantage." The minimum wage is therefore often set at a level that doesn't cover the basic needs of one person—let alone a family. The tragic result is that workers perform backbreaking work for long hours—and still find themselves mired in poverty.

What happens when large numbers of workers are subjected to harsh treatment for miserable pay? They rebel. And indeed, this is what garment workers around the world are doing. But attempts to organize are usually met with fierce resistance by management, who use threats, firings, and violence to keep workers from organizing unions. In some countries, such as China or Vietnam, there is only one government-controlled trade union and the formation of independent unions is illegal. In other countries, such as in Central America or Mexico, trade-union organizing is not prohibited by law, but owners set up company unions to keep real unions out.

Until the 1990s, when confronted with accusations of worker abuse, U.S. retailers like Nike, the Gap, and Wal-Mart would try to shield themselves by insisting that they were not responsible for factory conditions because they didn't own the factories—they were "just the buyers." But thanks to grassroots campaigns and media exposés, the abuses of the industry were catapulted into the public limelight, forcing companies to start taking responsibility.

SWEATSHOPS MAKE NATIONAL NEWS

The 1995 Department of Labor raid in El Monte, California, that uncovered seventy-two Thai immigrants making garments in a state of virtual slavery left the public in a state of shock.[3] Then in 1996, Charlie Kernaghan of the National Labor Committee charged that Kathie Lee Gifford's Wal-Mart line of clothing was made by underage, underpaid Honduran workers. Unbeknownst to Kathie Lee, her teary denial on national TV would help reintroduce "sweatshop" to the global vocabulary.

After that, media exposés about sweatshops swept the nation. TV news programs such as *60 Minutes, 20/20,* and *Dateline* took on the nation's favorite shoe and clothing companies. *New York Times* columnist Bob Herbert wrote numerous columns excoriating the greedy companies making millions off poor Third World women. *U.S. News & World Report* had a special feature titled "Sweatshop Christmas—Nice gift, but was it made by kids or exploited workers?" Teen magazines ran heart-wrenching stories about teenage garment workers; cartoonist Gary Trudeau devoted some twenty strips raking shoe giant Nike over the coals; and *Life* magazine did a devastating investigative report about young children in Pakistan making soccer balls.

To address the outpouring of concern on the part of consumers, companies took unilateral action by drafting codes of conduct laying out the conditions that factories producing for them would have to meet. These provisions included no child labor, no forced labor, a healthy and safe workplace, no forced overtime, and a commitment to abide by local laws regarding wages and overtime. Some of these codes also mandated that workers should have the right to freedom of association and collective bargaining.

Codes are just pieces of paper, however, if not implemented. In 1997, a group of companies, unions, and human rights, religious, and consumer organizations formed to develop a unified code of conduct and a means of enforcing the code. They later created an enforcement body called the Fair Labor Association. A firestorm of controversy arose, however, when the unions and religious group pulled out in protest over a code they considered too weak (it did not force companies to pay a living wage but only the local minimum wage) and an enforcement plan that allowed the companies too much control.

One of the most controversial points was who would do the monitoring. The companies preferred major auditing firms like Ernst and Young and PriceWaterhouseCoopers. But when an Ernst and Young audit of a Nike factory in Vietnam was leaked to the press, it showed that corporate auditing firms are too beholden to the companies to be impartial, rigorous monitors. Many antisweatshop activists therefore advocated for monitors who are part of local human rights and labor organizations with a track record of working on behalf of workers' rights. Companies, however, resisted the idea of using nonprofit groups they could not control.

Just as the Fair Labor Association was embroiled in these heated debates about who should monitor and how, the student antisweatshop movement erupted on the scene.

STUDENTS ENTER THE ANTISWEATSHOP FRAY

During the mid-1990s, students on campuses throughout the country joined various antisweatshop campaigns. Some worked with the garment workers' union UNITE in their campaign to organize workers in U.S. factories producing jeans for Guess. The students developed creative protests like collecting old Guess jeans, writing comments on them, and sending them back to the company. Others helped the National Labor Committee in the 1996 campaign to get Gap to put an end to union busting in a Salvadoran factory and allow for the first experiment in independent factory monitoring using local human rights and labor organizations. Yet another group of students worked on the campaign against Nike, exposing the abusive treatment of young women in its Asian factories.

The Nike campaign had particular relevance to students because some two hundred colleges had endorsed Nike in exchange for sports gear and financial contributions to their athletic departments. In the case of large universities like Duke, the University of North Carolina (UNC), and the University of Michigan, Nike had multimillion-dollar contracts. As students uncovered these connections, they hooked up with national groups such as Global Exchange, Press for Change, and the Campaign for Labor Rights to challenge their colleges' ties to the company. They brought Indonesian workers to their schools to give students insights into the life of Nike workers, leafleted athletic events, and sent hundreds of protest letters to CEO Philip Knight.

So worried was Nike by the student protests that it sent company reps on continuous tours of campuses to do damage control, took out ads in college newspapers, and offered research grants. CEO Knight even made a surprise guest appearance at a UNC seminar on Nike to explain the benefits of Nike jobs to foreign economies.

Other schools, like the University of Wisconsin (UW)–Madison, had contracts not with Nike, but with Reebok. At UW the students were outraged when they discovered that Reebok's contract with the university included an "antidisparagement clause" that stipulated that no faculty could publicly criticize the company. Students and faculty quickly mobilized a "Disparage Reebok" campaign that shamed the company—which prides itself on being a promoter of human rights—into eliminating the clause.

But there were problems associated with a campaign based on challenging university ties with the sports shoe companies. First of all, schools without Nike contracts could not be enlisted in the campaign. Secondly, students often encountered a negative reaction from fellow students who were sports fans. At UNC, the anti-Nike student group was confronted with a "Support the Swoosh" group of Nike lovers, and when students leafleted at ball games, they came close to being physically assaulted. Students also found that the contracts with the university were often so lucrative and so critical to the functioning of their athletic teams that there was little hope of getting the contracts cancelled.

Meanwhile, a strategy for addressing the broader collegiate apparel industry began to emerge among students who spent the summer of 1997 as interns with the AFL-CIO-sponsored "Union Summer." When John Sweeney took over the AFL-CIO in 1995, he reserved $3 million for a campaign to recruit students for paid internships during the summer months.[4] Modeled after "Freedom Summer" during the civil rights days, Union Summer was to designed to give students a firsthand look at union struggles and, hopefully, recruit future organizers.

During the summer of 1997, when a group of Union Summer students was interning at UNITE, the idea of looking at the links between antisweatshop activism and college clothing started to gel. The interns, who were from schools such as Yale, Duke, Columbia, New York University, and Rutgers, decided to investigate the origin and conditions of production of the apparel at their respective universities. They discovered that their universities earned royalties by giving companies—called licensees—the right to manufacture products using the university logo. Each university had many licensees, some of which were big companies such as Champion and Russell, and others were lesser-known companies such as Nutmeg Mills and Jostens. Most licensees then contracted out the actual garment production to dozens of U.S. and overseas factories. The students recognized that this contracting structure, which mimics the garment industry as a whole, is conducive to sweatshops because the licensees move production from factory to factory according to where they get the cheapest bids.

During the course of the summer, equipped with extensive research, personal tours of New York City's garment district, and fiery energy, the students established the base for a nationwide coalition against sweatshops. They came up with a plan to pressure their universities to adopt codes of conduct that would guarantee that licensees producing apparel emblazoned with their college logos would not use sweatshop labor. The code would call on companies to ensure workers a living wage, limited hours of work, the right to organize independent unions, and a safe and healthy workplace.

The students decided to also demand that the licensees publicly reveal the names and locations of the factories producing their products.

They felt that this "public disclosure" of factory locations would help lift the veil of secrecy that has characterized the apparel industry in this era of globalization. Students insisted that public disclosure was a prerequisite for setting up a credible system for monitoring the enforcement of their university codes.

STUDENTS CALL ON THEIR UNIVERSITIES TO PASS STRONG CODES OF CONDUCT

Returning to their universities in the fall of 1997, the students decided that their immediate goal was to demand that their administrations accept and implement a code of conduct. One of the leading campus activists was Tico Aumery Almeida, a junior at Duke University. He recounted how the activists built on their anti-Nike campaign to organize a broad antisweatshop campaign. The shift from anti-Nike to pro-worker resonated with a wide cross-section of the college community. Economics majors, human rights activists, and Latino, Asian, and women's student groups were all united on this issue, which is a rarity in the age of diversity on college campuses. Within a few weeks, Duke's newly formed Students against Sweatshops was educating students, mobilizing support, and swamping the college president with e-mails calling for new regulations to ensure that Duke clothing was not made in sweatshops.

Fortunately, Duke had a sympathetic licensing director who shared the students' concern about sweatshops. With a relatively supportive administration, students were amazed to find themselves included from the beginning in the process of drafting a code of conduct.[5] Unfortunately, creating a code that would be acceptable to both students and licensees proved to be a daunting task. The licensee companies put intense pressure on the administration to make the code "corporate-friendly." Moreover, communication between the corporations and the students was severely impaired by the fact that they only talked to each other through the administration, never face-to-face.

The code that emerged in March 1998 did not include everything the students wanted—for example, it failed to call for workers to be paid a living wage—but it was an amazing breakthrough. It recognized the workers' rights to freedom of association and collective bargaining, public disclosure of factory locations, periodic announced and unannounced factory visits, and an opportunity for workers to report noncompliance. After the code passed, Duke students began getting dozens of calls from students all over the country asking for advice on how to get a code passed in their schools.

Inspired by the Duke campaign and communicating through the

establishment of an active listserv, the antisweatshop movement erupted on universities across the United States and Canada. It resulted in an out-pouring of student activism unseen since the movement for divestment from South Africa in the early 1980s. The *New York Times* called it "the biggest surge in campus activism in nearly two decades."[6]

That following summer, some sixty students from about thirty schools got together and officially formed United Students Against Sweatshops (USAS). The schools involved ranged from the Ivy League's Harvard, Brown and Yale to the big state schools like UW, UNC, and the University of California. Also on board were religious schools such as Georgetown, St. John's, and Notre Dame, whose students claimed that without strong codes, their administrations were violating their religious teachings of fairness and respect for all.

The students were able to mobilize wide support on campus because perhaps more than any other issue, this one was so easy to connect the global with the local. "This is an issue that really moves a lot of people," said David Tannenbaum of Princeton. "The workers making our clothes are thousands of miles away, but in other ways we're so close to it—we're wearing these clothes every day."

The movement united students interested in a wide range of issues—women, immigrant rights, ethnic studies, labor rights, environmental concerns, and human rights. It also reached across political beliefs. As the University of Michigan's Rachel Paster reflected, "One reason we've been so successful is that opposition to sweatshops isn't that radical. Although I'm sure lots of us are all for overthrowing the corporate power structure, the human rights issues are what make a lot of people get involved and put their energies into rallies, sit-ins, etc. We have support not just from students on the far Left, but from students in the middle who don't consider themselves radicals. Without those people we would never have gotten as far as we have."

The students picketed college bookstores, held mock fashion shows, circulated petitions, and organized rallies. They communicated with each other through the listserv on topics such as coordinated national days of action, negotiating tactics, media strategies, and new developments in the industry. They shared their favorite chants and songs for rallies, and they held electronic debates over the group's mission, goals, and internal structure. "E-mail has been essential to the movement," said Peter Romer-Friedman from the University of Michigan. "It gives us a low-cost way to communicate with each other every hour of every day, all over the country. It allows different campuses to plan their strategies by drawing on the experiences and achievements of every other campus. I don't know how we would have organized without it!"

While there have certainly been key activists and dominating voices in USAS, the organization remained remarkably nonhierarchical—both as a network and as separate campus groups. "We wanted to build a coalition of campuses, but leave total autonomy for the individual universities," recalled Dan Hennefeld from Harvard. "We wanted to keep the structure open and democratic so new schools and new students could jump in. We also wanted to run by consensus, which certainly contributes to the length of our conference calls, but I think it was worth it."

Marion Traub-Werner from UNC agrees that consensus building is a critical part of the USAS identity. "When new people join our actions, they often say that what they like most is fact that we operate by consensus. And that's what I'd say that I like most about USAS, too—almost all proposals get circulated to everyone and you have a chance to participate on any of the issues you want." Thanks to this flexible organization, students from small schools like Oberlin, Vassar, Wesleyan, Bard, and Haverford were able to become leading players, even creating their own e-mail list to debate issues that didn't affect the larger schools.

As a student organization with no office, no staff, and no funding for the first two years, USAS relied heavily on support from the U.S. garment workers' union UNITE and from antisweatshop groups throughout the country. UNITE helped pay for conference calls and meetings. They also had a staff person, Ginny Coughlin, who did an amazing job helping the students strategize when events began to unfold at lightening speed. The National Labor Committee sent their fiery speaker Charles Kernaghan from campus to campus to inspire more students to get involved, and produced excellent publications and educational videos. The Campaign for Labor Rights provided activist materials and regular informational updates. Sweatshop Watch and Global Exchange drafted a model code of conduct for students to use, and organized a Living Wage Summit to better define the concept. With funding from these groups, some students even had a chance to travel abroad, meeting directly with factory workers and learning firsthand about the grueling conditions for workers in the free-trade zones.

The antisweatshop groups and the garment workers' union also helped bring workers from different countries to tour college campuses—an important step in building an international grassroots movement. One tour featured two young workers from a factory in the Dominican Republic that made baseball caps for dozens of major universities. Students were outraged to learn that workers made less than $1 for a cap that sold for $19.95![7] Another tour brought workers from a Phillips-Van-Heusen plant in Guatemala that closed down right after the workers had won a bitter battle to form a union. The workers solicited student support to pressure the company to reopen the factory. Other tours featured a Nike worker from Indonesia, a Gap worker from Saipan, and a representative of a women's association in Central America that organizes garment workers.

Given this outside support, some administrators and press tried to paint USAS as merely a tool of the unions. "Many in the education community are questioning whether the wave of anti-sweatshop protest is an indigenous resurgence of campus activism or the handiwork of a powerful outside agitator—organized labor," asserted a *Time* magazine article, "Campus Organizing." It quoted an administrator asking "How much of this student interest is really being influenced by unions whose main goal is to try to bring these jobs back to the United States?"[8]

Students get indignant when they hear this attempt to belittle their organization.[9] "It's such an insult," said Romer-Friedman. "We have benefited from the resources and expertise of many groups and unions in building our organization, but we aren't puppets of anyone. And our goal is not to bring garment jobs back to the U.S., but to provide decent working conditions for garment workers wherever they live."

STUDENTS TAKE MORE MILITANT ACTION

In the spring of 1999, a series of issues pushed students in a more militant direction. Many of their individual schools refused to pass codes that included key student demands of a living wage, public disclosure of factory locations, specific provisions for women's rights, and a serious monitoring plan. Students were getting tired of endless meetings with their administrations that went nowhere.[10]

Students also became embroiled in a battle with the Collegiate Licensing Company (CLC), an organization of some 170 schools that mediated between universities and licensees. Alarmed by the proliferation of different codes and pressured by its member schools, the CLC declared that it would come up with a uniform code for all its member schools. Students tried hard to have input into the content of the code, but while CLC officials met with them from time to time, they refused to give students a formal voice in the process. Students were therefore not surprised that when the CLC finally came out with its code in January 1999, it ignored key student demands for a living wage and public disclosure, and was almost identical to the code of the much-criticized Fair Labor Association. To make matters worse, in March 1999, dozens of schools, often behind the students' backs, began joining the Fair Labor Association as the mechanism for implementing their codes.

"We were furious when we found out that our schools were joining the Fair Labor Association," said Nora Rosenberg from Brown University. "First of all, we had had strong criticisms of how the association's monitoring system was biased in favor of the companies, not the workers. And secondly, here we were engaged in what we thought were serious talks with our administrators about how to pass strong codes and monitor them, when suddenly we turn around and discover that without our knowledge or consent, they joined an organization we are opposed to. It was an incredible slap in the face."

In response to this turn of events, the student movement altered course, becoming much more confrontational. Reaching back to 1960s tactics, students organized sit-ins in their presidents' offices. While this action would have been rejected by USAS earlier in the movement, it was now seen as not only acceptable, but necessary. First of all, they were determined to make the universities understand that the students would stand their ground. Secondly, students feared they were getting too bogged down in bureaucratic meetings with their administrations and losing their capacity to sustain the interest of the larger student body.

Duke's thirty-one-hour sit-in in March 1999 was the first to make headlines. Duke students invaded their president's office, calling for full disclosure to be added to the CLC code by February 2000 or for Duke to withdraw from the CLC. The sit-in, combined with widespread campus support and favorable coverage in the Sunday *New York Times*, was a resounding success.

With this victory, sit-ins spread like wildfire. One week after Duke's sit-in came Georgetown's, winning full public disclosure as well. The radical UW–Madison was next, with a sit-in winning full public disclosure, a clause in the code protecting the rights of women (prohibiting pregnancy testing and ensuring benefits for pregnant women), and a living wage. The living-wage provision included a commitment from the university to undertake serious research on how to define and calculate a living wage. "We started out with about thirty people and our numbers doubled each day thereafter," recalled John Peck. "The support from the community was tremendous. Students at UW–Stevens Point wore armbands in solidarity. Small businesses, co-ops, and local unions kept us fed and supplied with coffee. Professors wrote editorials in support of the occupation. After ninety-seven hours, we were victorious not only in bringing the chancellor around to our position but in building a powerful movement based on solidarity and direct action."

The action at UW–Madison was followed by protests at the University of Michigan and UNC, with both schools winning commitments on living wage and public disclosure. University of Arizona's ten-day sit-in, the last of the spring semester, resulted in acceptance of disclosure as well. "The sit-ins built off of each other and had a snowball effect," said

Dan Hennefeld from Harvard. "One campus would hold actions in support of the sit-in at another campus. There was an amazing level of solidarity. As a result of the snowball effect, some campuses got significant concessions from their universities without even having to sit in." This was true at the University of California statewide system, where students were preparing more dramatic actions in response to the administration's stonewalling. But after the nationwide sit-ins began, the students held a spirited rally attended by two local congresspeople, and the administration caved in on virtually every demand.

Although this intense antisweatshop campaign was approaching its third year, it was not until the sit-ins that the public and the media began to pay attention to USAS. All the major print, radio, and TV media covered the protests. The students were often portrayed as throwbacks from the 1960s, but without the violence. The *Boston Globe*'s headline, for example, read, "Campus Sit-Ins Recall '60s Minus Rancor." The media was enthralled by the fact that students brought their laptops into the offices and peacefully did their work during the sit-ins. "The press response was mostly surprised and shocked that students were doing anything at all," recalled Traub-Werner.

The sit-ins, the nationwide press conference, and the continued growth of the antisweatshop movement nationally served to get more and more schools involved. What started out as a mostly east-coast, Ivy League, and big-school movement blossomed into a broad national coalition. The USAS conference held in July 1999 in Washington, D.C., attracted some two hundred students from about seventy schools. There were graduating seniors, now veterans of this movement, who were handing on the baton to their younger colleagues. There were students from both "precode schools," (that is, schools that did not yet have a code of conduct for their apparel licensees), and "postcode schools" that were enmeshed in the controversy over how to implement the codes they had worked so hard to pass.

"It was amazing to listen as each student got up to say their name and where they were from," said Tom Wheatley from the University of Wisconsin, who was one of the main conference organizers. "There were representatives from big state schools, small private schools, schools like UW–Madison, known for their activism, and schools with no previous history of student activism. Together, there was this sense of power and excitement that we were part of a dynamic, nationwide movement."

CHALLENGES CONFRONTING THE
STUDENT ANTISWEATSHOP MOVEMENT

While the sit-ins were successful at mobilizing students and getting strong university codes, they were not successful in convincing schools to find alternatives to the Fair Labor Association for monitoring their codes. In fact, their schools were joining the Fair Labor Association in droves—by July 1999, 106 schools had joined—and the association was actively trying to woo the students to participate. "We want the students to work with us from the inside and have even offered them a seat on the board and participation in a separate University Advisory Council," said Pharis Harvey of the International Labor Rights Fund, one of the organizations that decided to stay in the association. "We agree with a number of the students' criticisms, and think that with their help, we can make the association stronger."

The debate among students on how to deal with the association was intense and centered around whether to "mend it or end it." Those in favor of mending it argued that students did not have the power to get their schools to withdraw from the association, nor did they have a credible alternative model put forth. Moreover, they argued, some of the noncompany members of the association were committed to making it a stronger process as time went by, and student participation would strengthen their hand. Perhaps their strongest argument was that the association was going forward whether the students wanted it to or not, and it was better to have a voice at the table then to be shut out of the process.

The other side contended that if the students formally participated in the association, they would be giving legitimacy to a procompany code and monitoring system and would prevent the development of alternative models. They wanted to see the association crumble and hoped that getting their universities to pull out would help accomplish this. Others said that even if the association continued and students could not pull their universities out, the most effective way to improve it was not to join, but to continue to mobilize students in protest.

A third group called for an inside/outside strategy that would try to raise standards within the association while at the same time working on alternative models.

The antiassociation stance won out, leaving students with the daunting challenge of trying to get their schools out of the association, coming up with a pro-worker alternative model, and then convincing their universities to go with this alternative.

With the help of UNITE and other antisweatshop groups, the students devised the Workers Rights Consortium (WRC). The WRC requires companies to publicly disclose information about their factory locations as well as workplace conditions. In terms of monitoring, unlike the Fair Labor Association, which is based on infrequent factory visits by outside monitors, the WRC is a worker-based model that encourages workers to voice their concerns and get local nongovernmental organizations to check up on workers' complaints.

Just like the waves of sit-ins succeeded in getting universitites to adopt strong codes of conduct, so, too, demonstrations, sit-ins, and even hunger strikes were used by students to get their universitites to leave the Fair Labor Association and affiliate with the WRC.

Sit-ins took place in Wisconsin, Pennsylvania, Oregon, and Kentucky; there was a hunger strike at Purdue, a fast at the University of Rochester, and a sleep-out at Yale. By the time of the WRC's founding conference in April 2000, students had convinced more than thirty of their universities to join. "It was an amazing accomplishment," said Marcia Roeper, a WRC staffer. "In March 2000, we had administrators around the country telling us there was no way they'd join. By April, we had thirty-five schools, including six of the Big Ten and three Ivy Leagues. I always thought that if we students used our energy and organizing power, we could pull this off, and we did!"

So much energy went into the struggle to create the WRC and get universities to join, however, that students had little time to focus on campaigns of the nonstudent movement that were shining the spotlight on particular companies like Gap, Wal-Mart, and Nike.

Many students hope they will be able to combine the narrow focus on university-based clothing with broader campaigns trying to change the entire industry. While college gear is big business, it represents just a tiny fraction of the garment industry. For students to keep up their energy and affect the larger industry, they have to engage in corporate campaigns that go beyond the campus boundaries.

Harvard's Dan Hennefeld agrees. "If our focus is too narrow, we'll lose momentum, since it's hard to mobilize students around the technical issues of monitoring. We have to follow through on enforcing our codes, but we also have to join fights against particular companies with name recognition to be part of the larger antisweatshop movement and to keep students mobilized. Our challenge is to find the right balance."

USAS also has to figure out how to relate to other labor and anticorporate struggles on campus, such as struggles for university-based workers to earn a living wage or to unionize. New student-based coalitions such as Student Alliance to Reform Corporations (STARC) have cropped up to take on the broader links between corporations and universities, and USAS has to find a way to collaborate while maintaining its own identity.

A related challenge for USAS is how to forge stronger ties to garment workers themselves. Few of the students have either been inside a factory or talked at length to garment workers. Carmencita Adad, who worked in a Saipan factory making Gap clothes, visited dozens of universities to give students a firsthand view of factory conditions. "The students have to build closer ties to workers to get a more realistic picture of what workers need," said Carmencita. "We have to get more garment workers to travel to U.S. campuses, and we have to get more students working with labor rights groups both in the U.S. and overseas."

Arlen Benjamin-Gomez, a UCLA student who traveled to Honduras to meet with garment workers and produced a video called *Sweating for a T-Shirt*, says stronger ties with workers are critical to keep students engaged. "It's one thing to read about abusive conditions. It's another to meet young women my age whose health has been permanently damaged from working in sweatshops making products for U.S. college students. More students need to have these direct experiences to make this struggle real for them and to keep up their energy over the long term."

The movement has to also become more internally diverse. Over 90 percent of the students are white and most are middle class, while most of the garment workers—both in the U.S. and overseas—are from poor Asian and Latin families. Recognizing the problem, the students created a diversity committee to find ways to reach out to people of color both on campus and in the broader community.

Finally, the students—and the antisweatshop movement as a whole— must find ways to move from voluntary codes and voluntary monitoring to mandatory rules that are enforced by governments and international institutions. They should insist the U.S. only sign bilateral or multilateral trade agreements that include the protection of workers' rights and have credible enforcement mechanisms. While we are a long way off from getting mandatory, enforceable rules for the global economy, the antisweatshop movement has to find ways to work in this direction.

In the meantime, students have become the vanguard of the antisweatshop movement. In an amazingly short period of time, they've helped sensitize consumers to the fact that the clothing they wear might be made in sweatshops. They've taken three concepts—public disclosure of factory locations, independent monitoring, and living wages—and put them on the table in a way that companies must take seriously. And they've proven that the young generation is not cynical or apathetic, but strategic and sophisticated organizers who are successfully challenging some of the largest apparel and shoe companies in the world.

NOTES

1. *Behind Closed Doors: The Workers Who Make Our Clothes*, a report by University students investigating factories in Central America, National Labor Committee, August 1998, p. 7.

2. *Mulan's Sisters: Working Conditions in Chinese Factories Making Disney Products*, Hong Kong Christian Industrial Committee, February 1999.

3. Paul Baerman, "Giving Voice to the Campus Conscience: Students against Sweatshops," *Perspectives* (September–October 1998): 2.

4. Jodie Morse, "Campus Awakening." *Time,* April 12, 1999.

5. Baerman, "Giving Voice to the Campus Conscience," p. 4.

6. Steve Greenhouse, "Activism Surges at Campuses Nationwide, and Labor is at Issue," *New York Times,* March 29, 1999.

7. Marc Cooper, "No Sweat: Uniting Workers and Students, a New Movement Is Born," *Nation,* June 7, 1999, p. 12.

8. Morse, "Campus Awakening."

9. Cooper, "No Sweat," p. 11.

10. "Sweatshop Issues Fuel Campus Protests," *IRRC Corporate Social Issues Reporter.* (March 1999): 9.

17

SCREW-U
The Anti-CETI Movement at San Francisco State University

Bert Levy, Adam Martin, and Joshua Wolfson

AN OVERVIEW OF THE CALIFORNIA EDUCATION TECHNOLOGY INITIATIVE

In September of 1997, the California State University (CSU) administration announced it was planning a partnership with four corporations—Microsoft, Fujitsu, GTE, and Hughes Electronics—in order to create a new for-profit entity that would provide technology improvements for all twenty-three of the CSU campuses. Called the California Education Technology Initiative (CETI), the partnership was to "self-fund the telecommunication infrastructure for CSU and to sell related services at a profit."[1] At its most basic, CETI was CSU's answer to providing needed information technology at a price it considered affordable. The CETI partners would, for a price, update and maintain the CSU's technology systems for ten years. In return, the corporations would be able market their products to students, faculty, and staff. Additionally, "CETI partners would also help train CSU employees and other businesses, as well as perform product testing and joint research projects."[2]

With a start-up cost of $300 million, the size of CETI was unprecedented; the "largest partnership ever between public education and private industry."[3] Revenue for the CETI corporations was projected to be in the *billions* of dollars, the bulk coming from sales of CETI services and products to CSU students and faculty, as well as contract fees paid by CSU.[4] CETI's ultimate goal is evident in its mission statement. The corporations would "meld technology and intellect to provide ubiquitous telecommunications service, improve education and *provide a reasonable return to the shareholders.*"[5]

To the CSU administrators and their corporate partners, CETI was a lucrative proposition for several reasons. For the four corporations, CETI held enormous profit potential, directly through the CETI partnership and additionally with the corporations' expanded rights to market products and services to CSU students and faculty. CETI would provide the corporate partners with a pipeline to advertise their products to a (captive) CSU audience of hundreds of thousands.[6] As a bonus, it would allow for the creation of a generation of students familiar with—and therefore more likely to purchase—the CETI partners' products. For the CSU administration, CETI offered a cost-effective solution to "Tidal Wave II," the dramatic enrollment increase expected to begin at CSU in 2005.[7] Instead of looking to state funds to provide the necessary resources to meet this predicted flood of new students, the CSU administration instead hoped to turn to private sources. As the *Golden Gater*—San Francisco State University's (SFSU) student newspaper—reported, CSU "Chancellor Barry Munitz advised the [CSU] system in a late October [1997] statement to 'continue its initiatives in . . . new public and private partnerships,' " as a "way to keep pace up with mounting enrollment."[8]

Under one proposed aspect of the CETI partnership, CSU campuses would be able to offer more online or distance learning through a "Virtual University" service.[9] In this way, CSU could avoid paying for the additional faculty and buildings necessary to meet increasing enrollments by providing students with less-expensive—and often inferior—online courses. CSU officials claimed that a public-private partnership like CETI was necessary because there was no other way for CSU to obtain the recourses necessary for information technology improvements. Don Scoble, SFSU's vice president of business and finance and CETI representative, said as much when he commented, "There is simply no state money available to provide these [technology] services."[10] This claim, however, is questionable, given California's budget surplus at the time, as well as the tremendous amount of state money being poured into the California prison industry, one the state's largest growth industries.

The man in charge of the university system planning to enter into an unprecedented technology public-private partnership was Barry Munitz, who had himself "never even used a computer" and vowed that he intended never to do so.[11] When taking into consideration Munitz's corporate past, it is hardly a surprise that CSU would seek a partnership with the private sector. Before becoming CSU chancellor he worked for nine years as a vice chairman of MAXXAM Inc.,[12] a Houston-based Fortune 200 holding company—and not without controversy. In 1995, a civil suit was filed by the Treasury Department's bank regulatory agency alleging MAXXAM, along with Munitz, MAXXAM chairman Charles Hurwitz, and others, contributed to the $1.6-billion failure of a Texas savings and loan.[13] The following year, the *Los Angeles Times* reported "Federal savings and loans regulators are investigating whether . . . Munitz 'may have committed criminal violations' by giving false statements to investigators looking into the $1.6 billion failure of a Texas savings bank."[14]

Ultimately, CETI represented an attempt to create a new style of higher education, one that incorporated business ideologies with the mechanics of traditional academia. Some in CSU's administration felt this would help state universities keep pace with the changing technological world, while at the same time providing a solution to the system's budget needs. Those who came to oppose CETI saw it as that latest and most glaring example of corporate America's intrusion into the public sector, a dangerous marriage that would undermine the integrity of the CSU system. At its most basic, this was a conflict between the corporate and academic worlds, and would set the stage for a battle that would rage throughout the following school year.

THE CAMPUS COMMUNITY REACTS TO CETI

Although a partnership between CSU and private industry had been discussed by the CSU administration for a few years prior to the September 1997 CETI announcement, it was only weeks into the fall 1997 semester that news of CETI became public. Given that the contract between the CSU and the four CETI partners was scheduled to be signed on December 15, 1997, those students, staff, and faculty skeptical of the plan had only a few months to postpone or prevent the CSU administration from handing over control of a significant part of their public university system to a for-profit entity. Students at several CSU campuses rapidly organized to fight the partnership, and campus newspapers began reporting on CETI and the growing controversy surrounding it. Soon faculty voiced their disapproval of CETI at academic senate meetings statewide, passing resolutions opposing the partnership or demanding that it be postponed.[15] Almost as soon as CETI was announced, a movement against it had begun to take shape.

At SFSU, criticism toward CETI began shortly after a university briefing in early October, when the initiative was introduced to the campus population by administrators and corporate representatives.

Many faculty members and students were quick to question the secrecy of the proposal, the lack of time allowed for its review, and more importantly, the broader implications of increased corporate control of the university. Some of the specific concerns included the possibility of students having to pay for technology services that were currently free (e-mail, Internet access, and so on), intellectual property rights, and a greater emphasis on distance learning.

With the planned CETI partnership, students and faculty alike worried the online class trend would increase substantially, reducing both the quality of education and the need for faculty jobs. Also, many disagreed with some of the practices of the proposed CETI companies. For example, they felt uncomfortable with the idea of San Francisco State University in a partnership with Microsoft, who at the time was being tried by the United States Department of Justice for antitrust violations. Furthermore, there was concern over the potential conflict of interest between the academic and private worlds. For instance, some students questioned whether they would be censored if they publicly voiced criticism of the CETI companies. Others were worried classes not considered to be "profitable" by the corporations would be denied technology upgrades or cut altogether. Indeed, many of those who would become participants in the anti-CETI movement at SFSU were pursuing degrees or teaching in subjects like philosophy, sociology, history, and other disciplines of little direct importance to the high-tech industry.

In a *Golden Gater* article on the October briefing, Scoble expressed the university administration's determination to push CETI through quickly, stating, "We've come this far because the whole project has been fast-tracked."[16] During the briefing, representatives from the corporations and CSU seemed unable, or unwilling, to respond to the concerns surrounding CETI. As Jo Ferneau, a primary organizer with the SFSU organization Student Peace Action Network (SPAN) who attended the briefing, said, "They just sort of brushed our questions aside like they weren't worth answering."[17] Apparently "fast-tracking" included turning a blind eye to the input of faculty and students.

THE GENESIS OF THE ANTI-CETI COALITION

In the weeks following the October briefing, members of SPAN decided to organize a student resistance to CETI. SPAN, the student branch of the organization Peace Action (formerly SANE/Nuclear Freeze) was started during the previous semester and had been involved in antimilitary and human rights issues.

After hearing about CETI in the fall of 1998, SPAN decided to devote its entire agenda to fighting the proposed partnership. This was an unprecedented move for a chapter of Peace Action, as the issue was neither directly antimilitary nor long-term. Posting flyers all over the campus, SPAN attracted students from the International Socialist Organization (ISO), the Peace and Freedom Party, Pan African Student Union, and other labor and environmental organizations, as well as several students with little or no experience in political activism. This group of concerned students began to organize into what came to be known as the Anti-CETI Coalition. In this essay we will follow the course of the movement against CETI from the perspective of three student activist/organizers involved with the Anti-CETI Coalition at San Francisco State University.

STUDENTS TAKE ACTION

Since Anti-CETI Coalition meetings were so much larger than SPAN meetings, and contained students from a variety of backgrounds in activism, they were a bit unruly at first. Also, many of us were relatively new to activism and unsure on how to proceed. We quickly discovered that the decision-making process of the coalition could get bogged down by circular, drawn-out, discussions (a natural byproduct of coalition building). One strategy we employed to circumvent this was that of the "five communicators," an elected group of five people who represented more or less a cross-section of the group and who would make snap decisions if necessary. This technique worked well for us, but the potential was always there for cumbersome and divisive meetings. This seems to be a very touchy part of operating a coalition: how to make decisions fairly, with equal input, and in a timely and effective manner. We in the coalition would have to learn to overcome these issues at each stage of our battle against the CETI partnership.

The administration's enthusiasm toward CETI made it clear to us that CSU would not abandon its privatization plans easily. In light of this, our immediate goal was to postpone the December 15 signing of the deal. We decided the most effective tool we could use to influence CSU decision making was a petition calling for a one-year delay of CETI. While the goal of our petition drive was to convince CSU officials to delay CETI's signing, the drive had other welcome results.

Perhaps most importantly, petitioning raised awareness of CETI among the student body, which had been for the most part left in the dark by the administration. Although the plan had received a fair amount of coverage in the *Golden Gater*, many students thought CETI was the

Search for Extraterrestrial Intelligence (SETI) program—which listens for alien messages from space—until anti-CETI activists explained the difference while asking them to sign our petition. Signing petitions also gave students a sense of involvement in the campaign and often prompted them to take further action. Furthermore, the large number of signatures gave us an effective way to illustrate both to the media and the SFSU administration that opposition to CETI extended well beyond the seventy-five to two hundred students attending any given anti-CETI event. By the end of the fall 1997 semester, more than twenty-five hundred students had signed the petition. This was a significantly higher level of participation than the seventeen hundred students who voted in student government elections in the 1997–98 school year.

In addition to the petition drive, another major plan of the Anti-CETI Coalition was to hold a protest rally at Malcolm X Plaza, located in the center of campus. Organizing a rally presented the coalition with numerous challenges. First and foremost, we had to choose a date for the event. This seems simple enough, but as we learned over and over again, everything about a demonstration or political action is a statement. Holding the rally too early would limit the amount of time we had to build support for the event. Holding the rally later in the semester would interfere with students' preparations for final exams, and would be dangerously close to CETI's signing date. The important thing was to send the loudest possible message to the administration as well as to educate the student body.

We also had to convince students that opposing CETI was just as important as the myriad other political and social issues of interest at SFSU. After all, for a student in San Francisco in search of a progressive political cause to support, there is no shortage of options. Efforts to end the death penalty, reinstate affirmative action, and defend bilingual education remain active on campus. Moreover, many of SFSU's students worked full-time. Our petitioning and flyering around campus had helped get people involved, but we needed other strategies. We decided it was necessary, therefore, to structure the anti-CETI campaign as an inclusive campus movement. We didn't want our campaign to be viewed as an issue that was only relevant to a narrow demographic of students. As CETI would affect the entire campus community, we felt it was important to reach out to those who wouldn't otherwise be involved, and toward this belief we tried—with varying levels of success—to attract a more diverse group of people into the Anti-CETI Coalition.

Learning that students at Humboldt State University (a CSU campus in the Northern California town of Arcata) were planning an anti-CETI rally for the second week of December presented us with a solution to the question of the rally's date. We decided to show solidarity with our fellow students by holding our rally the same week. While this was only one week before finals began, we agreed it was the best of a less-than-ideal set of options and chose December 10 as the day for our rally. Besides showing solidarity, we hoped this date also would allow the media time to report on the rally before the December 15 signing date.

To increase awareness and opposition to CETI, we held two events in mid-November. The first was a free showing of Noam Chomsky's documentary *Manufacturing Consent,* followed by a discussion on CETI and the efforts to oppose it. The second event, billed as "The CETI Teach-In" was a group discussion on CETI and privatization led by SFSU's California Faculty Association (CFA) chapter president Margo Kasdan, SFSU philosophy professor Ann Robertson, and student activist Rebecca Downer. We considered each event to be a success as they both informed an audience of around fifty people and led to an increase in the membership of the Anti-CETI Coalition.

During the time between the two November events, we learned the signing of CETI had been pushed back to January 29, 1998. Although moving the signing date from the beginning to the end of winter break did little to ensure there would be adequate time to review and discuss CETI, the postponement was a symbolic victory, evidence that CSU administrators were responding to campus pressure. In response, we increased our outreach efforts, covering all available bulletin boards and walls with multicolored flyers. Soon we began to hear our message discussed with increased frequency inside classrooms and around the campus.

By the beginning of December, growing opposition to CETI throughout California was making it quite embarrassing for CSU officials to follow through with their January 29 signing. Now they were scrambling to find support for the plan among faculty members. In an effort to increase support for CETI, the CSU administration devised a ghost-written letter campaign to illustrate faculty support for CETI. CETI representatives at each CSU campus were asked in an e-mail authored by Patricia Cuocco—who, according to the *Golden Gater,* oversees information technology for the chancellor—to provide the names of faculty and staff members who would be willing to sign prewritten pro-CETI letters that would then be sent to various publications. As it turned out, the SFSU administration found no takers, and once the plan was reported in the press it was immediately criticized by faculty, and as a result, quickly shelved.[18]

When December 10 rolled around, momentum had clearly shifted to our side. The future of CETI, which had earlier been considered a done deal, was increasingly less certain. To boost rally attendance, we hung colorful posters with messages like "CETI: Corporate Education Takeover Initiative." Still, as we set our banners in place, checked the sound system, and made other last minute preparations, a few of us felt a bit nervous at the sight of the sparse crowd milling around the stage. Fears of a low turnout, however, were put to rest after the first few speakers, as students began to fill up the plaza. In addition to speeches by SFSU students, Margo Kasdan and Berkeley-based high-tech industry watchdog Net Action's Nathan Newman spoke out against CETI. As our rally progressed and speaker after speaker denounced CETI as a danger to students and faculty, the roughly two hundred students in attendance became angry and energized, loudly cheering and chanting. At the climax of the rally, organizer and cofounder of the Anti-CETI Coalition Claire Tran led nearly one hundred students into an Academic Senate meeting at a nearby theater, where the executive director of integrated technology strategy for the chancellor's office, David Ernst, was addressing faculty members on the subject of CETI.

Ernst, along with Scoble, was there attempting to convince the faculty that CETI was a good deal for all concerned. Loudly chanting "The students are ready to shut down CETI," we marched into the theater and briefly disrupted the proceedings. Confused heads whipped about, and members of the audience whispered frantically into one another's ears. We remained unfazed, fueled by the momentum of the rally and the strength of our support. We were a wave of fresh voices and energy washing into what was becoming a stagnant discussion. Although we believed the faculty overwhelmingly opposed CETI, we had decided previously that marching into the forum en masse and chanting militantly would send a powerful message both to the faculty and to any CSU administrators present that students were prepared to take the fight against CETI beyond the level of polite, reserved discussion.

After a few minutes, we quieted our chants to let Academic Senate chair Mark Phillips speak. He reminded us of faculty reservation towards CETI, and welcomed us to join the meeting. At the theater's open microphone, teachers and students hammered out tough, well-articulated criticisms of CETI, and posed questions to both Ernst and Scoble, who spent the majority of the meeting adjusting their neckties and staring at their loafers. Their few responses to challenges against CETI were evasive and were usually greeted with our boos and catcalls. One faculty member summed up the feelings of many of those in attendance when he said, "The way this [CETI] has been laid upon us is wrong. It's reflective of the fundamental differences between the corporate and academic cultures."[19] By the end of the meeting it was clear that Ernst and Scoble were practically the only people in the room who favored CETI. Comic as the situation may have been, we had to keep in mind that while we may have outnumbered them in the auditorium, these men were some of the officials that had the power to push CETI through without any student consent. Much like teasing a snake through the bars of a cage, we had to make sure they never had the chance to bite back.

The next day, Ernst admitted in a *Golden Gater* article that protests and objections to CETI had made an impact. Citing pressure from students and faculty, he announced that "The issue of digital course work will not be part of the January [CETI] agreement."[20] Ernst also said that any further discussion on the subject would not occur until the summer and would be led by the faculty. This statement was a complete turnaround from the CSU's prior attempt to blitz the CETI partnership thorough without any real faculty input. Surely it was evidence that our movement was having some positive effect in, at the very least, slowing the CETI partnership down.

The events at San Francisco State University on December 10 were in many ways a turning point for the anti-CETI movement. For one thing, we could trade high fives over an event well done and analyze the successes and failures of our movement up to this point. Also, the increased media coverage on CETI following the rally placed the anti-CETI movement in the public spotlight. Two local television stations covered our rally on their evening newscasts, as did CNN. On the day after the rally, both of San Francisco's major newspapers published articles on our event, accompanied by photographs. We were surprised the mainstream press gave us so much attention. On our own campus, the *Golden Gater* printed four articles on our rally and other CETI-related developments which, along with photos of protesting students, nearly filled the front page.

While we felt the rally was in general a success, there was still room for improvement. A major mistake of ours was not collecting names and phone numbers of students at the rally for our contact list. This would have created a much more direct way to reach concerned students, as flyers and "grapevine"-style word of mouth are not the most efficient ways of reaching people. Some in the coalition expressed regret that the hundred of us at the Academic Senate forum trickled out quietly in small groups instead of chanting and marching out in unison as we had entered. Regardless, momentum was on our side as we planned for our next event, an appearance at the California State Legislature's hearing on CETI.

CETI UNDER FIRE AT THE STATE LEGISLATURE

Likely prompted by the increasing public opposition to CETI, a joint informational hearing on the proposed partnership was held on January 6, the first day of the California State Legislature's 1998 session, by three committees: the Assembly Higher Education Policy Committee, the Assembly

Budget Subcommittee on Education, and the Senate Budget and Fiscal Review Subcommittee number one. No votes would be taken and no final decisions made; the event was simply a forum for legislators to hear a number of selected views on CETI. While the Anti-CETI Coalition had not been invited to speak, the hearing was open to the public, and we seized the opportunity to express our opposition to CETI. The twenty Anti-CETI Coalition members who carpooled from San Francisco were joined by roughly an equal number of students from Humboldt State, as well as members of various CSU student governments who shared our beliefs.

Not long after we were seated in the hearing room, we began our chants of anti-CETI slogans. Raucous at first, our chants subsided after capitol guards repeatedly threatened to remove us, but we revived them again following especially outrageous statements by CSU officials. To our delight, it seemed that many of the people testifying were uneasy with the CETI partnership in its current form. California Faculty Association (CFA) and California State Employees Association (CSEA) representatives, for instance, spoke of how CETI placed their jobs, wages and working conditions in jeopardy. J.W. Jimenez, speaking on behalf of the CSEA, told the legislators, "The governor [Republican Pete Wilson] believes that the way you plan for Tidal Wave II is to plop hundreds of thousands of students in front of computers and TV monitors. This is no substitute for classroom instruction."[21]

Pia Jensen, a Sonoma State University student and Cotati city council-woman, also delivered testimony critical of CETI, stating, "The real effects of the upgrades and presence of corporations on the campuses could well be very disruptive to the educational quality and process due to construc-tion, advertising, research direction, and in general, market forces."[22]

Representatives of major Silicon Valley companies, including Netscape Communications Corporation, added their objections, testifying that CETI, "may compromise the academic integrity of the California State University . . . system."[23] Two students were also given the opportu-nity to testify, each presenting one side to the CETI issue. A San Diego State University student representing the California State Students Asso-ciation criticized the lack of student input in the CETI decision-making process, as well as the exclusion of students from CETI's proposed board of directors. Speaking in favor of CETI, a California State University Los Angeles student said he felt the partnership would bring new technology services and opportunities to his neglected campus.[24]

Most of the lawmakers present at the hearing did not seem to have an opinion on CETI—or much of an interest for that mater—as some appeared not to be listening to the testimony. A refreshing exception to this apathy was Debra Bowen, a Democrat representing part of Los

Angeles County. Bowen posed a slew of tough questions to CSU's CETI representatives, similar to those raised by students and faculty at SFSU. Bowen, along with Jim Cuneen, a Cupertino Republican, later wrote in a letter to CSU, "As proposed, CETI may lock the state into technological solutions that are likely to become obsolete before the term of the agreement runs out. We want to encourage CSU to move away from a process that effectively awards exclusive rights to any company."[25] When the testimony concluded, the only thing that seemed certain about CETI was its many uncertainties. The details of the deal had not been determined. To this end, some legislators said they hoped to hold a second hearing on the matter before CETI was signed.

CETI CRUMBLES

Whether as a result of criticism at the legislative hearing or our opposition to the partnership, the signing date for CETI was pushed back to March. Enthused, we began to plan for the second semester's anti-CETI activities. More than twenty-five people attended the first coalition meeting of the semester—our largest turnout ever. This was a great opportunity to increase the membership of the coalition and build momentum for the anti-CETI movement. Unfortunately we became bogged down in what would become a troubled topic for the rest of the semester: the long-term strategy of the group. Some members felt the coalition lacked direction, and that isolated rallies and teach-ins would prove futile against an opposition that seemed to have the resources and power to circumvent any individual expressions of criticism to the CETI plan. They felt we needed a way to appeal to a broader demographic, both on campus and off. The only way to succeed in halting CETI lay in the ability of the coalition to bring together a large group of concerned students and faculty; their specific political and social views were not important as long as they were concerned with the CETI partnership. In contrast, other members of the group felt threatened with the idea of expanding to a much larger demographic. They reasoned that in doing so, the coalition would be watering down its principles. This issue was never fully resolved, and consequently tensions between some members of the coalition would remain just below the surface for the rest of the semester.

This meeting illustrated one of most successful characteristics of the Anti-CETI Coalition: Its members could stay focused on solving the main issue even while disagreeing about other, peripheral issues. While people may have disagreed about things like long-term strategies and political affiliations, everybody helped with a cheerful smile and a kind word when we got together to paint banners, practice skits, and do the actual work that it takes to succeed. It was these get-togethers, as well as the occasional social at coalition members Bert Levy and Brian Eby's houses, that kept up our sense of camaraderie even as we disagreed with each other.

Despite the occasional disagreements and the lack of a long-term strategy, plans began for another anti-CETI rally, to take place in Malcolm X Plaza on April Fool's Day. We reasoned that a rally held on April Fool's Day would send the message that students were not going to be duped into a privatization scheme that was actually a detriment to their education. We also saw the rally as an opportunity to demand that SFSU president Robert Corrigan meet publicly with students to discuss the CETI issue, something he had continually avoided doing since CETI was announced in the fall. It was only fair, after all, that if our president chose to go along with the CETI proposal—which he openly had—he should defend his position to concerned faculty and students. In order to achieve this goal, we planned for the rally to culminate with a march to his office, at which time we would present him with a list of our demands regarding CETI and privatization in general, ask him to host a public forum on campus to discuss CETI with students and faculty, and deliver to him all the petitions we had been collecting.

Our spirits received a further boost in February with the news that the start of the CETI partnership was being pushed back once again, this time to May. This was a welcome relief for us; the whole anti-CETI campaign had been laden with a sense of desperation. For instance, during our December rally, there was great concern the proposal would be signed in a matter of days. Now we had time to refocus and analyze our efforts without the feeling of having our backs to the wall.

In March, there was more evidence that the now-shaky CETI partnership might be crumbling. CSU's new chancellor, Charles Reed, was quoted in the *Sacramento Bee* as saying, "It's 50–50 we'll be able to take the existing [CETI] partners, with the risks and revenue streams identified."[26] During the same week, the San Diego State University campus newspaper, the *Daily Aztec*, reported that some of the companies currently negotiating the CETI proposition were considering pulling out of the deal.[27] Although Chancellor Reed denied the report, it was apparent that CETI was indeed experiencing serious problems. Reed chose to blame the difficulties on financial uncertainties, although it was apparent that the mounting student and faculty opposition was causing the change.

With the encouraging news that CETI may be crumbling, the coalition made preparations for the April 1 rally. In an illustration of what had become a constant obstacle throughout the anti-CETI campaign, outreach for the rally was hindered because many in the student population still were unsure of what CETI was. One extremely effective technique we began using to defeat this problem was outreach within the classroom. We found most teachers were willing, if asked, to let us make a short announcement about our event at the beginning of class and to hand out flyers and circulate petitions to the students. This was effective not only because it involved everybody in our own classes, but because usually a few people from the class would become interested enough to take a stack of fliers and petitions to their other classes.

In order to attract a larger number of students to our rally, we decided to incorporate more entertainment features. This was not an attempt to water down our message; rather it strengthened it by showing people that activism could be enjoyable as well as have a serious purpose. To this end, we arranged for the SFSU Hip Hop Club to provide music for our event. This definitely paid off, as they helped attract a larger and more diverse audience. In addition, we performed a skit: an auction where students playing the CEOs of Fujitsu, Microsoft, Hughes, and GTE desperately bid with one another for the different SFSU academic departments while President Corrigan encouraged them. The "CEOs" wore suits and had paper money as props. In between rounds of bidding, students and faculty members gave speeches on the negative implications of CETI. During the auction, students attempted to get involved in the bidding, only to be punished for doing so by the CEOs and Corrigan. At the climax, the students stormed the stage and took back their school, sending the CEOs running and fake money flying everywhere. Building on this excitement, Jo Ferneau, the last speaker of the day, led a chant of "The students are ready to shut down CETI," as we, backed by the booming music of the Hip Hop Club, began to march to the administration building. Fifty chanting students stormed into President Corrigan's office, crowding into his main meeting room. To no one's surprise, Corrigan was conveniently away when we arrived. With the flashbulbs of photographers going off around us, we sat at his large meeting table and took turns expressing our views to Corrigan's assistant. We demanded Corrigan attend a student forum on CETI as well as publicly oppose the corporate partnership altogether. A letter expressing our opinions was given to his assistant after everyone in the room had signed it. Finally, in what had to be the highlight of the day, Corrigan was presented, in absentia, with the huge stack of petitions we had been circulating as well as the "Golden Screw" award, a mock trophy with an enlarged statue of a gold wood screw, for doing his best to screw the roughly twenty-seven thousand students at SFSU. Corrigan's assistant turned red in the face and smiled sheepishly as she accepted the award for him. What a sight!

The anti-CETI movement won its greatest victory soon after when, on April 17, the *San Francisco Chronicle* reported that Microsoft and Hughes had pulled out of the CETI partnership.[28] We began to discuss our next course of action, but ultimately it was unnecessary. By the beginning of June, the other corporations in CETI announced that after further consideration they were pulling out of the partnership as well. CETI was dead! We had succeeded! No amount of ideological difference could interfere with the jovial mood of the Anti-CETI Coalition at that point. Coalition member Adam Martin even made up a "CETI is DEAD" dance to celebrate our victory.[29]

THE CAMPAIGN IN RETROSPECT

Looking back, our campaign, while victorious overall, did have its successes and failures. We did well in organizing and executing our rallies, as well as getting a large number of students involved in and educated about the issue at hand. In October, hardly anyone in the school had heard of this strange new proposal called CETI, but after our April rally, CETI had become more or less a household word among SFSU students. At the same time, we handled the press poorly at times, for instance, and did not put enough emphasis on individual student outreach. Also, while we had faculty and staff support, we didn't organize with them as much as we could have, even though they, too, were fighting CETI.

As far as the media goes, we would have received more coverage if we had put together a press packet, giving concise, accurate information that was ready to report. If we had had something already prepared with a summary of the issue, our goals, and some catchy sound bites, perhaps we could have been mentioned more often in larger media outlets. Also, this would have cleared up some of the misrepresentations that we ran into with the press that covered us. For example, the *Golden Gater* sometimes misquoted people from the Anti-CETI Coalition, and on one occasion published completely erroneous information. While the misrepresentations of our group and events were not necessarily negative, it can never help to have inaccuracies reported by the press as fact.

Diversity—or lack thereof—was always a challenge for the Anti-CETI Coalition. There remained, unfortunately, a disproportionate number of white males in the group, which weakened the coalition internally. If we had had a more diverse group, there would not have been as much tension in the coalition; the uncomfortable feeling by some of the women and people of color of being outnumbered. We would also have had a broader spectrum of perspectives through which to view CETI. In addition, we would have more accurately represented the population of

San Francisco State University and therefore been more effective in presenting our movement as important to every student. In retrospect, while we reached out to many groups, we could have made an even stronger effort to include diverse perspectives in the coalition by making a more active attempt to network with other campus organizations. Similarly, we could have worked to make the connection that both CETI and issues like Proposition 209—the California ballot measure which ended affirmative action in California's colleges and universities—are similar in that they each limit the accessibility of higher education to many students. While we did produce some flyers and posters that made this connection, we could have focused on it to a greater extent.

We did not make the faculty and staff an integral enough part of the anti-CETI movement, even though CETI jeopardized them as much as it did students. Although we did involve them in our campaign to some extent, we could have included them much more meaningfully. If our coalition had done more faculty outreach, students and faculty could have worked as a united front, instead of as two parallel but separate movements. Similarly, we rarely coordinated our efforts with other CSU campuses. Unfortunately, with limited resources it is difficult to work effectively with students hundreds of miles away.

Our biggest successes were probably our two on-campus rallies, because we combined intelligent and insightful criticisms of CETI with entertainment such as music and theater. We showed students that activism can be more than just speeches and picketing. We had huge, colorful signs and props; lots of advertising beforehand; and persuasive, articulate, and energizing speakers. On both occasions, the accompanying marches were impregnated with people who had just stopped to listen, and were suddenly taking action for what they had just recently been convinced was right. The marches sent a firm message to the SFSU administration that we were not willing to sit idly by while CETI was imposed on our university.

LOOKING AHEAD

With CETI's sudden end, a new question presented itself almost at once: In what direction should the coalition go now? In our meetings we began to debate whether to expand our horizons beyond the CETI proposal or similar attempts to privatize the CSU system, and focus on the growing trend to privatize public institutions. We also discussed whether it was time the Anti-CETI Coalition stopped being simply against corporate influence in education, and start moving in a positive, proactive direction. It was difficult, after all—and a hindrance to our progress—to continue to be on the defensive all the time. After much debate we were no closer to solving the conflict over how to expand our focus. Instead of resolving the issue, groups inside the coalition went their separate ways. Some went back to their original organizations, while others decided to take a new approach.

It was at the end of April that the coalition was first presented with the idea of organizing a conference at SFSU, to take place during the fall 1998 semester. The conference was originally conceived as a way of bringing together students and faculty from all over the state to discuss the ever-increasing trend toward corporate influence in public education, not only in colleges and universities, but also in elementary, middle, and high schools. CETI would obviously be a main topic of discussion, but the conference would also be an opportunity to place CETI into a larger context. Students and faculty would be able to brainstorm and come up with effective ways to fight corporatization. Furthermore, the conference would provide long-term goals and strategies, something that had eluded the coalition during the anti-CETI campaign.

With the news in June that CETI had died, coalition members began to focus full-time on the conference. At the first organizational meeting, attended by five of the members of the Anti-CETI Coalition, the groundwork of the conference began to be framed. Names of potential speakers were optimistically thrown out: Noam Chomsky, Howard Zinn, Ani DiFranco, and other people who it would be difficult to get a hold of with just a phone call. The original plan was for the conference to take place over two days at San Francisco State University. The first day would feature workshops, speakers, and plenary discussions with three-to-four-member panels of students, activists, and experts; while the second day would involve some sort of direct action. Many of the ideas tossed out at the meeting were a bit far-fetched, but at the time no one on the conference organizing committee had an accurate idea of how difficult it would be to put on such an event.

It was during the second or third meeting that we came up with the name of our conference, "The Last Front: Corporatization and the End of Public Education." This was the point at which the conference began to seem more like a tangible project and less like a pipe dream. Now that we had a name we could open a bank account, have a mailing address, apply for school resources, and talk up our catchy-sounding project. The previous meetings were as much excuses to get together and drink coffee as they were actual progress-making conferences. This all changed, however, with the coining of "The Last Front."

As the summer progressed, the organizational committee for the conference began to grow in size as more members of the Anti-CETI Coalition became involved. Soon the outline for the conference weekend began to take form. Our goal was more or less clear from the beginning: We wanted to create an actively integrated network of individuals who would be committed to effectively educating and organizing against the corporatization of education. Now we had a plan. We decided to organize the speakers into plenaries, and to follow each plenary with a round of workshops. The plenaries and their accompanying workshops would cover different themes including the privatization of higher education, privatization in a global context, and examples of corporate intrusion into K–12 public education.

Besides plenaries and workshops, the conference was to include a groupwide brainstorming session, where we hoped to hash out goals for the future. Partly as a result of the positive feedback we received for including music and theater in our rallies, we planned to include an anticorporate art fair and an interactive play about privatization in the conference. We also decided on a date for the conference, the weekend of October 10–11.

On the Friday before the actual conference we organized a rally outside the "Friends of Milton and Rose D. Friedman Foundation Weekend Retreat" being held at the San Francisco Marriott. It just so happened that Steve Forbes, California governor Pete Wilson, and many other corporate heavyweights and their political pawns were attending a conference at the hotel to discuss the benefits of, and strategies whereby, corporate America could privatize schools to make a profit. As the goals of their conference and ours were diametrically opposed, we thought a protest was necessary. As it turned out, the rally was a shining success. There were between seventy-five and one hundred dancing, chanting, energetic people protesting in front of the hotel with signs and musical instruments and, to our delight, a sympathetic renegade baker actually put a pie in Milton Friedman's face.

The weekend of the conference itself changed shape somewhat from the original plan, since we had so many dynamic speakers. We had two plenaries on Saturday and one on Sunday, each followed by workshops. The antiprivatization themes of the plenaries and workshops remained the same, but each session was given more time than originally scheduled. This proved helpful because of the number of enthusiastic speakers, workshop facilitators, and participants we had. People came to attend and speak from as far as Wisconsin, New York, and Mexicali, Mexico. One of the highlights of the weekend was a slide show by Erik Drooker, an artist originally from New York, now residing in San Francisco. A play put on by a group of students from Humboldt State University was also a hit because of its use of planted audience members, which helped personalize the issues at hand. We had our brainstorming session on Sunday night, but by that time quite a few people had left for home, leaving a small and intimate group to discuss the goals our newly formed network would strive for, and the strategies it would use. Among these goals were stopping the privatization of another school, striving to increase the ethnic and gender diversity in the movement as a whole, and holding universities and corporations responsible for their actions by continuing to seek out and blow the whistle on the often-hidden moves toward privatization.

Guerrilla theater, nonviolent direct actions, demonstrations, and civil disobedience characterize Bay Area activism (and activism around the world, for that matter) and do not start or stop with "The Last Front." We hope, however, that our conference served as a catalyst for a greater student movement state-, nation-, and worldwide. At SFSU, we have already formed an organization called Students for Public Education (SPE) to serve as a watchdog against further privatization attempts. Groups like this are possibly the most important part of the student antiprivatization movement, as the main tactic used by the opposition is to sneak these deals through by making them technically public, but not actually making the information practically accessible—by mentioning the deal in the fine print of a student bulletin, for example, or bringing it up briefly at a student government meeting. Without student groups diligently keeping a close eye on these bastards, they will sneak off with our rights, resources, and educations.

SPE is just the beginning, however. Our ultimate goal in putting on "The Last Front" was to create a network where students worldwide can be in contact and organize together to keep their public schools free of corporate influence. If another "CETI" were to come around, students would be able to call on one another for assistance and support. This, of course, is a lofty goal for our small handful of activists and our insanely underfunded, understaffed conference, but through the snowball effect, and widespread student involvement, it may become a reality. It is certainly possible, especially considering that a bunch of students practicing learn-as-you-go activism were able to stop four powerful corporations from privatizing a major part of their university.

Student groups from other CSU campuses are already discussing the formation of a systemwide student lobby which, if created, would be one of the largest in the state, representing the largest university system in the world. This organizing strategy could be most effective because of its comprehensiveness: the individual organizes on his or her campus; the campus organizes with its sister campuses; the university system or consortium organizes within its state or league; and so on, so that no campus is left untouched, and no student is left uninformed. With a little bit of energy, a little bit of discipline, and a little bit of compassion, we can turn this relatively small movement into a worldwide phenomenon. Let's go, students; the time is now. Take back our schools!

NOTES

1. GTE Corp., *California State University's Technology Infrastructure Initiative: Business Plan CETI*, August 25, 1997, p. 2-2.

2. Jesse Garnier and Michele Thompson, "Corporate Deal Draws Criticism," *Golden Gater*, October 16, 1997, p. 1.

3. Michele Thompson, "Deal Draws Skepticism," *Golden Gater*, November 13, 1997, p. 1.

4. Garnier and Thompson, "Corporate Deal Draws Criticism."

5. GTE Corp., *California State University's Technology Infrastructure Initiative*, p. 3-1; italics added.

6. Courtney Macavinta, "Microsoft-CSU Deal Shaky," *CNET News.com* [online], www.news.com [March 20, 1998].

7. Sharon Lerman, "Tidal Wave Headed for Universities," *Golden Gater*, December 11, 1997, p. 1.

8. Ibid.

9. GTE Corp., *California State University's Technology Infrastructure Initiative*, app. B-2. This aspect of the CETI partnership was also termed the "University in a Box." See Garnier and Thompson, "Corporate Deal Draws Criticism."

10. Garnier and Thompson, "Corporate Deal Draws Criticism."

11. Jeff Ristine, "Munitz Looks to CSU Future," *San Diego Union-Tribune*, December 5, 1997, p. A1.

12. Amy Wallace, "The CEO Higher Learning," *Los Angeles Times*, January 19, 1997, p. 8.

13. Ibid.

14. Scot J. Paltrow, "Chancellor of Cal State Investigated," *Los Angeles Times*, July 12, 1996, p. A3.

15. Carolina Wolohan Jr., "Academic Senates Turning on CETI," *Golden Gater*, November 18, 1997, p. 1.

16. Garnier and Thompson, "Corporate Deal Draws Criticism."

17. Ibid.

18. Michele Thompson, "CSU Wants You, and CETI, Too," *Golden Gater*, December 11, 1997, p. 1.

19. Jesse Garnier, "Faculty Suggests CETI Slow-Down," *Golden Gater*, December 11, 1997, p. 1.

20. Ibid.

21. J. W. Jimenez, testimony before the Joint Informational Hearing of the Assembly of Higher Education Policy Committee, the Assembly Budget Subcommittee on Education, and the Senate Budget and Fiscal Review Subcommittee Number One concerning the California Educational Technology Initiative, January 6, 1998, Sacramento, Calif.

22. Pia C. Jensen, "Concerns Regarding the California Educational Technology Initiative," testimony before the Joint Informational Hearing of the Assembly of Higher Education Policy Committee, the Assembly Budget Subcommittee on Education, and the Senate Budget and Fiscal Review Subcom-

mittee Number One concerning the California Educational Technology Initiative, January 6, 1998, Sacramento, Calif.

23. Martin Haeberli, "Testimony of Netscape Communications Corporation on the California Educational Technology Initiative," testimony before the Joint Informational Hearing of the Assembly of Higher Education Policy Committee, the Assembly Budget Subcommittee on Education, and the Senate Budget and Fiscal Review Subcommittee Number One concerning the California Educational Technology Initiative, January 6, 1998, Sacramento, Calif.

24. As previously mentioned, the services offered under CETI—Internet access, e-mail accounts, computer lab use—were already available free of charge at most campuses. A few campuses, such a CSULA, lacked such services. As an alternative to CETI, the coalition recommended the CSU take a campus-by-campus approach to meeting new technology needs instead of a one-size-fits-all plan.

25. Pamela Burdman, "High Tech Venture by CSU Criticized," *San Francisco Chronicle,* January 22, 1998, p. A20.

26. Brad Hayward, "CSU's High-Tech Partnership Plan Stalled," *Sacramento Bee*, March 18, 1998.

27. Melissa Evans, "CETI Partners May Pull Out," *Daily Aztec*, March 16, 1998.

28. Pamela Burdman, "Microsoft Abandons CSU Venture," *San Francisco Chronicle*, April 17, 1998, p. C1.

29. For a printed transcript of the dance steps please send fifty dollars cash to Adam Martin, c/o the Prince House on 24th St., San Francisco.

18

LEARNING TO THINK LIKE A HARVARD ECONOMIST

Stephanie Greenwood

Every year, at the first lecture of Harvard's introductory economics class (Ec 10), the professor tells his 950 students that by the end of the course they will have learned to "think like economists" about various issues confronting the modern citizen. In 1996 I was part of the Ec 10 crowd, fulfilling a sophomore-year requirement for my department. Economics seemed like a stuffy, incomprehensible subject to me, and I had major political differences with the professor. So I was prepared to be hostile. We spent the year absorbing a logic that cast current trends in the economy—outsourcing, privatizing, the removal of rent control, increased inequality, corporate mobility, unsustainable industrial growth, and weakened unions—as healthy market successes. By the end of the course I was no longer hostile; I was totally disturbed. It seemed urgent that my classmates and I learn to think like economists in a much more politically self-aware, less academically one-sided context.

I wasn't the only one with reservations about Ec 10. In the final lecture of the year, a group of students went so far as to pass out leaflets raising questions about the limits of the course. One year and many meetings later, student discontent with Ec 10 had coalesced into Students for Humane and Responsible Economics (SHARE). The group combined weekly discussions aimed at economics self-education with a kind of guerrilla curricular project: making and distributing "alternative" lecture handouts to the Ec 10 class. Our goal was to open up some space for critical thinking about economic ideas that had been presented to us as if they were mathematical facts.

You might wonder, Why bother? With all the things in the world to get worked up about, why pick your basic economics curriculum? Even if the assumptions made about how people behave are unrealistic, they need to be in order to make the model usable. Information provided by simple models can help clarify issues that are often clouded by controversy from warring interest groups. The neoclassical framework used in most intro classes provides a set of tools and a method of analysis, not a brainwashing ideology—right?

Well, yes, but—like so much else in economics—only in an ideal world. Anywhere else, beware of an academic subject that claims access to objective, value-free information, especially when dealing with such fundamentally political topics as resource distribution and livelihoods. There are values embedded in the assumptions of even the most graphable models. The neoclassical framework's assumptions are not only poor descriptions of human behavior, the values underlying the assumptions are often socially and ethically problematic as well.

Briefly, the neoclassical view says this: Individuals are born with a set of preferences that they use to make choices that maximize their well-being. They have perfect access to information about products, other people's knowledge, and the future. In any transaction, each side has equal power to bargain or to refuse to buy or sell. In other words, there is no power or coercion in the market. All markets are perfectly competitive (no monopolies, prices settle naturally to an equilibrium where supply equals demand.) Finally, if everyone focuses only on maximizing personal benefit, society as a whole ends up with the greatest possible amount of well-being. In rare cases of market "failures," careful government intervention can be useful. But generally, economists guard against government interference since it almost always results in welfare-reducing market distortions. Economists analyze data to come up with facts that can hopefully be used to understand how society might be made better off. A few necessary assumptions obtain. But value judgments, decisions about who should be made better off and at what cost, are outside the realm of economics. Those of us interested in considering questions of value, inequality, power, democracy, and healthy development are encouraged to try other fields: sociology perhaps, or philosophy.

In Ec 10, we passed over the assumptions very lightly. Didn't we agree, the professor asked, that it would be preferable to be given $10 to go buy our lunch every day instead of being stuck on the meal plan, subject to some bureaucrat's idea of good nutrition? Consumer choice, we learned, was just about the best thing around. Also, more was better. Since markets were free of coercion, consumer preferences determined what sold well and what failed. The market mechanism rewarded ingenuity and punished the lazy and foolish. The idea that in the market, everyone got what she deserved slipped smoothly into the assumption that everyone deserved what he got. If you're poor, ran the subtext, it is probably your own fault. And if you're wealthy, no doubt you did something extremely clever for society.

In addition to the values lurking in the basic neoclassical model come the values of the professor, hidden or overt. Our professor had plenty of both. Lectures and homework assignments usually focused on the problem of government interference in perfectly good markets, or the clean solutions markets could provide to social problems. These ranged from health insurance (decrease subsidies), to education (vouchers), to pollution (create a market in tradable emission rights), to traffic (charge more during rush hour), to social security (privatize), to unemployment (eliminate minimum wage laws, weaken hiring and firing restrictions). All this was dutifully copied down in notebooks and repeated back on tests. Calculating the value of a university education only in terms of future income earning potential, or in terms of returns on investment in corporate sponsorship would have come naturally to us by the end of the course. After all, that's how an economist thinks.

Since the subject had been declared value-free, there was no need for discussion or debate. Review sessions, where much of the material was taught, were reserved for technical questions about how to make graphs and do calculations. The teaching assistants had no time to respond to more general questions about why the problems were set up as they were. Persistent questioning of basic assumptions was considered "disruptive" and not tolerated. Sometimes, though, the ideology latent in our material peeked through with alarming clarity. A friend of mine asked a question about how a particular graph would change if it were taken from the worker's perspective instead of the perspective of the firm. Her teaching assistant told her, half-joking, "We're talking about employers because you'll all be owners, of course." Of course.

So what happens when you teach economics using an unacknowledged set of values to a large group of elite undergraduates year after year? I think of it in terms of a ripple effect. First, the intro class acts as a filter. Those who are attracted to the kind of thinking offered in class are more likely to go into economics as a field of study, graduate as economists, and teach and advise policy makers. Those who find the course's logic disturbing tend to feel as if they don't understand the subject and flee. The students who might have provided the most challenging, invigorating criticisms to the field don't learn the language to do so "credibly." As an academic subject, economics contains a kind of internal self-perpetuating ideological mechanism.

Secondly, once filtered, academic economics helps determine which economic policies have the greatest political currency. Political trends and business interests often seem to dictate economic policy, rather than academia. But advisors trained in the paradigm of the day travel between universities and world capitals, giving policies a stamp of intellectual validation. The connection between how economics is taught and the status quo of economic policy seems especially strong at wealthy private schools. The change from socially-oriented economics to market-oriented that took place in the U.S. government over the last fifty years certainly saw both reflection and reinforcement in the Harvard economics department, which removed most of its non-neoclassically inclined faculty during the 1970s.[1]

Finally, there are all those people in the intro class who are neither greatly attracted nor repelled by the material. For most of them, the simplified market message (what George Soros called "market fundamentalism") will be their only exposure to economic thinking before they go out into the world as businesspeople, lawyers, government officials, professionals of various kinds, parents, and citizens. Through them, intro economics courses have a tertiary social influence. They help shape what people accept as normal in terms of resource distribution, personal behavior, and the relationship between profits and the public sphere. Innocuous-seeming classroom experiences can function to limit the questions people ask themselves about their own and others' economic situations. Again, this effect is probably most heavily felt from elite schools that turn out a disproportionate number of politically and financially influential people.

Altogether, intro economics education serves as a major point of entry into the reproductive cycle of the economic status quo. Happily, pressure on such a point can work in several ways. Learning passively to accept the market as the best arbitrator of resources may end up diminishing people's capacity for thoughtful, democratic decision making. On the other hand, a critically engaged economics education can be a crucial base from which to examine complicated social problems. An understanding of how certain markets come to be dominated by a few powerful firms, for example, can help guide rules for competition and prevent massive wealth polarization. In economics classes, students have a unique opportunity to deepen their own education, plant questions in the minds of classmates, challenge their teachers, and insist on controversy and debate. The costs of assuming away the social complexities of economic questions get higher as inequality and insecurity grow and more public space is taken over by the private sector.

That's why I helped organize SHARE, but others joined for many different reasons. Some were just bored and wanted more challenging material. Some bristled at the widely acknowledged conservatism of the professor. At least one member was an anthropologist who wanted to know what was all the fuss about consumption in United States culture. We got a few lonely leftist graduate students who had been working in ideological isolation for so long that even chatting with us neophytes appealed to them. Everyone who contributed to building the organization—there were about fifteen of us all together, rotating through a core organizing group of about six, as well as maybe thirty or forty more who attended discussions—shared a common frustration with the way economics was being taught.

At the weekly discussion meetings, we learned about ideas that were not raised in class: theoretical gaps in the neoclassical model, the ecological limits to industrial growth, worker-owned businesses, wealth inequality, prison labor, "fair trade" systems, problems with World Bank–directed "development," sustainable agriculture, social unionism, nonmarket cultures, the economics of child care—anything that began with the phrase "when the logic of the market doesn't apply." There were no shortages.

With the "alternative" handouts we hoped to bring some of the glossed-over assumptions and implications of the class material to the attention of the conveniently large, trapped audience of the intro economics course. We wanted to address the lecture topic from a different point of view—the labor market, for example, as an arena of contested power, not just a market like any other; or to raise ideas not even touched upon in class, such as the relationship between the social inequalities of gender and race and the neat economic model of neutral "individuals"; or sometimes simply to point out disagreements over questions that had been presented to us as settled, such as the assumed inverse relationship between unemployment and inflation. Initially, we had more enthusiasm than expertise at our disposal. But with advice, better research, and another year or so of economics courses, the handouts began to improve.

It worked in our favor that in huge, hour-long lectures any handout looking even remotely entertaining will generally be taken and at least partially read. We gave ours a competitive edge by including cartoons. Reception varied, but even in their earliest, least polished editions, the handouts had an interested following. The professor himself was kind enough on several occasions to dress them down. To his credit, he later took time to meet with us to discuss our plans and applaud our efforts—while deploring them as misguided, partisan, and unprofessional. But since many of our members were committed to continuing the handout series, our dialogue with the professor, who understandably wanted us to leave his class alone, was limited.

As our second year ended, we laid plans for ongoing meetings, speaker series and discussions, improved handouts, and the beginnings of a new intro economics curriculum, taught in a smaller, more discussion-oriented setting. To get all this done, we needed serious help. Through the hard work of one of our founding members and the generosity of several donors we were able to fund two students as SHARE interns during the summer of 1999. One of our faculty advisors helped us publish some information about our efforts in the journal *Dollars and Sense*. It turned out that people outside Harvard were far more enthusiastic about SHARE than people inside. The letters of support, contributed materials, and money donated to our copying budget reinforced our excitement about what we were doing and made us more ambitious. The *Dollars and Sense* office generously allowed SHARE's summer interns to use its space and resources, where we worked on building ties to local economists and student groups, setting templates for handouts, lining up speakers, developing the new curriculum, and plotting for the future.

In the middle of all this work, I graduated—a political economy student with a special focus on the World Trade Organization and every intention of going into economics graduate school. As a bored, resentful sophomore listening to a professor I found politically appalling tell me I'd learn to think like an economist, I'd had no idea that the class would give me a major educational, personal, and political shove. How economists learn to think, and how noneconomists learn about economics, does matter. With each graduating class it matters more. For every student who thinks critically about the social implications behind the graphs, there's about eight hundred others primed for the market, saying, "Isn't it all just supply and demand?" Corporations don't always need to make direct donations to benefit from the way schools operate. Sometimes the classroom does it for them—and students, and the rest of us, pay the bill.

ACKNOWLEDGMENTS

Special thanks to: Phineas Baxandall, Samuel Bowles, Matthew Ellman, Nancy Folbre, Noémi Giszpenc, Nien-He Hsieh, Alexis Karteron, Jane Martin, Derek McKee, Regina Mercado, Sanjay Reddy, Abby Scher, Juliet Schor, Ian Simmons, Claudia Sitgraves, and Adam Storeygard.

If you are interested in learning about SHARE or contributing materials for discussion or handouts, please contact SHARE@hcs.harvard.edu or SHARE, 4 University Hall, Cambridge, MA 02138

NOTES

1. In the aftermath of World War II, economics as a field was much less market-driven, and the faculty a Harvard—including Joseph Schumpeter, Wasaily Leontief, and Alvin Hansen—reflected that. As a result of student pressure and support of the '60's and early '70s, Ec 10 students could self-select into "radical" sections that covered the "standard" neoclassical material as well as critiques of it and other models. Even the regular sections used to include thinkers such as Marx and Keynes. The course offerings beyond Ec 10 were also much more ideologically varied than they are now. But during the '70s, virtually all the faculty members able to teach from non-neoclassical points of view were refused tenure, were asked to leave, or left on their own; only a handful of lecturers are left who would be sympathetic to the idea that non-neoclassical economic models have much to teach.

When the current Ec 10 professor took over the course in 1984 (returning from his position as chief economic advisor to President Reagan), its curriculum narrowed quickly. Radical sections were eliminated, allegedly because they required a distracting amount and range of study. Sections on economic history other than selected excerpts from Adam Smith and David Ricardo were removed from the curriculum. Guest lecturers who had previously offered substantial critiques of the neoclassical approach were no longer invited to speak regularly. Students seeking a socially and politically contextualized approach to economics would have been better off at the University of Massachusetts in Amherst or Boston than at Harvard.

19

CONQUERING GOLIATH
The Free Burma Coalition
Takes Down Pepsico

Zar Ni and Michael W. Apple

T here is a popular myth about student apathy on campuses across the country. Today's college students are often portrayed in the media and popular cultural discourses as less socially conscious and less politically involved than their counterparts a generation or two ago. The sixties are the cultural barometer against which the winds of today's campus activism are to be judged. Even with the proliferation of identity politics in society at large and the retreat of many otherwise socially and politically conscious academics into the realm of "theoretical politics," a considerable number of students and faculty fortunately continue to place their feet firmly in day-to-day local and global realities and remain committed to the still utterly important political struggle of countering the corporate agenda.

To say the least, the university has been increasingly integrated into this agenda, as a site for the production of the technical/administrative knowledge so necessary for "our" economic and cultural apparatus, as a major source of corporate legitimation, and as an arena for the generation of profit.[1] While this is not totally new,[2] it has intensified—as have the struggles to construct alliances to challenge such influence. In this essay, we present an account of the strategic building of one such alliance of students, educators, and community members at the University of Wisconsin (UW)–Madison, the Free Burma Coalition (FBC). We also point to some lessons we learned in the process.

THE FREE BURMA COALITION:
ITS ORIGIN, GROWTH, AND SUCCESS

The FBC is the first Internet-based grassroots coalition, linking groups and individuals in as many as twenty-eight countries. It has a large presensce in the United States, with members on more than one hundred college campuses. FBC groups have used various activist tactics including consumer boycotts, direct actions, street protests, civil disobedience, public education, and grassroots lobbying. Within a relatively short period of time, it has succeeded in getting more than two dozen U.S. and other multinational corporations out of Burma. It successfully lobbied the U.S. Congress for the passage of economic sanctions against Burma's pariah regime, which recently changed its sinister name from the State Law and Order Restoration Council (SLORC) to the State Peace and Development Council (SPDC). The regime's media in Rangoon have attacked the coalition and its members as "elements harboring negative views against the state with different attacks, axe handles relying on the aliens, lackeys of the colonialists, with negative views, cohorts of the colonialists, traitors and expatriates saying words of abuse. . . ."[3]

The FBC was founded as a registered student organization on UW–Madison campus by one of the authors in the fall of 1995; the other author served as the faculty sponsor. Its mission statement reads:

> Our mission is to build a grassroots movement inspired by and modeled after the anti-apartheid movement in South Africa. Our movement stands 100% behind the leadership of Daw Aung San Suu Kyi and the National League for Democracy (NLD), whom the people have recognized as the sole legitimate leaders of Burma.[4]

Its objectives are clear: "To weaken the grip of the State Law and Order Restoration Council (SLORC) by cutting its substantial flow of foreign currency provided by multinational corporations such as Total, Unocal, Texaco, and ARCO among others and to strengthen the position of the democratic forces within Burma by building up an international movement calling for the end of totalitarian rule under SLORC."[5] In the remainder of this section, we discuss the strategies that the "Free Burma" campaign used on the Madison campus.

While many of the people involved in the FBC had ties to national and international political movements, we were just as deeply concerned that the specific place where we lived, studied, and worked lived out a progressive politics. Thus, prior to the founding of the Free Burma Coalition in September of 1995, we met to generate ideas regarding the question of how "Free Burma" activists could exert pressure on the university administration here in Madison to divest from corporations with business ties to Burma's military junta. Since UW–Madison is reputed to be a faculty-run institution, we decided to first build a student-faculty alliance. We made phone calls seeking support from a smaller group of faculty. Further, in order to establish the credibility and legitimacy of the FBC, we negotiated with the chair of the Department of Curriculum and Instruction in the School of Education—the unit with which both authors were affiliated—to use the department as a host to a student organization such as the FBC. After we got informal departmental approval for the use of institutional space and name, the FBC sent out an e-mail request for a meeting with Chancellor David Ward informing him of the International Day of Action for a Free Burma and, more importantly, announcing that the FBC was to wage a grassroots campaign targeting the university's investment in corporations with business ties to the Burmese junta. Once again, the faculty-student alliance paid off as the faculty advisor to the FBC was able to work with members of the chancellor's Executive Working Team to persuade the chancellor to "drop-in" at the meeting where students and officials from the dean of students' office were to discuss Burma actions.

During the meeting, the chancellor gave a step-by-step explanation of how policies were made within the UW system in general and UW–Madison in particular. Although informative, his message was clear: Organize and build a broad-based grassroots campaign or no change would be realistically possible.

While the founding of the FBC was inspired by the historical victories of the South Africa divestment campaign on U.S. college campuses, the original members were fully aware of the limited scope of the South Africa divestment campaign. In spite of its success in forcing institutional investors such as universities and colleges to adopt "South Africa–free portfolios," the campaign resulted in no major general policy changes in terms of university investment. We decided that not only did we wish to accomplish the substantive goal of making the UW investment portfolio Burma-free, but we also wanted to push for more fundamental investment policy changes.

With this broader long-term goal, we set out to work with many groups, each of which had its own pressing immediate concerns, but each of which also wanted changes in the university's financial and investment priorities. This decision to form a broad-based coalition proved both worthwhile and strategic. We identified several communities who could become allies to our cause. Within the UW–Madison community, there were various "progressive" student organizations with concerns for labor, human rights, women's, and environmental issues. However, we also engaged in the difficult and time-consuming work of making connections to other groups outside the university setting. For example, there was a small but significant number of "socially responsible investors" who lent support. Furthermore, within the state of Wisconsin there were many small family farm communities that had suffered from the onslaught of corporate farming.

We were more than a little sympathetic to all of these groups' issues. Thus, in the first letter that was mailed to the Business and Finance Committee of the UW regents, the university's ultimate decision-making body, we incorporated the concerns of all of the aforementioned political communities. However, Burma was to be the springboard from which the assault was to be launched against the university's financial and investment policies, policies that did not very often take into consideration social, political, or environmental concerns. In order to pursue this wider goal, we formalized a loose coalition of campus and citizen groups called the "Coalition for Socially Responsible Investment," in which the FBC was to operate as the prime moving force. Within a matter of a few weeks, about twenty different community- and campus-based grassroots groups signed on to the campaign to make the UW system a "socially responsible investor." Among the more prominent allies within this coalition were the Teaching Assistants' Association, UW Greens, East Timor Action Network, Students for a Free Tibet, Family Farm Defenders' Association, Student Environmental Action Coalition, and Wisconsin Decade.

Given our knowledge that as a public institution the University of Wisconsin was sensitive to pressure from state legislators, we also sought support from representatives in the state legislature. Of particular import here was Tammy Baldwin, a widely respected and quite progressive member of the Wisconsin legislature. At the same time, we also built alliances with social activists from a number of church organizations with a history of progressive stands.

Often the pluralistic nature of such a coalition—with its diversity and strongly held concerns—can act as an obstacle to the formation of an effective campaign. However, in our campaign the organizers were able to keep the tensions that arose from this pluralism to a minimum. We learned early on that, along with some other social and strategic factors, attributes such as genuine interest in and concern for the causes of other coalition members, integrity, and a consistently open process of communication on the part of the leading organizers played an important role in expanding and solidifying such a grassroots coalition. It also helped when both the founding members of the campaign and those who joined it as it progressed all agreed on the short-term and long-term goals of the campaign: Burma divestiture and adoption of socially responsible investment.

BUILDING ON PAST HISTORIES AND VICTORIES

As mentioned earlier, the FBC drew its inspiration from the economic action campaign in support of South Africa's antiapartheid movement. Some of the key organizers in the FBC had been involved in the campus antiapartheid divestment movement. In addition, faculty and community members who had witnessed the successes of that movement were optimistic and generally supportive of our campaign. A number of us did archival investigations into the strategies both of the advocates of past divestment campaigns and of the conservative proponents of "constructive engagement" (the term the Reagan administration coined and helped popularize during the period of antiapartheid activism in the United States). Members of the FBC spent considerable time in the university archives examining minutes and speeches by university authorities, as well as documents pertaining to the original mission of the University of Wisconsin. Through intergenerational interactions with sympathetic professors and community members, younger members of the FBC learned a great deal about these past social-justice campaigns and movements, their strategies, their shortcomings and successes, and hence about the possibilities and limitations of our local Free Burma/Socially Responsible Investing campaign.

The advantages of knowing the institutional history, as well as the changing discourses of various political communities associated with the university, became clear. Not only did it direct us to those who were potential allies and supporters, but also we were able to come up with more historically grounded arguments. This type of historical knowledge allowed us to engage in educational work about the issues through widely publicized public forums. It also made it clear to a wider public that we were not only deeply committed, but that we had done considerable research to back up our arguments. (This was in keeping with the admonition of the dean of students who advised us in our meeting with the chancellor to above all "do your homework.") The hard work of learning the history of local activism also enabled the FBC to avoid repeating some of the worst of past mistakes, including internecine fights and turf wars.

Of major importance as well, while we were organized around egalitarian lines, we were quite conscious of not wanting to commit the all too common "sin" of pursuing an unwieldy and unworkable "false" form of egalitarianism where everyone does everything at the same time. While democratic in terms of decision making, once a decision was made everyone was clear about the division of labor. Both leadership on the various aspects of the campaign and each person's role on a particular task were clear. This hardly seems worth stating, but it proved crucial. From previous political mobilizations, many of us had witnessed what could happen if "simple" things such as clarity and specific responsibilities were taken for granted and not overtly focused upon.

The extensive historical knowledge we accumulated also enabled us to stay ahead of the administration and to anticipate their often procorporate rhetoric and slow bureaucratic response. It also gave us insight into how to capitalize on the supposedly "liberal" discourse that one often hears from institutional leaders, especially university administrations and their governing bodies. Finally, this historical sensitivity allowed us to better understand the nonmonolithic nature of the board of regents and to be able, through our campaign statements, speeches, and meetings, to connect with the conscience of those regents who, in spite of their official Republican affiliation and conservative tendencies, did have populist leanings and a serious distaste both for overtly repressive regimes and for policies that harm ordinary people.

ACTIVIST EDUCATION: ACTING LOCALLY, THINKING GLOBALLY

As the campaign proceeded, we built an increasingly comprehensive information data bank on the subject of socially responsible investing. We made it available to members and anyone interested in learning about the subject, and encouraged our colleagues to study it. We kept audiocassette copies of our meetings with the regents or their representatives, which were in turn listened to by other interested members who could not be part of the negotiating team. And once again we made efforts to brief other members through the Internet.

This last point is important. Perhaps the element that distinguished the Free Burma campaign is the extensive use of the resources of information technology, such as the World Wide Web and e-mail. While we were taking local actions, including educating ourselves about the subject of divestment and waging a grassroots campaign, we benefited a great deal from our daily, and sometimes hourly, contacts with other student, community, and shareholder activists. Without the Internet, that would not have been possible. Usually, telecommunication costs are beyond what campus activist communities can afford, and the Free Burma Coalition at UW–Madison with its shoestring budget was no exception. Access to "free" university resources at our disposal, such as the Internet and e-mail, then, proved vital.

In addition to the local alliances among Free Burma activist students, faculty members, community leaders, and local representatives, we were also building a national network of people who shared our vision of a uni-

versity that took policies for socially responsible investment truly seriously. Many of our out-of-state allies included clergy who were involved
in various social justice campaigns using shareholder activism (for
example, the New York–based Interfaith Center on Corporate Responsibility), high school teachers and students, sympathetic shareholders, managers and researchers for socially responsible funds, lawyers with progressive politics, law professors in various schools, and even some corporate employees. These individuals shared useful information with us
and provided us with feedback, advice, suggestions, and help for further
networking. For instance, when the regents consistently tried to delay
action with their "carefully worded" arguments crafted by the office of
the university general counsel, we would scan these official letters and
post them both on our Free Burma listserv and on other progressive list-
servers so that legal experts and other activists could help us generate
ideas and strategies for the next part of the campaign. Thus, although it
was not necessarily originally planned or designed this way intentionally,
over time this truly became a two-way critical educational project. In this
way, a number of generations of activists could join together in ways that
cut across a spectrum of theoretical and political concerns.

On the Madison campus, perhaps these commitments were also
heightened by the fact that on their way to the main library on campus,
most people had to pass by the university bookstore, where nearly every
single athletic consumer item displays the Reebok Corporation's logo.
Like other comparable public universities across the country, such as
UCLA, Michigan, Iowa State, Minnesota, and so on, the supposedly "progressive" University of Wisconsin sold Reebok exclusive rights to market
on campus, on the bodies of our campus athletes and our coaches, and on
our athletic facilities. Thus, particular signs of the corporate agenda's
reach were not all that hidden and daily reminded people of how capital
reached into our taken for granted lives at the university.

PUBLIC EDUCATION AND THE USE OF CORPORATE MEDIA

In our efforts to counter the growing influence of capital on campus, we
found some allies in the media, including the corporate media. We knew
that regardless of its internal heterogeneity, various right-wing groups
saw the progressive agenda aimed at eroding the growing corporate influence on our educational institutions as a real danger.[6] We also were well
aware that the corporate media and even the public-owned media have
often been quite effective in discrediting and delegitimating the Left at

every opportunity. Yet even in the face of such media representations, the Free Burma struggle was perceived positively by both Democratic and Republican party leaders (including Jesse Helms, Mitch McConnell, Bill Clinton, and Daniel Patrick Moynihan) at the national level. The mainstream media—from the staunchly pro-capital *Wall Street Journal* to the supposedly more "liberal" *New York Times*—responded positively to the grassroots divestment campaign. This support was mirrored in the local media in Madison. Both the liberal *Capital Times* and conservative *Wisconsin State Journal*—owned by one corporate entity—supported the Free Burma campaign. Even the conservative "independent" campus paper, the *Badger Herald*, lent its support to the Free Burma campaign. Thus, a political umbrella was formed under which groups who would otherwise not agree on most issues could gather.

The fact that we did not pitch our anticorporate polemic too high may account for the reception of the Free Burma campaign and its ultimate call for socially responsible investing. Our public education campaigns, in which a considerable number of student organizers, labor leaders, academics, community groups, and local lawmakers participated, were able to construct an image of the campaign that was quite positive. We worked hard at this. Even though it was clear that a significant part of the campaign was largely led by those with a strong anticorporate agenda, we consistently strove to ensure that our message was clear and aimed at widely shared goals. Even when we banged on the doors of the regents' executive meeting room in Van Hise Hall to bring attention to the exclusion of both public scrutiny of their decision-making processes and ethical concerns in their financial decisions, we were not seen as "mindless" anticapitalists but as a coalition that was genuinely concerned about Burmese atrocities being committed with the implicit support of and funding by an identifiable group of American corporations such as Texaco, Unocal, ARCO, and PepsiCo, among others.

For the local media, Free Burma was a good "liberal" cause to support. Furthermore, in the conservatives point of view, Burma was a source of drugs that destroyed many American families. For instance, at a national level, Sen. Jesse Helms (R–N.C.)—clearly no friend of progressive causes to say the least—supported tough measures against Burma, including sanctions and an arms embargo, simply because of his own brand of conservative ideology that called for "acting tough" against both authoritarianism and drugs.

In addition, the utter ruthlessness and murderous nature of the Burmese regime itself was ideally suited to catch the media's attention. When a junta represses the majority of its citizens and arrests eight hundred peaceful activists and democracy supporters in a matter of forty-eight hours, or engages in a calculated, vicious, and ethnically polarizing campaign against Aung San Suu Kyi, the Burmese opposition leader and Nobel Peace Prize laureate, this is indeed appalling. Of all the authoritarian regimes in the world, the one in Burma has been among the most brutal. It has deservedly received critical attention and condemnation in the world media. While we wished these events were not happening and wanted the media to be even more critical of the junta, these factors helped our campaign.

Finally, one of the authors of this essay, a leading activist nationally and internationally in the Free Burma struggle, is a native of Burma and the organic link he has with the struggle there strengthened the call to local action on the Wisconsin campus. As one reporter put it, "You are from Burma and I can understand why you would be concerned about the issue. But these people are white liberals. They are do-gooders." This may be true, but it is also important to recognize the capacity of a wide range of people to understand brutality and to want to act against it. Ethnicity and national affiliation here seemed to have worked in the interest of our campaign. Wisconsin media, especially the ones in Madison, closely followed the campaign, in part because of the fact that one of its leaders was a graduate student who was a political refugee and would be subjected to severe reprisals if he ever returned to Burma.

GRASSROOTS TOOLS AND LIMITED GAINS

All of this work and trust ultimately paid off. Earlier in this essay, we mentioned that a more detailed understanding of past mobilizations helped our efforts in waging a well-coordinated campaign on the Wisconsin campus. This history of past struggles left us with legacies. One of the most positive aspects of this legacy was specific legislation, Wisconsin State Statute 36.29 (5). This law was enacted after a long series of radical actions by student, faculty, and community activists during the South African antiapartheid divestment campaign. This statute bars the University of Wisconsin system from doing business with any business entities that knowingly condone, either directly or indirectly, the practice of discrimination on the basis of race, gender, creed, or religious beliefs. While a number of the members of the FBC were trying to make a parallel legal case for Burma, others remained skeptical of the possibility that the attorney general's office would read the statute this broadly. Such a reading would have qualified Burma for state sanctions, since U.S. corporations have entered into business contracts with the military regime in spite of their prior knowledge of various forms of rights violations, including discrimination on the basis of ethnicity.

Ultimately, we decided that even if we could not get such a broad reading of the statute, it was still a crucial tool in the campaign. It established an important precedent for challenging a state institution to adopt more humane standards in investing and managing its endowment funds. At the time of our campaign, the University of Wisconsin had a nearly $230-million endowment. While this was a relatively small package compared to other institutions, such as the University of California (nearly $2 billion), Harvard ($8 billion), and Stanford ($5 billion), it was still no small amount of money. The fact that Wisconsin had begun a long-term effort to build a much more extensive endowment also meant that the establishment of progressive precedents now would echo throughout the coming years in even more powerful ways.

With this statute in mind, we began to step up both media and direct-action campaigns on the Madison campus, as well as on other UW campuses where we had activist colleagues and friends, both faculty and students. We focused on the Madison campus simply because the office of the board of regents is housed here; Madison is also the flagship university within the larger UW system. In November of 1995, the campaign officially informed the board of regents Business and Finance Committee of our demands. These included:

(a) the adoption and implementation of a rigorous set of "socially responsible investment" policies;
(b) the creation of a committee representative of campuswide interests that would be empowered to do research on university's existing business and financial interactions; and
(c) the divestment of stocks from the two most powerful companies which were in Burma, namely PepsiCo and Texaco.

After much media coverage in prominent national newspapers and magazines and in local media coverage over a period of one-and-a-half years (November 1995–April 1997), the board of regents decided to divest itself of all Texaco stocks.[7] While the chair of the regents publicly denied that the decision had anything to do with the intense grassroots pressure we had initiated, the director of university relations later acknowledged that it was the Free Burma campaign that persuaded the regents to make that decision.[8]

In its annual list of the top ten activist campuses in 1997, *Mother Jones* ranked the University of Wisconsin–Madison as the number one activist campus in the nation. It said the following in its citation:

Borrowing a page from campus anti-apartheid protestors of the 1980s, Madison students continued their campaign against human rights abuses by urging the university to divest companies doing business with Burma. In 1995 they launched the Internet-based Free Burma Coalition, and last spring they helped convince the university to unload $239,000 worth of stock in Texaco, which has business ties to Burma.[9]

Among the major effects of the FBC campaign was not "only" the successful struggle to convince the university to divest. The efforts also led to a rebuilding of wider coalitions among groups on campus, a greater connectiveness between the campus and community activists, and the growth of activism around a range of issues. The campaign also made it clear that the global and the local can be successfully joined if the tools made available by technologies such as the World Wide Web and e-mail can be used in creative and mobilizing ways.

In September of the same year, Texaco sold its business to the UK's Premier and withdrew from Burma. PepsiCo has recently done the same. And in Madison the campaign for even stronger policies on socially responsible investing continues.

NOTES

1. M. W. Apple, *Education and Power*, 2d ed. (New York: Routledge, 1995).

2. C. Barrow, *Universities and the Capitalist State* (Madison: University of Wisconsin Press, 1990).

3. Kyaw Gaung, "The New Light of Myanmar," *Skyful of Lies*, BBC and VOA, March 13, 1997.

4. Free Burma Coalition at the University of Wisconsin–Madison, mission statement [online], www.wicip.org/fbc [1995].

5. See the Free Burma Coalition Web site, www.wicip.org/fbc.

6. See M. W. Apple, *Official Knowledge*, 2d ed. (New York: Routledge, 2000); *Cultural Politics and Education* (New York: Teachers College Press), 1996; A. Molnar, *Giving Kids the Business* (Boulder: Westview, 1996).

7. See J. Nichols, "UW Dumps Stock Linked to Burma," *Capital Times*, May 10–11, 1997, p. 1A.

8. D. Orzech, personal Internet communication with the authors, fall 1998.

9. "Top 10 Activist Campuses," *Mother Jones* (October 1997): 19–20.

20

SOCIAL CHOICE
FOR SOCIAL CHANGE
Campaign for a New TIAA-CREF
Neil Wollman and Abigail Fuller

Socially responsible investing (SRI) is coming of age. Nearly one out of every ten investment dollars now sits in a socially responsible fund. A recent issue of *Co-op America Quarterly* listed forty-three of them. Several important studies have refuted the notion that doing good means doing worse financially, and big investment houses like Salomon Smith Barney and Dreyfus have socially responsible funds. Now SRI is evolving toward more sophisticated and stronger ways to use money for positive change. Mutual funds and pension funds are increasingly moving beyond "negative screens"—avoiding companies that pollute the environment or do business in tobacco, alcohol, nuclear weapons and energy, or the military—to actively seek out companies that have exemplary records with regard to various social and environmental concerns. Such "positive investing" is the wave of the future, according to some in the field.

In this context, we began a campaign in early 1997 to persuade Teachers' Insurance and Annuity Association–College Retirement Equities Fund (TIAA-CREF) to begin positive investing a small portion of the assets in the Social Choice Account, its socially responsible fund. This would mean $200–400 million invested in companies and other financial institutions (such as community development corporations) that are models of social and environmental responsibility—a way to reward and promote corporate responsibility toward consumers, the environment, employees, and local communities. TIAA-CREF is the nation's largest private pension system, serving two million employees, principally in higher education. It was started by Andrew Carnegie to insure that college teachers would not retire penniless. In 1989, an earlier campaign succeeded in persuading TIAA-CREF to provide a socially responsible option for its investors, creating the Social Choice Account. This five-year effort, like the current one, pitted David against Goliath: Our annual budget ($400) was less than the CEO's salary for one hour. We succeeded by framing an appealing argument and conducting a grassroots effort that included gaining endorsements from professional organizations and activist groups, circulating petitions, and getting TIAA-CREF participants, mostly college faculty, to write to the company. Today, one-tenth of all TIAA-CREF investors have money in the Social Choice Account, and its returns are comparable to those of TIAA-CREF's similar accounts.

Our current campaign is based on four strategies: persuading TIAA-CREF officials of the merits of positive investing for all concerned (the company, participants, and society at large); putting pressure on TIAA-CREF by getting participants and others to write the company in support of the campaign and sign petitions, and by securing the endorsements of various organizations and groups; gaining local and national media attention; and, if necessary, taking some type of more direct action. We have made heavy use of the Internet to spread the word, including the creation of a Web site. We have distributed brochures at conferences, written letters to the editors of newspapers, passed around petitions, been featured in the *Wall Street Journal* (August 24, 1999) and in two short pieces in the *Chronicle of Higher Education*, as well as other media, and notice of the campaign has appeared in various newsletters and publications.

Our campaign seeks for TIAA-CREF to invest 5–10 percent of SCA assets—$200–400 million—in progressive, typically small companies and in community development corporations. Community development loan funds and banks, like South Shore Bank in Chicago, direct capital into low-income communities, where it is used to build affordable housing and provide loans for small businesses. Progressive companies may be identified by, for example, exemplary relations with employees (equitable salaries, family-friendly policies, union relations, and the like); consumers (product safety and quality, truthful advertising, and so forth); communities (low-income housing, community development, and so on); and the environment (recycling, pollution control, life-cycle analysis and design, and the like).

Companies also exist that are pioneering socially and environmentally responsible products and services. Kafus Environmental produces tree-free paper. Bellway builds energy-efficient homes, many on recycled industrial land ("brown fields"), that minimize the use of nonrenewable hardwoods.

Investment in progressive companies, especially by prestigious TIAA-CREF, adds to their credibility and puts them in a stronger position to expand their operations. Consequently, it enables them to serve as models for newer companies and thus promote corporate responsibility more generally. And some assets could be invested directly as "venture capital," aiding companies more directly.

During the past year, we have exchanged a number of letters with John Biggs, CEO and chairman of TIAA-CREF. He has made various objections to the proposal, which we feel we have adequately addressed. Regarding his concern that positive investing would negatively affect the fund's rate of return, we responded that knowledgeable people have assured us that investing such a small portion of the fund's total assets in progressive companies would entail minimal risk. Biggs wrote that positive investing is beyond the account's stated purpose; yet, as we pointed out, the prospectus states that the social criteria of the fund "can change from time to time." He objected to the extra costs involved in administering positive investing, but we responded that lists of progressive companies already exist, that TIAA-CREF already hires outside advisers for the negative screens, and, in any case, that the cost, relative to the size of the account, would be minimal.

Perhaps most significantly, Biggs was clearly in error when he argued that there is not strong support for positive investing among Social Choice Account participants. A survey that TIAA-CREF itself conducted found that an overwhelming percentage of participants support positive investing, and are even willing to lose some money if it means contributing to building a better society. Additionally, Biggs argues that positive investing is too vague a concept to be practically administrable; that is, how can one determine what are "good" companies? However, several funds have already set up specific criteria for determining which companies to invest in. Again, TIAA-CREF arguments fall flat.

After months of exchanging letters with Biggs, we are ready to up the ante. In addition to drumming up support among TIAA-CREF participants, we are more aggressively seeking national media attention. We are in the process of contacting other TIAA-CREF officials and trustees in hopes of garnering their support. A tactic we have waiting in the wings is to advertise to Social Choice Account participants those funds that do engage in positive investing, and encourage them to withdraw their money from TIAA-CREF and invest it there.

As we told TIAA-CREF, we are in it for the long haul. If we succeeded in helping create the second largest socially responsible fund in the United States, we can succeed in helping make it a stronger force for positive social change.

If you are interested or can help in any way—and there are numerous ways to contribute, small and large—contact Social Choice for Social Change: Campaign for a New TIAA-CREF, Box 135, Manchester College, North Manchester, IN 46062; (219)982-5346/5009; or e-mail Neil Wollman at NJW@Manchester.edu or Abigail Fuller at AAF@Manchester.edu. Our Web site is located at ARES.manchester.edu/ department/PeaceStudies/njw.disclaim.html.

Part Five

EDUCATION WITH REPRESENTATION
Union Organizing on the Campus, Incorporated

21

TAKE BACK THE UNIVERSITY
Only Unions Can Save Academic Life

Henry Steck and Michael Zweig

*L*est there be any doubt, the authoritative word has come down from *Business Week*: "Higher education is changing profoundly, retreating from the ideals of liberal arts and the leading-edge research it always has cherished. Instead, it is behaving more like the $250 billion business it has become."[1] Nor is there any doubt that a buzzword of the new model university is "business." The president of Columbia Teachers College writes that "colleges and universities are not in the campus business but the education business."[2] William A. Wulf takes a step further when he writes that "universities are in the information business,"[3] as though there is no difference between higher education and Time-Warner. More bluntly, John V. Lombardi, president of the University of Florida, has declared, "We have taken the great leap forward and said: 'Let's pretend we're a corporation.' "[4]

But it's not "let's pretend" anymore. As university managers look to the future they are redefining the ideology and the operating code of the modern institution of postsecondary education. As our colleagues document elsewhere in this collection, for professors and higher education professionals,[5] it's a new world out there. Neoliberal talk is everywhere, markets are everywhere, corporate-style management strategies are everywhere.

The widespread introduction of corporate management practices into higher education has occurred in an era when capitalism has triumphed, both in Cold War competition and in relation to the labor movement in the United States, its raw power now entering the most precious institutions of democratic society. The dramatic changes in higher education policy and practice parallel the most striking shift of resources and power in the private economy since the Great Depression. The political shift from liberal to conservative dominance is a sign and consequence of the more fundamental shift of economic power from labor to capital over the last quarter-century.

At the same time that workers have experienced a steady decline in living standards,[6] teachers and other education professionals have been feeling the burden of corporate power in increasing workloads, proliferation of part-time and non-tenure-track employment, and, most important of all, challenge to independent scholarship and teaching. In the new entrepreneurial university, faculty are increasingly dependent on corporate support for research activity.[7]

A university for hire is no university at all. A university bought and paid for by business interests, or any other particular interests, necessarily loses in its faculty the autonomy of mind that critical thinking and creative work requires. In the entrepreneurial university, what happens to knowledge that is inconvenient to those with power and money? It cannot thrive.

Managing a university is an academic task, not a business task. What is scholarship? What deserves support? What is bogus? What is interesting or important to know? These are questions whose answers cannot be allowed to depend on market values and corporate sensibilities. People cannot do creative work looking over their shoulders for signals in the smiles or frowns of the rich and powerful.

The university has never been a pristine place. Thorsten Veblen described the power of business interests in academic life as early as 1918,[8] and the 1960s were marked by struggles against the multiversity and the military-academic complex. Our current concern is not based on nostalgia for some mythical past of ivory-tower seclusion. Our concern is to understand the contemporary shape of an age-old problem: how to protect basic academic values from power that seeks to subvert them.

We do not want to keep external or corporate funds off campus altogether, nor do we want to break all ties between universities and the business community. Rather, the problem lies in setting and enforcing terms of engagement between the academy and the larger corporate world. We have identified nine challenges to academic freedom arising from corporate funding that we believe require special vigilance.

We are concerned with challenges to:

- the integrity of research design and the place of peer review in corporate-funded research;
- the integrity of the content of undergraduate, graduate, and professional curricula;
- the integrity of academic work itself, arising from "unbundling," in which the preparation, presentation, and evaluation of courses are separated in a new division of labor that destroys the academic craft and subjects academic labor to central authority in the tradition of Frederick Taylor;
- university employment from outsourcing and overreliance on part-time faculty and staff;
- tenure criteria, especially the weight given to raising money as a condition of tenure;
- peer and public access to research findings, instead of their proprietary control;
- the neutrality of campus space through commercialization in public advertisements and deals for exclusive access;
- priorities for decisions about allocation of public monies among university departments and programs at state universities; and
- the language used to characterize academic life, in which the search for knowledge and critical thinking are subordinated to a new language of students as customers, or as investors out to get the maximum market return.

If we do not pass through this period of intense turbulence with a university independent of market forces, we will not have an institution that affords the peace of mind and physical resources needed for independent scholarly work of any kind. We face the challenges of capitalist power alongside workers and professionals throughout this country and abroad. We believe that rescuing the university from corporate domination and those who would pay for knowledge only as a private asset *must* come as part of the larger task of rescuing society in general from corporate domination. We therefore believe that faculty and other academic professionals must find ways to work with and contribute to a larger social movement, including a larger labor movement, whose goal is to muster sufficient force to put needed limits on capital. We believe that academic unions are a vital institutional component in this process.

Academics as a group have been slow to register the scope and source of changes to the university, often seeing them as the perversity, mediocrity, or stunted imagination of this or that provost or chancellor or this or that governor and his budget priorities. We have not always understood that improved government fiscal conditions will not mean an end to corpo-rate-style management because corporatization is designed to bring the faculty under control independent of finances. Why else would manage-ment gurus and their academic fellow travelers be so intent on eliminating tenure; reducing the prerogatives of faculty governance; displacing fac-ulty authority over curriculum; and interjecting market values, flexibility, and efficiency into the lexicon of academia?

There is no good reason to believe that these transformations in higher education are transitory adaptations to yesterday's fiscal crisis. The fiscal crises of the midseventies to midnineties may have been an opening to "restructuring," an excuse to subject higher education to scrutiny. But there is a deeper corporate agenda at work that will continue even as fiscal pressures subside. It is the agenda that has subjected ever-wider aspects of modern society to market logic and the specific needs of capitalists since the earliest days of capitalist development. As Marx and Engels observed over 150 years ago when describing the effects of capi-talists' revolutionary energy in society, "All that is solid melts into air, all that is holy is profaned."[9] Their insight is a reminder that the rapid pace of economic change dissolves, transforms, and reconfigures existing social institutions. The university is no exception.

Indeed, what is happening to academics parallels the pressures doc-tors face in managed care, leading them to unionize, even with the sup-port of the American Medical Association. These developments arise from the same corporate management attitudes that drove Boeing engi-neers to strike in early 2000, declaring on their banners "No Nerds, No Birds" and "No Brains, No Planes." Sociologist Craig Little recently summed up the situation well: "As the wealth and associated power of capital's owners expands, the relative power and authority of society's professionals are tending to decrease. Today's professionals are learning, just as industrial laborers learned more than 100 years ago, the only effec-tive counter to the power of capitalist expansion and domination is union organizing for collective bargaining."[10]

Amid the current changes, two vital traditional aspects of higher edu-cation are being torn away. First, corporate managers who would reduce faculty to employees seek to wreck the university as a community of scholars and center of critical study, self-directed by the norms of schol-arship and free inquiry. Second, higher tuition, reduced financial aid, and attacks on remediation all work to undermine the democratic opening of higher education to working people dating back to the establishment of land grant colleges with the Morrill Act in 1862.

These two changes are related. In the guise of greater access, our stu-dents are encouraged (in practical terms, forced) to borrow to pay higher tuitions and fees. On graduation, access to higher education turns into intense pressure to pay back the loans by finding high-paying jobs in a kind of debt peonage or forced indenture, to work on behalf of corporate interests upon graduation. As education has been conflated with earning power in the market, our students, their parents, and public officials have come to expect marketability from us instead of the capacity to think critically. We cannot leave it to the market and market-oriented leaders to organize an intellectually vibrant, scholarly college system.

Academic unionism is a natural vehicle to rescue our traditions as higher education goes through inevitable changes. We say it is natural, despite the reluctance of many faculty members to think of themselves as union members, because unions have been a tested and proven vehicle for faculty power with respect to their administrations and because the labor movement in general has a long history of support for democratic traditions and opening society to working people.

Unions are good for faculty in all the ways unions benefit any working person. In the new world, in which administration treats faculty increasingly as employees rather than colleagues, this is no small point. Through collective bargaining agreements, academic unions protect the terms and conditions of faculty employment, regulating such basic matters as pay, benefits, job security, and grievance procedures to deal with arbitrary treatment. Where academic professionals are unionized, they do better in these matters compared with similarly situated colleagues in nonunion settings. In recent years, the importance of unions for professional people has become increasingly evident, with doctors organizing against HMO management with the blessing of the American Medical Association, and lawyers and computer programmers also turning to collective bargaining for protection.

In addition to these commonly recognized benefits, unions are good for the university as an institution. As a matter of professional honor and self-defense, faculty must work to recover and restore a university that best serves the complex purposes of scholarship and humane learning. We want to instill the values of service and opportunity, values that strengthen democratic civil society. This is what we mean when we say "take back the university."

The problem is one of power as well as understanding. Administrators can no longer automatically be seen as members of the family. Individual managers, however humane or scholarly they are, often no longer act as "colleagues" according to the codes of "collegiality" that have long prevailed. Instead, they are becoming bosses. In this setting, we academics must engage questions of power as well as intellect. Our vision of academic unionism extends beyond the basic negotiation of collective bargaining agreements that protect faculty with respect to management. Effective academic unionism must also defend and advance the needs of the academic mission.

In terms of the size of their workforce, colleges and universities are part of a major American industry, well represented by a tight network of management organizations. The higher education establishment and its corporate allies cannot be expected to give unions featured space or attention when questions of higher education are discussed.[11] The leading academic journal, the *Chronicle of Higher Education*, for example, has a regular section titled "Money and Management" and "Faculty," but not "Faculty and Unions."[12]

Academic unions are not part of the national academic conversation, despite the fact that over 250,000 faculty and academic professionals in the United States belong to unions and are represented by collective bargaining agreements. Academic unions are a presence, however, despite the widespread belief that faculty will show no interest in unions. Academic unions have been most successful in the public arena, where the American Federation of Teachers (AFT), the National Education Association (NEA), and more recently the American Association of University Professors (AAUP) represent 80 percent of unionized faculty members, 96 percent of whom are in four-year and two-year public institutions. In 1995, only 11,000 members were in private institutions, a reflection both of the crushing impact of the *Yeshiva* decision[13] as well of the culture of higher education in the private, often elite sector.[14]

There is, however, an important caution in thinking about the success of academic unions in public colleges and universities. In 1996, collective bargaining agents represented faculty in thirty-two states (plus the District of Columbia and Guam), but nearly 50 percent of all unionized faculty were concentrated in just two states, California and New York. Ninety percent of unionized faculty are concentrated in ten states[15] and public four-year and two-year colleges are nearly equal (52 percent and 48 percent). Six of the "top ten," it is worth noting, are either in the Northeast (four) or Pacific Coast (two) and only one is in the South. All, except perhaps Florida, have been traditionally regarded as important industrial states with significant labor movements and with liberal and Democratic politics. Southern and Sun Belt states are notably not represented, while the Midwest and Prairie states show only scattered pockets of academic unionism.

UNIONS ARE GOOD FOR THE UNIVERSITY

Corporate values are not academic values. Entrepreneurial values are not the appropriate values for a learning community. A liberal education—that is, one that frees and enlarges the person and trains the mind —is different from training in job skills, and should be part of the experience of every person.

How, then, to take back the university from the forces of retrenchment, restructuring, reconfiguring, and management intrusion into the lives of faculty and academic professionals? We set out below four reasons why unions can play this role: (1) unions embody values that challenge corporate practices; (2) unions have a formal power to negotiate as equals with management; (3) unions speak on a national scale; (4) unions have leverage in the political arena.

UNIONS EMBODY VALUES

First, unions come from a tradition of struggle that embodies values of fairness, dignity, and democracy.[16] Just as in the 1930s, when the case for unions was cast in ethical terms as well as economic terms, so today academic unions can make both the material *and* the moral case. Academic unions can express core values in ways that speak to the need to empower faculty and professionals at the workplace, secure a measure of dignity (an especially important point for part-timers, for example), and assure simple fairness.

We believe these values correspond to what academics want. The most common cries we hear from our member colleagues when they have problems are, "They're treating me like dirt," "It's not fair what they're doing," "They won't listen to us," or "These guys are wrecking the place." Empowerment, dignity, fairness, community—these are the ethical and social values that unions must place along side the goals of good wages, job security, and benefits.

Academic freedom is one of the most important embodiments of college life. Whatever their rank or place, faculty understand full well that the defense of academic freedom, which all academic unions are committed to, is part and parcel of the defense of the idea, mission, and institution of the university.[17] The right of free and critical inquiry is central to the dignity and fair treatment of faculty; it is a cornerstone of democracy. Corporate values undermine academic freedom through the subjugation of the university to the bottom line, through attacks on tenure and through the privatization of knowledge. Unions are uniquely able to defend academic freedom, through collective bargaining agreements and with resources devoted to political and cultural campaigns that raise the issue before the general public.

Unions are positioned to speak for the *general* interest of the faculty and the academic community, in the way that corporatized managers no longer can, *and* for the *particular* interest of individual faculty members, professionals, or sectors within the academic community. The question of voice is crucial: there are numerous trade associations of top administrators (for example, American Council on Education), and management has the *Chronicle* to speak for the Establishment. Management has many voices, many outlets, and ample funding. What, by contrast, does the faculty have? Academic unions have the potential and the obligation to give voice to the faculty and to the vision of a university as a place of learning and knowledge, a potential so far barely effective in the wider world.

UNIONS HAVE FORMAL AUTHORITY

Second, unlike other forms of faculty organization—senates, departments, committees, or discipline-based academic associations—unions, where they are recognized as a bargaining agent, have legal authority to engage academic administrators on behalf of the faculty. More generally, academic unions have a legitimate voice in national discourse related to academic life. This double authority is essential even in the context of a generally cooperative relation between faculty and administration.

Based on our experience at SUNY, we can report that labor-management cooperation can be a key ingredient in strengthening the academic work of an institution. Labor-management cooperation can and does work in a number of key areas to win resources and carry out programs. But this can happen *only* when the faculty enters the process as a strong, independent force, not beholden to administration for its seat at the table. Because of their legal status, academic unions make this possible in ways that traditional governance structures cannot.

Due processes can diminish the nastiness that often accompanies difficult personnel decisions or discipline. Administrators are grateful beyond measure when unions lobby for better budgets with state legislatures. In new areas such as e-technology, unions and administrators have made strides in working together and in developing contractual relationships to protect academic values and the faculty. Academic unions are concerned with a range of issues—pedagogy, research, governance—that further the well-being of institutions. At times, of course, management is so ideologically intoxicated that it cannot see the value of unions in an institutional context; no doubt, our union sisters and brothers can also sometimes be unduly stubborn. Despite the stereotypes of clash and confrontation shared by many faculty and administrators, the pattern of labor-management relations is complex and nuanced. Much, of course, depends on the will and personality of individual leaders on both sides as well as particular institutional or political contexts.

An academic union belongs to the faculty and professionals themselves and not to trustees or presidents or rectors.[18] It stands on a foundation of public law (federal labor law, state public employee law), contractual arrangement, and the free choice of its members. In a formal sense it meets the claim of democracy and empowerment as an association of self-directing individuals. While faculty may recognize, respect, and respond to administrators as both colleagues and officials of an institution, the union as such is beyond the reach of administrators in a way that faculty senates, departments, programs, and centers typically are not. Senates tap the tradition of shared governance, but shared governance involves the sharing of power; the trouble is that when unequals share, the result on key issues reflects this disparity.

This is not to disparage faculty senates or to suggest that shared governance is of no value. It is or can be particularly valuable on issues related to immediate academic concern or even to the broad stewardship of an institution. Unions and senates can play complementary and mutually supportive roles, as we have shown at SUNY, where the United University Professions (UUP) and SUNY Senate worked together to effectively challenge the board of trustees when they sought to impose curriculum reform on the faculty and students. Table 1 compares the roles of academic unions and traditional governance bodies.

Management would not be so filled with complaints about faculty governance if it were not an effective expression of faculty judgment. This is why there is a strong belief in contemporary higher education administration circles that boards of trustees should have their authority strengthened vis-à-vis faculty governance. The Association of Governing Boards of Universities and Colleges now calls for the expansion of the circle of "stakeholders"—the latest buzzword in administration circles. The faculty is denigrated by being seen as just another "stakeholder," along with nonacademic staff, "non-tenure-eligible, part-time, and adjunct faculty" (as if exploited contingent faculty—already underpaid and overworked—were not truly "faculty" members).[19] And on the assumption that trustees can define the parameters of governance, the Association of Governing Boards takes dead aim on unions by urging consideration of a "formal policy regarding the role of union officials in institutional governance," including "limitations [that] the existence of a bargaining agreement may

TABLE 1: COMPARISON OF ACADEMIC UNIONS
AND FACULTY SENATES

Unions	Senates
Autonomy defined by state or federal labor laws and by negotiation contract.	Contingent and dependent autonomy; bounded by trustees and institutional rules.
Relations with management defined by contract, campus support, and relative political position.	Relations with management defined by tradition of governance (e.g., shared), by level of faculty support, by management deference.
Culture and tradition: equality between members (faculty) and between faculty (union) and administrators	Culture and tradition: deference within a hierarchical structure and culture of collegiality, civility, comity
Core self-image: union represents the faculty; willing to challenge administration	Core self-image: senate represents faculty and is willing to challenge administration
Traditions: accepts conflict as normal; poses differences of interest within academic and labor-management framework	Traditions: views conflicts (as distinct from "differences of opinion") as destructive; sees differences within academic framework
Issue area: labor-management relations and terms and conditions of employment, broadly defined	Issue area: academic issues and issues of governance
External relations: can draw (generally) on external political, financial, legal, organizational support and can reach out to form alliances with noncampus groups	External relations: does not generally reach out to form alliance with noncampus groups
Consistent presence in political arena (e.g., state legislature)	In political arena: variable by institution and tradition
Resources: member dues; support from state and national affiliates; paid staff; organizational expertise; access to internal media (e.g., union newsletters, newspapers, etc.)	Resources: from members and from administration in some cases

place on participation in governance by union officials."[20] Truly, it seems, a specter is haunting governing boards, the specter of unionization.

Unions have resources that senates do not. As Table 1 shows, unions can often do what senates cannot. Unions have the organizational and legal clout and the external independence to be the check and balance against management. Unions have the right and the duty to project themselves into decision making when terms and conditions of employment are considered; and what could more directly affect terms and conditions of employment than sweeping policies of restructuring, mission change, program termination, and so forth?

But this leverage points to a challenge unions face if they are to exercise the advantages they have. They must stop merely reacting to what is happening around them and they must go beyond negotiations over terms and conditions of employment to shape the broad agenda of academic decision making across the country.

Whether one speaks of the AFT and its locals, of the NEA and its campus organizations, or of the AAUP, unions are organized, are continuous, and command financial resources. They can draw on professional expertise to do their work, and, above all, have a legal and moral duty to fairly represent their members. Unions are on the other end of the 911 call; they are the academic hot line. Unions, and only unions, are on the job twenty-four hours a day, 365 days a year to defend and advance the interests of their members and the interests of academe itself. Even where a particular campus local or chapter may be weak, it can turn to its national affiliates.

UNIONS OPERATE ON A NATIONAL SCALE

Third, unions have the potential to provide faculty with a voice in the national discourse over higher education. As we write, our desks are covered with reports from this, that, and the other academic association: the American Council on Education, the Council for Aid to Education, the American Association of State Colleges and Universities, the National Association of College and University Business Officers, the American Association of State Colleges, the American Association of Community Colleges, the Association of Governing Boards of Universities and Colleges, the Pew Charitable Trust, the American Association of Higher Education, the Carnegie Foundation for the Advancement of Teaching, the Business–Higher Education Forum, WICHE, and more. There is a rich network of higher education trade associations that dominate the agenda and it is clear that they set the terms of national discourse. To take one example: the New Pathways working paper series (fourteen papers in all) of the American Association of Higher Education clearly delineates the emerging consensus. By reading the titles we can get an idea of what is in store. Just note the following seven titles: *Tenure Snapshot, Campuses Without Tenure, Uncoupling Academic Freedom and Academic Tenure, Innovative Modifications of Traditional Tenure Systems, Practices in Other Professions, Post-Tenure Review, Voluntary Incentive to Forego Tenure.* Administrators have rich—in both senses of the term—access to publishing outlets. The recent volume, *Strategy & Finance in Higher Education: Surviving the '90s*, published by Peterson's Guides and edited by directors of the Stanford Forum for Higher Education Issues, contains no article by a unionist or even by a faculty scholar who writes on this subject, as if faculty and professionals have no interest in "surviving the '90s."[21]

A complex network of overlapping administrative elites, tied to multiple constituencies and interests, dominates the American higher education community. The world of academic managers is peopled with overlapping circles of influence that provide tight linkage of people, publications, listservs, and the like. New ideas travel fast in these circles: Mention "post-tenure review" or "academic accountability performance measures" at Harvard and within the month the words will be heard in Kansas and Georgia. Academic unions are not in the loop.

While these networks and groups do serve higher education policy in important ways and while their reports, testimony before Congress, and public pronouncements often serve laudable goals, they also set the institutional agenda. But the fact is, labor is rarely part of the agenda-setting network while major national corporate policy institutions are.[22] They have channels to the media. When the press calls, when Congress calls, when the PBS *Newshour* calls, it is rarely if ever that academe is represented by a professor from a faculty union or faculty senate or, for that matter, by a student representing a student organization. Corporate representatives speak instead.

Here the major academic unions have a rich potential to provide a counternetwork, an alternative voice. The NEA and the AAUP dispense important and excellent publications—*Thought and Action, Almanac (NEA), and Academe* (AAUP)—which provide a base for influencing the national debates. We use the word "potential" because the unions have yet to find a breakthrough strategy to propel themselves onto the national stage in a fashion that provides an effective voice for faculty and for labor. Another tired PR campaign or position papers for a small group of academic readers will not do. The AFT, the NEA, and the AAUP have the capacity to reach out to progressive think tanks, public interest groups, and, if the effort is made, the general public. They can bring to center stage concerns about the quality of higher education, make the case for tenure, rebut the delegitimation of the university, address the problem of part-time academic labor, and seek to join with those concerned about college costs and access. In doing so, academic unions can bring the wider public to see these concerns as their own, not those of some "special interest" seeking to preserve perks and privileges.

Through its link with the AFL-CIO, the AFT has a special capacity to reach out to nonacademic unions. Under the new leadership of John

Sweeney, the AFL-CIO has taken a number of steps to reconnect labor with potential academic allies. Many areas of cooperation exist, from research to holding universities to fair labor practices as employers of many different kinds of workers, both directly and through contracting relationships. Part of this common agenda quite naturally involves the defense of higher education as a resource for working people, both through wide access and through the exercise of academic freedom in the pursuit of knowledge and critical thought.

In short, *academic unions have the capacity to address both the academic community and the general public on the basis of core values of the academy.* Because the major academic unions are national, they have the advantage of money, expertise, and solidarity that is not available to ordinary faculty senates scattered in hundreds of American colleges. Faculty and professional colleagues are disconnected one from the other, especially those in the vast number of nonelite private colleges and universities. The normal round of meetings—disciplinary associations, specialists' conferences—do not fully address issues of "the profession."[23] The reverse side of that famous individualism and craft "autonomy," so treasured by teachers and scholars, is "isolation." Managers have their national connections but faculty do not. The discourse of denigration that the academic profession has been subject to—unproductive, lazy, irrelevant research; no concern for teaching; coddled with tenure; overpaid; and so on—is something that unions have failed to answer effectively. Yet academic unions have the means to answer these claims by explaining the realities and promise of college life both to the academic community itself and to the general public.

UNIONS HAVE POLITICAL LEVERAGE

Fourth, academic unions have a degree of leverage vis-à-vis the political system. In New York State, the UUP's affiliate, the New York State United Teachers (NYSUT), representing over four hundred thousand unionized teachers, is a powerful political lobby. Thanks to the UUP and the NYSUT, SUNY has managed to fend off some of the worst efforts—supported by conservative trustees—to cut budgets, reduce access, raise tuition, cut student aid, and in general to dismantle the university. The UUP's lobbying efforts over the years put public higher education on the statewide political agenda and, with assiduous bipartisan lobbying, kept it there. When, for example, the SUNY board of trustees launched its well-advertised attack on a women's studies conference at SUNY New Paltz and demanded the syllabi and vitae of the faculty and the job of Roger Bowen, the college president—a president of uncommon courage, it should be said—UUP's efforts were decisive in the struggle that got key legislators to stand with the faculty in defense of academic freedom. Elsewhere the story is similar. In California, to take one example, the California Federation of Teachers secured passage of legislation in the assembly that would provide "equal pay for equal work," paid office hours, paid health insurance, and seniority rights for part-time community college faculty.[24]

Meanwhile, of course, legislatures have placed devastating demands on public universities.[25] There is no doubt that faculty need to be forcefully represented in the political process, to explain the mission of the university and the reality of academic work, and to win legislators and the broader public to the defense of higher education. Politics is treacherous territory, but unions, under the democratic control of their members, are an essential institution for working people, faculty included, in the political arena. Rescuing the university from the grip of market forces is a social priority, not a special interest. Academic unions are uniquely able to bring to the wider public the issues and the stakes.

SOME PRACTICAL STEPS

Before presenting some specific proposals for an action agenda, we turn to the general circumstances in which union organizing on campus will unfold at the start of the twenty-first century. Many academics considering union activity think that the *Yeshiva* decision means that faculty in private colleges and universities cannot organize unions. But this is not true. When the U.S. Supreme Court agreed with Yeshiva University management that the faculty there were also management because the faculty had influence over hiring, tenure, nonrenewal of contracts, and curricular matters,[26] the result was *not* that the faculty could not organize. Rather, the decision meant that the faculty did not have the protection of the National Labor Relations Act (NLRA), which requires management in the private sector to recognize unions voted for by their employees and then to bargain in good faith to reach a collective bargaining agreement.[20]

Nothing in *Yeshiva* says that faculty cannot organize. Losing the protection of the NLRA was a serious blow that should be repeatedly tested, not taken for granted. The first practical consideration, then, is that faculty have every right to organize unions and to apply collective pressure on management for relief against corporate practices in the university. If management resists the union, all the more reason to organize it, and all the more opportunity to do so as well. Nothing prevents academic unions from seeking their natural constituency in private colleges and universities to bring them into the battle in a multitude of ways other than direct collective bargaining.

Even if there is little prospect that management can be forced to recognize the union and bargain a contract, faculty organized through union activity can help to set a climate of activism on academic issues that can help change the balance of power in the longer run. In the same vein, academic unions need to speak for more than their own immediate membership. Through their activity among and on behalf of faculty in general, unions can have an impact even on campuses where no union will take root in the near future.

Organizing efforts should focus on junior faculty. The current generation of young faculty have little lived experience of unions, having grown up in a social environment where unions have been marginalized. That may now be changing; there may be a growing base of academics receptive to the message that a reinvigorated academic union movement can deliver. Graduate students, junior faculty, contingent faculty and professionals, medical students, and those struggling for tenure understand well the erosion of the profession, the bleak opportunities they face, the callous treatment of faculty by university CEOs, the low wages and limited job security, the barriers thrown up by the "get rid of tenure and hold their noses to the grindstone" crowd. Moreover, given the dynamic spread of organization by graduate students and adjunct contingent faculty—movements that must build and sustain themselves from the bottom up to win recognition—the new generation of scholars coming into academic life understands organization and struggle. All of this, taken in the context of a newly revitalized AFL-CIO, gives reason for optimism.

Scholars, Artists, and Writers for Social Justice (SAWSJ) is an organization of intellectuals, mostly campus based, that grew out of the 1996 labor teach-in at Columbia University. National labor leaders and labor-oriented intellectuals came together to explore the possibilities for cooperation after John Sweeney and his new leadership team were elected to guide the AFL-CIO. Faculty can do much to promote academic unionism besides trying to organize a union on their own campuses. In many places, that step must be prepared over time with other activity designed to bring the issues and possibilities to the attention of the academic community. The kind of labor scholarship and labor-oriented social activism SAWSJ (pronounced "sausage") facilitates can make important contributions while helping to create better conditions for academic unionism at the same time.

Meanwhile, the academic unions themselves—the AFT, NEA, and AAUP—must overhaul their strategies. Internally, they have tended to be top-down business unions rather than bottom-up mobilizers of their rank and file. Externally, academic unions have simply not been able to get the attention of a public that has for years been treated to a nonstop discourse of denigration of the academy.[27] Academic unions need to state the positive case. They need to project a vision and outlook that will inform the public and appeal to working peoples' aspirations for access to education.

On the political front, academic unions typically engage in the type of conventional electoral politics, which, in CUNY professor Nancy Romer's words, "relies on a combination of Democratic Party loyalty, back channel maneuvering, acceptance of political 'realities,' and an uninformed and demobilized membership; in short, business unionism."[28] An effective politics must also reach out to faculty, students, and communities, with a principled set of appeals that expands the base of popular support for universities.[29]

This is not a polar proposition: either principled mass movement *or* backroom politics. It is, rather, a matter of a nuanced sense of a struggle on two fronts: expanding active constituencies in defense of the university, its workers, and its students, *and* the conventional politics of interest and elections.

The entire labor movement is, of course, confronting these issues, as are community groups and student associations. As academics wrestle with the variety of issues that come up in unionization, we are in a position to form coalitions with others facing the same underlying social problem: capital triumphant. Working with other organizations, academics have the opportunity to participate in the two-way street of social mobilization. We can learn more about how society works, helping to develop understandings and organizational strength for the larger social movements in which we are necessarily embedded. And we can bring our situation and needs to the attention of other sections of society and win their support for our own particular battles.

In addition to these general observations, many examples of practical activity come to mind. If the AFL-CIO can move from Meany and Kirkland to Sweeney, academic unions can shift from Shanker to a new model of academic unionism. We present below in short form a number of ideas for action.[30] Some look outward to the academic community, the labor movement, and the general public; some look inward toward internal reform of academic unions to make them more democratically responsive and so more effective. All are meant to be implemented in the context of academic unionism that addresses both the particulars of terms and conditions of employment and the academic mission to which we are professionally committed.

- Unions should mobilize faculty and professional staff to organize union activity and promote conferences that bring the academic skills of the profession to bear on the problems we face in the academy and the larger society.[31]

- The AFT, NEA, and AAUP should jointly create and develop an imaginative, creative, intellectually credible think tank or policy institute; provide support and fully funded fellowships for working faculty to spend a year or a semester engaged in research, seminars, symposia; and provide a publication program similar to that of the AAHE, described above.
- Academic unions and labor-oriented academic groups should explore ties with the Labor Party to help build an independent labor politics.
- Academic unions and labor-oriented academic groups should be present at professional society meetings to provide information, organize, and help create a new climate among academics.
- Academic unions should reach out to medical, legal, and other professional union-organizing efforts for mutual support.
- Academic unions should develop a more aggressive strategy for becoming a presence in the media.
- Union leadership should encourage the empowerment of members, encourage democracy, and not fear dissent.[32] In the cyber age there are new modalities of democracy available and leaders must be willing to challenge both laws and old shibboleths, for example, that there cannot be expanded debate over contracts and all other elements of the union's agenda through union publications, Web sites, listservs, and so on.
- Unions should utilize to the fullest the new information technology both to distribute information and, more importantly, to facilitate open discussion. Unions should support this activity even for those campuses, private or public, where there is no "official," organized union presence. How else can academic unions penetrated the walls of the private schools and the public schools in what we call right-to-work states?
- Unions should reach out and work intellectually with graduate student unions; these militants and activists are, after all, the leaders of the next generation.
- Academic unions should support bottom-up and not just letterhead coalitions with other unions, citizens groups, and advocacy groups.
- Academic unions should find ways to meet and dialogue extensively and intensively with campus administration leaders from the other side. At a time when labor-management cooperation over common concerns is so widely stressed, there is no reason why the AFT-NEA-AAUP should not host conferences for faculty unionists, nonunion faculty, and management.

- Academic unions should develop programs that create a presence on private campuses, even in the face of *Yeshiva*.
- Faculty and professionals have billions of pension dollars invested with TIAA-CREF, Aetna, and other funds. Academic unions should be part of the wider national movement to use pension holdings as leverage for socially responsible corporate behavior.

CONCLUSION

We in higher education are not just experiencing a rightward shift in politics. We are suffering from labor's weakness and the associated increased strength of capital, which has brought the country into an unbridled quest for private money and power, the public (and public servants) be damned. This means that the future of higher education is tied to the future of labor as an organized force in society. Academics have every interest in helping to redefine the labor movement and recreate and strengthen unions as a vital, democratically controlled force.

Academic unionism can contribute to reclaiming the university in many ways. First, our unions can defend our institutions and our faculty through collective bargaining and in the political process. Second, we can safeguard the university as a place for strong individual scholarship in the context of a creative atmosphere of debate secured with academic freedom. Further, through academic unions we can support other unions and the broader social labor movement that will be needed to create a new climate in the country. Finally, a strong union presence among academics can contribute to labor scholarship in the research, writing, and teaching we do. The university, whatever its problems and faults, is a core institution of civil society. Reclaiming it for our students, our profession, and our society is an urgent task worthy of our every effort.

NOTES

1. "The New U: A Tough Market Is Reshaping Colleges," *Business Week*, December 22, 1997.
2. "The Soul of a New University," *New York Times*, March 13, 2000.
3. William A. Wulf, "Warning: Information Technology Will Transform the University," *Issues in Science and Technology* 11, no. 3 (summer 1995): 46.
4. "The New U."
5. A note on linguistic usage in this paper. For convenience and from custom, we will use the terms "faculty" or "professors" or "professorate." But we understand—and importantly so—those terms to refer to more than classroom

teachers or researchers and scholars in research universities. We also include the ranks of what, in our own union, we term professionals. These are the nonclass-room professionals who provide not simply support but also direct services to the mission of any postsecondary institution: financial aid, counseling, career coun-seling, residence hall professionals, art gallery directors, computer personnel, admissions staff, administrators who are not "managers," directors of various programs (e.g., multicultural and diversity programs), laboratory workers, non-physician health-care workers in medical schools and teaching hospitals, student union personnel, etc. Under New York's public employee relations law (the Taylor Act), faculty and professionals constitute the bargaining unit.

6. See, for example, Michael Zweig, *The Working Class Majority: America's Best Kept Secret* (Ithaca: Cornell University/ILR Press, 2000), chap. 3.

7. See, for example, Eyal Press and Jennifer Washburn, "The Kept Uni-versity," *Atlantic Monthly* (March 2000): 39–54. It is typical of the dominant approach to the subject among faculty concerned with the growing influence of corporations on campus that this important, well-received, and broadly noted article makes no reference to academic unionism.

8. Thorsten Veblen, *The Higher Learning in America* (1918; reprint, New York: Hill and Wang, 1957).

9. Karl Marx and Frederick Engels, *The Communist Manifesto* (1848), in *The Marx-Engels Reader*, 2d ed., ed. Robert C. Tucker (New York: W. W. Norton, 1978), p. 476.

10. Craig Little, private communication to authors, September 16, 1999.

11. There is an illustrative anecdote here. At the June 16, 1999, meeting of several subcommittees of the SUNY board of trustees (Academic Standards and General Education Subcommittees), Karen Arenson of the *New York Times* was present. She was introduced to the Academic Standards Subcommittee by Trustee Candace DeRussy as "an ex officio trustee" and by Provost Peter Salins as someone "we think of as the sixteenth trustee." When materials were distrib-uted at this open meeting, copies were given to Ms. Arenson, but not to a member of the public from United University Professions, the union representing SUNY faculty, in possible violation of New York's open government laws. At this same meeting, Provost Salins provided a report on his plan to require all SUNY syllabi to be placed on the World Wide Web or the Internet in a standardized format. When asked about the purpose of this policy, Salins replied that it would benefit students and "allow the provost to see what's happening around the university." Six months earlier, without full consultation with the faculty and in violation of their own policies, the trustees had mandated a university-wide core curriculum for SUNY, the action that precipitated votes of "no confidence" from the senates of nearly all of the thirty SUNY units and a joint vote of "no confidence" by the University Senate and United University Professions, the first action against con-servative "activist trustees" in the nation. Tom Kriger, UUP Research Depart-ment Memorandum (shared with authors), "Summary of Trustees Subcommittee Meetings, June 17, 1999," June 18, 1999. See also "SUNY Faculty Groups Lack Faith in Board," *Chronicle of Higher Education*, May 14, 1999.

12. It is worth noting that in the section on "faculty and staff" in its annual "Almanac" the *Chronicle* does not provide data about academic unions, e.g., number of faculty represented by bargaining agents, number of campuses with recognized bargaining agents, etc.

13. *NLRB* v. *Yeshiva University*, 444 U.S. 672 (1980). In this case, the Supreme Court held that faculty at Yeshiva University were not protected by federal labor law in their attempts to organize a union because they were essentially management. Since that time, faculty unionization at private institutions has been limited to a small number of places where the administration has raised no objection to union recognition if the faculty vote for it.

14. These figures are rough. For total faculty numbers, "Almanac," *Chronicle of Higher Education*, August 28, 1998. For data on faculty represented by unions, see Richard Hurd, Amy Foerster, and Beth Hillman Johnson, *Directory of Faculty Contracts and Bargaining Agents in Institutions of Higher Education* (National Center for the Study of Collective Bargaining in Higher Education and the Professions) 23 (January 1997).

15. California (67,223), New York (55,020), Wisconsin (29,637), Pennsylvania (11,329), Minnesota (11,017), New Jersey (10,731), Michigan (10,530), Washington (10,308), Florida (10,162), and Massachusetts (9,563) for a total of 225,520. See Hurd, Foerster, and Johnson, *Directory of Faculty Contracts*.

16. See Zweig, *The Working Class Majority*, chaps. 5 and 6.

17. It is worth noting that the defense of tenure rests on the proposition that tenure is a necessary institutional mechanism for assuring academic freedom. The new thinkers in the higher circles of administration are currently wont to argue that academic freedom can be defended by the First Amendment and that tenure is not necessary for this. Richard Chait, for example, argues that we should "decouple academic freedom and academic tenure." See "Academic Tenure: Between All or Nothing" in *Proceedings. Twenty-fifth Annual Conference of the National Center for the Study of College Bargaining in Higher Education and the Professions*, Baruch College, CUNY. April 1997.

18. A serious and important problem is this: For many good unionists the phrase "an academic union belongs to the faculty and professionals themselves" does not ring true. Given the prevalence of business unionism and of the service model and given the entrenched position of a number of union leaders, the point is made—one of the oldest issues in unionism—that the union has been captured by leaders and that ordinary members are disempowered. The struggle for union democracy is an old union struggle, and not just in the Teamsters. Given the scope of this article, we can only note the importance of this issue without delving into the complex topic of union democracy. The literature of political sociology provides ample discussion on the sources of nondemocratic tendencies in unions. In his classic work, *Political Parties* (1910), Roberto Michels formulated the "iron law of oligarchy" that holds that democracy is impossible in organizations like unions. On the resistance of AFL-CIO leaders to the change in the Sweeney era, see Arthur B. Shostak, "On the Revitalization of the U.S. Labor Movement: Can 21st Century Cyberunions be Created in Time? Or Will

Cyberunions Compute?" *Proceedings. Twenty-fifth Annual Conference of the National Center for the Study of College Bargaining in Higher Education and the Professions*, p. 22.

19. Association of Governing Boards of Universities and Colleges, "Statement on Institutional Governance" [online], http://www.agb.org [November 8, 1998]. For a critique, see Cary Nelson, "War Against the Faculty," *Chronicle of Higher Education*, April 16, 1999, pp. B4–B5.

20. Ibid.

21. William F. Massy and Joel W. Meyerson, eds., *Strategy and Finance in Higher Education: Surviving the '90s* (Princeton, N.J.: Peterson's Guides, 1992).

22. For more detailed analysis, see Barbara Ann Scott, *Crisis Management in American Higher Education* (New York: Praeger, 1983); and Sheila Slaughter, *The Higher Learning and High Technology* (Albany: State University of New York Press, 1990).

23. This may be changing. Disciplinary associations do have committees and commissions to address professional and pedagogical issues and the report on part-timers by eight disciplinary associations represented a major intervention on the policy discussion on the part-time issue.

24. California Federation of Teachers, "Educators Applaud Passage of Equity for Part-Time Professors," press release, *News from the CFT*, June 3, 1999.

25. See, for example, Peter Schmidt, "A State Transforms Colleges with 'Performance Funding,'" *Chronicle of Higher Education*, July 2, 1999, p. A26.

26. *NLRB* v. *Yeshiva University* has been adjusted somewhat in recent rulings that have granted legal protection to faculty union efforts at some private institutions. See Donna R. Euben, Associate Counsel, AAUP, "Annual Legal Update," prepared for the Twenty-eighth Annual Conference of the Baruch College (CUNY) Center for the Study of Collective Bargaining in Higher Education, March 20, 2000.

27. For an example, see the discussion of the attack on tenure, what Finkin sees as "a massive assault . . . a veritable mugging." Matthew W. Finkin, "The Assault on Faculty Independence," in *Proceedings. Twenty-fifth Annual Conference of the National Center for the Study of College Bargaining in Higher Education and the Professions*, p. 50.

28. Nancy Romer, "The CUNY Struggle: Class and Race in Higher Education," *New Politics* (winter 1999): 47–56.

29. For a model of community organizing and community politics sparked by a faculty union group (The New Caucus, a caucus within PSC at the City University of New York), see Romer, "The CUNY Struggle," pp. 55–56. On California, see the article by Jeff Lustig in this volume.

30. The interesting discussion by Shostak, "On the Revitalization of the U.S. Labor Movement," has been helpful here.

31. The experience of the authors is illustrative. For several years they have been pleased to have been invited participants to the AFT's annual higher education conference. These are usually well-organized and intelligently planned,

with excellent outside speakers who raise the level of discourse significantly. The problem is that there is no follow-through. The final sound and impact is that of one hand clapping.

32. See Romer, "The CUNY Struggle," pp. 50–51 for an account of the almost pathological anxiety of some leaders toward opposition perspectives. Granted that Romer herself is a leader in an insurgent caucus and therefore a less than disinterested observer, but her account rings true as one observes the techniques of leadership domination to be found in the AFT. Cooperation between the three unions—the AFT and its locals, the NEA, and the AAUP—should provide openings for new internal structures. The sense of union democracy that underlies this article is, roughly, based on two propositions: (1) that a democratic union is characterized by an "effective" electoral and "party" or "caucus" system that gives members de facto secret ballot choice between competing candidates and groups; (2) a culture, with supporting and encouraging mechanisms, of open discussion, empowerment of members at all levels.

22

PERILS OF THE KNOWLEDGE INDUSTRY
How a Faculty Union Blocked an Unfriendly Takeover

Jeff Lustig

It is a testament to the continuing promise of a university education that despite long-running charges of its impracticality and widespread questions about its purpose, Americans still eagerly send their children off to college each fall, and their tax dollars each spring. The institution's honor has often been tainted by special interests, its departments swamped by passing fads, its budgets bled by stingy legislatures, but still the ideal remains. This dissonance between ideal and reality will soon disappear, however, if current reorganizers have their way—not because the compromises will cease but because the ideal will be altered beyond recognition. The question those reformers raise now is not just about the right "uses" of the university, to recur to Clark Kerr's famous title,[1] but about what the university itself will be.

The essays in this book trace different routes to the corporatization of the American university, a transformation proceeding by both conscious intent and by inadvertence, by design and by default. If it runs its course universities will be turned into higher-education equivalents of HMOs, with deprofessionalized faculties, abandoned chambers of self-governance, and standardized student prescriptions. Universities will be separated from their public mandates just as corporations were severed from their chartered origins a century ago. That fate, however, is not inevitable. It can be fought. And it was fought with a great deal of success by California State University (CSU) faculty in their contract struggle of 1998–1999. I want to trace here the main routes of corporatization as charted by the CSU, a lead institution in the national effort, then summarize the course of the contract dispute and explain why faculty unions are emerging as the best check against the threatened takeover of higher education. Lessons from this struggle are applicable in other universities and, in light of events like the American Medical Association's recent decision to unionize, other professions as well.[2]

THE UNIVERSITY BESIEGED

That business interests play an inordinate role in the life of American universities has been known since the time of Thorstein Veblen and Upton Sinclair. Chairs have been endowed, institutes founded, and professors feted to serve the interests of wealthy industrialists. Private foundations have played a role too, helping shape the modern university and, at mid-century, drafting resources they had previously nurtured for the often covert business of area studies and foreign policy.[3]

Business leaders and higher-education policy makers today are moving beyond random raids and annexations to assault the very nature of the institution. They threaten to turn it into something that first became visible in Kerr's *Uses of the University*. Commentators had already noted the mushroomlike ascendance of campus administrations—of whose growth Kerr was chief prophet and ornament. UC's President Kerr explained the academy's managerial revolution as an expression of the larger transformation of the old community of scholars and semiautonomous faculties into the modern "knowledge industry." New forms of federal contract research and corporate funding were giving birth to large, bureaucratized facilities for knowledge "production and distribution."

Kerr admitted some downsides to all this. The authority of teachers would be eclipsed in the knowledge industry by administrators and academic "entrepreneurs." "Power [would] move from inside to outside the original community of masters and students," he predicted, to the administration and "leadership groups in the society," though he denied that this would invite "control in any deleterious sense." (He failed to see the high costs already being incurred by academic obeisance to those leadership groups with such things as the Vietnam War and nuclear development.)[4] The faculty, he continued, would "shift their identification and loyalty" to new funding sources and become "tenants rather than owners" of the new university. He could have added as a lesson from American industrial history that the grant of greater powers to the managers would also mean the expropriation of initiative and judgment from those who actually do the work, and increasing control and supervision of people who had expected intellectual autonomy.

With a clever expository sleight-of-hand, Kerr presented this process as the depoliticized workings of an irresistible history. Though the product of that process might be utilitarian in its purposes, insatiable in its fiscal appetites, and promiscuous in its alliances, he wound up approving of it because it was, above all, "productive."[5]

ANATOMY OF A MAKEOVER

Faculty on the twenty-two campuses of California State University have seen what Kerr predicted coming to pass over the last decade. The effects of long-term trends have been accentuated by a dysfunctional "merit"-pay plan, a high-tech information technology partnership (CETI, discussed in another essay in this book), a redesign for instructional methods according to the dictates of "outcomes assessments," and a belligerent, private-industry approach to collective bargaining. Taken together these initiatives reveal the presence of a new, stealth Master Plan for California higher education, a plan as troubling in its delivery as it is in its content. Each of its components was announced peremptorily from above by system managers, lacking public input, legislative mandate, or even documented necessity.[6]

The cunning of history actually delivered none other than Barry Munitz, Clark Kerr's former protégé, to launch these changes. Munitz, fresh from the MAXXAM takeover of Pacific Lumber (he was MAXXAM's vice president) and a looted Texas S & L (costing taxpayers $1.6 billion) was Kerr, however, with blinders removed. Where the UC president had envisioned a "postindustrial society," CSU's raider-cum-chancellor frankly appealed for business leadership. Where the former still honored college decorum, the latter tried to manufacture elite status by force of salary accretion. (The president at my campus, CSU, Sacramento, saw his salary jump a phenomenal $73,000; in the same three years mine rose $2,500 and lecturers' inched up $300). And where the former still sought to debate his ideas with colleagues, Munitz candidly turned to manipulation, calling for "leverage and constraint mechanisms . . . to effect change and improve client orientation in response to consumer and patron expectations."[7]

The CSU experience reveals three main roads by which the process of corporatization is proceeding: an instrumental, a structural, and a functional. The first, instrumental route is an extension of the old practice of raid and annexation. Businesses and cooperative university CEOs propose forms of contract research that go beyond anything Kerr imagined and will reduce many faculty into fee-for-service providers of "customized" outputs. CSU's notorious Cornerstones plan proposed farming students out to local businesses for credit. The CETI plan proposed to turn over students and faculty as captive markets to the high-tech consortium in a pattern David Noble found replicated by agreements struck by UCLA, UC Berkeley, USC, and the University of Colorado.[8]

Business *values* also penetrate the campus as never before. Campus managers eagerly take up neologisms from the "reinventing the corporation" literature along with its underlying view that administrative entrepreneurship, consumerism, and short-term productivity are the apotheoses of organizational values.[9] Students become "customers" (for current chancellor Charles Reed); teaching is regarded as an "Influence over Product" (former chancellor Munitz); and graduating seniors are invited back to realize the "value-added" potential of graduate work.[10]

Lest anyone doubt the ultimate potential of what Kerr called the movement of "power from inside the original community of masters and students" to administrators and "leadership groups in the society," the Kafkaesque tale of one gifted researcher is instructive. The event took place at the University of South Florida (USF) on Charles Reed's watch, before he came to the CSU. Petr Taborsky, the researcher in question, was a USF student who had worked on a project funded by a grant from the Florida Progress Corporation, and continued to wrestle with the problem identified by the project on his own time after the grant ran out. Taborsky eventually discovered a solution to the problem and, refusing to hand it over to the corporation and university as requested, applied for and received his own patent. He had not signed an agreement requiring him to do otherwise.

The university was not impressed and decided to prosecute. Reed, a paid member of the Board of Directors of the Florida Progress Corporation at the time, favored its interests more than those of his student to such an extent that he authorized an expensive prosecution of Taborsky on two felony charges. His concerns were not merely admonitory. The university pursued the case zealously and the lone researcher was eventually convicted on both counts. Taborsky was sentenced to a three-and-a-half-year prison term, the first months of which were actually spent on a chain gang—a scientist in leg irons providing a cautionary warning to anyone foolish enough to think about bucking the external service agreements of the Brave New University.[11]

The partnership between higher education and business is thus a fateful one, and the men and women promoting it are dead serious. Some have explained their zeal as a simple response to state budget cutbacks. But fiscal austerity is only a pretext for an agenda that was developed elsewhere, for other purposes, and would shift the strategy of instrumental usage from occasional ploy to permanent relationship.

Businessmen have always complained, as magnate Joseph Wharton put it a century ago, that

> college life offers great temptations and opportunities for the formation
> of superficial lightweight characters, having shallow accomplishments
> but lacking in grip and hold upon real things. . . . [12]

Now a new agenda is spelled out starkly in a volume written by two IBM employees, appropriately if infelicitously titled *What Business Wants From Higher Education.*[13]

The book updates Wharton's vintage charge and proceeds to recast the university as society's mechanism for escaping such lightweight characters and training more down-to-earth members of its labor force. It also recasts the university as a business best judged by standards of productivity and efficiency. This agenda seeks to socialize major job-training costs of the knowledge-based industries, though not, of course, their profits. The authors of *What Business Wants* see diploma mills like Phoenix and National Universities as pointing the way and challenging them to quicken the pace and cheapen the product of a university career.

CSU leaders have embraced this program. (Munitz is the last person quoted in the book, while his old CSU assistant, Molly Broad, authored the preface.) They claim that despite the prospect of burgeoning enrollment they will maintain "access." Even if the claim were true (which is doubtful), it is a matter of bitter irony that just when many members of California's working-class and minority families for the first time gain entry to higher education, the quality of that to which they are gaining "access" will be degraded by this agenda and a real university education again put beyond reach.

THIS WAY TO THE KNOWLEDGE FACTORY

In order to attain these objectives, top administrators at CSU and elsewhere are, secondly, attempting a structural transformation of the university. They are impatient with the ability of academic senates and maverick departments to block their initiatives and constrain the flexibility demanded by business partners. They want lines of command to be simplified and strengthened. The new Captains of Erudition (Veblen's term) therefore are trying to graft corporate organizational methods onto an institution that had always been distinguished by procedures for shared governance. The university is not only to be subjected to but modeled after the corporation. Joanna Scott has noted how

> [a] wide variety of campuses . . . are experiencing the gradual displacement of regular faculty governance in favor of a hierarchical, corporate decision-making structure. . . . Faculty governance through traditional, selected councils takes second place to a parallel track of [informal] "task forces" and "ad hoc committees" as values are shifted from academic freedom . . . to cultivating academic "consumers" and cost savings.[14]

Most recent university initiatives seek, beyond their stated objectives, to shift power and control on the campuses. The so-called merit-pay plans, beyond rewarding merit, transfer power from peers to administrators over key aspects of professional advancement, conferring it on people with little knowledge of what faculty members do in their disciplines and classrooms. This grant of powers, along with fantastic salary raises, are intended to transform people who had been essentially functionaries and expediters of operations into CEOs—bosses with authority over teaching and research. Munitz sought a new "structure of incentives." Merit pay provides the answer. No matter that the studies show that this kind of merit pay will not work for its stated objectives. It *will* augment presidential powers for patronage and cronyism, undermine academic freedom for dissidents and tenured Taborskys, and subvert traditions of collegiality by pitting faculty against each other for scarce dollars and status.

At CSU, Chancellor Reed tried to secure campus presidents new powers by denying faculty rights to appeal their merit awards. This effort to dispose of due process might seem to clash with his stated objective of increasing accountability.[15] But if it was mysterious in its logic it was nevertheless clear in its lineage. The idea harks directly back to the old Taylorite scientific-management assumption that employees need to be disciplined and controlled, and decision-making power concentrated in the hands of management.[16] Accountability only applies to those below. Those who accept these assumptions today seek consciously or unconsciously to move faculty from the center of the university to its periphery —from a key role in its governance to the status of one "stakeholder" among many, a petitioner invited to submit periodic claims to administrators who themselves will make the decisions.[17]

The outcomes assessments and "demonstrated learning" approach, announced in the Cornerstones Report, also fits in with this restructuring effort. Such assessments will also work to strengthen top-down controls. The complaint about them is not only that they will dumb down course work as students are "taught to the test"; not only that they are defective means for appraising educational results. The deeper objection is that they will lead to the eventual control by those who do the testing of that which is being tested. That, too, is a lesson of American industry.

The call to increase productivity by means of outcomes assessments masks an unacknowledged strategy to narrow "productivity" to that which is susceptible to quantitative and immediate measurement. Subjects that can be tested in this way will flourish (such as business and engineering); those that cannot will founder (for example, English, history, and ethnic studies). This is the epistemological cost of the restructuring. The forms of knowledge and ways of thinking represented on campus are to be restricted, because the tests will drive future funding allocations. The real significance for comprehensive universities is summarized succinctly by Molly Broad:

> [H]igher education must stand ready to measure institutional performance in terms of the demonstrated learning of our students, particularly in the areas deemed relevant by prospective employers.[18]

It should be noted in passing that the emphasis on outcomes assessment accomplishes something of even greater importance. The assumption that increased testing produces better teaching serves to redirect attention from what goes on in the classroom to how it will be viewed externally. It shifts concern from students' and faculties' satisfaction with what they are doing to how they will be rewarded for doing it. This tacit shift of attention from the use-value to the exchange-value of learning is obviously functional in the prevailing political economy and will be useful to students in their careers. It constitutes an attempt, however, to deal with the destruction of proper teaching conditions by institutionalizing the loss and shifting faculty members' calculus of what counts. This transformation was forced painfully on other American occupations long ago, and is now being attempted with a broad array of professional workers beyond the university.

The restructuring of the university thus strikes at the role and rights of faculty in a number of ways. It reduces their place in governance and subjects them to system apparatchiks, as we saw at CSU. By redefining the purposes of higher education, it constrains the scope of their professional judgment and pedagogical authority. By viewing universities as businesses and making cost-cutting a priority, it reclassifies faculty as variable rather than fixed costs of enterprise—thus "liquefying" the faculty, in the unsettling argot of the accountants.[19] Faculty are reduced from being citizens of the institution to being simple factors of production. Efforts in this direction underlie their recent experiences of salary cuts, speed-ups, two-tier job structures (with burgeoning ranks of lecturers), and performance-pay plans, all of which serve to remind professors of class forces most had hoped to escape.

The third route to corporatization consists in efforts to make campuses direct sites of capital accumulation. This is an attempt to alter the *function* of the university and convert teaching and learning experiences into forms of profit-making activity. CSU's CETI epitomized this approach. Beyond promising expanded profits to high-tech firms from the sale of products, its deeper significance was that it would have prepared CSU campuses for the commodification of different aspects of teaching and learning. CETI was defeated, but numerous successors wait in the wings. There are profits to be wrung from the capitalization of higher education and from the breaking-up of the educational experience into discrete pieces (syllabi creation, course design, test preparation, and so on) to be marketed as commodities ("courseware," online classes, and the like.)

This route throws into bold relief a key point that Kerr missed. The emerging knowledge industry is not an expression of secular imperative toward "modernization," or largeness. The processes that created it were not neutral, and the finished product is not a neutered "postindustrial" institution. The product is a capitalist institution intent on accumulating profit and commodifying human relations—a "knowledge factory," as students called it in the sixties.[20] Capitalist corporations have steadily extended their influence since the end of World War II beyond the marketplace proper to medicine, entertainment, sports, and even prisons. The university is no exception. It offers one of the last available sites for the self-expansive energies of capital. Exploitation of this opportunity is a main engine of current corporatization.

A UNIVERSITY IS NOT A CORPORATION

Public opposition to the transformation of the university first surfaced in the sixties. Mario Savio's famous declaration of resistance during the free speech movement, which launched the sit-in in Kerr's administration building, in 1964 has been justly remembered. "There is a time," he declared, "when the operation of the machine becomes so odious, makes you so sick at heart, that you can't take part. . . . You've got to put your bodies on the gears. . . . " What is forgotten, however, is the exact operation he was talking about. In the sentences directly preceding this passage, he spoke of an emerging managerial "autocracy" and the growing use of corporate references, concluding with a request. He asked the thousands gathered in Sproul Plaza

to consider if this is a firm, and if the Board of Regents are the board of directors and if President Kerr is . . . the manager, then . . . the faculty are a bunch of employees, and we're the raw material! But we're a bunch of raw material[s] that don't . . . mean to be made into any product, don't mean to be bought by some clients of the university. . . .[21]

It was the prospect of being processed for use by external clients that made students who had come to Berkeley for an education "sick at heart." It was the knowledge factory in which they refused to take part. Thousands of educators throughout the nation supported their decision.

A student is not a commodity. A university is not a corporation. First, the job of the corporation is to produce commodities for profit. The job of the university is to teach men and women about particular professions and ranges of human experience to help them grow as people. It is to "liberate their initiative" and "fulfill [their] own best powers," Paul Goodman wrote, and also to teach them about "the ongoing activities and culture of society, so that [their] initiative can be relevant." It is to promote "the free pursuit of knowledge both for the public good and for its own sake." As a profit-making institution, the corporation is responsible to investors. But a university's responsibilities are multiple: to the public, to generations yet unborn, and to the goals and standards of the independent professions housed on its campuses. Kant held that scholars' "agreement" with the citizenry was to free the mind. If this is an investment at all (and the older idea was that it was a public endowment or trust), then it is a long-term investment whose payoff defies immediate assessment.[22]

It follows, secondly, that students are not customers. They don't buy degrees; they earn them. They are not the authorities on the disciplines they study, whereas the customer is always right. Customers generally know the usefulness of what they buy before they spend money on it. But most of the value of that to which students are exposed is incalculable at the time. The deepest distinction between the two identities, however, is perhaps still the ancient one noted by Socrates in the *Protagoras*: "You cannot buy knowledge and carry it away in another vessel," he explained. "When you have paid for it you must receive it into the soul and go on your way, either greatly harmed or greatly benefited."[23] What is acquired in higher education has a much more lasting effect and more deeply shapes a person's life than a packaged commodity.

It is also important to remember that customers and students reside in different ethical worlds. The corporation, driven by the need for profits, favors salesmanship, bluster, and impersonality, and is not averse to adulterations in product quality to make a buck. The rule is caveat emptor. But the ethic of the university, derived from its obligation to help people find "their own best powers," embraces care, personal trust, and candor about defects in either students' or professors' work. A university governed by the entrepreneurial spirit and devoted to extruding as many graduates as quickly and cheaply as possible would not be a corrupted university; it would be no university at all.

We saw, thirdly, that corporations and universities have different institutional forms.[24] Universities are distinctive social institutions because of the plurality of their governing structures and internal standards. History professors do not appraise performance like engineers, nor art departments like business schools. Universities are governed by a rich fabric of different standards to meet their different objectives, for the weaving of which faculty senates, unions, departments, and administrations have been created. The new order being sought by current reorganizers would dispense with all this and impose a narrow form fashioned for a more linear function.

If those reorganizers are successful, then the university, a living heir of an older corporate form, would be gutted of its internal complexity and rich external mandates, converted into a launching pad for academic entrepreneurs, and forced by the business corporation down the same narrowing path it blazed for itself a century ago.[25] Different areas of study currently nurture different kinds of cognition—aesthetic interpretation in literature, positivist precision in physics, empirical analysis and qualitative judgment in history and politics, imaginative vision in art. But the triumph of the corporate form would reduce all this to the narrow ways of thinking approved by campus managers.

Fourth, organizational fashions in business change every few years. It proliferates "panaceas du jour." Universities, by contrast, are heirs to long traditions of self-governance. They modify themselves only on the basis of long experience. "We have had the conservative responsibility," explains Professor Michael Clarke, "of preserving the truths worth keeping and at the same time the radical responsibility of continually subjecting those truths to the changing circumstances of modern life." "Faculty as the core of the university [also] have an obligation to the future," adds another CSU professor, "to teach students about that which is of long-term value."[26]

Assimilating the university to the new business fashions would work a profound reversal of its traditional and expected purposes. This is clear from *What Business Wants*. What seems at first only a restatement of Wharton's old lament about "superficial lightweight characters . . . lacking a hold upon real things," turns out to be a tract for our times. It is a primer for the era of mergers and acquisitions, when American production skills have declined and the helm has been grabbed away from Captains of Industry, like Wharton and Rockefeller, by "raiders," like Milken and Munitz.

Diana G. Oblinger and Anne-Lee Verville, the authors of *What Busi-*

ness Wants, frame their arguments in the larger picture of a global, knowledge-based economy that rewards "value added" rather than "volume produced." Because opportunities for value-adding activity move and shift rapidly in this highly organized world, they predict, current students will have to get ready to move. They will presumably hold an average of thirteen jobs in their lifetimes, spanning three to five careers.[27] It is no surprise, then, that the modern cure prescribed for superficial lightweight characters dispenses with the need for learning any specific subject matter (aside from information technology), and consists instead of learning formalistic skills like "communications," "problem solving," "teamwork," and the critical "flexibility." Graduates will need to keep their intellectual bags packed; no wonder they travel light. They follow in the wake of corporate raiders who have also dispensed with any training in the production techniques of the industries they capture, reorganize, and strip of assets. The way to "get a hold upon real things" in the current era, then, is precisely to lose a hold on real things. It's a long way from the older bourgeois desire for confident, autonomous solidity. In fact, in the new outlook, "[t]he autonomous culture of higher education may even work against developing these [marketable] skills." The prize now goes to "adaptability."[28]

This program entails the most wrenching reversal of the intended institutional dynamic. It proposes that students come to college not to find their own best powers but to be sorted and trained for others' needs (as Savio foresaw in 1964.) The university becomes a tool in the first instance not for education (e-ducing or drawing out potential), but for social engineering. The society supports universities not to gain a critical perspective on its activities and values, but to train youth to be uncritical servants of prevailing values.[29] These reversals capture perfectly the shift from classical to corporate liberalism. "In the past the man was first," Frederick Winslow Taylor announced. "In the future the system shall be first."[30]

To remake the university in the corporate image would thus exact a permanent toll on American universities. To accomplish this, however, the new bottom-line mandarins would have to destroy the arrangements that have defined higher education in America. Shared governance, collegiality, tenure, faculty unions, and intellectual property rights would all have to be tossed out for the university to be reinvented along the lines prescribed. Faculty would have to be demoted to the status of "resources to be managed" in order to be "directed and deployed" by others.[31] That's what the recent talk about remaking faculty culture is all about.

"A STRONG CONTRACT MEANS QUALITY EDUCATION"[32]

That's the effort that hit a snag in the contract dispute of 1998-1999. The bases for the dispute had been laid during the nineties as management introduced the initiatives described above. Negotiations for the new contract proved to be the flashpoint for resistance, reawakening a tradition of faculty activism in California that runs back to UC's loyalty oath controversy of 1950, San Francisco's anti-HUAC demonstrations of 1960, the Berkeley faculty's decisive support of free speech strikers in 1964, and the prolonged San Francisco State strike of 1968.

CSU faculty have since 1982 been represented by the California Faculty Association, affiliated with the National Education Association (NEA) and the California Teachers Association (CTA), the American Association of University Professors (AAUP), and also, via affiliation with the Services Employees International Union (SEIU) and California State Employee Association (CSEA), the AFL-CIO.[33] It faced a negotiating team ultimately led by Chancellor Reed, who had just arrived fresh from Florida State University praising three-to-five-year contracts in place of tenure, and announcing that despite CSU's heavy teaching loads, "everyone can do more." The problem for CSU faculty, of which the present author is a member, is that we were already doing more—for less. We were teaching eight courses a year—25 percent more than faculty at comparable universities—for 11 percent less in pay. We were also angered by scarce salary dollars going to a bogus merit-pay plan and by the fact half the CSU teaching load was now being carried by underpaid and poorly protected lecturers.

Negotiations got off to a rocky start when the Chancellor's Office demanded a doubling of merit pay (to 40 percent of new salary monies), a reduction of regular salary step increases, removal of workload limits, transfer of department chairs into management, and removal of certain lecturer protections. The talks deadlocked, stalemated, dragged through the expiration of the old contract on June 30, and gave way to impasse and mediation that ended unsuccessfully at the end of the year.

The union protested the chancellor's position in all the usual and a few not-so-usual ways. It held meetings, disseminated leaflets, encouraged letters to editors and circulated petitions. Together with well-organized students and angered legislators it was able to quash CETI.[34] It began to attract new campus leadership, drawing in many veterans of past higher education struggles. Members became more vocal. Effective full-page ads opening the conflict to public view were published in the western edition of the *New York Times*.

But this at first had little effect. The chancellor and trustees were playing a new game. Unions expect to participate in normal collective bargaining practices and are proud to have earned a seat at the table. Reed upset those expectations, changed the rules of the game, and tried to remove the seat. Faculty opinion counted for nothing. Something more than opinion was needed. But who would supply it?

Not the professoriat as a whole. Though we pride ourselves on self-governance, few faculty really take part in its forums and committees. The rights professors enjoy are products of collective institutions, but few faculty dwell on that fact or are prepared to defend those institutions. They generally enjoy the pleasures of university citizenship without its burdens, and are no more likely than other individualistic Americans to take the lead on issues not of palpable private importance.

Faculty senates play a more active role through their oversight of academic and curriculum policies and of peer review processes. The university would not exist without their dedicated efforts. Their authority, however, has become limited on most campuses, is ultimately advisory, and is exercised within others' budget controls. Shared governance tends to be "split governance," one analyst concludes. "Senates tend to be deference cultures."[35] In their collective as in their individual capacities, professors therefore enjoy autonomy without power. And they are loath take the lead, even against programs that threaten their status and rights.

A union does potentially possess the capacity for this leadership. It has the power to block polices that endanger workload limits and teaching conditions because its contracts have the force of law. They are not simply advisory. A union also possesses weapons to force access to the financial and budgetary data on which so many current university decisions are made. But the CFA was at first inhibited from asserting in these ways itself by handicaps it shares with many other American unions.

Since its inception it had tended to focus on narrow salary issues and CSU funding politics. It had not been a presence in public-policy discussions or in larger efforts to influence the direction of the university. The CFA's mode of operation led most of it members to see it not as a vehicle of their own activism but as something like an insurance agency or off-site provider, a third party. Members paid their money and *it* handled representation. Like other practitioners of services unionism, finally, it had grown increasingly bureaucratic after its early struggles and its leaders had fallen out of touch with the membership. The effects were evident in a steadily eroding membership, falling from around eighty-three hundred members at its peak in early 1991 to sixty-three hundred members by late 1997.[36]

Unlike other unions, faculty unions are often required to act in concert with management—for example, in influencing state budget appropriations. In the process their leaders run the risk of beginning to see themselves as a *part* of management, accepting its worldview, and ceasing to develop an independent perspective from which to take stock of their situation and the university's options. The CFA proved susceptible to these dangers. Used to thinking primarily about salary and benefits, its leaders did not see the structural significance of the chancellor's new methods. Accepting management's views of inexorable trends, many joined the ranks of the volitionally impaired, relying on phrases about "done deals," unavoidable trends, and "what everyone else is doing." Believing they owed their successes to the legislature, they had declined to mobilize their base or public support in years. Political action for them meant campaign contributions and legislative lobbying. They clung to the old model while the world around them was changing.

Faced with unsuccessful mediation in January 1999, CFA's incumbent leaders prepared to make concessions. They knew that CSU's offer was a bad deal but saw no alternative. Under California law the chancellor can impose terms and conditions of employment if mediation fails. This had never happened and many feared that embarking into the terra incognita of grievance handling under the old education code would spell disaster for the union. Against members' instructions union leaders had already capitulated to the chancellor's 40 percent merit-pay demand. Now they decided to present members with what they knew was a weak contract.

But their choice met unexpected opposition. Many faculty had grown aware of the larger trends discussed in this volume and openly warned of the structural implications of the chancellor's demands. Hundreds of new members had joined the union. Campus chapter presidents had become more militant and begun to develop the independent analysis that had been missing so far. They decided to lead a fight against the contract proposal and after a month's hard efforts, succeeded in decisively defeating it. It was a turning point for the struggle, and for the union.

The old leaders had a month to mull this over before being defeated in a regularly scheduled election. Susan Meisenhelder, a comparative literature professor from CSU San Bernardino and former CFA vice president, was elected president. The union selected a lecturer as vice president for the first time in its history, signifying growing commitment to the plight of Cal State's second-tier faculty. The chancellor made good on his threat by attempting the unprecedented imposition of the terms and conditions of employment on the system's twenty thousand faculty. Far from spelling disaster, however, his effort provoked a month of escalating activities by faculty and students.

Led by the new leaders, angry faculty launched informational picket lines, demonstrations, and teach-ins. The union invented and declared a "State of Strike" to announce an end to business as usual and preparation for a real walkout. The new use of the "s" word eased hesitant faculty into consideration of more serious action and elicited press coverage, for the first time critical of the chancellor. Campus chapters sought and received strike sanctions from local labor councils. Academic senates fielded "no confidence in Reed" referenda. CFA's labor affiliates showed their support. Students declared themselves ready to support a faculty strike and at Sonoma State enthusiastically jumped the gun with a two-day walkout. Particularly threatening were CFA plans to discourage local contributions and donations for campus fund-raising efforts. And new members continued to join, surpassing 1000 for the year in April 1999.

The chancellor took a second look at his cards, saw the bets being raised, and decided to reconsider. By late May the new leaders were able to present a contract that contained concessions from the CSU. It cut merit pay back to 26 percent, imposed due-process review of presidents' merit awards, granted 3.6 percent general raises, retained workload limits and chairs in the faculty unit, and provided new protections for lecturers and counselors. It was not a perfect agreement and contained some bitter pills, but it shored up important gains and provided the foundation for further struggle. This contract was overwhelmingly ratified in late May.

CONTRACTUALLY PROTECTED ACADEMIC FREEDOM

What had happened? What accounted for a relative victory just six weeks after the union seemed destined for fruitless stalemate or certain defeat? How was it that the CFA harvested the fruits of its earlier fight *after* the familiar, well-mapped scenario had ended and did better in terra incognita than the CSU management?

A number of things are obvious. The chancellor clearly wanted to prevent a further escalation of activities and tone things down for his trustees, the last bastion of the previous Republican governorship. The tide of media reportage was turning. The public was beginning to see that low faculty salaries were impairing the university's ability to renew itself by hiring high-quality young faculty. The palpable support of labor allies was increasingly evident. And the threat to contact donors was taken seriously by CSU campus presidents. The feat of provoking an unprecedented systemwide strike in the first year on the job, in any case, might not have looked so good on a manager's résumé.

But to note all these things is only to say that the chancellor responded to increasingly mobilized power. Most faculty, like most Americans, would rather not think about power. They prefer to think that appeals to reason and dispassionate reports will do the trick. To talk about power is unseemly, impolite, and, well, unprofessional. But it was the assertion of power that, paradoxically, persuaded the chancellor to reason. It was only the mobilization of members, students, and affiliates that accounted for Reed's sober consideration of proposals that had been sitting on the table for six months.

For power to be exerted like this, however, people have to act. They have to become physically engaged. Protest power, in fact, is people acting together. And getting faculty to act is difficult given current understandings of professional identity. They are more comfortable, again, adopting resolutions, forming committees, and honing arguments. By temperament and training most of them prefer to wait until all the data is in—to wait, that is (as William James and Hannah Arendt both noted), until the time for acting is past.

The burdens this imposes on a union are great. On one hand, it has to take the lead, to stake out positions and plan actions in its members' interests. On the other, it may have to do this before its members are fully clear on their interests. If it defers such leadership, it fails in its responsibility. So at times like the present, when the rules and stakes are changing, it has to take the initiative but also to stay in close touch with its grass roots and admit mistakes if it is wrong. All this requires, again, that it possess its own analysis and is challenging the intellectual hegemony of the new-breed university administrators. That the new California Faculty Association leadership is succeeding for the present in these multiple tasks is clear from the increasing support it is receiving and the fact that it is becoming an intellectual presence on CSU campuses. It is ceasing to be a third party.

Many of the older leaders doubted at first that the union had any power to exert. It might adopt organizational positions, and it might score an occasional debating point. But when push came to shove, it could hardly be expected to hold out against opposition. Hence the inevitable last-minute capitulations. And hence the acceptance of the familiar view in which legislatures are seen as the deliverers of labor's rights, and resources are expended almost entirely on lobbying rather than organizing.[37] But this is a mistake, for reasons C. Wright Mills explained long ago in *New Men of Power*. A labor leader, despite his or her self-conception, Mills wrote,

is in conflict with the powers [that be] . . . : He is a rebel against . . . [the] unmolested exercise of the powers which property conveys. In his timidity and fear and eagerness to stay alive in a hostile environment, he does not admit this, . . . but the fact remains that he is. . . . Unlike the corporation, the union is usually . . . on the defensive in a sometimes actual and always potentially hostile society.[38]

If a union is always in potentially hostile terrain, then it must always be organizing its power. A faculty union may hope to operate in a collegial fashion and normally succeed in doing so, but the potential for conflict remains. Its capacity to mobilize its power, its members' willingness to become engaged, is the precondition for any real success it can have in the legislature or at the bargaining table.

To assume that faculty are powerless entails a fundamental misunderstanding and amounts to seeing them through management eyes. Faculty and students possess a great deal of power, latent though it normally is, for the simple reason that they essentially *are* the university. What they do is its basic work. If they don't do it, it doesn't get done. It was the rediscovery of this fact in late spring 1999, that exhilarated CSU faculty and produced a new firmness, spirit of camaraderie and collective pride among them.

The course of this conflict also provided a needed lesson about the relationship between unions and academic senates. Academic senates exercise primary authority over academic policy and are the normal defenders of academic freedom. But their role is advisory, as already noted. Had Chancellor Reed succeeded in implementing his preferred merit-pay plan in the contract conflict it would have transferred control over a significant part of career advancement from peers to administrators and undermined shared governance. It also would have subjected campus dissenters and disciplinary innovators to potential retaliation. The union prevented this. It was the union that won a faculty-based appeals process over the campus presidents' merit-pay decisions. The conflict thus revealed that union and senate powers are complementary, and those who would preserve shared governance and academic freedom in the present period will have to work to defend both.

RESISTING THE GREAT LEAP BACKWARD

The tasks that confront faculty unions and other professional unions are slightly different from those confronting other unions. While most American unions seek to protect working conditions and raise members' wages, professional unions are engaged in a struggle to keep the value and rewards of their work from being reduced to simply wages. While most unions have been confined to procedural channels and deprived of a role in governance, faculty, doctors, and many public workers are trying to retain a role in the direction of their institutions. Like other workers, however, faculty unions are committed to protecting their members' rights, defending job standards and realizing their collective values.

Fulfilling these tasks is leading the CFA away from the services model to a more activist, organizing model of unionism. Long-term efforts to win agency fee legislation bore fruit in fall 1999, making it the largest faculty union in the country and capable of playing a more active, initiating role. The union has also launched a "Future of the University" project that will hold public hearings throughout the state to develop the vision of a People's University in contrast to that of a Corporate University and establish that the CFA is not a special interest, but an expression of the public interest.

For these efforts to be successful, however, faculty will ultimately have to come to a new understanding of their identity. The old days of passive collegiality and the easy exercise of established rights are gone. The illusion that faculty membership is an individual status is no longer tenable. The CEOs of the education industry have changed all that. A "war has been declared against faculty," Cary Nelson writes; and they will need a "re-education . . . to resist it." Disputes like the one in the CSU system are providing that reeducation. They are teaching faculty that they have to become activist professionals or they will soon cease to be professionals at all.

They are also leading faculty to challenge administrators' narrow notions of accountability by affirming other obligations to their students and the public. An increasing number of voices dispute the proposition that the public university's main purpose is job training and that the market should be its guide. There have been two more important reasons in America for public higher education. The first and fundamental purpose was political, to develop democratic citizens and prepare them to become participants in a democratic public life. The obligation to develop qualities of citizenship is an obligation to enable students to understand their society, to locate themselves in history, and to see what's at stake in the conflicts of their time. It is to prepare them to act and to think about ends so they do not remain simply means or tools of others' designs.[39]

The second purpose of intellectual enrichment has been to aid in self-development. It is to help people grow, in Paul Goodman's terms, to broaden themselves and get ideas about how to live meaningfully in the world. That colleges and universities today offer many credentialing programs only makes these tasks more challenging; it does not reduce campuses to industrial placement offices. It was Mills, again, who captured both purposes when he explained that a liberal education

> includes a sort of therapy in the ancient sense of clarifying one's knowledge of one's self. It includes the imparting of all those skills of controversy with one's self which we call thinking; and with others, which we call debate.[40]

If John Dewey's program for citizenship and self-development was a program of Progressive Education, then the current plan for job training and spineless adaptability should be recognized as a design for Regressive Education. It offers the prospect of a Great Leap Backward.

Such a leap would threaten the values of the society as a whole, for the university responds to some of the vital impulses of American democracy. For all its reputed elitism and confusions about its role, the university remains a critical and respected repository of democratic opportunity. The insistence that everyone can be a citizen of the republic of letters, that people can raise themselves by learning, that well-roundedness is preferable to narrow specialization, and that anyone can become an informed critic of high policy—all this finds its grounds for fulfillment in the promise of the comprehensive university. The struggle emerging on American campuses is important, then, not only because it pits new-risen managers against masters and scholars. It is important because it will also reveal whether the corporation will be permitted to thwart social plurality and dictate to an entire culture, or whether a beleaguered bastion of social promise will continue to broaden human possibilities and aid other centers of democratic activity in the society.

Had business-oriented CEOs been successful in California they would have given the green light to their associates nationwide. But they did not succeed, and the lesson, conversely, is that the Great Leap Backward can be stopped. The CFA was able to stop it because it was able move its faculty to act, involve allies, develop its own independent analysis, and mobilize its power. The agreement it eventually won was reasonable and fair. But it took more than reasonable arguments to win it.

NOTES

1. C. Kerr, *The Uses of the University* (1963; reprint, New York: Harper & Row, 1966).

2. In July, the AMA voted to form a union to represent its members in health plans, hospitals, and universities. Michael Weinstein, "If Doctors Win the Right to Organize, Patients Could Lose," *New York Times*, July 8, 1999, p. C2. Public defenders and other state and county lawyers throughout the country are also examining the option.

3. D. Horowitz, "Billion Dollar Brains," *Ramparts* 7 (May 1969): 36–44; and "Sinews of Empire," *Ramparts* 8 (October 1969): 32–42.

4. The ethos of secrecy introduced by nuclear development in Kerr's own UC system was inimical to university openness and free inquiry, with grave long-term costs to the public. The classic Vietnam-era case was provided by Michigan State University, led by its president—a former assistant secretary of defense and

a chair of the Rockefeller Foundation–sponsored American Council of Education (current sponsor of the Oblinger volume, n. 13 below)—to collaborate with the CIA in propping up South Vietnamese president Diem. Horowitz, "Sinews," p. 38.

5. Kerr, *Uses of the University*, pp. 42, 45, 54–59, 90. The troubling and recurrent allusions to prostitution were Kerr's, as in his use of the limerick:

> There was a young lady from Kent
> Who said that she knew what it meant
> When men took her to dine,
> Gave her cocktails and wine;
> She knew what it meant—but she went. (p. 69)

Also see pp. 94 and 122.

6. Even the 450 faculty invited by the Chancellor's Office to a three-day retreat to help draft the Cornerstones Report worked within a framework devised by Munitz and his advisors. "Cornerstones: Choosing Our Future," CSU Chancellor's Office, 1998.

7. B. Munitz, "Managing Transformation in an Age of Social Triage," in *Re-inventing the University* (New York: Wiley, 1995), chap. 3.

8. David Noble, "Digital Diploma Mills: The Automation of Higher Education," *Monthly Review* 50 (1998): 38–52. On Cornerstones, see n. 6.

9. Linda DeLeon and Robert Denhardt, "The Political Theory of Reinvention," presented at the American Political Science Association, Washington, D.C., August 1997.

10. Letter to graduating seniors from CSU, Sacramento, CSUS association vice president for research and graduate studies Ric Brown, August 18, 1998. "Influence over Product" is a subsection in Munitz's "Managing Transformation in an Age of Social Triage."

11. Florida Progress Corporation paid Reed $30,000 a year to sit on its board. The university spent over $300,000 prosecuting Taborsky for felony theft of his own notebooks (!) and felony theft of trade secrets. S. Shulman, "A Researcher's Conviction," *MIT Tech Review*, February 24, 1997, p. 24. Also, J. Nicklin, "Struggle Over a Patent Brings Prison Terms for Former U. of South Florida Student," *Chronicle of Higher Education*, August 4, 1993, p. A25; and L. Jaroff, "Intellectual Chain Gang," *Time*, February 10, 1997, p. 64. I am indebted to David Noble for this information.

Reed was called before the state Ethics Commission during the Taborsky affair on a different conflict-of-interest matter involving the very same corporation, and was cleared in a controversial decision. L. Dunkelberger, "Ethics Commission Clears University Chancellor," *Sarasota Herald-Tribune*, October 15, 1993.

12. Horowitz, "Billion Dollar Brains," p. 37. Further anticipations of the current outlook are MIT president (and later Carnegie Foundation president) Henry S. Pritchett's "Shall the University Become a Business Corporation?" (1905), and Morris L. Cooke's Taylorite *Academic and Industrial Efficiency* (1910).

13. Diana G. Oblinger and Anne-Lee Verville, *What Business Wants from*

Higher Education, American Council on Education and Oryx Press Series on Higher Education, (Phoenix: Oyrx Press, 1998). Oblinger is manager of academic programs and strategy for IBM's Global Education Industry; Verville held that post until 1997. Looking beyond short-term measures, even in economic terms the CSU has not done so badly with productivity. One study that looks beyond the marketability of graduates' skills to the synergies and contributions of the institution as a whole is "The Economic Impact of the California State University and the California Economy, 1993-2002," by Robert Girling, George Goldman, and Sherry Keith (CSU Chancellor's Office, 1993). It found that the B.A.s CSU awarded since 1960 (over half the state's), its forty thousand nonfaculty employees (who generate an additional fifty-one thousand jobs), and direct addition of over $4.5 billion to the state's GSP make major contributions to the state's economy and "boost its competitive advantage in key knowledge intensive export sectors." The report recommends not campus cost-cutting but restoration of older levels of funding, predicting that an investment of $842 million would generate $7.6 billion in GSP in the next decade (a benefits-to-costs ratio of 9:1) pp. 1–3.

14. J. V. Scott, "The Strange Death of Faculty Governance," *PS: Political Science and Politics* 29 (December 1996): 724–26. Report on 1996 AAUP conference, Shared Governance versus Corporate Management. Scott, currently at Eastern Michigan University, was formerly a professor at CSU Long Beach.

15. Reed himself did not have to prove his merit for the chancellorship of the nation's largest site of higher learning because the job search that found him was uniquely secret. That was convenient, for his academic qualifications are modest. CFA members found that his 1970 Ph.D. thesis, titled, "Doctoral Graduates in Education of the George Washington University, 1960–1970," offered simply a 129-page summary of answers by 133 respondents to a questionnaire about their postgraduate careers.

16. "The war against the faculty entails identifying and separating all the roles that faculty members perform, eliminating those that inconvenience administrators, and contracting for the others as piecework." Cary Nelson, "The War against the Faculty," *Chronicle of Higher Education*, April 16, 1999, p. B4. Taylor's emphasis on individual, material incentives has been largely discredited in industry. See Jeff Lustig, *Corporate Liberalism, The Origins of Modern American Political Theory* (Berkeley: U.C. Press, 1982), chap. 6; and Christopher Newfield, "Recapturing Academic Business," *Social Text* 15 (summer 1997): 44.

17. Nelson, "The War Against the Faculty."

18. Oblinger and Verille, *What Business Wants from Higher Education*, p. vii.

19. Christopher Newfield is lucid on the limits of this cost-cutting approach. "Financial accounting's tendencies are stark. It sees costs as negative, labeling them as investments only if they can be linked to a quantifiable expected return. If costs yield nonquantifiable goods of the kind common in research and education . . . it will be hard for finance to certify them as valuable investments" ("Recapturing Academic Business," p. 48).

20. Kerr did see that the educational estate was "merg[ing] its activities with industry as never before" (*Uses of the University*, pp. 86–91), but he did not take the capitalist character of that industry seriously.

21. Cited in D. Goines, *The Free Speech Movement, Coming of Age in the Sixties* (Berkeley: Ten Speed Press, 1993), p. 361.

22. Paul Goodman, *Compulsory Mis-education and the Community of Scholars* (New York: Vintage Books, 1964), pp. 139–40, and regarding Kant, p. 203. The remark about knowledge is from B.A. Sethuraman, "Running the Business of Knowledge," *Los Angeles Times,* April 4, 1999, op-ed page. Already in 1964 Goodman noted, "The *ultima ratio* of administration is that a school is a teaching machine, to train the young by pre-digested programs in order to get pre-ordained marketable skills" (p. 172).

23. Plato, *Protagoras* (New York: Bobbs-Merrill Reprint, 1956), p. 10.

24. On this, see also Sethuraman, "Running the Business of Knowledge."

25. On the history of the university, see Goodman, *Compulsory Miseducation*, pp. 191–208.

26. Professor Rice, San Jose State University, writes on the changing fashions and transient loyalties. Review of *What Business Wants from Higher Education*, [online] www.amazon.com [March 8, 1999]. Clarke ("Why Stay with the CFA," *CSU-SB,* October 12, 1998) is professor at CSU San Bernardino. The last phrase is Professor Ted Hornback's (CSU, Sacramento campus leaflet, January 21, 1997).

27. Oblinger and Verville, *What Business Wants from Higher Education*, p. 26.

28. Ibid., pp. 82, 18. Kerr made the same point: "The process cannot be stopped. The results cannot be foreseen. It remains to adapt." (*Uses of the University*, p. 124).

29. The coordinator of MSU's Vietnam project later attributed his and others' "appalling" participation to the fact they had "been conditioned . . . not to ask the normative question. . . . We have only the capacity . . . to serve the policy" not to "question and judge" it (Horowitz, "Sinews of Empire," p. 42).

The reversal of expected university purposes finds a grammatical corollary in a curious diction that recurs in the Oblinger volume. Universities, it explains, have "a unique responsibility for . . . maintaining the . . . resources [for] our economic growth." Employees are "increasingly empowered with the responsibility for their own ongoing education." What sounds at first like a declaration of powers and opportunities is quickly revealed as a statement of function and duty.

30. From Frederick Winslow Taylor, "Principles of Scientific Management," in *Corporate Liberalism*, p. 2. The Oblinger sentences, *What Business Wants from Higher Education*, pp. v and 26.

31. Nelson, "The War against the Faculty." The antifaculty offensive is apparent to Nelson in reports from the American Association of State Colleges and Universities, the Association of Governing Boards of Universities and Colleges, and the American Association for Higher Education; he refers also to Pew and Mellon researches.

32. CFA's slogan in the 1998–1999 contract fight.

33. Though legalizing unions in the UC system, HEERA also limited labor's scope of representation in such a way as to preserve most issues as the exclusive prerogatives of campus senates. UC's nonsenate faculty (lecturers, librarians, and special-education faculty) remained as the constituency with a stake in union organizing. Article 1, Sec. 3562, q. UC Teaching assistants were omitted from the purview of the act altogether, but gained representation rights in 1998.

34. In addition to its other flaws, CETI would have violated state constitutional bans on gifts of public resources to private profit-making entities. Constitution of the State of California, Article XVI, Sec. 6.

35. Newfield, "Recapturing Academic Business," pp. 57, 60. "Senate members are especially good at seeking *autonomy without management*. Unions are better at knowing that *autonomy requires defense against management*" (p. 59; emphasis in original).

36. The peak was May 1991. CFA Treasurer's Report, September 1997. Services unionism is similar to business unionism but weaker, at least in the public sector, because it cannot use the threat of a strike to profits to get raises. It has to lobby the legislature to seek raises, and do so in collaboration with management.

37. "The model is based on the false assumption of equality of bargaining power. Using it . . . [therefore] results in the continuation of management's dominance rather than in the creation of work-place democracy." Deborah A. Ballam, "The Impact of the NRLA on the U.S. Labor Movement," *American Business Law Journal* (February 1995): 460. See also Kim Moody, "American Labor: A Movement Again?" *Monthly Review* 49 (July–August 1997): 77.

38. C. Wright Mills, *The New Men of Power: America's Labor Leaders* (New York: Harcourt, Brace, 1948), pp. 8, 154.

39. See Sheinbaum's remark, n. 29. A public education is one which gives "individuals and publics . . . confidence in their own capacities to reason." (C. Wright Mills, *The Sociological Imagination* [New York: Oxford University Press, 1959], p. 189; also pp. 4–5, 185–87).

40. C. Wright Mills, *The Power Elite* (New York: Oxford University Press, 1957), p. 318. I am indebted to Hornback for the title of this section (January 21, 1997).

23

JUSTICE FOR JANITORS
Organizing Against Outsourcing at Southampton College

Corey Dolgon

I t was the perfect job. As a recent Ph.D. committed to political activism and social movements, I could not have hoped for a better academic position than assistant professor (tenure-track) in the Friends World Program at Southampton College of Long Island University (LIU). Once an independent Quaker college, Friends World's mission was based on the pedagogical proposals of founder Morris Mitchell, who wanted to encourage students from all nations "to treat the entire world as their university; take the most urgent human problems as the basis of their curriculum; seek together designs for a more humane future; and consider the whole of humankind as their ultimate loyalty."

In 1990, financial problems forced Friends World to merge with LIU. As an alternative educational program within the confines of a larger corporatized university, Friends World experienced new conflicts over its educational direction and social mission during the years that followed. In particular, a series of administrative decisions over personnel, curriculum, and recruitment challenged (and substantially damaged) the program's traditional commitment to shared governance and a social-justice agenda. During my first two years at Friends World, it became increasingly evident that the program we advertised to capture the spirit and passion of idealistic young people was being eroded by LIU administrators more concerned with profit and hierarchy.

In the winter of 1998, however, a Southampton College decision to contract out its custodial work instigated a crisis concerning the structure and nature of the entire campus community. In a different context, the college itself began to experience tensions and conflicts similar to those already happening within the smaller Friends World Program. The outsourcing of custodial work suddenly forced students, faculty, and staff to question what kind of community the college was and ought to be; what kind of responsibilities an institution has to its employees and the surrounding community; and what role the students and other campus groups should play in the decision-making process that impacts their surroundings.

For eighteen months, a coalition of campus and community people, under the guise of the Southampton Coalition for Justice (CFJ) fought to have the custodians rehired by the college. I was one of the founders of this group, whose rotating and fluid membership was often comprised predominately of Friends World students and college custodians. This article tells the story of the coalition's struggle and ultimate victory. More importantly, though, I think our experiences demonstrate a possible vision of community that challenges the corporatized model of universities. In particular, CFJ members overcame many class, cultural, and ideological differences to work collectively in pursuit of a specific goal. In doing so, we created a context and process for honesty, democracy, and justice that countered the cynical and hierarchical business mentality at Friends World and LIU.

COLLEGE OR K-MART?

On February 14, 1997 the custodial operation at Southampton College of Long Island University was sold to the Laro Management Company, an outside firm that specialized in providing maintenance services. While the custodians' union representatives had been notified a few days earlier in order to renegotiate contractual terms with the new employers, custodians were not informed and suddenly found themselves forced to fill out new job applications for positions some had held almost thirty years. Laro supervisors told custodians that no one's job would be guaranteed as changes in workforce, schedules, and procedures would soon follow. As one custodian told the local press a few weeks later, "We felt like dogs kicked onto the sidewalk."

This administrative decision came as part of a chain of events that had exposed the college's increasingly corporate nature and agenda. In 1996, administrators began regular breakfast meetings with local business leaders to determine ways in which the institution's curriculum and policies could address the "educational and training needs" of area businesses. Throughout the mid- and late 1990s, the college leased its facilities to a variety of vendors (including J. Crew and the Maslow Group) for a series of warehouse-type sales. Local businesses protested this unexpected competition and forced town officials to cite the provost for violating zoning ordinances. In response, the provost explained to the *Southampton Press*: "[We are] an enormously powerful economic force, bringing in at least $30 million worth of business to the East End [while our payroll] adds $26 million to the East End economy. . . . The broader perspective is that we are decidedly pro-business."

The decision to contract out the custodial unit, though, was a blatant act of corporate banditry. Even Laro executives admitted that they were in the business of driving down wages. Laro's vice president, Lou Vacca Jr., explained to the *New York Times*, "How do you do it cheaper? You take it out of labor." One custodian had worked for Laro at a local K-Mart and told others about the poor wages, benefits, and conditions he experienced there. Laro's specialty, however, was busting unions. The company's president, Robert Bertuglia Jr., told the *Times* how he cut the New York City Port Authority bus terminal's workforce by bringing in four hundred replacement workers after the company was "tipped off" about a surprise walkout. He boasts, "They wanted to get rid of, I don't want to use 'get rid of,' phase out the union cleaners. We were low bidders."

Within this context, then, the college provost sounded a lot like a tobacco CEO when he defended his decision to outsource custodians as "budget-neutral." At a faculty meeting a few days after the contract was announced, a professor protested the move, asking whether the custodians had been involved in the decision. He also wondered aloud what the ramifications would be of inviting "sleazy" outside companies onto campus to exploit workers who had been part of the college's community for so long. The provost scolded him for commenting on the character of the college's new "partner" without any background knowledge. While custodians were not part of the decision, he continued, the conditions of their employment "would remain much the same." No other faculty spoke on the issue.

By the next week, however, the provost's comments proved curious at best. Background research by the custodians showed that Laro had a history of National Labor Relations Board (NLRB) violations and had tried to bust union locals throughout the New York metropolitan area. Meanwhile, the work conditions and compensation for custodians changed significantly: They lost eligibility for TIAA-CREF retirement benefits; they lost tuition remission benefits; they lost access to emergency loans and other "perks" offered to college employees; and they experienced immediate changes in work, pay, and vacation schedules.

Laro threatened and intimidated custodians, asserting that they "knew" some of them were "lazy workers and thieves." Laro also warned custodians that "fraternizing" with students, faculty, and staff would not be permitted. It became clear that the custodians' conditions of employment had not only changed, they had been radically transformed.

FIGHTING BACK!

A few days after their contract was sold, custodians passed around a petition among students and faculty. It called on the college's administration to cancel the new contract. While the petition did not circulate for long, it did succeed in garnering student support, and illustrated that workers were unhappy with the new situation and would work to change it. Custodians also tried to find out what role their union had played in the process and remained frustrated in the lack of accessibility and accountability from their local's business agent. The union maintained its satisfaction at having "saved" the custodians' jobs despite the obvious threat that Laro posed.

During the next week, I sat down with Michelle Wattleton,* a junior at Southampton College, with whom I had worked as part of a welfare rights organization in the previous year. Michelle was a "nontraditional" student in all aspects of the description. She was twenty-nine years old, part Native American and part African American, and a single mother of three children. She worked part-time at the school's switchboard and part-time at the campus Center for Racial and Cultural Diversity, making barely enough to support her family and pay tuition. The custodial situation also affected Michelle in a direct way, as she was engaged to the custodians' shop steward, Malcolm Day.

Michelle and I decided that a group comprised of students, faculty, staff, and community residents might help the custodians pressure the college by publicizing the situation. Michelle discussed this with Malcolm, who agreed. We then contacted a friend and former Friends World student who was working at a local newspaper and asked him to announce a meeting we were scheduling for the next Monday night. We also asked him to convince his editor to cover the event.

The first meeting's turnout was much larger than expected: The professor who had spoken out at the faculty meeting, a couple of students, a campus secretary, and about eight of the custodians showed up. Immediately, the coalition and its work took shape around the custodians talking about their situation and experiences. Meanwhile, Michelle and I tried to

---

*The names of all students and custodians have been changed to protect their anonymity.

adapt those experiences by laying out a variety of strategic and political options for the group's work. What was clear from the first meeting, though, was that custodians were angry about the way that they had been treated, wanted to act in some way, and appreciated the support from others on campus and in the community.

The first meeting also demonstrated that the situation was a complicated one and there were many different analyses for what had happened and why. I offered research evidence that outsourcing had become a common institutional strategy at places like Yale, Weslyan, and the University of Pennsylvania. In particular, we looked at Tufts University where, in 1994, custodial work was contracted out to one firm, UNICO, and then again in 1997 to another. The second contract allowed the university to claim no responsibility to its former workers, who were now UNICO employees. We all thought that Laro could have been hired to play that same role in Southampton.

Some custodians, however, argued that the decision had important racial dynamics, too. Their unit was, after all, the only one on campus comprised predominately of people of color. In fact, under the leadership of Malcolm Day, the custodians had been pressuring the administration to create what they called a "promotional pipeline." For thirty years, only two custodians had ever been promoted to the next level—mechanic—within the Physical Plant Department, and neither of them had been people of color. Custodians were sure that the increased pressure from their leadership had inspired the administration to find a private management company and, in the words of the physical plant manager, "Wash our hands of all of you."

While the custodians had already dropped the petition, the group decided to meet again the next Monday and embark on a letter-writing campaign to the local press. Everyone agreed that the more pressure the college received from local people and groups, the more likely it would be to terminate the contract. We also began collecting more information about Laro and about other colleges and universities that had experienced similar labor problems. In essence, part of our strategy was based on educating the community about the issue, while another part was to educate ourselves by conducting research on subjects integral to better analyzing the struggle.

Over the following weeks, the coalition brought together students, faculty, staff, and concerned members of the community to work with custodians. The group leafleted the campus, coordinated a letter-writing campaign, held the first political rally at the campus since the 1960s, and took the issue to the local AntiBias Task Force and County Human Rights Commission for political pressure. But the most powerful action was to intervene in the college's attempt to get $5 million in funding from the

Town of Southampton for a swimming pool. The college proposed to make the pool available for public use (with a $500-per-year family membership) but it would be located at and operated by the college. The coalition informed the college that we would publicly oppose the pool project because the college had acted as poor local citizens by negatively affecting the employment conditions of residents. In fact, we argued that the college's policies could influence a downward spiral for employment conditions throughout the region if the wages and benefits fell for unionized workers in maintenance and service positions.

In response, the college offered numerous concessions to the custodians: (1) restoring tuition remission; (2) revisiting the promotional pipeline issue; and (3) incorporating the coalition in the college's evaluation of Laro's performance. The coalition accepted these concessions and decided not to publicly oppose the pool project. This was a difficult decision, however, as some members of the group believed that the pool represented a strategic opportunity to expose the college's duplicity in claiming to be "good citizens" and part of a "caring community" on the one hand, but (according to one of the custodians) "treating its employees like slaves at the auction block" on the other. In the end, however, it was the custodians themselves who swayed the coalition to accept the concessions and back off of the pool project. The workers believed that students and faculty wanted the pool and that public opposition would damage the coalition's support on campus.

EVERYTHING WE NEED TO KNOW WE LEARN IN STRUGGLE

The Coalition For Justice not only confronted the college's administration, it also had ramifications for the Friends World program, which had become the source of most of the students who joined the CFJ. Students began pressuring program faculty for more activist-oriented courses. In response, Friends World hired an adjunct faculty, Bob Zellner, to teach a fall semester course on the history of social activism in the United States. Zellner, who had recently moved to Southampton, may be best known as the first white field secretary for the Student Nonviolent Coordinating Committee (SNCC) and has remained a civil rights activist for the past thirty years.

Zellner had attended coalition meetings and was a guest speaker at our demonstration the preceding spring. At that event, he said that race relations in Southampton were similar to the conditions he experienced in the South during the 1950s. He continued, "both on campus and in the community, whites seem to have a plantation mentality and African Americans are relegated to the mop-and-bucket brigade." Later, Zellner would explain that groups such as the coalition comprise today's civil rights movement. He explained that although "the general polity believes there is no civil rights movement going on right now, if you take the aggregate of all the activities going on around the country (single issue campaigns and multi-issue groups), that's the movement." Zellner saw two very strong roles for the coalition and similar groups: "One is that they are providing training and experience for people who want to be active in their communities. Two, they provide the platform from which a more synthesized and energized national movement can occur."

The timing of his hiring could not have been better, as I had decided to leave LIU and take a position at a state college in Massachusetts. Although I maintained my commitment to the coalition and attended regular monthly meetings, Zellner's presence added both new life and a consistency that might have been lost without a strong faculty presence. His course introduced students to a variety of social and political movements and the roles they played in shaping the contours of American life. But the class also had an important action component that required students to engage in some form of community activism. According to Zellner, this emphasis on experiential education forced students to contemplate the practical and emotional dynamics of political work. As part of the course, Zellner invited students to attend a meeting of the New York chapter of the National Civil Rights Coordinating Committee (NCRCC), a fledgling group that he had founded to try to reinvigorate a national civil rights movement.

At the NCRCC meeting, Michelle Wattleton recounted the plight of the custodians and the coalition's work. Maggie King, a first-year student from Texas, attended the meeting and says that she was really "upset and disgusted" at the way in which custodians were treated by the college. Another student wrote in his journal that the custodians' situation was part of a larger problem with racism and segregation on campus. He explained: "Since my first days at LIU I have been aware of the lack of minorities within the student body and the faculty, and the segregation within the dorms. I have seen 'rent-a-cops' [campus security], and I have yet to see one of them be a minority. On more than one occasion I have seen them pull aside an African American man from a group to check for ID with no apparent reason." Zellner agreed that students could join the coalition for their action projects. Because of this, almost two dozen Friends World students became coalition "members" and attended the first mass meeting of 1997, held in early October.

The mass meeting began with introductions and announcements, and proceeded to a discussion of what the coalition was and who the custodians were who inspired its formation. After a long recounting of the group's history, we talked about our goals and potential strategies for accomplishing them. Over the summer, the coalition had decided to meet monthly. New students, however, wanted to be more active. The coalition agreed that students should form a separate task force to take on particular actions that the coalition could support, but that perhaps might be too risky for custodians and others to participate in directly. The desire to be more active would be a growing source of frustration for new students. While custodians had reluctantly settled into their identity as Laro employees, they still wanted the coalition to maintain a steady presence to protect them from Laro's intimidation and union busting. Students, on the other hand, wanted the college to terminate the Laro contract immediately and were anxious to organize direct actions to accomplish it.

Throughout the fall of 1997, students engaged in an education campaign to reacquaint the campus with the custodians' struggle. Students from the coalition also met independently with the provost to discuss their concerns, but they were generally dissatisfied with his responses. At a coalition meeting, one of the students, Casey Stanton, explained that "the provost basically whined about how it wasn't fair that his name was being used and that he was getting the brunt of our attacks . . . that we see him as part of the institution and don't listen to him as an individual." In response to the provost, King wrote in her journal that although he was probably right about the coalition's bias against him, "If he wants the job of provost and all the benefits that go along with that position he must face the responsibilities that go along with it, too."

Although frustrations over general campus apathy and administrative intransigence ebbed and flowed throughout the semester, those students who participated in coalition activities and attended meetings regularly developed an important identity as coalition members and as local/campus activists. This identity was nurtured by a synthesis of active, collective engagement and personal, emotional response. As Brian Williamson, another first-year Friends World student, wrote in his journal: "Wow! I can't think of any better words to describe how I am feeling after today's class and meeting. I got a feeling today that I don't ever recall having before. It happened during the Coalition for Justice meeting. I felt a deep emotional excitement mixed with a feeling of power and a new sense of realness and seriousness."

Friends World students generally spend their spring semesters participating in internship projects at various locations across the country. As some admitted, the prospect of leaving campus without having "won" the struggle for the custodians' jobs intensified their desire to increase pressure on the administration. But other students contended that it wasn't until the end of the semester that they really understood what it meant to be a part of a political struggle. As one student wrote in her evaluation of the activism course:

> Throughout the semester, many of the students in this class became involved in their own activism, the main way being with the Coalition for Justice right here at Southampton College. . . . I feel as though the energy was constantly growing in the class. When I say that the energy was constantly growing, I mean that it was not until the end of the semester that we all seemed to become excited about activism, people wanting to get involved and it was exciting to see the change in many people.

While both dynamics were probably at work, students did organize a demonstration late in the semester at the main gate of the college. The action received important media coverage and support from the local community. Holding signs such as "Honk If You Love Custodians" and "Humanities: Practice What You Preach," students again disseminated information to the community and spread the message that the coalition would continue its struggle.

The semester ended with coalition students holding a sit-in at the provost's office. They confronted him on many issues, including the custodial contract. The most significant exchange, however, addressed the problems of racial discrimination in general, and the college's role in propagating it. Two students of color, over a dozen white students, and a white provost discussed whether or not the administration could or should be accused of racism. From the beginning of the coalition's effort, the provost had defended himself and the college against such charges. The *Southampton Press* and its all-white editorial staff jumped to the college's defense by stating that the administration could not be held responsible for problems that "sadly exist" in our larger society. But as the coalition continued to point out that no custodian of color had been promoted in thirty years, even the town's Anti-Bias Task Force agreed that the situation appeared to be a prima facie case of discrimination.

The provost took these charges personally, so much so that he began to defend himself against charges of racism—charges that the coalition had never made. He began explaining to the press and to the campus community that he was not a racist and that it was unfair and "biased" of the coalition to single him out in such a way. He made this same defense during the sit-in. At the sit-in, however, Maggie King (who had become one of the most active students in the coalition) brought up the issue of institutional racism and discrimination. She attempted to explain how the college had been led by white men for thirty years and that they had established hiring practices and procedures that reflected the white-dominated social dynamics of the Hamptons. By incorporating these conditions into the everyday policies and practices of the college's operating culture, she stated, administrators had maintained a racially discriminatory system where people of color were seen as custodians and, regardless of their skills and abilities, could not find access to higher levels of employment. This condition did not mean that any particular administrator was or wasn't a "racist." It did mean, however, that the college and its leadership were responsible for discrimination and had an obligation to actively dismantle such a culture. The video footage of the sit-in shows the provost, impressed with this description, markedly silent in response.

Still, some of the students who left the sit-in persuaded by the provost thought that racial issues were not that significant a part of the custodial problem. Many could not separate the individual provost who seemed reasonable, unprejudiced, and trustworthy, from the historical and institutional discrimination against custodians. Even King, in retrospect, was not entirely comfortable with her depiction of institutionalized racism. She explains:

> Before the semester I wasn't even familiar with the term "institutionalized racism." I still don't know the depths of the effects and signs of institutionalized racism. I don't like hearing that part of the video because I am a little embarrassed about terminology I used and the ignorance I displayed. For example, I use the term "entitled" instead of "privileged." Of course, I did what I could at the time and I do not regret that I spoke. It was the only thing said that day that the provost did not have a brisk response to. Despite my lack of eloquence, I do think that he understood what I was saying and perhaps it made him think a little bit about the institutionalized racism and his role in it.

For a first-year student, King's eloquence is actually quite striking despite her self-deprecation.

The issue of institutional discrimination and how it impacts on the policy and practices of the college in particular and the society in general was one of the most important educational conversations that emanated from the coalition's work. Therefore, it is not surprising that those students most vulnerable to the provost's denials were the ones who did not attend regular coalition meetings. The power and depth of understanding institutional racism was inspired by the active engagement with the custodians as educators. Students who shared experiences of long meetings and difficult discussions with custodians became the best equipped to grasp the ways in which institutional disrespect and discrimination worked.

This discrepancy was also true among those students who had

attended student task-force meetings but had not attended full meetings of the coalition with custodians and faculty. The custodians' ability to act as teachers and define the practical and emotional conditions of knowledge about racism were diminished by some of the fragmentation that occurred within the coalition because of the different meetings. While some students might identify with the injustice over the custodians' overall treatment, those who did not participate in the open discussions about race and discrimination with the custodians could not fully identify with their own place in the struggle or the complexity of issues involved. In fact, I would argue that they were much more likely to identify with a white professional male who felt guilty and defensive about racial issues.

BUILDING NEW IDENTITIES

The most educational conversations the coalition produced included talks that allowed all members, especially the custodians themselves, an opportunity to understand the complexity of history, identity, politics, and community. The custodians, too, had been divided by racism and racialized identities. While infrequent resistance from communities of color in the Hamptons (especially Native American and African American) had occurred, the overall tenor of race relations remained one of liberal/elite complacency on the part of whites and a quiet but resolute steadfastness on the part of minorities. For the custodians, even with union protection and representation, open and organized resistance to job discrimination and racial indignities was rare. As one custodian put it, "We were used to being ignored or put down by white employers and supervisors, and we mostly just let things roll off our backs. We had some of the best jobs around and there wasn't any need to make a big deal about it." Still, not all of the custodians of color reacted in the same way. Ella Hamer, an African American woman who has worked at the college since it was founded, had a reputation for speaking her mind, and admits to more than once telling a student, colleague, or even supervisor how she felt about being treated with disrespect. Mostly, though, custodians would individually or collectively weigh the merits of open protest versus silent deference and find some manner of action between the two poles that maintained both their dignity and the relative peace of their day-to-day workplace.

Some tensions existed between Native American and African American custodians, and one unit member said that "even before the Laro contract, people tended to stick to their own camps." The most significant divisions, however, remained between white and nonwhite workers. These tensions resulted in a lack of unity that kept unit members from any serious collective action. Although white custodians did not receive any significant advantages, they were often referred to informally by supervisors as "the good workers" who didn't "make trouble." In return, white workers did receive unofficial perks like the use of college vehicles and supplies, and certain overtime jobs.

Because race was such an important issue, not only to the coalition's analysis of what had happened but also in the process of creating solidarity where little had existed before, we decided that meetings had to include open and honest discussions of race whenever appropriate. In the beginning, conflicts arose over analyzing how important race actually was in the administration's decision. White workers felt betrayed by the college and figured the administration wanted to save money and perhaps break their union. Workers of color argued that race was the most crucial reason for the outsourcing. Some workers (both white and nonwhite) thought that the more militant custodians of color were actually to blame for the decision. Thus, although some whites acknowledged race as an issue, they did not blame the administration for a history of discrimination and wanted more vocal members to "stop making waves."

When the unit was contracted out, many workers responded in different ways: The most militant of them protested immediately and accused the administration of racism and betrayal; those less militant did support protests but blamed the militant activists for the situation; and some of those who were most antimilitant refused to get involved in any action and hoped that they could still do well if they supported the administration and Laro. Generally, custodians of color fell into the first two categories, while white workers belonged to the second and third groups.

The most interesting ways in which these divisions can be observed, though, is in connection with one of the two Yugoslavian immigrant workers. Manny, who spoke English well but with an accent, was one of the newer and younger custodians. Although he was very angry about being outsourced and wanted to protest openly and militantly, he was reluctant to go along with other custodians who felt that race had played a part in the college's decision. In fact, Manny had been told by supervisors on numerous occasions that he was "not like the lazy ones." He believed he might have a future at the college, especially since he was taking business courses there. While not exactly the beneficiary of white privilege, Manny made it clear that he did not think of himself as "nonwhite," and that others had encouraged him to identify with the management's conception of a good (read: "white") worker. As one custodian explained during a meeting, Manny was in the process of becoming white and receiving the "perks" that came with it.

Two discussions are particularly informative on how some custodians had sophisticated understandings of class and race identities. While they did not previously employ their analyses as part of a unified action, their knowledge did inform daily interactions and eventually helped to characterize the fluidity of new identities shaped by the coalition's collective struggle. For example, in our second meeting, we discussed strategies for publicizing our fight. We decided to start a letter-writing campaign to the press and talked about going to the town's Anti-Bias Task Force. Some of the white workers were apprehensive about making race a significant issue: Some didn't think it was really important and others were reluctant to "press any buttons" since "so many people are overly sensitive about race." Manny agreed with both sentiments, although he did acknowledge that there was much racial discrimination. He was also concerned about his own status and didn't want to upset supervisors.

Leonard Parsons, a Shinnecock Indian, had been described to Manny as one of the "bad workers," and the two were not on speaking terms. Management had successfully played them against each other by convincing Manny that his best interests lay in identifying with their agenda, while at the same time they convinced Leonard that Manny was really "management's boy." At the meeting, Leonard argued that race had separated workers for too long and, while the custodians of color always got the short end of the stick, white workers had not benefited all that much either. Manny came to realize that the identity of "good worker" was generally a racialized and politicized one that had more to do with his skin color and obedience than with his hard work or performance. When Manny said that he still felt discriminated against because of his accent, Fred Johnson, an African American custodian, explained that Manny, as a European immigrant, was only part white and that until he could blend in better and move out of a custodial job, he would never be completely white. Another custodian, Jesse Ames, compared the situation to an earlier story I had told about the provost yelling at me when I wrote a letter to the press critical of the Laro contract. The provost had scolded me for not talking to him first and said, "I thought we were colleagues." Jesse explained that "what he really meant was he thought you were one of them [faculty and administrators] not us [custodians]."

Weeks later, Manny and Ella got into a verbal spar over an incident that had occurred on the job. While the actual event was never fully described at the meeting, it was clear that both had used harsh and "racist" words in fighting with one another. Many of the custodians intervened and tried to extrapolate what had actually happened. Jesse looked across the circle at Manny and said, "Manny, you know I've never said anything bad about you and I've always been with you, but you can't say things like that. We have to be able to argue and disagree without talking like that. Ella was hurt and responded in kind." Ella was still hurt and told Jesse to "forget about it." But Jesse continued, "We have to fight like we're a family, you know? We can't let arguments break us up."

One of the greatest successes from our coalition organizing was our ability to embrace conflicts over race and class identities as part of the struggle itself. The meetings and actions became sites where strict and limiting racial and class identities were challenged. I believe this process may be exactly the kind of "opening up" for radical democratic politics that Howard Winant writes about in his recent work "Racial Dualism at Century's End," where he declares:

> To acknowledge racial dualism is to understand the malleability and flexibility of all identities, especially racial one. . . . One of the recognitions hard-won by the movements of the 1960s . . . was that identity is a political construct. Not carved in stone, not 'sutured' (Mouffe and Laclau, 1985), our concepts of ourselves can be dramatically altered by new movements, new articulations of the possible.

While our country struggles to produce such mass movements in the 1990s, the coalition's work and its meetings created a new place that nurtured the convergence of personal honesty and collective commitment that allowed for at least the temporary testing and challenging of racial boundaries.

REBUILDING COMMUNITIES

When Friends World students returned in the spring of 1998, they once again held a demonstration. I came down for a final coalition meeting in April, and we decided to plan a conference for the fall that would bring together local and regional labor and community organizations that worked on social justice issues. The strategy would be one of expanding the solidarity we had created to build a network of support throughout the area. The custodians' union contract would also be coming up for negotiation in November and they believed strongly that Laro would try to force a strike and use replacement workers to bust the union.

From the beginning of the outsourcing, the custodians thought their union had "sold them out" by agreeing to the Laro contract. Most felt the union had never really represented them well. Yet the unit had lacked commitment or solidarity needed to make any significant changes. As the coalition's struggle progressed, however, many members began talking about changing affiliations. By the summer of 1998, they were ready. By a unanimous vote, the custodians selected a Teamsters local to represent them in the fall. The Teamsters had not only promised strong support for contract negotiations, but had thrown full support behind the coalition.

It is impossible to know the impact of this new affiliation, but in conjunction with the prospect of another fall barrage of bad press, campus demonstrations, and direct actions, the college finally agreed to terminate the Laro contract in early September. The administration rehired the entire custodial unit under the same terms they had before the outsourcing and agreed to begin negotiations for a new contract. The college also promoted an African American custodian to mechanic, breaking the campus color line. While the provost told custodians not to think of the contract termination as a "victory," custodians later told a coalition meeting, "It felt like a victory to us."

The victory was multidimensional, though, and shared by everyone in the coalition. In our struggle, the group had attained more than just the tangible goal of having custodians rehired by the college or even of breaking the discriminatory hiring and promotion practices. We had all participated in a process where structural and preconceived identities were challenged. And from these activities, we began creating visions of what universities and their surrounding communities could be. What Jesse termed "staying together as a family" and what many of the students spoke about as "community" were references to a kind of solidarity that inspires thinking about good relationships and institutions where people are not isolated from each other or marginalized from the power to maintain dignity and security.

Some of the most important lessons from the coalition are, as King explained, that "social conformities could be broken." She continued in her journal:

> The custodians were very grateful toward the students for wanting to be involved and for caring about the situation. I was taken aback by their compassion at first; I considered it my duty and responsibility to become part of the coalition. For it was not "their problem" but our community's problem. Moreover, the situation on our campus is a microcosm of what is happening throughout the country.

The more students, faculty, and custodians worked together, talked together, argued and fought together, the more socially constructed barriers were challenged. This isn't to say that race and class prejudices and divisions did not remain salient; they were always with us. But by openly confronting them, we began the long process of reshaping their contours and meaning. That students who attended regular meetings would be able to comprehend the complexities of institutional racism better than those who did not have frequent communications with custodians attests to some of the power of this process.

In some ways, the future of the university derives from this political struggle over the production of knowledge. When students learn as part of a coalition or community of commitment that not only challenges discriminatory practices but accepts the multivalence of authoritative voices (in this case, recognizing custodians as teachers, too) they break down the compartmentalization of knowledge production that has become so prevalent in higher education. This fragmentation of knowledge is a necessary part of the university's corporatization and a key component of what Barbara Ehrenreich has called the "moral numbness" that allows the academy to teach humanities at the same time that it treats its employees like tools of production.

Working in coalitions that struggle for social justice teaches different lessons, as King explains. She writes:

> In retrospect, I think that there were no greater learning experiences than being active in the coalition. . . . My religious and spiritual beliefs teach me to seek a better, more egalitarian, nonhierarchical society. In a sense we are all interconnected, it is easy for me to see that in working with the custodians . . . in all the ways that I know how I am helping myself and weaving a stronger web for all.

When groups such as the Coalition for Justice contest such compartmentalization and corporatization, they create a glimpse of how the university might be reconstructed; a vision of mutual responsibility that might rise from what Bill Readings has called a "university in ruins." For me, this means that such work must be conducted at all academic institutions and carried out by diverse coalitions of representatives from all aspects of campus and community life. For a college professor to be involved in these efforts and to write about them for a larger audience helps establish the conditions for and possibility of new visions of community. And, perhaps, this process sets the standard for what would indeed be a "perfect job."

24

STUDENT UNION
Labor, Community, and Campus Unite to Fight Defunding

Thomas Ehrlich Reifer

*In memory of my brother,
Matthew Benjamin Ehrlich, 1974–1999*

Since the 1994 elections, a national assault on public spending has radically threatened social spending for publicly funded universities, health care, workers, middle-income groups, and the poor as deficit-cutting, budget-balancing politics rule the day. Instead of funding for public higher education being increased with the money from the peace dividend, universities are facing savage cuts even as military spending remains near Cold War levels. The deficit, largely created by the $5–6-trillion program of militarization of the Carter-Reagan-Bush-Clinton years, which provided massive corporate subsidies to private and public universities and corporate research, is now being used to whittle down the democratic possibilities of universal education envisioned by John Dewey and brought about through the struggles of American activists. Indeed, the federal abandonment of aid to the cities and states from the late-Carter years on took place concomitant with the explosion in the military budget, financed both through regressive borrowing offshore and from the domestic rich awash in funds from tax cuts.[1]

For decades, the Cold War served as a pretext for the expansion of U.S. business, war against the Third World, and the containment of U.S. enemies and allies, while providing through the Pentagon system a domestic welfare state for the upper classes and a mechanism of controlling the labor movement and the public as a whole, under the ideological guise of national security. Thus the Cold War system of state-corporate system power lives on, despite its ostensible end with the collapse of the USSR and the Warsaw Pact.[2] Though this ended the ideological justification for roughly half the U.S. military budget, military spending stands at more than 85 percent of Cold War levels, higher than during the Nixon administration and still accounting for half the discretionary budget of the United States. Here, the Persian Gulf War provided for what some have called an operational budget shield, protecting Pentagon funding going to subsidize corporate arms production and high-technology development, while aid for education and human services are slashed.

In the fiscal year 1998 budget for higher education and science, only $12.7 billion went for student aid, including loans at interest, roughly 75 percent of the $75.5 billion for R & D that goes to the Pentagon and allied agencies. On January 1, 1999, Clinton announced planned increases of yet another $100 billion for the military budget. This perversion of resources recurrently passes without critical comment in the *Chronicle of Higher Education* which, with no sense of irony, reports the nearly $1 billion appropriated for the University of California managed labs to ensure "that the nation's nuclear arsenal is safe and in working order." Those programs not deemed essential to the military-academic-industrial complex face severe cuts.[3]

The very force of this budget-cutting assault, though, in the context of the new unionism—notably the graduate student employee unions that serve as a bridge between public workers and students, uniting two groups that are bearing much of the brunt of the budget cuts—has shown the potential for transformative struggles that link graduate student employees, undergraduates, adjuncts/teachers, and other workers in common coalitions. This potential has already found expression in coalitions around the country. This essay explores the experience of the 1995–1996 Citizens' Mobilization to Save New York, which organized a broad-scale coalition of well over sixty graduate student employee, public, and private sector unions, and religious and community activist groups against Governor Pataki's assault on the university and the general corporate attack on the public sector. The process is examined for the lessons it holds up—negative and positive—for successfully resisting the corporate assault on higher education.[4]

In fact, there is a new potential for rainbow coalitions of social movements with the nominal ending of the Cold War, which presents the possibility of tearing down the barriers that have cut off U.S. unionism from the energy of student and other social movements. For the first time in the lives of many activists there are possibilities for a new social-movement unionism that unites students, graduate student employees, faculty, and other university workers, as the union movement seeks to make inroads especially among low-wage and white-collar workers. For while the labor and civil rights movements have historically been the most important democratizing forces for equality and social justice in the United States and throughout the world, the incorporation of elements of these groups within the state-corporate system has limited their independence in important ways. Freeing these movements from the historic straitjackets that have limited the power of all progressive forces in the United States is the major task before us.

The ultimate goal here is the democratization, transformation, and politicization of higher education as part of the struggle for social justice and democratic renewal in the United States and world society. The new harsh political environment in the United States ironically creates opportunities for organizers to break down the walls between universities and workers under assault in ways that transform the politics of the possible in the process. A key goal of our movement is to challenge the nexus between corporations and the national security state in order to free up money for a peace dividend. Only then can we realize the potential of universal free education for all necessary for a new democratic politics oriented toward meeting the needs of people, not profits.[5] More than ever, if social movements are to transform our lives, they must be oriented toward both social change and intellectual understanding as a guide to action.

The stakes described above are illustrated poignantly in the budget battles of 1990s New York. After the 1994 elections, New York voters ousted one of the most articulate spokespersons of liberalism, Governor Mario Cuomo, who had, however, carried out a steady program of austerity and prison expansion, plus billions of dollars in tax giveaways and subsidies for the rich. A frustrated electorate thus chose the unknown George Pataki, a public relations creation of his corporate sponsors. The new right-wing administration was helped along in staffing and policy by the now-dominant right-wing think tank in New York, the Manhattan Institute, started over a decade ago with the help of William Casey, a lawyer and investment banker who would later become Reagan's CIA director, and his allies from the land of Thatcherdom.

A key aspect of Pataki's agenda was to capitalize on New York's economic and political decline by deflecting attention away from corporate power while mobilizing middle-class anger over taxation as a battering ram to destroy the public sector in health, education, and human services. Among the first items on this agenda, after restoring the death penalty, was to confront New Yorkers with the most devastating budget cuts since the Great Depression, including a proposed $290-million cut to the great multiuniversity, the State University of New York (SUNY), and millions of cuts to the City University of New York (CUNY), including the destruction of remedial education and other harsh new regulations that would virtually eliminate the possibility of attendance for the large number of poor students enrolled.

This unprecedented attack on the public budget and the resistance it engendered, however, allowed for some unique politics to come into play.[6] Caught squarely in the headlights of the oncoming budget train was the Graduate Student Employees Union/Communication Workers of America 1188 (GSEU). After fighting for decades for union recognition at SUNY campuses, including a graduate student employee strike, the statewide union had finally been granted legal recognition. With four thousand teaching and graduate assistants, the GSEU became at once the only statewide graduate student employees union—with major campuses in Binghamton, Buffalo, Stonybrook and Albany, and smaller ones from Syracuse to New York City—and the largest one in the country.

In 1994–1995, just after the budget cuts, the GSEU, having just negotiated its first contract with improved wages, health benefits, and student-employee rights, was just beginning to shoulder the responsibilities of helping to administer and organize around the enforcement of the contract. This was especially difficult for a union spread throughout New York State at four major campus centers and more than a dozen smaller campuses. Indeed, at the time the GSEU had no statewide office and what local offices tenuously existed were the result of sporadic guerilla action against university officials.

Suddenly the budget crisis confronted the GSEU with a much bigger problem. The papers carried daily quotes from members of the Pataki administration, who were very open about their strategy. They clearly articulated that they wanted to spread the pain far and wide so they could divide and rule, by getting all the various constituencies to fight against each other, at which point they would steamroll over the opposition. There was an additional problem. The massive budget cuts were driven by the huge so-called tax cuts the governor proposed, which in reality were tax hikes, as the cuts meant increases in the costs of tuition, transportation, and health care for working people. The Democratic assembly response to the governor's proposal exacerbated this situation by increasing these very "tax cuts" by taking money away from education, health care, and other human services, hence forcing up the costs of these programs. While Democratic Party politicians later came out against the budget cuts, this was all political theater, as their own tax breaks for large corporations, the wealthy, and now the middle classes were driving budget executioners' axes. This generated a real need for a political movement with real social anchoring, independent of both parties, that struck at the heart of right-wing populist ideology by mobilizing a countercrusade against corporate power in favor of public sector spending on health, education, and human welfare.

At the time the battle erupted, I was a graduate student employee in sociology at SUNY Binghamton, home to one of the finest and most progressive historical sociology departments in the world, specializing in the study of large-scale, long-term social change, which came out of the Columbia student uprising of 1968.[7] My own political experience included being a former National Student Organizer for the Committee in Solidarity with the People of El Salvador and cochair of the student mobilization committee for the National Demonstration for Peace and Justice in Central America and South Africa in 1987. This demonstration, which had widespread labor and student support, brought some 150,000 people to Washington, D.C., and some 50,000 to San Francisco, including a massive civil disobedience of more than 700 at the headquarters of the CIA, the latter an outgrowth of the CIA off-campus movement.[8]

My own previous work in the movement had helped me to garner considerable organizing experience and a network of political connections, which as the president of the GSEU made me feel compelled to at least try to build a mass coalition against the budget. As the budget hatchet came down I moved to Albany to see what could be done. Discussions between the GSEU and the independent Student Association of the State University (SASU), headed up by then-president Kazim Ali, led to plans for a massive demonstration in Albany against the cuts. SASU was funded by fees from students and had a long history of radical, independent student activism on a host of progressive issues, notably the struggle for student power, diversity, and universal higher education as a right, not a privilege. At the time, I had just recently met the SASU activists, but my chief organizing partners, Chis Vestuto and Tim Dubnau, had long worked with the group on issues of common concern to undergraduates and graduate students.

Ali, quite a charismatic figure in his own right and a powerful speaker, had been a longtime student activist himself. Indeed, Ali would eventually go onto the presidency of the United States Student Association, which provided an independent network for the student movement, with greater autonomy than the student government groups it continued to work with. Initially, the GSEU-SASU partnership meant moving in with SASU, given that the GSEU had no office. Moreover, the alliance forced us to try to function as a single team in the budget battle, in a relationship that eventually led to SASU's renting the GSEU their downstairs basement as our statewide office after the rally.

The key aspect of this mass protest rally was that rather than focusing only on higher education, which in fact various groups did early on and throughout the process, we wanted to unite with all other organizations opposed to Pataki's cuts and his politics of divide and rule. Originally, a meeting in New York City, which the GSEU and SASU attended, seemed to solidify plans for a unified demonstration date and multigroup coalition. With the GSEU's statewide staff person, Chris Vestuto, we came up with a name, the Citizens' Mobilization to Save New York, and a simple mission statement, which read:

> On March 27, 1995, citizens from across New York will converge on the Capitol in Albany to demand the full restoration of the currently proposed massive cuts to education, health, and other public services. The so-called "tax cut" is actually a tax hoax, which would produce nominal benefits for the wealthy, while ordinary New Yorkers suffer skyrocketing property taxes, college tuition rates, and devastating cuts in essential services. We are firmly opposed to any fiscal policy that would bargain away New York State's long-term economic vitality and the future of our children for a pocketful of spare change.

With this simple call in hand, the GSEU mobilized its own membership and started calling up other organizations for endorsements, using the new technology of faxes and modems to spread the momentum. Innumerable graduate student employees put long hours into budget resistance while teaching and taking classes. Across the state, despite numerous problems and errors, the GSEU's membership and its elected officials, working in coalitions, created impressive momentum against the budget locally and for the Albany mobilization. With the Communication Workers of America (CWA) District One's endorsement of student groups, others slowly began to sign on. What really turned a steady stream into a rushing river, however, was that Pataki threatened massive layoffs of public employees unless the legislature accepted the budget.

At the time, the Citizens' Mobilization was one of the few groups that had a call on the table for solidarity among all the different groups affected by the budget. Overnight, along with numerous religious, community activist, and student groups, most of the major public-employee unions in New York State, and numerous private ones as well, signed on to the call. This was truly amazing, as historically the Cold War divide had separated unions from larger social movements, especially that of students. The Citizens' Mobilization thus represented a unique and perhaps unprecedented development in the struggle over the New York State budget. The joining together of these forces in a coalition was made possible by the fact that the coalition was led by graduate student employees who were both students and trade unionists, with a foot in both the labor and the student movements.

Numerous multicultural coalitions and organizations came on board, including the Same Boat Coalition of a hundred or more groups in New York City. This snowballing of support was a testament to the power of the coalition, its message of solidarity, and its effort to be as inclusive as possible while still maintaining a strong position opposing the budget cuts and attacking the tax hoax driving them forward. Organizing New York City was made easier with the help of District One of the CWA. GSEU's international representative, Steve Early, helped to secure resources from District One through its vice president, Jan Pierce, one of the leading progressive labor leaders in the country.[9] Pierce also helped raise the financial resources so students and others from New York city could attend the rally. In a memo to other unions calling for financial help and attendance at an ultimately successful meeting, with representatives from Local 1188 in their Citizens' Mobilization clothing and the major unions of New York City, Pierce underscored that:

> The idea for the rally was developed by CWA Local 1188. . . . They are a unique group bridging two of the major constituencies which will be devastated by the Pataki cuts—students and public workers. It was quite natural for them, therefore, to plan a rally, which instead of focusing on the individual demands of a particular group, attempts to enhance our common fight by bringing together everyone to speak with a unified voice.

The demonstration in Albany, attended by over ten thousand people, was one of the largest and most diverse rallies seen in that city in years. A major theme of the effort, as noted above, was to create an independent political movement to put pressure on both parties and expose all those who were wielding the budget axe to better mobilize opposition; as one labor leader in the New York City meeting noted, quoting Dylan, one of our problems was that "the executioner's face is always well hidden."

The joint efforts of students, labor, religious, and community organizations represented a real step toward a politics of solidarity. The presence of and speeches by religious figures working with feminist, gay, lesbian, and AIDS activists, along with labor officials, rank-and-file workers, a broad-based student movement, groups representing people of color, and a host of other causes, was really something that made this no ordinary protest. A high point of the rally was the whole crowd singing "Which Side Are You On?" Figures such as Daniel Ellsberg, the former Pentagon and State Department official who released the Pentagon Papers, addressed the relationship between the diversion of money to the military budget and the crisis of the cities and states. And as Ellsberg noted, the one difference between the Albany demonstration and antiwar protests during the Vietnam era was that now the unions and the workers were marching with the students arm in arm.

The demonstration was unable to turn around the budget cuts, though it did represent a high tide of opposition. Indeed, the largest public-employee union in the state, the Civil Service Employees Association, signed the contract that would set the pattern of bargaining for the other unions, not coincidentally, the night before the rally, as the threat of telling all its public workers to leave work and attend the mobilization made this its maximum moment of pressure. And the *New York Times*, the day before the March 27 rally, had as its lead editorial a piece called "Time to Rethink the Tax Cuts," which chastised both the Republicans and Democrats for their complicity in the budget cuts, noting:

> The student protests against his education cuts put Gov. Pataki in a ped-agogical mood. He lectured the students fiercely about the need to "bring desperately needed fiscal sanity" to the task of reducing the $5 billion deficit. If only the Governor would listen to his own sermon. He would realize that now is not the time to aggravate that deficit with a nonsensical tax cut. . . .
>
> The current wave of protests represents the rebellion of reasonable minds. The reductions in health care, social services and education have hit the outer limit of conscience . . . .
>
> For their part, Assembly Speaker Sheldon Silver and the Democrats should abandon efforts to outdo the Republicans with a more progressive tax cut of their own and look more to heading off the worst budget cuts.[10]

Our efforts temporarily hurt Pataki's poll ratings and provided an alternative perspective on the budget independent from the corporate ven-triloquism of both parties and their constituencies. Our efforts also led many organizations in New York to think about the possibility of coali-tion actions in the future. And in fact, the following year, the Citizens' Mobilization returned again, with even more endorsements, to work in coalition with other groups carrying out local actions across the state. In addition, the GSEU hosted the National Conference of Graduate Student Employees in 1996 and worked in conjunction with other groups to host a conference and lobby day with students from CUNY and SUNY, which was a major step forward in uniting upstate and downstate constituencies. The GSEU also played an active role in Jobs with Justice and sent a team of delegates to the first annual convention of the Labor Party, as part of its efforts to build an independent political party representing the interests of the broad sector of working people in the United States.

The coalition failed to reverse the corporate onslaught against the stu-dents and workers of New York. The budget was indeed cut, though much less than originally proposed. The formation of an independent Citizens' Mobilization coming out against the logic of two parties' politics and business-as-usual unionism was a major step forward. The efforts thus demonstrated the hope of a new social-movement unionism through building coalitions and alliances based on mutual respect and awareness of common interests. And indeed, though the coalition failed to consolidate itself in New York, the work led to numerous initiates and alliances which built on the success of getting together such a mobilization at all. For example, the close cooperation between the GSEU and SASU on the budget issues solidified a working relationship that has since continued. Unions and community groups met after the rally to work on new initiatives for fighting the budget battles in a more coherent way.

At the same time, the impact of mobilizing for its second contract during all of the budget cuts, in the face of a totally hostile Governor's Office of Employee Relations (GOER), took a toll. Permanent mobilization of our own membership for a decent contract and to preserve the budget for education and human services put our union under enormous strain. The close working relationship the GSEU had with other unions, political leaders, and other groups did help put pressure on the state to grant us the right to grieve and arbitrate violations of the contact, a standard right for most unions denied to Local 1188. Still, with a right-wing administration in power, the GOER refused to budge.

Today, with a long history of an active rank and file, the GSEU is working to rebuild its base, building a strong union and contributing to social-movement unionism, especially the struggle for universal access to higher education and the battle over the public budget. What role the GSEU will play in the future, however, is up to a new generation of leadership, who can hopefully learn from the successes and mistakes of those who came before them.

The experience in New York shows some of the opportunities and difficulties of organizing against corporate and state power as we enter the new millennium. This period has witnessed an extraordinary effort by corporate-subsidized right-wing think tanks and politicians to destroy the public sector, especially education, and with it the dangers of democratic and critical thinking. Graduate student employee activism in New York, as in other states, has enormous potential, for these unions represent public-sector workers on the front line of budget cuts, with feet in both the labor and student movements, providing much energy for cross-fertilizing efforts. And as the Yale Graduate Employees and Student Organization (GESO) has shown, organizing efforts at private Ivy League universities, in cooperation with students and Yale's other unions, has the potential to challenge the attack on labor within the confines of the ivory tower.[11]

Breaking with business unionism and the two-party system beholden to corporate interests will not be an easy task, however, as it means nothing less than overcoming the historical separations between the civil rights, labor, student, and community movements in the United States.

For an alternative, leftist project of social movement unionism to succeed, breaking down the Berlin Wall constructed between unions and the progressive left during the Cold War will be an essential task.[12] The opportunity that remains open in the current conjuncture, especially with the recent thaw in the Cold War orientation of the AFL-CIO[13]—notwithstanding its recent support for NATO expansion—has been expressed most eloquently and succinctly by author and activist Daniel Ellsberg, and thus is quoted at length here.

The breaching of the Berlin Wall could lower the wall between American unions and the multitude of social movements that continue to emerge and grow in the U.S. despite disappointments.

The ending of the Cold War opens the prospect of conversion of the economy that would break the dependence of the labor unions on arms spending, hence permit the shattering of the alliance between union leadership and the national security establishment. At the same time, with the threat of global Communist expansion removed, the direct role of the CIA and of labor officials who share a CIA-like anti-communist perspective in the international departments of major unions and the labor federation could be ended, likewise freeing union energies for alliance with progressive causes both at home and abroad.

In turn, activists in a wide variety of partly-overlapping, now uncoordinated movements could be encouraged for the first time in a generation—for many of them, the first time in their lives—to add to their personal and organizational agendas the strengthening and broadening of the American labor movement and its political role. . . .

Unions in the U.S. represent mainly Northern blue-collar workers —a decreasing fraction of these—who are in turn a declining fraction of U.S. workers.

Every existing and potential movement for improvement in our environment and society—potentially encompassing the vast majority of Americans—has a stake in bringing about this conversion as dramatically and as swiftly as possible. In no other way can their resource requirements be met even partially; but in this way, with no lessening in the military security of this country, the fundamental material requirements of all of them can be covered! . . .

[T]he ending of the Cold War—with the freeing of resources from the arms race, and the potential freeing of unions to join other social movements in directing the reinvestment of those resources—is just the time to get started. It is a time for new strategies and new alliances, the latter a possibility that could hardly have been conceived even one year ago. And perhaps, for a broad range of "progressive, leftist" activities, a new sense of our own political identity.[14]

The Citizens' Mobilization and other new initiatives between students, labor, and university employees represent perhaps some of the first stirrings of this process. These initiatives must ultimately be built and organized at a national and international level if we are to succeed. Of course there will be mistakes and problems along the way for groups fighting with meager resources against the wealthy and powerful. Bold initiatives, however, along with basic grassroots organizing, are necessary to push the limits of progressive transformation of politics and to change the debate to create real movements that can be built upon in the future. Moreover, we must initiate a dialogue between the family of movements on maintaining solidarity among our forces, working in common when we can. Problems in organizing should be a first step in an ongoing effort to talk and work honestly and openly about how to move forward in the struggle. This means honest and open discussion, the willingness to put down egos and listen to and learn from each other.

Before some of the latest round of budget cuts, I was allowed to speak before Pataki's new right-wing corporate SUNY board of regents, in the grand tradition of giving persons five minutes to speak and a cigarette before their execution. After stating the budget cuts were carried out in favor of and at the behest of corporations and the wealthy, many of whose representatives, I noted, were among us, I quoted the following from radical educator John Dewey, whose organic contributions to the United States Left have recently been rescued in Robert Westbrook's *John Dewey and American Democracy*.[15] I was first thinking of Governor Pataki, who knew nothing of public school but instead went to Yale:

> Nothing in the history of education is more touching than to hear some successful leaders denounce as undemocratic the attempts to give all the children at public expense the fuller education which their own children enjoy as a matter of course.

I then spoke the words of Dewey again, as he pinpointed clearly the task at hand:

> The price that democratic societies will have to pay for their continuing health is the elimination of an oligarchy—the most exclusive and dangerous of all—that attempts to monopolize the benefits of intelligence and the best methods for the profit of a few privileged ones, while practical labor, requiring less spiritual effort and less initiative remains the lot of the great majority.

NOTES

1. For an analysis of decline of aid to the states and cities, see Mike Davis, "Who Killed LA? A Political Autopsy," *New Left Review* 197 (January/February 1993): 3–28.

2. For a review of the Cold War system and its legacy, see Thomas Reifer and Jamie Sudler, "The Interstate System," in *The Age of Transition: Trajectory of the World-System, 1945–2025,* coords. Immanuel Wallerstein and Ternece K. Hopkins (London: Zed Press, 1996), pp. 13–37. See also Gabriel Kolko, *The Politics of War* (New York: Vintage, 1968); Gabriel and Joyce Kolko, *The Limits of Power* (New York: Harper & Row, 1972); and Noam Chomsky, *Deterring Democracy* (New York: Verso, 1991).

3. For an early account of the formation the military-academic complex, see Clyde Barrow, *Universities and the Capitalist State* (Madison: University of Wisconsin Press, 1990). For a long historical view of the origins of military-industrial complexes in the modern world system, see Giovanni Arrighi, Po-Keung Hui, Krishnendu Ray, and Thomas Ehrlich Reifer, "Geopolitics and High Finance," in Giovanni Arrighi, Beverly Silver, et al., *Chaos and Governance in the Modern World System* (Minneapolis: University of Minnesota Press, 1999), pp. 37–96. See also Giovanni Arrighi, *The Long Twentieth Century: Money, Power & the Origins of Our Times* (New York: Verso, 1994).

4. See also my piece, "Mobilizing to Save New York State," *Against the Current* (May/June 1995): 3–4.

5. Readers should consult the voluminous and fundamental writings of Noam Chomsky on the relationship between military spending, corporate domination, and the attack on democracy. See especially Noam Chomsky, *Towards a New Cold War* (New York: Pantheon, 1992) and *Profit Over People: Neoliberalism and Global Order* (New York: Seven Stories Press, 1999). On the militarization of the universities, see also Jonathan Feldman, *Universities in the Business of Repression: The Academic-Military-Industrial Complex in Central America* (Boston: South End Press, 1989).

6. For an analysis of an earlier round of public budget battles, see Sidney Plotkin and William E. Scheuerman, *Private Interests, Public Spending: Balanced-Budget Conservatism and the Fiscal Crisis* (Boston: South End Press, 1994).

7. For a synopsis of this unique experiment, see the short book on one of the program's founders, who died in 1996, *Mentoring, Methods, and Movements: Colloquium in Honor of Terence K. Hopkins,* by his former students (Fernand Braudel Center, 1998).

8. For an account of the demonstration along with the campus-based CIA organizing, see Tony Vellela, *New Voices: Student Political Activism in the '80s and '90s* (Boston, Mass.: South End Press, 1988).

9. See Steve Early's "Membership-Based Organizing," in *A New Labor Movement for a New Century,* ed. Gregory Mantsios (New York: Monthly Review, 1998), pp. 82–103.

10. "Time to Rethink the Tax Cuts," *New York Times*, March 26, 1996, p. A14.

11. See Cary Nelson, ed., *Will Teach for Food* (Minneapolis: University of Minnesota Press, 1997).

12. For one of most penetrating analyses of the U.S. labor movement, as well as the landscape of Reaganism and its afterlife, see Davis, *Prisoners of the American Dream*. See also Paul Buhle, *Taking Care of Business: Samuel Gompers, George Meany, Lane Kirkland, and the Tragedy of American Labor* (New York: Monthly Review, 1999).

13. See Josh Lyons and Tom Reifer, "AFL-CIO-Endorsed Expansion of NATO Will Hurt Workers," *Labor Notes* (April 1998): 10. For another attempt to outline an visionary alternative to contemporary politics, see Roberto Mangabeira Unger, *Democracy Realized: The Progressive Alternative* (New York: Verso, 1998).

14. Daniel Ellsberg, "Unions, Conversion, and Social Democracy: A Line of Advance for the Post–Cold War U.S.," unpublished. Quoted with permission of the author. This analysis should be compared with the brilliant piece of Giovanni Arrighi, "Marxist Century, American Century: The Making and Remaking of the World Labour Movement," *New Left Review* 179 (January/February 1990): 29–64. See also Giovanni Arrighi, Terence K. Hopkins, and Immanuel Wallerstein, *Antisystemic Movements* (New York: Verso, 1989).

15. Robert B. Westbrook, *John Dewey and American Democracy* (Ithaca: Cornell University Press, 1991), pp. 173, 178.

Part Six

MUCKRAKING 101
Advice and Resources
for Campus Organizers

25

GREED IN THE GROVES

Ralph Nader

The aggressive spread of corporate priorities and mercantile values respects few boundaries in our society—and academic traditions and values are not among the few. The corporate mentality views colleges and universities as valuable testing grounds for business-defined technologies, as valuable trade schools for corporate recruits, as valuable research centers for further corporate products, as valuable instruments for legitimizing corporate ethics, and as valuable terrain to possess in the drive against challenging alternatives to corporate-think. For corporations, universities and colleges are facile mechanisms for converting tax-supported wealth into private profit, institutions vulnerable to reshaping through the cooptation of grants and deals.

Pressing the corporate model onto the university world jeopardizes the preservation of precious academic values, as well as broader democratic rights. The corporate model concentrates power; restricts the production and application of knowledge; and increases uniform behavior, self-censorship, and—when needed—outright suppression. Thomas Jefferson warned Americans about the "excesses of the monied interests" when he urged representative government. Higher education is another one of those crucial countervailing powers to the dominance of the "economic government." Universities, as described in a recent Carnegie Foundation essay, perform "an integrative function, seeking appropriate responses to life's most enduring questions, concerning themselves not just with information and knowledge, but with wisdom." Everywhere the generation of knowledge for the uses and enlightenment of humanity is slowed, stalled, or stopped by a business mentality unable to tolerate criticism or pause to consider alternative models for economic activity. The growing business regulation of government has pulled these two major social institutions into an unhealthy, tight convergence lubricated by government contracts, subsidies, and business campaign contributions. The overall result is the dissipation of accountability, untreated problems, and ever more serious risks. Our country has more problems than it deserves and more solutions than it uses. The unleashed desire for the unlimited acquisition of wealth skews all priorities.

Ensuring that knowledge and progressive principles *matter* in our society is an urgent necessity that demands collaboration. The controversial issues of these turbulent times merit a systematic response from concerned faculty members working in concert. The talent, care, and potential exists among thousands of thoughtful and progressive faculty members at campuses throughout the nation. But, for the most part, these concerned people do not know one another.

There needs to be a mechanism that facilitates concerted action on serious matters among the members of this most significant but unconnected population. That, at least, is the conclusion I find inescapable after listening to hundreds of faculty members express their desire to wed knowledge to action and theory to practice. Again and again, on major issues from civil rights to the arms race, from Agent Orange to auto safety, from soil erosion to acid rain, from corporate monopoly to government violations of the law, from automation dislocation to the corporate looting of America, precious time passes with painful results to many people before knowledge is brought to bear on the misfortunes that afflict our nation.

With our support, a national coalition for universities in the public interest will begin this year to bring together thousands of Americans from higher education who want to make a difference with knowledge by making knowledge the difference between bewailing the present and shaping the future.

For more information, write: National Coalition for Universities in the Public Interest, Box 19367, Washington, D.C. 20036, or e-mail ncupi@ earthlink.net

26

IN THE HANDS OF YOUTH
The Growing Struggle for Democracy and Education

Ben Manski

"We are the university!"
"Hey, why can't you see? We need more diversity!"
"Schools not jails!"
"This is what democracy looks like!"
"Corporate-free university!"

. . . sounds of the '90s

This essay is an offering of tools for organizers and for would-be organizers. Its purpose is to provide an understanding of how a democracy and education movement has come into being on university, liberal arts, technical, and community college campuses across North America. Rather than serving the rigid principles of academic inquiry, my intent here is to offer the reader some practical perspectives gained from personal experience in campus organizing. I also intend to offer the reader hope for the future. Although the corporatization of education represents a grave crisis, it is a process that is being effectively confronted on a growing number of campuses.

Most of what appears here was written in 1998. At that time, the title was "The Coming Struggle for Campus Democracy"; today, in the aftermath of Seattle, the struggle is already here. The reader may wish to consider this essay as both a framework for future action and a social movement history of what has come already.

CHANGING CONDITIONS IN THE '90S

Twenty thousand students march on city hall in New York City, strikes rock campuses in Ontario and Quebec, May Day demonstrators descend on the Wisconsin branch of the National Association of Manufacturers and set its marquee afire, and students across California occupy buildings and fast for ethnic studies and civil rights.[1] The scene so described, as any observer of campus organizing well knows, is that of campus movements in the 1990s. Yet the fact that the public relations industry has gotten away with replacing the phrase "student power" with that of "student apathy," in the face of all facts to the contrary,[2] says something about today's movements. For all our recent sit-ins, strikes, and successes, students in most parts of North America have yet to gather our energies to help create a general education movement that is a decisive political force.[3] Nonetheless, there are efforts underway today to do just that.

What is different about today's efforts? If we were to look back several decades in an effort to find some example against which to compare today's student movement, it would be difficult to uncover evidence of a conscious, generalized pattern of campus organizing; rather, the student movement of those years was fractured. The following examples will illustrate this point. In 1983, students mobilized as part of more general efforts to resist the draft, halt the nuclear arms race, protest President Reagan's gutting of social welfare programs, free political prisoners, support the revolution in Nicaragua, and so on.[4] Five years later, we find another array of issues emerging on campuses as part of larger struggles carrying on at the time: mobilizations for reproductive rights, against apartheid in South Africa, in support of the rebels in El Salvador, against racism locally and nationally, against U.S. interventions in Panama and the Persian Gulf, for gay rights, and so on.[5] Recently, in the early years of the 1990s, as the so-called new social movements[6] have come to the fore, we find evidence of student participation in the emergence of new political parties, resistance to NAFTA and GATT, environmental justice and wilderness defense campaigns, gay rights activism, Chiapas solidarity work, protests against the Ku Klux Klan, indigenous rights campaigns, and farmworker support.[7]

The point here is that the many surges of student activism throughout the 1980s and 1990s could more truly be attributed to organizing happening off campus rather than on campus; the student movement at that time served chiefly to support and reflect the broader movement. I do not intend to claim that no substantive efforts around on-campus organizing took place: Certainly organizations such as the United States Student Association and other education lobby groups focused on fighting for what have been traditionally labeled "student issues" in education policy, such as financial aid, diversity programs, tuition rates, and so on. In fact, it is worth pointing out that at various points over the past several decades, various student organizations engaged in fairly radical direct action campaigns to kick the ROTC and CIA off campus; to win fair contracts for campus workers; to force their schools to divest from South Africa; and to establish ethnic studies, women's studies, and other similar programs.[8] Yet it seems to have been generally true that the lessons of these instances of targeted on-campus mobilization were lost amid a sea of momentous issues and emergencies. Until now, there has been no ongoing student-based campaign principally aimed at radically restructuring education for the needs of the people.

Today, therefore, we witness two very different conditions on campuses across the United States. We witness first that for all the efforts of organizers of the past, student activism passed into the 1990s in a sorry state. The face of student activism in the early to mid-1990s, with some notable exceptions, was that of fractured organization, a dwindling resource base, and no common frame of action. Second, we are witness to the transformation of education by administrators, foundations, and politicians in order to meet the demands of the corporate sector. Furthermore, we can see clearly that in recent years, students, educators, labor unions, and members of the general public have begun to respond to the increasing corporatization of education with growing protest. Many people don't want their schools to promote the politics and values of a corporate society.

For the moment, these two conditions of student disorganization and of the corporatization of education coexist. Meanwhile, the response to corporatization is taking on a more organized and radical character that threatens to end the era of so-called student apathy.

Let's explore the recent rise of an expressly countercorporate, pro-democracy direction in student and education movements, and briefly discuss the Democracy Teach-Ins as an example of work based in this orientation. I'll conclude by outlining a series of strategic organizing principles that I believe to be particularly well-suited to efforts to overcome our current challenges.

SOURCES OF THE NEW DIRECTION

Few would have predicted a decade ago that the emergence of a pro-democracy direction in student organizing would be taking place today. Yet at the moment a new direction is emerging, it is being taken up by various constituencies within the campus community, and the only question that clearly remains is how far they will take it. We might as well ask: Under what conditions did this come to be?

On close examination, three recent trends across many United States campuses appear to have contributed to the emergence of a campus democracy movement. These are:

(1) *Proactive Trends*—Progressive organizations have been taking a proactive interest in campus politics to further their own specific agendas.

(2) *Reactive Trends*—Students, faculty, labor activists, and members of the general public have reacted defensively against attacks on education.

(3) *Transformative Trends*—Education sector activists and anticorporate organizers have developed a comprehensive response to the corporatization of education.

Proactive Campus Campaigns

The first of these trends is hardly new. The antiwar and civil rights movements in particular have historically engaged in on-campus organizing, with the express purpose of expanding their influence, bringing in new activists, and confronting the complicity of the education establishment in supporting war making and/or in institutionalizing discrimination. One slogan of the antiwar movement in the late 1960s was "Bring The War Home."[9]

In the latter half of the 1990s, international solidarity, environmental, and labor organizations, among others, have engaged in campus campaigns aimed at furthering their respective causes. Many organizations have engaged in on-campus organizing campaigns aimed at engaging students in efforts to get their schools to divest of particular corporations or to cease procuring particular products.[10] At the same time, organized labor has invested significantly greater resources, to great success, in expanding the ranks of unionized campus workers and in delivering greater benefits to those workers.[11] These types of on-campus campaigns have tended to boost both student and community organizing efforts: Students gain hands-on organizing experience, as well an understanding of how decisions are actually made on their campus; community and labor organizations gain greater publicity for their causes and a strong link to a new generation of organizers.

Reactive Campus Campaigns

At the same time that proactive on-campus organizing campaigns have taken off, students and others in education have been forced to be reactive in defending the social gains of the past. Affirmative action programs, ethnic and gender studies, campus labor unions, first generation and immigrant students, multilingual education, and civil rights policies for the queer/gay community have all come under attack. The general perception is that these attacks are coming from conservative organizations, and that the obvious motivations of those organizations are sexist, racist, nativist, and homophobic in character. While this perception is certainly well-founded, an additional element in these attacks is becoming public knowledge: The funding for these organizations, and for the politicians implementing their agenda, generally has come from within the corporate sector.[12]

Unfortunately, it's not enough that the gains of four decades of social progress are crashing everywhere around us; education is also facing attacks of a different kind. University, college, and public-school administrations almost everywhere are caving in to an onslaught of so-called education reforms for the 1990s: corporate promotional contracts, taxpayer subsidies for private corporate schools, privatization of campus services and student programs, monopolistic technology contracts, and, finally, an intense lobbying effort on the part of such organizations as the National Association of Manufacturers to cut state and federal support for public education. In each of these cases it is also exceedingly clear to a growing number of students that large corporations are behind the attack on education.

In a bid to halt these attacks on education, students have joined in coalition with interested members of the general public, faculty, and other campus workers. As significantly as the proactive on-campus campaigns, these reactive campaigns have boosted student and campus organizing in various parts of the country.

Transformative Response to Corporatization

Amid the growing storm of conflict descending on campuses in the 1990s, the great majority of students and educators have been caught unprepared; it is no surprise that recent campus movements have generally had a reactive character. Yet some people were not caught completely unaware by the arrival of the storm; these people had their intellectual fingers to the wind, so to speak. One of the first significant rumblings of the struggles ahead was the publication in 1995 of *Leasing the Ivory Tower*, by Larry Soley, a professor at Marquette University in Milwaukee, Wisconsin:

Corporate, foundation, and tycoon money has had a major, deleterious impact on universities. Financial considerations have turned around academic priorities, reduced the importance of teaching, degraded the integrity of academic journals, and determined what research is conducted at universities. The social costs of this influence have been lower-quality education, a reduction in academic freedom, and a covert transfer of resources from the public to the private sector.[13]

In short, education is being reconstructed to serve the priorities of corporate profit, and is in the process being destroyed as an institution of democracy. Public education theorists such as Soley have developed an analysis that explains in detail what is changing in education today, who is behind these transformations, how they are going about achieving their goals, and what they hope to achieve by their machinations. This analysis is hardly new, of course. Mario Savio, a member of the 1960s Berkeley free speech movement challenged the notion of the industrial university in his famous "Machine" speech from the steps of Sproul Hall. Countless others have remarked on and written on the rise of the corporate influence on education.[14] Yet it has arguably only been in recent years that this analysis has become as widely available or as clear and articulate as it is today. What has changed?

In the 1990s, the question of corporate power came to the fore. In the arena of trade, the 1990s were marked by the establishment of NAFTA, the World Trade Organization, the European Union, the contemporary Multilateral Agreement on Investments negotiations, and numerous regional trade federations. On the labor front, strikes against Caterpillar, Staley, UPS, Trailmobile, Gannett Newspapers, and General Motors all took national stage as the so-called Labor War Zone of central Illinois stretched across the continent. Prison building and the privatization of the justice system doubled and quadrupled in pace. Welfare was transformed into a government-run union-busting temp service for corporations. The move to implement universal health care, popular with the public, was killed by industry lobbyists and their campaign contributions. NBC/GE was joined by ABC/Disney and CBS/Westinghouse, as the national news media continued to consolidate with other sectors of industry. And a twin strategy of co-optation and suppression was unleashed by the mining, oil, and timber giants as efforts were stepped up to eliminate ecological resistance movements. In the 1990s, there was no question that the corporation had moved to consolidate its hold on power.

Some people saw it coming. Among those who, in the late 1980s, came to the conclusion that the coming consolidation of corporate dominance was inevitable were Richard Grossman and Ward Morehouse, who formed what later became the Program on Corporations, Law, and Democracy (POCLAD). Since 1993, POCLAD has organized over one hundred weekend "Rethinks," short for "Rethinking the Corporation," at which organizers from diverse social movements have come together and figured out that, in Grossman's words:

> In the final analysis . . . it is useless to try and reform corporations. Corporations do whatever they want and remain by and large entirely unaccountable. The key educational struggle if we work in this premise as activists is to educate ourselves in coming up with a "new story" which will redefine people as holding dominion over and above the corporations.[15]

Until recently, the struggle against corporate power has indeed turned out to be an educational struggle. Among the new democracy activists, education, rather than direct action, has been the primary means of achieving change. In large part this may have been because the problem of corporate power now looms so large and runs so deep that the new democrats are wary to look before they leap. Given the tendency of many people to rely on conventional ways of doing things in the face of new challenges, it became necessary to focus on education as well as action. As POCLAD researcher and corporate anthropologist Jane Anne Morris put it:

> There is no reason why grassroots activists can not insist that we once again impose . . . laws to direct corporate actions. But because education and media corporations are silent about the power of the sovereign people literally to dictate terms to corporations, we instead spend our time fighting in regulatory agencies and courts where the odds are against us from the get-go.[16]

Meanwhile, of all the fronts of the corporate war on the world's peoples, among the most stark contests has been that over education itself. Amid the attacks on labor unions, social welfare programs, immigrant rights, environmental regulations, wilderness protections, and affirmative action policies, and during a time of mass imprisonment of millions of U.S. citizens, the institution of education could hardly be left alone. The strategic importance of education in the war over who shall rule could not be overlooked.

Examine what is at stake. U.S. universities provide the corporate sector with trillions of dollars worth of research and development. The ranks of tomorrow's corporate management are prepared and stratified in the schools of today, and the undesirables are weeded out. Tomorrow's popular culture is refined, commodified, and distributed en masse from the bowels of the college scene. Schools continue to play the twin roles of centers of both resistance and status quo policy making, and to influence politics disproportionate to their populations. Even the sheer market potential of public education as a private for-profit multitrillion-dollar industry is at play.

Education is in crisis.

Given these trends, how could it be surprising that among the first constituencies to join the ranks of the new democracy movement are those directly involved in the field of education? In fact that is what is happening, as those same students, educators, and workers engaged in proactive and reactive campus struggles have joined with the democrats and education intellectuals to prepare the way for a new campus democracy movement. This confluence of conditions, this common sense of crisis, is what is different about education in the 1990s. It is out of these conditions that one collaborative effort has emerged: the Democracy Teach-Ins.

DEMOCRACY TEACH-INS

Until recently, the Democracy Teach-Ins (DTIs) have been a work in progress. The teach-ins arose out of a need to address disagreement over that perennial question, "What is to be done?" Since the teach-ins were first proposed in February of 1996, they have grown in focus, participation, method, and leadership with each passing year. Today, disagreements over what is to be done still persist, yet the broader campus climate in which those disagreements are taking place has been transformed. In some ways, the teach-ins have been instruments of that transformation.

In February of 1996, some fifty activists from across North America met at a conference sponsored by the Coalition for Socially Responsible Investment at the University of Wisconsin–Madison to discuss possible courses of action. Participants included student activists, human rights campaigners, policy makers in the area of social responsibility, and community-based anticorporate campaigners. In this gathering, then, were present some of those involved in the trends—proactive, reactive, and transformative—I've previously identified as leading to a broader campus democracy struggle.[17]

After a weekend of discussion and debate, it became clear that a consensus would not be reached as to a common course of action. The participants were divided on numerous questions: Should the focus be on social responsibility or on corporate power? How fast could a movement be pulled together to address these questions? Who would do it, and by what authority? Was this to be a student, campus, community, or joint effort? What kind of tactics were to be adopted by this movement? There was little agreement on these questions, and the discussion was lost in foggy weariness. And so, in the waning hours of the conference, instead of a course of action, the group found that it could agree only on a course of education, the teach-ins, and on a set of dates for those teach-ins, October 13–19, 1996.[18]

Without entering into a play-by-play account of the work involved in building the teach-ins, it would still do some good to explain how the effort grew and changed over the years. The teach-ins, as they were originally conceived, were intended always as an intermediary step along the way to something bigger. The idea, in simple terms, was to engage in an extensive educational program aimed at getting to the bottom of that same old question, "What is to be done?"

By holding teach-ins on college campuses and in high schools, community centers, and union halls, we intended that two kinds of essential education take place. First, organizers hoped to foster the kind of mass outreach and education that takes places all too rarely in our society. We developed a common question that could be asked of teach-in participants everywhere: *"Can we pursue democracy and social justice when corporations are allowed to control so much power and wealth?"* The idea was to spread the net wide, and to draw in all the thousands of interested people who are not reached on a daily basis in the somewhat insular world of activism as usual.

The other central purpose of teach-in organizers was to educate ourselves. We sought to learn more about what it would take to successfully build a mass movement for democracy. What would it take to reach and involve new circles of people in civic action? To develop our own communication, learning, and work skills? To find common agreement among different communities as to what must be done? What was the true nature of the problem we were so busy organizing teach-ins about? These questions all are permanent features of any dynamic movement, and so they have remained questions of the teach-ins to this day.

With such questions in mind, some aspects of the Democracy Teach-Ins have changed since February 1996, mostly for the better. Certainly the number of teach-ins increased from the first round to the second, with some forty-five having taken place in the fall of 1996, and more than one hundred in the spring of 1998. The name of the teach-ins themselves has changed, from the "National Teach-In on Corporations, Education, and Democracy" to the shortened "Democracy Teach-Ins."[19] In a sign of some success, the circle of people involved in organizing the teach-ins has changed markedly, as students and campus organizers have increasingly taken over from community-based activists in playing a lead role in the development of the project.[20] Perhaps the most significant change in the

Democracy Teach-Ins has come in focus. The 1996 teach-ins were only loosely connected events, tied together more on paper than in practice. The 1998 teach-ins, on the other hand, more consistently dealt with the future of education as a question in and of itself.[21] These shifts in size, participation, and focus demonstrate in their coming the success of one component of the teach-in educational program, in that those of us involved in organizing the teach-ins were able to apply the lessons we learned along the way, some of which are articulated in this essay.

For all the dynamism of the DTIs, certain recurring issues have continued to define aspects of the effort. Chief among these is the often problematic issue of race, specifically dealing with the issue of control over the DTI project. The overwhelming majority of teach-in organizers and participants have been white college students, who are therefore doubly privileged by race and by class. While the ranks of leadership both at the general and the local levels of DTI organizing have become somewhat more inclusive over the years, the problem still remains. The DTIs have remained too distant from the work of majority–student of color organizations, which often have had their hands full leading campaigns around affirmative action, prison building, immigration, and—yes—the corporatization of education. As on the labor and ecological fronts, the question of race and nationality continues to pose a powerful practical and ethical challenge to those students and educators who support building a united democracy movement in this country.

Similar struggles have taken place over the role of women in the teach-ins. As with the issue of race, the question of gender has remained a recurring theme of the teach-ins, in particular as far as process questions have been taken up. By process questions I mean those such as, but not limited to, these: Who speaks? Who is spoken to? Who is seen to be in charge? Who takes charge? Such questions remain fundamental to any claim to democracy. A major criticism of the teach-ins has been that the assumption of a focus on corporatization versus democracy as such has ignored more long-standing and pervasive struggles over power. For example, organized systems of domination of women by men, or patriarchy, continue today, and go back a long, long time, predating the emergence of corporations and capitalism itself.[22] Such criticisms must be understood and acted upon by those who carry on the teach-ins and similar projects. Specifically, those who raise the banner of democracy and education must be positive that antiracism, feminism, and gay/queer liberation, among other essential struggles, are part and parcel of what they are about. An understanding of the corporatization of education does not subsume these struggles in its wake; instead, it is a contribution to a larger struggle of which all these are integral and ever-linking parts.

A final and no less frustrating difficulty encountered by teach-in organizers has been that of a lack of resources and experience. Throughout the teach-in project, the majority of funding came in through small contributions that amounted to just barely enough to cover printing, phone, and similar costs. The majority of labor for the effort was done on a volunteer basis, as funding for staff time was donated only briefly for a total of two months at the beginning of the three-year effort. Only a very few of the many people directly involved in coordinating the teach-ins over the years possessed any previous experience in national or international organizing; many lessons at this level of organizing had to be learned through the school of hard knocks. Finally, the DTIs were concentrated heavily in the United States's Midwest and South; we found ourselves marginalized by what we perceived to be a bicoastal bias on the part of funders, other activists, and the media.

Have the Democracy Teach-Ins been a success overall? Are the student movement and campus organizing stronger today than they were before the teach-ins? Did the teach-ins have anything to do with that? Are students, educators, and members of the general public more aware of what is being done to subvert education and to suppress democracy in this country?[23]

By most measures, the answer to these questions is "yes."

Yet in a very real sense, the teach-ins remain a work in progress. At the 1998 Campus Democracy Convention, a turning point in the Democracy Teach-In effort, a significant change in direction and in scope occurred. Participants at the Campus Democracy Convention decided to form a new chapter-based organization: the 180 Movement for Democracy and Education (180/MDE). That's a "movement" fighting for a "180"-degree turn toward "democracy," and for "education" as a fundamental right. The members of the 180/MDE are currently organizing teach-ins and actions targeting the World Trade Organization's (WTO) attempts to globally corporatize education.

Putting the 180/MDE, WTO, and the rest of our 1990s alphabet soup aside for a moment, it's worth recognizing that already something important has been accomplished. On North American campuses, after a century of misuse and abuse, democracy is coming into its own as a radical challenge to corporate power.

CAMPUS DEMOCRACY: WHAT IT IS—WHY IT'S IMPORTANT

Until now, there has been no ongoing, student-based, large-scale campaign aimed principally at radically restructuring education for the needs of the people. Today something has changed. I've explored how it is that a campus democracy theme has emerged out of various proactive, reactive, and transformative strands of North American campus and student movements. The question on the table is: What does this "campus democracy" look like?

Fundamentally, the heart and soul of campus democracy reside with the question of power, especially power on the campus: Who holds it, who is benefited by it, and to what ends. We could probably look at the question of campus democracy from any number of perspectives. We'd be best served here, however, by putting our version of campus democracy together the way it appears to have come together, which is out of the experience of those who are now creating it. Six major elements have been fundamental to the creation of a campus democracy orientation: Social responsibility, diversity and civil rights, the right to organize, access to education, research/curriculum/technology issues, and campus governance. These are campaigns actively underway on hundreds of campuses across North America.

Social responsibility campaigns generally seek to alter a school's investment, procurement, or merchandising policies so as to reward corporations whose actions are more conducive to the general welfare. These are proactive campaigns in that they aim to direct a school's funds away from corporations that cause social injury, and toward those that promote social good, as measured against particular standards of corporate conduct (typically these are environmental, labor, human rights, and/or civil rights standards).

A stunning example of this kind of campus campaign was the recent wave of antisweatshop building occupations and sit-ins. These actions were aimed at forcing campus administrators to require that any apparel sold featuring the college's logo be "sweatshop-free."[24] Social responsibility campaigns generally speak to the values an educational community upholds; unfortunately, these campaigns often illustrate just how little say students, educators, and members of the public have in campus policy.

Diversity and civil rights concerns have recently become even more central to campus struggles, as the orchestrated attacks on affirmative action, ethnic studies, and multiculturalism proceed apace. These attacks have forced students and educators to organize reactive campaigns in defense of these policies. At the same time, proactive efforts to expand civil rights guarantees have continued in the form of domestic partnership benefits, increased faculty and administrative hiring and retention of women and people of color, and campus police oversight boards, among many other examples.[25] Together these efforts constitute a struggle to expand on the traditional civil rights movement.

In the spring of 1999, the Third World Liberation Front (TWLF) was reborn on the University of California, Berkeley campus as a reaction to an administrative announcement that the Ethnic Studies Department was to be gutted. The protests began as a hunger strike and building occupation, grew to involve mass demonstrations and arrests, and ended in the capitulation of the administration. The questions before us on this front of campus struggle are chiefly about "who counts": Who gets in to the academy? How far do they get? How much do they get rewarded for their labor? What are they taught? Where do they get tracked to? How much weight does their voice carry in education policy?

The right to organize of students and campus workers is under direct attack in the 1990s. Wherever student power is strong, it is subject to a deliberate and continuous assault from those who consider themselves to be the defenders of conservative principles and Christian morality. The most targeted of these attacks have come in the form of lawsuits designed, as described in the propaganda of one foundation, to force elected student governments to "defund the Left," which apparently includes service groups for women and for the gay/queer community, cultural and national organizations, environmental and labor groups, and so on.[26] Students have been forced into reactive positions by these assaults, yet have been able in the process to build a national response, coordinated by the Center for Campus Free Speech, which clearly identifies their assailants for what they are: religious fundamentalists allied with corporate funders whose common goal is to destroy student activism.

Furthermore, organized campus labor, as with labor almost everywhere, is subject today to an unrelenting assault, as university administrators across the United States invest tens of millions of dollars in union-busting firms and management-restructuring schemes aimed at destroying campus labor organization once and for all. The labor response: renewed efforts at organizing campus labor and an increased militancy in contract negotiations.[27]

Access to education is becoming ever more restricted. Over the past several decades, tuition has increased on average at over twice the rate of inflation. Financial aid programs have shifted 180 degrees away from gifts and scholarships in favor of loans. Meanwhile, college administrators have consciously made efforts to reduce the number of students admitted into college each year. Due in part to attacks on college minority recruitment and retention policies, the majority of those who are admitted continue to be white and/or students from middle- or higher-income families. Together, these trends amount to a crisis of accessibility, a crisis that is tearing at the traditional liberal promise of equal opportunity. The response to this crisis has been reactive to the extent that students have campaigned for reductions or at least a freeze in tuition rates; for increases in direct financial aid; and for the maintenance of more open admission, recruitment, and retention policies.

Ontario has emerged as a recent flashpoint in the struggle over access. There the reaction against education cuts has taken the form of student strikes on multiple campuses, as well as the occupation of bank and government buildings.[28] In regions such as Ontario and Quebec, it has it has become clear that the promise of public education itself has come under attack. As a result, students and others increasingly are campaigning expressly on behalf of education. Increases in tuition rates, cuts in financial aid, and declining admissions are all a function of reduced public funding for education. Access to education is declining as public education comes under attack. Yet it is not the public that has been clamoring for reduced funding. Corporate lobbies such as the National Association of Manufacturers (USA) have been largely responsible for the cuts in education spending over the past several decades. At the same time, the corporate sector and its think tanks have been promoting prison building as a solution for the so-called crime problem. It's a grim picture: Government prisons have been going up while our public schools fall apart, and both are being replaced at an ever faster pace by privatized prisons and privatized schools, all paid for by the public.[29] It is this situation that today's campaigns on behalf of access to education must combat.

Research, curriculum, and/or technology-oriented campaigns go right to the core of the crisis brought on by the corporatization of education. On the campus of today, public and student needs increasingly have come into conflict with private corporate profit. All too often corporate profit proves the more powerful force in these conflicts. Yet as the corporate sector has increasingly come to rely upon higher education for information-age workers and technological development, education intellectuals and activists are beginning an organized response. Where corporations have used "grants" and "partnerships" to control the content of research projects and gain ownership of the products of that research, students and faculty have fought them.[30] Where information technology companies have pushed for exclusive monopoly contracts with particular campuses or entire university systems, they have consistently met with resistance, and in some cases been defeated, as was the case with the California Education Technology Initiative (CETI) program at the California State University system.[31] Where liberal arts programs are eliminated or demands for ethnic, gender, or sexuality studies are frustrated, departments favored by corporate executives are baldly subsidized.[32] These struggles over public need versus corporate greed are occurring everywhere. As these struggles mount, the issues become less and less subtle: Can for-profit corporations interact with educational institutions without exploiting them?

Campus governance campaigns deal most directly with the question of "Who rules?" Traditionally, the answer to this question on most any college campus has been "The rich and powerful rule." How little some things have changed! The modern campus is ruled from on high by a governing board of regents or trustees, which sets policy on everything from tuition to research. The majority of these governing boards are neither elected nor representative, and are stacked instead with corporate executives and/or the patrons and friends of powerful politicians. Noticeably underrepresented on these boards are women, people of color, openly lesbian/gay/ bisexual/transgendered people, people of low or middle income, or for that matter, anybody with experience in the field of education. Ultimately, students, campus workers, educators, and the general public do not rule the campus of the 1990s, corporations do.

At the administrative level of campus governance, wherein hundreds of faculty members and staff administrators sit on scores of policy-making committees, it is rare to this day to find students or nonacademic staff that have much or any voice at all. Even institutions that employ some form of "shared governance" policy that includes students still deny those same students access to the more important decision-making bodies. Anyone involved in campus organizing long enough, whether it be via proactive or reactive campaigns, soon discovers what those involved in a transformative democracy politics have come to know: The campus is governed today as it always had been governed—as a corporation. The remedy for this situation, and for all the harm caused by it, comes in a transparent bottle with a simple label on the front that reads, "More Democracy."

More democracy is what organizers at the University of Wisconsin system have called for in their campaign for an elected board of regents. When it was revealed that a newly appointed regent and his wife were each $10,000 contributors to the governor's election fund, the campus 180/MDE chapter began to raise money to "Buy a Regent." Eventually the group organized an open primary election, and marched with the victor of that election, Jon Effron, on the governor's office to present the governor with a check. Two weeks later, the establishment regents fled their monthly meeting rather than face Regent-elect Effron. Most recently a "Regent Election Bill" has been introduced to the Wisconsin state legislature. Such campaigns to transform campus governing boards and administrative committees into elected and representative bodies are becoming more common today, as they are spurred on in large part by the truly dangerous decisions so many of these decision-making bodies are making.[33]

Why are these campaigns so important? Because together they constitute a democratic agenda for college and university campuses that is inherently threatening to the corporate sector. Movement toward greater democracy on campus will inevitably come into conflict with those who today control our schools. Movement to democratize education by making it more accessible, internally democratic, and responsible to the public will inevitably conflict with corporate designs to privatize and dismantle public education, reinforce class and racist segregation, and transform our campuses into research, development, and employee training centers. The stakes are very high in this conflict, not only for the corporate sector, and not only for students, educators, and campus workers, but for all the people of this era.

PRINCIPLES FOR ORGANIZING DEMOCRATICALLY

Weather signs tell of a storm on the horizon. The corporate sector has invested billions of dollars in campus research programs, infrastructure, and recruitment efforts. Billions more have been poured into corporate think tanks, lobby firms, and legal foundations, as well as the two dominant political parties. Meanwhile, student and labor organizing are on the rise in response to the ever-mounting crisis of education and democracy. A major confrontation for power is emerging, and compromise is not an option. At some point, one side will either bend or break. The confrontation requires us all to get our act together and learn how to conduct effective organizing campaigns.

Following are some democratic organizing principles for others to look at, respond to, adopt, reject, or modify.

Education Base

Education must be tackled as a basic frame of reference for our organizing, not as an afterthought. A purpose of our efforts must be to organize educational institutions and communities themselves, to democratize them, to win them away from corporate power, and to insure that they play a positive role in the larger fight for democracy everywhere.

This movement is not solely a student movement, or a youth movement, or a movement of intellectuals and academics. It is instead a movement that unites all people who are concerned about the prospects for education and democracy. Effective organizations like the University of Arkansas' Campus Democracy Collective have made such unity an express goal, stating that they exist to "educate, organize, and mobilize the student body, faculty, and staff of the University of Arkansas and the surrounding community . . . [to] move the University of Arkansas toward a more liberatory education in which the students, faculty, and staff participate equally. . . ."[34]

Inclusivity

The issues raised in efforts to win campus democracy affect so many people that the potential for effective coalition work is very strong. If we wish to take advantage of that potential, we must make conscious efforts to be inclusive in our organizing, and to maintain a focus at the same time on issues of common concern. Wherever possible, those who are privileged enough to have greater flexibility and opportunity in our organizing must be sure to assist those who are not. We also should be careful not to make the mistake of allowing political and/or geographical boundaries to separate us in this struggle.

Long-established organizations such as the United States Student Association (USSA) and the Canadian Federation of Students (CFS) are models of racial inclusivity both in process and in outcome. For example, the USSA employs a sophisticated yet simple affirmative action policy in selecting delegates to the organization's events. Additionally, the USSA's people of color, gay/queer, women's, class, and allies caucuses are the most central feature of its decision-making processes. As a result of these policies, and the decisions that in part result from them, the USSA is unique among national student organizations in that it is a truly inclusive organization.

Functionality

In the arena of campus democracy it is uniquely important that we take an approach to organizing that places function before form. Universities and colleges being what they are, we've got to be careful of the common tendency to overintellectualize and underpractice. Our ideas regarding what is to be done should be guided by our organizing experience, rather than the other way around.

The Democracy Teach-Ins are one example of this kind of approach. In the development of the teach-ins, there was no "five-year plan" that someone copied out of a text or drafted late at night. Instead, the DTIs were developed step-by-step, and each step was itself a lesson that helped us to figure out what to do next.

Dynamism

Campus democracy advocates must be willing to create and embrace new methods of organizing that the powers that be have not yet learned to counteract. We can do this in part by actively relearning our own history, and by adopting those methods from the past that seem appropriate to the present. A more difficult task lies in developing truly new and more effective methods for achieving social change.

One example of such dynamism is the Free Burma Coalition (FBC), which pioneered the art of Internet activism. Via the effective use of e-mail listservs, Web page design, and mass e-mailings, the FBC was able to inspire and coordinate numerous days of action throughout the mid-1990s. The Burmese SLORC dictatorship, and its corporate sponsors in North America, were never able to respond quickly enough to the FBC's actions to be effective.[35]

Practice of Democracy

Democracy must be expressed as much in our actions as in what we say. We've got to look for democracy in our process, in our language, in our priorities, and in the product of our labors. We should be sure to balance democracy of process with democracy in outcomes, and not allow either priority to overwhelm or impede the other. Otherwise we risk the twin dangers of parochialism on the one hand, and of unaccountable hierarchy on the other.

We can find democracy at work in many communities and organizations. Some labor union locals practice an old-style, highly organized form of rank-and-file union democracy. Most housing, production, entertainment, distribution, and office cooperatives are rooted in democratic values, tools, and traditions. We can also tell when democracy is missing. There are a lot of groups out there that talk big and claim hordes of members, but that are incapable of accomplishing anything that really matters. Why? Because their members aren't involved in the organization.

Sustainable Growth

This is a massive conflict that campus democracy organizers are entering into. As much as we might not like it, the conflict is likely to last a long time. We, too, must prepare our movement to last a long time, which means that we need to pick our battles carefully. We've also got to ensure that our movement continues to grow over time, not only in understanding, but also in numbers. Longtime campus-based movements such as the Student Liberation Action Movement (SLAM!) in New York City have placed a priority on long-term organizing, and in mobilizing large numbers of people; small isn't always beautiful. In New York City, there are tens of thousands of people who have participated in SLAM!-sponsored events.[36] As much as sometimes we might prefer to work with small, workable numbers of people, we will need to learn to work with large movements of people if we are ever to succeed.

Agenda Setting

In the short term, our task must be to set the agenda in this conflict. The conflict can be about whether education will serve people or corporations, or it can be about whether our colleges and universities are wasting tax money. The conflict may be carried out individually on campus after campus and capitol after capitol, or it may be a conflict joined globally and locally at the same time. We've got to change the rules of engagement as we wage this struggle, because as things stand now, we are bound to lose.

A stunning example of such radical agenda setting is the strike at the National Autonomous University of Mexico (UNAM) in Mexico City, which was entering its fourth month at the time of this chapter's completion. A mass strike called in reaction to the imposition of tuition at the UNAM was transformed into a struggle for power. Students and campus workers turned the table on the administration, demanding a democratic "reconstitution" of the university. Hoping to avoid a long struggle, the administration caved in on the tuition issue, but it was too late. The strike is now about control of the university.

No Compromise in Defense of Education!

The struggle for campus democracy requires determination most of all. With a deeply rooted will to carry forward it's possible that we will succeed; but without that determination we will certainly fail. Because corporations cannot achieve their basic purpose of unchallenged supremacy without dominating our colleges and universities, they will not yield in this conflict. It is only our own dedication and ability that is still at question: Will we yield? In a passage often cited in early Democracy Teach-In literature, Frederick Douglass warned us of the cost of submission:

> Power concedes nothing without demand—It never has and never will. Find out just what any people will quietly submit to, and you have found out the exact measure of injustice that will be imposed upon them, and these will continue until they are resisted with either words or blows, or with both.[37]

Campus democracy campaigns are universally radical in nature, as are all such efforts to alter relations of power. The broad strategy of these campaigns has been to press demands for radical education reform, to seek the involvement of ever-larger circles of people in pressing these demands, and to raise new demands for more radical reforms as our movements have gained in support and strength. The short-term measure of our success will be the extent to which we build democratic power. So long as we never yield in our work for democracy and education, the scope and intensity of our struggle will continue to grow. The answer to the original Democracy Teach-In question will become ever clearer:

> We cannot pursue democracy and social justice when corporations are allowed to control so much power and wealth.

> We cannot allow corporations to control power and wealth.

As democracy movements come into their own across the planet, campuses everywhere are playing a vital role.[38] This age of global corporate consolidation has made the democracy movement that much more necessary, as corporations move increasingly to colonize every aspect of our lives.

Will corporations be allowed to colonize education?

Our actions may provide the answer. While the struggle moves ahead for democracy at work; in markets; in media, government, and religion; and elsewhere, we also must press our demands for campus democracy.

Information regarding issues that are not specifically documented in the notes is available from 180/MDE and the Center for Campus Organizing (see Appendix). Please contact the author for an extensive set of notes elaborating on many of the concepts in this chapter.

NOTES

1. *The Struggle at CUNY: Open Admissions and Civil Rights,* a publication of CCNY Student Liberation Action Movement, spring 1998; *Student Activist,* March 1999; *Infusion: Tools for Action and Education,* a publication of the Center for Campus Organizing, 1996–1998; *Midwest Headwaters Earth First! Journal* 1995; *Against the Current* 71 (November/December 1997).

2. By only one mark are the students of the 1990s at all apathetic, and that is by the measure of voter turnout—which only goes to show that students don't vote as much as other age groups, which by and large don't vote. Additionally, in recent elections the overall youth vote, of which students are the majority, has played a significant role in advancing unconventional candidates, especially candidates of the Green, New, and Reform Parties. Better indicators for activism would be found in an examination of indicators of involvement in demonstrations, community service,

and so on; by these standards, campus activism in North America is at an all-time high, and significantly further along than it was in the 1960s. Besides, as an IWW of old once said, "If elections changed anything, they would be made illegal."

3. Very little attention will be paid in this chapter to the situation faced by those involved in education between kindergarten and the twelfth grade. Please excuse the oversight.

4. *Student Voice*, a publication of the Progressive Student Network, May 1983.

5. *Progressive Student News*, a publication of the Progressive Student Network, January 1988, October 1988, January 1990.

6. *Capitalism, Nature, Socialism: A Journal of Socialist Ecology* 8, nos. 29–32.

7. *Progressive Student News*, September 1991, April 1992, January 1993, 1994. *Student Insurgent*, a publication of the Student Insurgent Collective, University of Oregon, 1995, 1996; *Threshold*, a publicatio nof the Student Environmental Action Coalition, 1994–1996.

8. *Progressive Student News*, May 1983, January 1988, January 1990, October 1990, September 1991, January 1992, 1994.

9. Dennis O'Neil, in his pamphlet *SDS: 101—From the Inside*, wrote: "The school year started, October, 1967, at a quaint little school with an SDS chapter, the University of Wisconsin at Madison. There was a demonstration against the Dow chemical corporation, manufacturers of napalm. . . . It was a good, big, successful demonstration, and it was attacked by campus and local police. They beat the hell out of people. They dragged them off to jail. More people got outraged. There was a total boycott of classes, lasting two or three days and completely successful. It petered out, but the level of struggle was escalating way past what it had been" (p. 20). Available from the Freedom Road Socialist Organization, Student Commission.

See also "A Causeria at the Military-Industrial," a speech by Paul Goodman published in Walt Anderson, ed., *The Age of Protest* (Pacific Palisades, Calif.: GoodYear Publishing, 1969).

10. Examples of such procurement and/or investment campaigns have recently included: Free Burma Coalition (PepsiCo, Texaco, UNOCAL), Free Nigeria Movement (Shell, Mobil, Coca-Cola), United Farmworkers (strawberries), Pineros y Campesinos Unidos del Noroeste (Gardenburger, NORPAC), Students for a Free Tibet (China), Student Environmental Action Coalition (Burma, tropical hardwoods, Exxon, Nigeria), East Timor Action Network (Indonesia), and Jobs with Justice (union busters), Global Exchange/National Labor Committee/UNITE! (sweatshops), Democratic Socialists of America (DSA) Youth Section (various).

11. Labor unions and labor organizations that have recently taken an active interest in campus organizing drives include: United Auto Workers (UAW), American Federation of State County & Municipal Employees (AFSCME), American Federation of Teachers (AFT), National Education Association (NEA), United Food & Commercial Workers (UFCW), Teachers for Democratic Culture (TDC), Coalition of Graduate Employee Unions (CGEU), Industrial

Workers of the World (IWW), and the AFL-CIO Organizing Institute (*Infusion: Tools for Action and Education*, 1996–1998; *Against the Current* 71 (November/December 1997).

12. Nari Rhee et al., *Guide to Uncovering the Right on Campus*, 2d ed. (Houston: Public Search, 1997); *The Feeding Trough*, a report on the Bradley Foundation by the Milwaukee branch of the A Job Is a Right Campaign, 1997.

13. Lawrence Soley, *Leasing the Ivory Tower* (Boston: South End Press, 1995).

14. Anderson, *The Age of Protest*.

15. Richard Grossman, presentation at Chicago Organizing Conference, August 16, 1996.

16. Jane Anne Morris, "Fixing Corporations, Part 1: Legacy of the Founding Parents," *Rachel's Environmental & Health Weekly*, no. 488.

17. Some of the chief organizations represented included the Student Environmental Action Coalition, Free Burma Coalition, Students for a Free Tibet, Democracy Unlimited of Wisconsin Cooperative, Earth First!, Student Labor Action Coalition, the Greens, Wisconsin's Environmental Decade, and the Interfaith Center for Corporate Responsibility.

18. For a full history of the first few years of the DTIs, check out the Web site at: corporations.org/democracy.

19. By way of illustration, another name change has been that of the transition from the intentionally vague "Chicago Organizing Conference" of August 16–19, 1996, to the "Democracy Teach-In Organizing Conference" of October 29–November 1, 1997, to the fairly specific "Campus Democracy Convention" of November 5–9, 1998.

20. In the second round of teach-ins, dozens of organizations came on board officially as cosponsors of the effort; eventually some thirty-four national and international organizations signed on. Also, the Center for Campus Organizing (CCO) in Boston came to play a pivotal role in the second round of teach-ins, and played a kind of partner role to the UW Alliance for Democracy in serving as a clearinghouse for DTI organizing.

21. Democracy Teach-In Organizing Packets 1 and 2; People's Tribune, 1996–1998; *Infusion: Tools for Action and Education*, 1996–1998; A. S. Zaidi, "Students on the Move," *Z* (March 1998): 22; Mary Beth Marklein, "Students Challenging Corporate Cash," *USA Today*, March 5, 1998; Benson Gardner, "Campus Democracy Convention," Wisconsin Public Radio, transcript, November 13, 1998.

22. Patriarchy is defined by Gerda Lerner as "the manifestation and institutionalization of male dominance over women and children in the family and the extension of male dominance over women in society in general." Gerda Lerner, *The Creation of Patriarchy*, (New York: Oxford University Press, 1987), p. 239.

23. One interesting mark of the reach of the teach-ins in organizing going on beyond the campus is the recent passage of a City of Arcata referendum, which reads, in part, "[W]e request that our City Council co-sponsor (in cooperation with the drafters of this initiative) two town hall meetings in the five months following the passage of this ballot measure on the topic: 'Can we have

democracy when large corporations wield so much power and wealth under law?' " City of Arcata, California, Advisory Measure on Democracy and Corporations, *Alliance Reports* 2, no. 11/12: 22. This language was clearly adopted from the original language of the Democracy Teach-In question, "Can we pursue democracy and social justice when corporations are allowed to control so much power and wealth?"

24. The United Students Against Sweatshops home page is located at www.asm.wisc.edu\~usas.

25. See www.ethnicstudies.com/home.html. Other campuses where campaigns of this kind have been highlighted in the media include the University of Texas, University of Michigan–Ann Arbor, University of California system, University of Washington, and the New School.

26. Here I am referring the Alliance Defense Fund's $500,000 lawsuit against the University of Wisconsin, in which they advertise their campaign to "defund the Left." Similar lawsuits have been filed against students in Oregon, California, and New York, and are winding their way through the court systems to the U.S. Supreme Court (www.alliancedefensefund.com/). Also check out Rhee, *Guide to Uncovering the Right on Campus*.

27. Some campus labor unions have begun to form on-campus labor federations to strengthen interunion solidarity. On the University of Wisconsin–Madison campus, the UW Federation of Labor is now entering its third year. See www.sit.wisc.edu/~uwwf

28. *Student Activist*, March 1999. The most stunning recent examples of these kinds of campaigns in the United States have taken place at the City University of New York system and at the University of North Carolina Chapel Hill, where students have mobilized by the thousands and taken their protests into the streets.

29. "Notes on The Prison Moratorium Project," *Activist*, a publication of the DSA Youth Section, p. 26.

30. Campuses include: UW–Madison (Exxon, Monsanto, Cargill, ConAgra, etc.), UW–Stevens Point (Rio Algom), UW–Oshkosh (Exxon), University of Texas (Freeport-McMoRan), University of Oregon (animal testing), University of Minnesota (Medtronic), Penn State (Procter & Gamble), and others.

31. California State University system (Microsoft, GTE, Hughes, Fujitsu), University of Texas (Microsoft), and others. According to Mary Beth Marklein, "Owning PC Becoming College Requirement," *USA Today*, March 5, 1998, the University of Florida, University of North Carolina at Chapel Hill, and Stevens Institute of Technology, among scores of other campuses, have all established requirements that students purchase personal computers.

32. University of Chicago (Education School axed), New York City Technical College (NYNEX curriculum developed), Columbia University (Library School and Linguistics Program both axed), University of Wisconsin at Madison (English as a Second Language slashed, Fluno Executive Training Center created).

33. Campaigns for elected board of regents/trustees have met with varying success at the University of Arkansas, University of Massachussetts System, University of New Mexico, University of Illinois System, and Western Con-

necticut State University. An additional source on the ties of university presidents to corporations is the November 1997 issue of the *Multinational Monitor*, titled "University Inc."

34. University of Arkansas Campus Democracy Collective Constitution: comp.uark.edu/~cdemcol/consti.html.

35. Free Burma Coalition Web page: www.freeburmacoalition.org/education.html.

36. Student Liberation Action Movement Web page: www.geocities.com/CapitolHill/Lobby/6353/.

37. This quotation comes from a Douglass speech marking West Indies Emancipation Day on August 4th, 1857. Milton Meltzer, ed., *Frederick Douglass: In His Own Words* (San Diego: Gulliver Books, 1995), p. 104.

38. In the months that this chapter was written, millions of students and campus workers were involved in general strikes on campuses in Israel, Mexico, Korea, Indonesia, Zimbabwe, Puerto Rico, Turkey, France, and elsewhere. These mass actions were universally about the same kinds of issues addressed by campus democracy campaigns in the United States. This presents the possibility that grassroots organizers in the United States might join with, and learn from, existing international education movements. We might begin by looking next door to Canada, Mexico, and Puerto Rico.

27

DO YOUR HOMEWORK
Research and Organizing Advice for Corporate Combatants

Sonya Huber

MUCKRAKERS, ORGANIZERS, AND VISIONARIES

Student activists understand that in the broadest sense possible, as well as on the day-to-day level, the corporate world shapes what education has become. In an economic situation where no security is guaranteed and staying competitive is the mantra, the educational system appears to accept the mandate delivered by the corporate world. Although the media tends to (and is paid to) portray student activism as narrow, misguided, and destined for failure, students have achieved encouraging and consistent gains in the last few decades. If students are able to connect with this history, find fellow activists on campuses near and far, and build alliances with community members and faculty, they have the potential to be one of the strongest forces in the fight against the corporate university. To wage a successful campaign, students need to do the work of analyzing a local situation, coming up with a strategy to achieve goals that the community needs, and organizing.

Research is crucial: Student anticorporate organizers are teaching themselves to be investigative journalists because tracking their corporate foes requires careful scrutiny. Students understand that in order to be taken seriously in their communities and in the media, they need to have accurate facts and figures as well as a broad analysis. On a "Democracy

Teach-In" online discussion list, organizers regularly trade information about how to file a Freedom of Information Act request, how to request information on a target company from the Securities Exchange Commission, and how to use the readily available university and corporate brochures and balance sheets to analyze the links between universities and corporations, between administration, trustees, and corporate boards. Nikki Morse, a student at University of Massachusetts Amherst, discovered connections between her university and the Monsanto corporation, a biogenetics giant that is the target of many environmental activists' campaigns. Morse said, "I thought it was going to be difficult, but the research took us a day and a half. Who knows what else we could have come up with if we had more time."

The Center for Campus Organizing, the Reporters' Committee for Freedom of the Press, and Fairness and Accuracy in Reporting have all published excellent resources for helping activists with this sort of research. Another option, if students can find faculty members or local nonprofit organizations to support them, is to petition for internships or independent studies that may appear innocuous enough in proposal form, but that will give them a semester's worth of time—and academic credit—while they dig into the university's financial background. Once students begin to uncover connections, it can be worthwhile to let campus newspapers, radio stations, and activist groups know about their findings.

This research is essential for refuting the claims of the university administration. The corporate university has a number of stock arguments to use against student activists. These arguments are used to reframe the debate, denying that the university has any responsibility regarding how its money is made, and denying the fact that corporate involvement presents a host of negative prospects for education. Administrators or trustees may say that if corporate dollars didn't fund research, the university would go bankrupt or that various program would have to be cut. They may say that government funding cuts force them to look for corporate funding. They may say that student demands such as the continuation of financial aid, need-blind admissions, or ethnic studies programs, or faculty and staff demands such as union wages or benefits, require that they look for corporate funding. A common argument heard from administrators and corporations is that the wasteful U.S. education system is not competitive enough for the twenty-first century, and that public education has let down America in terms of preparing a competent workforce.

Understanding the opponents' viewpoint is particularly vital as students do outreach and attempt to organize in their communities. Many potential supporters may initially have doubts based on what they have heard from official sources. And the people students see every day on campus have more information about the school than is contained in any book, so a vital part of research is listening and asking questions, particularly of people who have been with the university for a few years or more. Who paid for the new science center? Why did the English department lose two faculty members? What happened with complaints of harassment among employees at the food service contractor? Which faculty members and trustees sit on the boards of directors of corporations? The general information and the often astounding web of connections that students uncover will be a huge help to any activist group on campus, because, luckily, corporations have many enemies.

Although a university may take for granted that connection with Reebok or Pepsi means that money will be spent efficiently and wisely, these assumptions can be refuted with research. The amount of waste generated by the average multinational corporation casts serious doubt on the claim that a corporation could run a university efficiently (and the corporate agenda itself is largely responsible for the current state of public education, as billions of dollars have gone to corporate welfare while our public schools have languished for years and our jobs were moved to sweatshops overseas). When students challenged the University of Pennsylvania's investments in Burma, the administration responded that "universities in general have avoided taking positions on issues not directly related to their academic mission." Students in this situation knew their history: Students had forced Penn to divest from South Africa in the eighties.[1] Make the mission of the university, and its financial decisions, open to debate!

VISION AND ORGANIZING

Students can crack the code of corporate doublespeak by organizing community members to speak in human terms about their experiences. A primary method for doing so is to make public the experiences of students and university employees. At University of Massachusetts Amherst, students held a speak-out in spring of 1998 to talk publicly about the ways that their economic situations made it difficult for them to attend school. This action was a part of the Democracy Teach-Ins that took place across the country.

Seeing that corporate control affects us all, students from the Alliance for Democracy at the University of Wisconsin–Madison launched the second Democracy Teach-In Campaign in the summer of 1997. Tracing the ways that students in the 1960s and 1970s up through today have battled against corporations for their rights, organizers ask themselves and their communities the question, "Can we pursue democracy and social justice when corporations are allowed to control so much power and wealth?" Many activists around the country have answered that corporate power, on and off the campus, is a major obstacle to democracy. More than 250 student organizers gathered in Chicago in October 1997 to teach each other about how to research university-corporate ties and how to hold anticorporate teach-ins. It is estimated that one hundred campuses held simultaneous teach-ins on March 1–8, 1998. At the University of Wisconsin–Oshkosh, students went on a "Corporate Crap Detection and Scavenger Hunt," a tour through the campus that pointed out examples of corporate influence.[2]

In these campaigns, students have thought of creative and fun ways to involve their communities in the anticorporate critique. Activist Cedar Stevens helped to organize a "Corporate Monopoly" game on her campus at the University of Texas at Austin:

> We laid out a life-sized monopoly board that people could move around on to different corporate logos. A Vanna White figure handed the dice to players, and a game-show host in Uncle Sam garb narrated what happened to people as they landed on the squares. Unless you rolled doubles, your chances in the corporate game were not favorable, but lucky tycoons who rolled doubles got to cheat and move around the board and rake in all the profits. Hundreds of people gathered to watch this game in the "free speech" area of UT Austin.

Stevens described the first "Ending Corporate Dominance" workshop she attended as part of an Earth First! gathering in 1994 as "a real 'a-ha moment' for many activists who were weary of the battle-by-battle style of eco-activism, where we win some/lose some, but the perpetrators of environmental destruction remain constant, thriving, and growing more powerful all the time."[3]

Corporations are too huge to tackle without strength in numbers and the combined intelligence and strategy of a large group of people. Therefore, it is vital to build alliances on and off campus. Even if employees do not have votes in the boardroom of a corporation, they are still the essential force that makes the university function. If staff, faculty, or graduate students and teaching assistants on campus are unionized, students can make contact with the union representatives to learn about the history of the union's struggle with the university. Students can ask employees how their jobs have changed in the last few years, and if there have been any labor disputes. If staff and faculty are not unionized, students can make contact with any employee clubs or organizations that exist, and be ready to organize students in support of staff if a union struggle develops. Members of such groups may have surprising access to information. For example, Harvard University clerical workers, as part of their job responsibilities, often arrange travel itineraries for administrators. During a contract dispute, clerical workers used this information to coordinate campaign actions. Key administrators were surprised to be met at airports around the country by Harvard union allies, who pressured administrators to concede to workers' demands. Especially working in coalition with other groups on their campus, students may be surprised by the information and resources on-campus allies can provide.

From the first conversations with peers and members of the community, it is essential and also inspiring to talk about alternatives. If the university is currently contracting its custodial services out to a contractor that pays minimum wage, what would the employees want in an ideal situation from the university? If courses are overcrowded and students have to drop out to save for tuition, what would be a better situation? The more exactly students can describe what their community wants, the easier time they will have both formulating a campaign and generating energy and the will to change. Members of the Canadian Federation of Students attribute their recent success with the "income-contingent loan repayment scheme" campaign to the fact that they had a vision to which they held to strongly, instead of saying "let's negotiate" without a clear idea of their goals.

Given the increasing financial burden of attending college, increasing discrimination against many students who want to enroll, decreasing financial aid, and decreasing chance of finding a decent job after graduation, many students and parents will be willing to listen and respond to a focused critique of the university and of the education system at large. Lower-income students and students of color, many of whom are also lower income, are being weeded out of higher education and told that their place is in GED classes, at vocational schools, or not in school at all.

The mass student mobilizations of the 1960s and 1970s, as well as the student movements in the 1980s, all faced struggles with the question of how to do real solidarity work and support each others' struggles. It is essential for the students of the year 2000 and beyond, particularly white and class-privileged students, to use their resources to investigate and support struggles going on in their neighborhoods and cities, across the lines of race and class. Community colleges and technical schools specifically are on the front lines of corporatization. Faculty in these institutions are the most overworked and underpaid, and students here are seeing directly that they are being given only educational choices that relate to specific low-paying careers. For students to mount a challenge to McUniversity, they will need financial, organizing, and infrastructural assistance from outside the university, from older organizers who can help them take on this formidable adversary and also deal with internal challenges such as the ever-changing, transitory student population. As students further explore the meaning of the word "solidarity," they can form a united force that may truly be effective in changing education in this country.

NOTES

1. Peter Chowla, "The Ethics of Investment: Students Demand that Administrators Take Action," *PANic* (University of Pennsylvania), March 1998, p. 4.

2. *Infusion* 3, no. 2 (March–April 1998): 9–11.

3. E-mail interview exclusively for this article, via contacts of the Center for Campus Organizing (1997).

28

KEEP YOUR ROOM CLEAN
How to Uncover Corporate and Military Influence on Your Campus

John E. Peck

Many students probably remember getting helpful advice from parents, relatives, and friends as they set off for their academic adventure in the ivory tower—study hard, meet new people, keep your room clean. Actually, these tired clichés can be a rather good game plan for the campus activist interested in challenging corporate/military influence. Despite their reputation as institutions of higher learning and progressive idealism, colleges and universities are now being taken over by the dark side of the force—namely, the military-industrial complex. School cafeterias, laboratory facilities, classroom materials, sports programs, and even college officials themselves have succumbed to the corrupting influence of the profit motive in our higher educational system. In a period of runaway tuition and taxpayer backlash, it is tempting to have a "take-the-money-and-run" attitude toward military contracts and corporate handouts. Yet with all the strings attached, your school is more likely to end up an academic puppet—held hostage by someone else's bottom line. As the infamous (and recently pied!) Chicago School economist Milton Friedman once admitted, "The corporation can not be ethical. It's only responsibility is to turn a profit."

WHAT'S THE BIG DEAL—SCIENCE IS SCIENCE, RIGHT?

There are several standard excuses apologists trundle out for the unbridled corporatization of higher education that campus activists should learn to recognize and be ready to counter. The first is that there's a fundamental difference between basic (pure) science and applied (dirty) research—and that any pursuit of the former is somehow apolitical and value-neutral. This is total bunk—all scientific investigation is a conscious product of social values and political decisions. As another well-known economist, Robert Bell, notes, "The American scientific community is as 'pure' and unbiased as the political machinery that dispenses its patronage and its funding." Hitler's Third Reich endorsed and financed all sorts of gruesome Holocaust studies in the name of science, and the United States has a similar sordid public research legacy. A current example is the National Institute of Health's "Violence Initiative" that's providing millions in federal funding to university researchers to identify and isolate the genetic "cause" of violence among inner-city youth so as to then develop improved drugs to treat this "disease"[1]—another case of a misguided quest for a biotechnological solution to a sociopolitical problem. Researchers getting military money in disciplines like physics and mathematics are especially prone to justify their work in the noble cause of advancing knowledge. Yet it is hard to see the Pentagon as a disinterested benevolent patron of science—after all, knowing everything about the performance characteristics of metallic alloys and the explosive capacities of chemical agents has tangible life-and-death consequences down the road.

Another argument one often hears is that corporate/military funding improves instructional opportunities at the university. In other words, teaching stands to benefit from all the taxpayer-subsidized infrastructure required for state-of-the-art research—like nuclear fusion laboratories, three-dimensional-atom probe microscopes, interactive distance education classrooms, digitizing tablets for audiographic presentations, and so on. Of course, this assumes that such pricey trappings are accessible and relevant to all members of the university community and their respective fields of study—which they clearly are not. Given limited resources, public funds leveraged by private gifts to improve such cutting-edge disciplines as mechanical engineering or biotechnology simply translates into less money for other programs—say, ethnic studies or environmental science. Like other schools, the University of Wisconsin (UW)–Madison reflects this trend, with over 50 percent of the total budget now devoted to research and barely 33 percent to instruction—and the gap widens each year.[2] To make matters worse, such edificial facilities are often privatized and off-limits to the average undergraduate student or common taxpayer citizen—at UW–Madison, for instance, no one ever expects to have a class or even a field trip to the new primate laboratory addition or the soon-to-be-completed $22-million Fluno Center for Corporate Executive Education.

BUT EVERYONE BENEFITS FROM DONATIONS TO EDUCATION—DON'T THEY?

Public/private partnership is the latest buzzword on campus, with the benefits supposedly trickling down to even the poorest homeless person half a globe away. Of course, this is based on the patently false notion that *any* activity that expands market turnover—that is, increases gross domestic product—must be inherently "good" for society (like trafficking cocaine, dumping toxic wastes, peddling weapons, exploiting children in sweatshops, and so forth). Most people less indoctrinated in neoliberalism know better, though—as one rural Midwest saying goes, "There's no money to be made studying something that saves other people money." This is especially true for many family farmers, who have witnessed the hijacking of public science research and university extension services by corporate agribusiness in order to engineer their dependence upon costly external market inputs—like hybrid seeds, pesticides, fertilizers, hormones, antibiotics, heavy machinery, global positioning system technology, and so on. A U.S. Department of Agriculture survey of land grant colleges between 1993 and 1996 found less than 5 percent of research projects geared toward sustainable agriculture.[3] Likewise, UW–Madison officials hardly questioned the altruism of Cargill when it recently donated $200,000 in the form of student/faculty internships, a sponsored biotech professorship in chemical engineering, and a full-time business school recruiter. After all, anything that facilitates Cargill's control of the world's food supply *must* be beneficial for all of humanity.

Lastly, there is the old constructive-engagement idea, whereby institutions are thought to gain an enlightening influence over corporate practice and/or military policy by playing the game and not divorcing themselves from the real world of greed and conflict. Following this fallacious argument, it would have made perfect sense for universities back in the early nineteenth century to invest in slavery and try to reform the system from within—since if *they* didn't have a stake, someone worse probably would. Of course, anyone familiar with the more recent history of the antiapartheid movement realizes just how easily constructive engagement became a camouflage for complicitous profiteering, and school officials today should be more worried about the potential liability once their corporate patrons find themselves in court for aiding and abetting criminal activity and state terrorism. The recent $1-billion class action lawsuit filed in January 1999 in U.S. Federal Court on behalf of fifty thousand indentured Asian women workers against such Saipan sweatshop corporations as the Gap, Tommy Hilfiger, Wal-Mart, J Crew, the Limited, and others is a case in point.[4] If—for example—UW–Madison is actively licensing, buying, and, hence, officially condoning products from Saipan and the oppressive sweatshop conditions under which they are produced, could it not also be sued for damages in federal court?

BEWARE—READ THE FINE PRINT BEFORE YOU RESEARCH!

What most cheerleaders for corporate/military research on campus won't tell you is often hidden deep within contracts or conducted behind closed doors. University scientists, graduate student researchers, part-time project assistants, and other campus employees must now navigate a whole array of gag rules and academic embargoes as their work increasingly becomes the private property of some corporate sponsor or falls under the thumb of the military's definition of national security. Peer review has been literally thrown out the window as software programs, chemical processes, testing protocols, genetic sequences, and so forth are licensed and rendered immune to external scrutiny. Increasingly, professors are hired (and fired) based upon whether they can entice corporate dollars and produce marketable results—to the point where many faculty buy their way out of teaching altogether, so they can focus full-time on for-profit tinkering and outside consulting instead. The result has been a drastic decline in instructional effort and quality—as shown by over-crowded classrooms and overworked teaching assistants—as well as crass neglect of scientific research in the public interest. What was once a noble quest for truth and reason has become a rather selfish endeavor of dubious standing and social purpose. To give but one egregious example, the UW–Madison business school recently completed a $40,000 study paid for by Exxon to prove that poor people of color actually prefer to live next to petroleum refineries and chemical plants in Louisiana's "Cancer Alley," thereby whitewashing the notion of environmental racism.[5]

For a real horror story of corporate power in the ivory tower, just talk to Petr Taborsky, a graduate research assistant at the University of South Florida, who was released in April 1997 after three-and-a-half years in jail—including eight weeks on a chain gang(!)—for allegedly stealing his own research work from a private sponsor, Florida Progress Corporation.

Back in the summer of 1988, Taborsky was working in a laboratory at $8.50 per hour when he came across the superabsorbent capacity of a heated clay compound, clinopotilolite, that could revolutionize water treatment. Unfortunately, when Taborksi took home his personal notebooks and successfully patented his discovery, the university, at the behest of Florida Progress Corporation, had him arrested and imprisoned for grand theft of trade secrets worth in excess of $20,000.[6] Another recent case study of corporate influence corrupting academic freedom involves students at the Environmental Law Clinic of Tulane University in Louisiana. When the clinic successfully appealed to the EPA on behalf of a predominantly African American community fighting a $700-million Japanese-owned plastics manufacturer in their backyard, Governor Mike Foster and the Louisiana Supreme Court intervened, making it illegal for the students to freely associate with community organizations. It just so happens that the Japanese corporation, Shintech, was a major financial backer of Governor Foster and other influential state politicians.[7]

As David Shenck disturbingly documents in a recent *Nation* article, a veritable flood of shoddy science is now issuing from once-reputable universities as corporate dollars erode the quality and integrity of public interest research. Since passage of the 1980 Bayh-Dole Act, which allowed public schools to patent (and profit from) research work, as well as the 1981 Recovery Tax Law that enabled corporations to count gifts to schools as federal tax deductions, private funding to universities has increased fivefold—topping $1.7 billion in 1997, according to the National Science Foundation. Meanwhile, corporate licensing of university inventions is estimated to generate $21 billion in revenue annually, with a recent survey of private industrial patents finding a whopping 73 percent to be derived from public science research—there's taxpayer-subsidized corporate welfare for you! In 1997 alone, the top ninety research schools in the United States earned $446 million in patent royalties—a 33 percent increase over 1996.[8] Given the fortune to be made, it's not that surprising to hear the director of the Wisconsin Alumni Research Foundation at a recent patenting seminar bluntly instruct an audience of campus researchers that the school "was no longer interested in the scientific value of their work, merely its commercial value." Last fall, scientists within the UW College of Agriculture and Life Sciences quietly signed over all their findings on the next promising generation of biological pest control agents (*Photorhabdus* bacteria) to Dow Elanco—as required in their original one-sided research contract. Feeling charitable after such university largesse, Dow turned around and gave a tax-deductible donation of $500,000 toward a new $40-million UW chemistry complex—most of which will end up being paid for by Wisconsin taxpayers anyway.[9]

BUT UNIVERSITY RESEARCH IS IMMUNE TO CORPORATE CORRUPTION—ISN'T IT?

Violations of academic freedom and scientific method are rife when corporations set the rules on campus. Shenk cites one 1997 survey of corporate contracts that found 58 percent of university researchers subject to a six-month embargo on publication of findings, pending clearance by the sponsor, and 33 percent denied access to work of their colleagues due to private proprietary claims.[10] As an example, one recent $25,000 contract between Exxon Production Research (EPR) and a UW–Madison professor in geology and geophysics even included this ominous clause challenging the First Ammendment of the U.S. Constitution: "The university will avoid any real or apparent impropriety in connection with the research performed under this agreement or any adverse impact on the interests of EPR or any of its affiliates."[11] So much for ever biting—or even badmouthing—the hand that feeds you! Yet another survey found a third of all scientific journal authors to have a personal financial interest in their results—yet there was almost no public reporting of such conflicts of interest. In a lucrative discipline like pharmaceutical science, 98 percent of researchers ended up publishing articles that essentially endorsed processes and products of the corporations from which they had originally received money.

Even more insidious is how this corporatization phenomenom siphons off taxpayer subsidies and corrupts public mandates. Rarely does a company pay the full overhead cost of subcontracting a university to do its research bidding, and many now have their own tax-exempt foundations through which to launder their dollars and avoid any overhead expenses whatsoever. At UW–Madison, corporations are supposed to pay 44 percent of overhead costs, yet the loophole in a recent $144,000 grant between the Exxon Education Foundation and the UW–Madison Biotech Department is increasingly typical: "The foundation does not typically provide funds to cover lump-sum overhead fees . . . [and believes] it is appropriate for the grant recipient to absorb these costs as one demonstration of its commitment to the project for which funding is sought."[12] A 1996 study at the University of Rhode Island revealed that as much as $390 per year of undergraduate tuition was directly paying for private research on campus.[13] In other words, runaway corporate influence is making higher education less a right and more of a privilege. A blatant example from the University of Minnesota actually had school officials shifting funds from other academic programs to bankroll a new business school—and also evicting student organizations to make room for corporate franchises in what was once a student union and is now a shopping mall![14]

ALL RIGHT—BUT ISN'T MILITARY FUNDING FOR THE COMMON GOOD?

Much the same critique can be levelled against the military, where mandated educational programs such as the Reserve Officer Training Corps (ROTC) and the National Security Education Program (NSEP) siphon off scarce federal monies and force desperate students into serving the Pentagon in order to go to school. One of the requirements to receive federal funding for the land grant college system is a provision of military training and, since its creation in 1916, ROTC has fulfilled that function. Unfortunately, as a campus wing of the military itself, ROTC remains a bastion of underground racism, sexism, and overt homophobia—in blatant violation of many school (and even state) antidiscrimination policies. Created more recently, the NSEP draws on a $75-million Pentagon trust fund and often commits scholarship recipients to future work for the Defense Department or the U.S. intelligence community. For example, a few years ago UW–Madison's engineering school received a generous $3-million NSEP grant for Japanese language and cultural training, as well as internship opportunities in Japan, ostensibly to widen access to competitive Japanese corporations (that is, industrial espionage for national security). One of the requirements for student participants was a post-trip debriefing with military officials.[15]

On many college campuses, military research is now at higher levels than during the Vietnam War—a sure sign that there's no peace dividend at the end of the Cold War rainbow. Through the so-called Academic Strategic Alliances Program, the Clinton White House is pushing $45 billion worth of fresh nuclear and military-related research programs and facilities at universities over the next ten years. Since 1995, one UW–Madison professor in industrial engineering and computer sciences alone has received over $429,000 from the Pentagon to research competitive trade-off modeling for improvement of conventional and nuclear war game scenarios—sadly reminiscent of the former UW Army Math Research Center's work that led student protestors to bomb the building back in 1970.[16] One is left to wonder just how much of the basic research originally conducted at universities is now being ruthlessly applied by the Pentagon in warfare against the people of Yugoslavia and Iraq. Even scarier is recent news that the National Science Foundation and the Defense Advances Research Projects Agency are teaming up to bankroll UW–Madison scientists interested in attaching DNA strands to gold-coated glass plates—the first step toward creating cybernetic databanks for hyperactive info processing.[17] It's a brave new world on the high-tech campus battlefield of the future.

WHAT ABOUT FIDUCIARY VERSUS SOCIAL RESPONSIBILITY?

Through amoral investment and procurement policies, many colleges are also directly profiting from abusive corporate practices with regents, administrators, coaches, and professors skimming off their own benefits in the form of kickbacks, dividends, and so on. UW's unelected board of regents is largely composed of right-wing corporate executives—most of whom also happen to be wealthy, white, straight men with massive portfolios, real estate holdings, and personal fortunes of their own. One such CEO, Guy Gottshalk, a Wisconsin cranberry grower and patron of a $1.2-million UW–Madison chair for cranberry research, was appointed to the UW board of regents after donating an extra $7000 to the governor's political campaign.[18] In 1996, the UW athletic department signed a $7.9-million exclusive contract with Reebok, which requires all Badger coaches and players to wear its clothing and violates their free speech rights by requiring signing of a nondisparagement subclause. Since then, the UW has become a full-blown public relations agent, sending out Reebok press releases and even ordering campus police to harrass and arrest anti-Reebok protesters.[19] Campuswide monopolies, catering to the vital educational needs of pacified student consumers for soft drinks (Coke or Pepsi), sweatshop clothing (Reebok or Nike), fast food (Taco Bell, KFC, or Pizza Hut), and software products (Microsoft), are cropping up everywhere. And then there's the disturbing cognitive dissonance between educational mandates and capitalist imperatives as played out in university endowments. The UW Trust Fund, for example, in violation of its own supposed social responsibility policy, is still investing millions in sweatshop operators (Disney, the Gap), tobacco pushers (Philip-Morris, RJR Reynolds), landmine makers (Raytheon, Lockheed Martin), prison industries (Wackenhut, Corrections Corp.), toxic dumpers (Chlorox, Exxon), and biotech meddlers (Pfizer, Du Pont).[20] Sadly enough, this gives a reputable institution of higher learning like UW–Madison a vested interest in global instability, low-intensity conflict, and full-blown warfare, since the dividends from $8 million worth of defense contractor holdings helps build up the all-important—albeit blood-drenched—endowment. A bottom-line policy of fiduciary responsibility basically lets schools profit from anything that's still legal.

HOW TO TACKLE THIS MESS? FIRST, HIT THE BOOKS!

Uncovering and challenging insidious examples of corporate/military influence on campus is actually much simpler (and more fun!) than most people would think. The first step—like your parents said—is to study hard. If you're at a public school, much of this information is available as an open record. For instance, each UW regent must file a "Statement of Economic Interests" with the Wisconsin State Ethics Board before she can take her seat. This statement conveniently lists all of her stock options, real estate properties, corporate directorships, and so on—a veritable dirty laundry list! Researchers receiving federal money have to file their own "Financial Disclosure" forms with the graduate school, though this is often seen as just a perfunctory formality. Similarly, you should be able to obtain a public copy of current investment holdings and research contracts, rubberstamped by your board of regents, from your school's archive or the principal research investigator. If the office machinery turns exceptionally slowly, you may want to have a civic-minded lawyer make follow-up inquiries on your behalf. At a private school this process can be more difficult, but finding a sympathetic trustee (or secretary or graduate student) to leak the necessary information is not impossible. Tipping off a local investigative reporter about suspicious behind-the-scenes activities can also often get insiders talking. Like turning on a light at night, a brewing scandal is a good way to expose the hidden cockroaches on campus.

Careful sifting and winnowing of university press releases and news stories (often indexed on your school's Web site), as well as in-house departmental publications, will uncover other interesting happenings. Less modest university administrators can often be caught bragging about their latest corporate connections and some have even frankly written about how they sold off their school's reputation to the highest bidder.[21] Another quick sleuthing routine is to surf the Lexis/Nexis database at your library and simply type in the names of your school (or more specifically, a regent, dean, or professor) and a suspect corporation to see in what context they both appear—be it a press story, congressional testimony, federal lawsuit, whatever. In the case of federal military research, you can submit a separate Freedom of Information Act request for work unit summaries at your school.[22]

In order to get more general dirt on a particular corporation, there are many other Internet resources at your fingertips, as well as informational clearinghouses geared toward campus activist types. If the corporation is publicly traded, then it must file various reports with the Securities and Exchange Commission, such as the 10K and shareholder proxy statement, DEF14A. These are good places to find out just who the major stockholders are, which lawsuits are pending, what shareholder resolutions are being considered at the annual meeting, and so on. If your school has more than $100 million in holdings, it must also file a 13F with the

SEC outlining these investments, which may be another route to obtaining this information if your school is private and/or not respecting open records requests for its portfolio. (Be sure to ask for a 13F both under your school's proper name and "Trustees of ———— School.") If you are a bona fide shareholder yourself (and all it takes is one share!), you are entitled to a glossy annual report—though these can sometimes be obtained directly by contacting the corporate headquarters to get the latest breaking information for that business class term paper. Corporate recruiters on your campus and your career advising office may also have such materials to share—just ask in an friendly, innocent manner.

GOT THE INFO?
NOW SHARE IT WITH YOUR MANY FRIENDS!

Once you've unveiled several examples of corruption on campus, the trick is finding the best way to share the information to build a campaign—which is where the next piece of college advice, make new friends, comes into play. The corporatization/militarization of higher education is a great coalition-building issue, since it adversely affects almost everyone! Be ready to think outside the box regarding who may be potential comrades in your corporate-free-campus campaign. Believe it or not, many conservative organizations will go ballistic when they hear your public school is waist deep in taxpayer-subsidized corporate welfare. Other more natural allies would include labor unions, family farmers, people-of-color groups, religious organizations, and social justice networks, to name but a few. Also, be sure to get your exposé out in a variety of forms—not just the usual press release or public forum. Why not try a series of "unwanted" posters or even trading cards with your favorite corporate factoids about university regents and administrators? When activists at UW–Madison realized many of the regents had literally bought their seats through $10,000 donations to the governor's reelection war chest, they launched their own "Buy a Regent" educational fund-raising campaign, soliciting over $1000 in spare change from students, faculty, and workers on campus! Or better yet, as a summer project, compile and publish a "disorientation manual" to distribute the first week of school, countering the university's Welcome Week propaganda and exposing all the corruption on your campus.[23] And don't forget to make some friends with legal expertise along the way—such as local affiliates of the American Civil Liberties Union or the National Lawyers Guild—since you never know when you might suddenly face a Stategic Lawsuit Against Public Participation filed by an angry corporation seeking to intimidate you from such good detective work.

THE WORD IS OUT—
NOW IT'S TIME FOR A CLEAN SWEEP!

The final friendly advice—keep your room clean—applies just as well to the rest of campus. Universities and colleges exist to satisfy the educational needs of students and provide knowledge for the common good—not to subsidize profits of corporations or facilitate atrocities of the military. School administrators and professors are public servants accountable to citizens—not renegade mercenaries on the free-market auction block. Your school's own legacy will support this perspective if you take a moment to review its mandate and the wise words of its far-sighted founders. At UW–Madison activists have grown particularly fond of rubbing the nineteenth-century "Wisconsin Idea" in the face of ignorant, embarrassed technocrats. Such history, though, is routinely (and conveniently) forgotten by most campus officials today, and part of your duty is to remind them of their place and purpose. To get in the right mental state, just remember, whenever you have to challenge the arrogant hypocrisy of authority figures on campus, that as a student, *you* are their *boss*! Without your presence, they would not have a paycheck, and hence they are directly answerable to you for any of their actions. Like a civic-minded King or Queen Midas, you should be able to touch any aspect of your university community and make it not only socially responsible—but also democratically accountable.

As you come to grips with your school's rather sordid status quo, ask yourself a few simple questions: (1) Who is framing the agenda? (2) Who is making the decisions? (3) Who is benefitting from the outcome? If "community" (that is, students, faculty, workers, and citizens) is not part of the answer, then your university is suffering from an acute bout of creeping corporatization and needs a revolutionary overhaul! Don't accept reformist diversionary tactics, like another ad hoc committee to do another fact-finding study ad nauseum (unless your token presence is a sneaky strategy to get an inside scoop for your real activist work). As concerned students, educators, and sovereign citizens, we deserve more: a shared-governance principle mandating equitable representation of students and workers on all decision-making bodies now dominated by administrators and professors, a fully elected board of regents or trustees, an independent ombudsperson position, a citizen review board for campus investment and procurement policies, an oversight committee for campus police, a revolving no-strings-attached funding pool for public interest research, and so on. Back in the late nineteenth century, a New York Supreme Court justice wrote that "the life of a corporation is worth less than that of the humblest citizen," and this is the same basic value we should adopt in our ongoing campus struggles for social change.

NOTES

1. Daniel Pendick, "Natural Born Killers?" *Isthmus*, January 28–February 3, 1994; International Committee Against Racism (INCAR), "Biological Determinism Feeds Fascism—Oppose Racist 'Violence Initiative,'" position paper, 1994.

2. University of Wisconsin–Madison, annual report, 1997–1998.

3. Brian DeVore, "Sending the Land Grants to School," *Land Stewardship Letter* (April–June 1998).

4. Steven Greenhouse, "18 Major Retailers and Apparel Makers are Accused of Using Sweatshops," *New York Times*, January 14, 1999.

5. Kerry D. Vandell, "Environmental Justice—An Economic Perspective," Center for Urban Land Economics Research, University of Wisconsin–Madison School of Business, working paper series, August 1996; Dan Rodman, "Buying a Good Reputation," *Badger Herald*, October 11, 1996.

6. Jeanne DeQuine, "Volatile Mix of Corporate Cash and Academic Ideals," *Christian Science Monitor*, July 11, 1996; "Man Imprisoned in Patent Fight Finishes Term," *New York Times*, April 3, 1997.

7. Frank Wu, "Motion Denied—Louisiana Retaliates Against Tulane Law Students," *Progressive*, March 1999.

8. David Shenk, "Money + Science = Ethics Problems on Campus," *Nation*, March 22, 1999; Julianne Basinger, "Universities' Royalty Income Increased 33% in 1997, Reaching $446 Million," *Chronicle of Higher Education*, January 8, 1999.

9. Dow Elanco and University of Wisconsin–Madison, research contract, July 24, 1995, obtained through open records request; University of Wisconsin–Madison Office of News and Public Affairs, "New Bacterium May Aid War on Insect Pests," press release, December 18, 1997; University of Wisconsin–Madison Office of News and Public Affairs, "Public/Private Partners Support Chemistry Building Project," press release, September 14, 1998.

10. Shenk, "Money + Science = Ethics Problems on Campus."

11. Exxon Production Research Co. and University of Wisconsin–Madison, research contract, November 11, 1993, obtained through open records request.

12. Exxon Education Foundation and University of Wisconsin–Madison, research contract, January 7, 1997, obtained through open records request.

13. Ron Grossman and Charles Leroux, "Research Grants Actually Add to Tuition Costs, Study Reveals," *Chicago Tribune*, January 28, 1996.

14. Drew Hempel, graduate student, University of Minnesota, personal communication with the author, December 1998.

15. U.S. Department of Defense and University of Wisconsin–Madison, work unit summaries, 1992–1998, obtained through FOIA request.

16. Ibid.

17. Vincent Kiernan, "DNA-based Computer Could Race Past Super Computers, Researchers Predict," *Chronicle of Higher Education*, November 28,

1997; Lee Bergquist, "Computer Researchers Harnessing DNA for a Brainier SuperProcessor," *Milwaukee Journal Sentinel*, June 7, 1998; U.S. Department of Defense and University of Wisconsin–Madison, work unit summaries, 1992–1998.

18. Jeff Iseminger, "UW–Madison's Cranberry Connection," *On Wisconsin*. (Univ. of Wisconsin–Madison Alumni Foundation), March–April 1997.

19. Reebok International Ltd. and University of Wisconsin–Madison, marketing contract, July 15, 1996, obtained through open records request.

20. University of Wisconsin System Trust Fund Portfolio, quarterly reports, March 1996–April 1999.

21. For example, read Clark Kerr, *The Uses of the University*, 4th ed. (Cambridge: Harvard University Press, 1995).

22. Send a letter to: Defense Technical Information Center, 8725 John J. Kingman Road, Suite 0944, Fort Belvoir, VA 22060. There's also a Web site at www.dtic.mil. Be sure to have a Dr. Science type on hand to decipher all the technogibberish you'll receive!

23. Many of these strategies have been big hits at UW–Madison. Contact us if you would like copies: UW Greens Infoshop/Alliance for Democracy, 731 State Street, Madison WI 53703; (608) 262–9036; www.studentorg.wisc.edu/greens/ or www.sit.wisc.edu/~democrac.

29

POCKET CHANGE OR SOCIAL CHANGE?
University Investment Responsibility and Activism

Seth Newton

Many people are taken aback when they hear that Stanford University has a contingent of its student body active on social and political issues. How could such an elite institution cultivate deeply felt concern for the inequalities and unsustainable nature of our society, while at the same time upholding the very power structure of this society? Students at Stanford itself might also be taken aback by the assertion. However few the numbers, it's undeniable true: Students at Stanford—and at universities of all shapes and sizes—are increasingly disillusioned with our society, and are taking it upon themselves to change the structures both supporting and supported by our educational institutions.

Activism at Stanford currently addresses issues from faculty diversity and U.S. foreign policy and war, to old-growth purchasing and gay/queer awareness. This spring Stanford held a conference on the potential for student contribution to the labor movement, simultaneously with conferences at Harvard, Yale, and Kent State. These conferences established a national youth-labor solidarity and action organization. Yet another issue that has commanded students' attention for three decades has been Stanford's lack of investment responsibility. From a 1980s South Africa–divestment campaign to current efforts to adopt policies on corporate labor standards and climate change, Stanford students have made many attempts—some successful, some not—to address the social irresponsibility of investments.

The demand for socially responsible investment is growing on campuses around the nation, as seen in the formation of a national student organization, Student Alliance for the Reform of Corporations (STARC). National student groups come together because they recognize the common aspirations on campuses across the nation, and the value in shared experiences and coordinated efforts. It is my hope that a peek at Stanford students' array of approaches and strategies in investment responsibility activism will offer insight and ideas for activists on other campuses and strengthen these efforts.

First, I look at the intellectual arguments that consistently uphold a status quo of corporate complicity, and prevent universities from adopting socially responsible investment policies. Not only is this an important practical exercise, but it also begins to illustrate the extent to which our universities are influenced by corporations and a much more fundamental corporate consciousness. In addition, through a greater understanding of the state of our universities, we are more capable of changing them. Next, I offer a spectrum of possible actions students might take—many of which go beyond criticism and toward solution-oriented actions—based on Stanford students' efforts over the years. We by no means claim to have exhausted the possibilities out there, or even succeeded in our goals (in fact, we are far from them).

Yet the more we analyze, act, and reflect, the more the process of activism gains importance. This is the democratic process—one that is devalued and almost absent from campuses across the United States. Whatever the issue at hand, this is the process we want to see validated, and the process we shall win back.

OF RESPONSIBILITY, NEUTRALITY, AND THE STATUS QUO

Stanford students undoubtedly realize that the opportunities available to them come at an enormous financial cost—to themselves and/or their families. What too few students realize, however, is the social costs of their education and institutional affiliation. Stanford's facets are due in no small part to its colossal endowment of $4.7 billion. Incorporated for the sole purpose of managing Stanford's endowment, the Stanford Management Company invests this endowment in domestic stocks, international stocks, and real estate equity, among others.[1] Though many believe investments to be financial transactions disconnected from social, political, or environmental ramifications, this couldn't be further from the truth. In providing capital for approximately twenty-five hundred corporations, Stanford University and its constituents support socially detrimental, economically inequitable, and environmentally destructive activities not mentioned in the Stanford's Annual Report.

While some administrators will continue to debate a university's responsibility for such corporate activities (and will even question the corporation's responsibility for the social injury), the responsibility for a university to exercise its role as a shareholder to correct destructive activities is not a point of contention. In *The Ethical Investor*, John G. Simon, Charles W. Powers, and Jon P. Gunnemann assert that "the 'moral minimum' responsibility of the shareholder to take such action as he can to prevent or correct corporate social injury[2] extends to the university when it is a corporate shareholder."[3] Even scholars such as Derek Bok (president of Harvard for twenty years)—who are more conservative when it comes to the social responsibility of institutional shareholders—do not deny responsibility for investments. Some level of responsibility exists by any standard; the question is how this responsibility is interpreted within the context of a university.

Unfortunately, we at Stanford have not been able to get our president, Gerhard Casper, to even agree to this much.[4] His basic argument is that the university is a unique institution that as a community cannot determine what is socially responsible, and that efforts to do so would detract from the university's primary responsibility. He also argues that the university is not set up to "adjudicate" the countless social issues associated with investments, and thus taking any action to influence the corporations in which we are invested violates Stanford's institutional "neutrality" and links Stanford with the making of political statements.[5] Stanford should therefore refrain from even the slightest attempt to implement a socially responsible investment policy. Derek Bok says that this position conveys "the awkward message that it is simply too much trouble to take ethical positions on important issues even when there is no other means that is nearly as effective in expressing an opinion that will have a constructive influence on corporate management."[6] While there isn't room here to systematically counter President Casper's peculiar argument (I've begun to do so during his office hours), his argument points to a greater problem at Stanford—and other universities—that extends beyond our responsibility as shareholders to vote shareholder resolutions.

Two points of contention are particularly relevant: the notion of neutrality (and the making of political statements) and academic freedom. With greater connections to the outside world and economy than ever before, it's virtually impossible for a university to remain neutral.[7]

President Casper claims that this can be done by investing based only upon financial returns and by abstaining from shareholder resolutions.

Yet these, too, are choices that endorse a certain set of values—in this case the prevailing economic status quo. This status quo is one that values profits above all else, supports the unregulated flow of capital across borders, prioritizes the individual and his ability to fend for himself, and tolerates externalizing costs on society and the environment.

The university supports its "neutral" stance in investment matters by defining university functions parallel to economic principles. For example, just as a corporation claims it cannot take socially oriented action without impairing its economic role in society, universities claim that they cannot address social issues in investments without compromising their strictly educational role. Similarly, corporations must focus all effort on the goods and services for which they have a comparative advantage. University resources are often seen in the same light. Furthermore, both corporations and universities claim they do not have competence to address such issues, and that socially motivated action would be unfair to some (in the case of the corporation) and infringe upon faculty academic freedom (in the case of the university), and that only government can legitimately deal with social problems.

President Casper claims that the university's primary responsibility is to its students, and other responsibilities must not infringe upon this one. His consideration is greatly appreciated, but we must not fall into the economic logic of Milton Friedman, who claims that a corporation's responsibility is to its shareholders. A noble end cannot justify injurious means. Receiving a highly regarded education will not be well served if it was made possible through social and environmental irresponsibility. This concern can not be understated; students have considered dropping out of Stanford because of the university's contribution to social and environmental injustices, and the associated feeling of personal responsibility for the destructive practices being supported.

To revisit the assertion of neutrality, by not choosing within the context of the economic status quo, we are still making a choice. In his own words of welcome to my Stanford class two years ago, President Casper explained why any choice is not neutral, referring to our choices as students at Stanford. He said: "I should like to make a few suggestions about how to think about making choices. First, not choosing is in itself a choice. In some circumstances, like not voting, that often means abdicating the choice to others."[8] Stanford's investment policy is one such circumstance. Not choosing to vote shareholder resolutions and not choosing to act against social injury will abdicate the choice to others, usually in favor of a corporate management that has allowed, and refused to mitigate, social injury. Derek Bok aptly warned of the danger in this position when he said that "the university may be attacked for clinging to a specious neutrality that amounts to little more than a tacit endorsement of the status quo and a willingness to support initiatives defined by the wealthy and the powerful."[9] Though mentioned in a section detailing the "activist view," his is an insightful warning.

Not only is investing solely for financial reasons and without exercising the normal responsibilities given to shareholders a nonneutral decision, it is not out of the question to believe that acting to mitigate and prevent social injury might be based on more widely shared public values of human rights and environmental sustainability—and thus less of a political statement—than the prevailing economic status quo. Unfortunately, these points are difficult to get across in part because of differences in values and in a basic understanding of social injury. Those who would support the concept of neutrality and inaction in investment responsibility decisions see universities as innocent bystanders when corporations cause social injury. As innocent bystanders, the social injury is no more their responsibility than that of the general public. To those who understand an endorsement of the value system contributing to social injury, as well as a more interconnected relationship with the victims suffering social injury, however, the bystander is not innocent. The bystander is complacent, even helpful, and thus responsible. As long as the Stanford community perceives itself as individual actors disconnected from the impacts of financial transactions and dollar votes, we will fail in our responsibilities as citizens and as an institution that was founded "to promote the public welfare by exercising an influence on behalf of humanity and civilization."[10]

In all this discussion of neutrality, it's easy to forget the nature of social injury in the first place. It's not worth documenting the social and environmental abuses resulting from corporate activities in the United States and abroad—they are all too apparent. However, we must ask our administrations why upholding international norms of decency—such as human rights and environmental protection—are considered partisan. I'm well aware that these may not reflect the values of all those in the Stanford community, yet they are norms that have been adopted by international institutions. Stanford has a responsibility to uphold values other than a deceiving political neutrality.

To address one last criticism, these choices toward investment responsibility need not violate academic freedom nor infringe on the academic context—both more critical components of universities than institutional neutrality. President Casper claims that academic freedom is at stake when the university decides to implement socially responsible investment policies. Yet scholars have devised methods of separating investment decisions from the academic community, primarily by giving the board of trustees the final decision on investment responsibility matters.[11] Again, we should be more concerned with complicity in the prevailing economic status quo and its impact on academic freedom. The Declaration of 1915 established the concept of academic freedom to protect faculty from outside influences and internal discipline.[12] Today outside influences in the form of corporations are more present than ever, not only through investments but even more directly through purchasing contracts, donations, and sponsored research. The very purpose of academic freedom—to protect faculty from outside interests—is being undermined by the growing role of corporations in universities.

FURTHER YET FROM DEMOCRACY

The economic status quo embraced by Stanford and other universities is at the heart of investment irresponsibility. This status quo runs so deep that it becomes apparent that universities such as Stanford have more than a corporate influence; they have a corporate consciousness. This consciousness goes hand in hand with the lack of democratic student participation in university decision making, as well as a healthy academic context. In addition to drawing a correlation between the values of the economic status quo and university values, an even more fascinating and disturbing parallel appears between the growing political disconnectedness of the greater U.S. public and the power structure of universities. It appears as though the growing disenchantment with political life is reflected in the Stanford administration's fear of entering into any debate that might have political implications. This is manifested in a climate of silence and lack of debate, in zealous individualism, and in the governing structure of our university. The administration may claim institutional neutrality within this corporate system, but its basic characteristics are antithetical to the necessary academic context where healthy debate can be cultivated. This climate is reminiscent of the national trend just described.

True, President Casper and other administrators will encourage the investment responsibility activism of its students—but only as individual and isolated citizens. Someone once said that "everybody has an alibi for silence." Not only does everyone have an alibi for silence, but also for inaction. In the context of the university, two of the strongest alibis for inaction are President Casper's prized virtues—neutrality and individualism. In the context of the economic status quo, these values have contributed to the systematic devaluation of political experience. It is no wonder they are so highly prized: While preventing more socially responsible policies and more democratic decision making, they quell student concerns and maintain Stanford's economic powerhouse. This individualism runs deep, at colleges and universities nationwide, encouraging success in the corporate world as rugged individuals. Yet, true success—success removed from the grips of our current status quo—is perhaps more measurable not by the degree of personal achievement and the accomplishment of individual aspirations, but by the ability to understand one's integral relationship to all other humans and things, and to live by and act on this awareness.

FROM DIALOGUE TO DEMONSTRATION

It is not enough to criticize the state of our universities, even the state of our democracy. As activists, perhaps we do this too often. What must come next are visions of what we might like these institutions to look like, and what solutions we might propose. This is the basic premise behind investment responsibility. We have an affirmative duty to correct and prevent social injury caused by those corporations in which we are invested. I do not mean to imply that socially responsible investing will succeed in restoring our democracy and achieving social justice, or even in reforming corporations for that matter. Clearly the forces and power structures maintaining injustices and unsustainability are greater than any corporate dialogue, shareholder resolution, or divestment could aspire to achieve. Nonetheless, the gap between here and there—between our present situation and our goals—is so great that the first steps will necessarily feel insufficient and overly compromising.

With a greater understanding of the arguments involved in preventing more socially responsible investment policies, I turn to the history of investment responsibility activism at Stanford. I list a series of strategies and efforts available to student groups, seen through Stanford students' experiences over the years. This list is by no means exhaustive. While our successes have been few and far between, they are significant. In addition, the scarcity of grandiose victories is a well-known reality on U.S. campuses. This shouldn't prevent us from learning from these experiences, and even trying them again (many know the disheartening feeling of being told that something has already been tried, and thus cannot work). Repetition and persistence have paid off. Due to the difficulty of maintaining activist institutional memory, many of the specific lessons learned over the years will not be included—though they may be inferred from the outcomes. More importantly, my knowledge and experience in the investment responsibility movement is dwarfed by the collective efforts of countless dedicated students. It is with humility that I attempt to share their work, and strive to contribute myself.

Before delving into strategies for activists, a point connecting the two main themes of this chapter—the intellectual pursuit of understanding the current state of our universities and the active pursuit of changing university policies—must be bound and reinforced by making political and social activism integral components of our education. Organizing should no longer be considered extracurricular. Activism is a fundamental part of our education, just as education is an essential piece of effective activism.

The more we recognize social and political activism as an essential ingredient in our education, the less administrations and trustees will be able to deny, criticize, and separate our activism from the normal operations of a university. It's a reassuring irony that our efforts to change our educational institutions constitutes a central role in our education. This valuation of activism and political experience ties in directly with goals of socially responsible investing. Bok says that "[u]niversities are concerned with education, and their response to social issues will affect the education of their students just as surely as the lectures and the readings that go on in their libraries and classrooms. If we would teach our students to care about important social problems and think about them rigorously, then clearly our institutions of learning must set a high example in the conduct of their own affairs."[13] In reading the following, notice both the value students took from these experiences, and the systematic denial of Stanford University's responsibility on two fronts: in valuing university activism as education and in the conduct of its own affairs.

The following are some possible steps to take toward investment responsibility. They constitute a list of options rather than a "how to" guide, because approaches will necessarily be specific to the school and a group's interests, and developing the method of action is an essential component of investment responsibility activism.

Push for a trustee committee on investment responsibility.

In response to a student demonstration led by the Black Student Union (BSU) and national concerns regarding investment responsibility, the Stanford trustees created an ad hoc Committee on Investment Responsibility in 1973. This constituted some of the first investment responsibility activism. The Committee on Investment Responsibility and subsequent committees were guided by Stanford's Statement on Investment Responsibility.[14] In response to broadened campus and national concern, in 1977 the trustees established the Select Committee on Investment Responsibility, and later that year created the Commission on Investment Responsibility. This two-committee system is essentially the framework that exists today, with what are now the Special Committee on Investment Responsibility (SCIR) and the Advisory Panel on Investment Responsibility (APIR). The APIR is a committee composed of faculty, students, staff, and alumni, and serves to make recommendations to the SCIR, a trustee committee.

This framework aims to gather input of all the various groups within the Stanford community, while at the same time separating the decision on investments from the academic context of the university. While it takes a lot of time to advance investment responsibility issues through this committee system, and at times even appears inactive, creating and working within these committees is an important step in providing an institutional voice for students. In addition to student representation, these committees have advanced important investment policies that are currently in place.

Initiate a class that investigates a specific social/political issue, or investment and corporate responsibility.

Through the 1970s a movement began to gain momentum regarding the apartheid system in South Africa and the contribution of U.S. corporations in support the oppressive regime. In winter quarter 1977, students taught a course on apartheid through a program called the Stanford Workshops on Political and Social Issues (SWOPSI). This class examined the relationship between South African apartheid, multinational corporations in South Africa, and Stanford's investments in these corporations. Through their class and a research paper, students argued that the corporations in South Africa weren't a positive force, as some claimed, but were rather supporting the existing regime. The paper was then distributed to trustees, administrators, and in dorms.[15]

Starting a class, whether through a program like SWOPSI or with a faculty sponsor, has many advantages: it provides credit, allows students more time to work on issues with social and political implications, validates student activism regarding investment responsibility, and provides a forum for investment responsibility concerns and research. Unfortunately, President Casper has recently cut SWOPSI because of the supposed lack of academic rigor, as well as funding difficulties. This contributed to the lack of support and value ascribed to social and political issues at Stanford, and student-run and public-service-oriented programs more generally.

Twenty years after the SWOPSI class on apartheid, Kelly Naylor, a student activist, started a class called Corporate Responsibility in the Local and Global Environment. This class has been offered for two years, and will be offered for a third time in winter of 2000. While it is more comprehensive than examining a single issue or focusing on Stanford's investments, it provides the forum for this discussion. The chair of the

APIR (and staff member at the Stanford Management Company) and I are interested in connecting this class more directly with Stanford's investment responsibility by encouraging students to write research papers that can be used to create policies for the APIR. Furthermore, the chair is attempting to extend this concept of investment responsibility based classes and research to other departments, interested faculty, and students.

Start an investment responsibility student group on campus; network with similar groups on other campuses.

Around the time of the SWOPSI class, students formed the Stanford Committee for a Responsible Investment Policy (SCRIP). Through the campaign on South African apartheid, SCRIP built a consensus with other groups at Stanford, including the Half the Sky (a women's group coalition) and the Stanford Organizing Committee (an umbrella group). According to one observer, SCRIP was effective because women and racial minorities were supported and encouraged to speak out, new members were taught the basic skills, and students were eager to take on leadership roles.[16] In addition, the BSU continued to be active on apartheid in the 1980s, including a sit-in in support of divestment from Motorola in 1985, which was selling equipment to South Africa's military and police.

Student groups became active on investment responsibility again in the 1990s, when concerns grew about the oppressive military regime in Burma and Stanford's contribution to maintaining this regime through its investments. Students were active through Students for Environmental Action at Stanford (SEAS, a Student Environmental Action Coalition group), as elected representatives in the Associated Students of Stanford University (ASSU), and through the formation of another organization: SR-squared (which stands for "social responsibility and student representation"). Those working on investment responsibility today continue to do so through SEAS. A critical part of beginning a new organization or campaign is researching the history of investment responsibility activism at your campus, as well as connecting with existing groups who might be active on investment responsibility issues.

As mentioned in the introduction, STARC is a national student group that will prove a powerful organization for future investment responsibility campaigns. STARC is currently negotiating a merger with the 180 Movement for Democracy and Education (180/MDE). Tapping into what is now another growing national movement for investment responsibility through these organizations will build strength and influence on each of our campuses.

Organize teach-ins, guerrilla theater, and if necessary, sit-ins around an investment responsibility campaign.

Following the SWOPSI class in 1977, SCRIP organized a campaign around Stanford's investments in South Africa that led to a sit-in at which 294 students were arrested. The campaign called for Stanford to vote its shareholder resolutions regarding apartheid and investment in South Africa, and if the resolutions did not pass, they called for Stanford to divest from these companies. SCRIP began its campaign with educational outreach based on a paper that was written in the SWOPSI class. Students prepared leaflets, walked door-to-door, talked to students, showed a film on apartheid, gathered almost three thousand student and eighty faculty signatures on a petition, gained support from twenty student groups, wrote letters to the editor and columns in the *Stanford Daily*, held rallies in the main plaza, acted out guerrilla theater, played music, and displayed posters. The amount of public outreach and campus visibility was outstanding. In response to student concerns, the trustees only agreed to abstain from voting shareholder resolutions.

On May 2, 1977, students began a three-day vigil and thirty-eight students fasted in response to the trustees' decision. The next day SCRIP held a rally demanding that the trustees reconsider their position. They met with opposition, and decided to plan a sit-in at Old Union, one of the main administrative buildings. Students occupied Old Union on May 9th, and broke up into groups to weigh the costs and benefits of peaceful arrest, while many others gathered outside in support. After thoughtful deliberation, 294 students decided to remain in the building, and were systematically extracted from Old Union by the police that night.

While Stanford did not immediately divest from corporations in South Africa, in subsequent years the trustees began voting shareholder resolutions in support of eventual withdrawal from South Africa. It wasn't until the mid-1980s, under the more supportive President Donald Kennedy, that Stanford began to seriously consider divestment.[17] One protester's reflection on the SCRIP campaign attributed its success to the group's ability to bring in students, faculty, and other groups to its side; its interest in reasoned dialogue; its nonviolence; its trust in new membership; and finally, the ability to expose the undemocratic and hierarchical structure of the university.[18]

Prevent irresponsible corporations from profiting off your campus; pass a selective purchasing resolution.

Following the campaign for investment responsibility in South Africa in the late 1970s and 1980s, the APIR turned to tobacco industry and environmental issues in the early 1990s. Then, in the mid-1990s, students began to raise concerns regarding investments in Burma that supported the oppressive military regime. Stanford began negotiations to bring a Taco Bell franchise to the student union in 1992. Taco Bell is owned by Pepsico, which was invested in Burma. When talks resumed in 1996, SEAS rallied around the opportunity, asserting that Stanford should not be supporting corporations doing business with what was then called the State Law and Order Restoration Council. In March of 1996, activists collected more than two thousand signatures opposing the Taco Bell on campus. In April, the advisory board overseeing the decision granted a local fast-food chain—Pollo's—the lease. Taco Bell had been denied the spot. As was expected, the dean of students claimed that in no way was the decision affected by student protests or Taco Bell's connection to Burma.[19] Students are inclined to believe otherwise—and such a campaign surely raises student awareness beyond traditional investment responsibility issues.

A related effort was to have the ASSU, Stanford's student government, pass a resolution that prevented Stanford from purchasing products from corporations doing business in Burma. While critics undoubtedly claim negligible impacts from such a decision, their symbolic, educational, and institutional value makes them worthwhile extensions of university investment responsibility.

Propose a socially responsible endowment fund.

While still highly concerned with Stanford's investments in Burma (students were pressuring the APIR to vote shareholder resolutions regarding Unocal), students realized that due to the number of corporations Stanford is invested in, and the time it takes to address but one of these corporations, they should pursue a more general policy on investment responsibility. Their plan: create a new endowment. Instead of attacking individual corporations or even individual oppressive regimes (amounting to isolated negative screens), in October of 1996 students proposed that Stanford create a separate "progressive endowment fund" (based on a mixture of positive and negative screens). This fund would receive money from donors who wanted their money invested in a socially responsible manner. The trustees rejected the proposal because they didn't think it would increase alumni giving, as the students proposed; they believed it overlooked the fact that the endowment is already invested in socially responsible corporations; that it would politicize the act of asking people for money; and that it would be confused with another fund at Stanford.[20]

In protest, the student group SR-squared gathered one thousand signatures in support, and began their own socially responsible fund through the ASSU. Students gathered over fifty donations, at which point the trustees granted them the opportunity to resubmit a revised socially responsible endowment proposal. Based on the aim of increasing the efficiency with which the trustees exercise their responsibility as ethical investors, students submitted the proposal in May of 1997, calling for a more efficient committee process; a formal procedure to allow members of the university community to bring concerns and requests for divestment to trustees; and the adoption of a policy that enables them to freeze investment in a given corporation so as to respond to community concerns, invest 5–10 percent of the endowment strictly in socially responsible corporations, give donors the option of directing their donation to this socially responsible fraction of the endowment, perform marketing research on the potential of attracting donors by a social responsibility option, and hire a student intern to help the APIR research issues. When the APIR and SCIR finally responded to the second proposal for a socially responsible endowment in 1998, they rejected each and every proposed policy.

Though drawn out and rejected, the proposal for a socially responsible endowment fund brought investment responsibility activism to a new level. Based on the available data showing that socially responsible funds (for example, Domini Index) make just as much or more profit than the S&P 500, gradually moving toward a socially responsible endowment more effectively addresses both trustees' fiduciary and social responsibilities.[21] Even though it has yet to gain approval at Stanford, convincing other universities to adopt this course is not out of the question. This might be most appropriately accomplished through the process adopted by the second proposal, above.

As mentioned above, after the proposal for a socially responsible endowment fund had been submitted, students began to establish their own endowment fund. Yet another option is to invest student governments' endowments in socially responsible corporations. While yet to be attempted at Stanford, establishing a socially responsible student government endowment fund (the ASSU currently holds approximately $7 million) could have a considerable impact, and is definitely closer to students' sphere of influence.

Make sure students who are active and aware maintain a presence in the committee(s).

While activists often balk at working within "the system," there is a lot to say for covering the bases both within and outside the system. Such is the case for the investment responsibility committee system. Over the years,

Stanford students affiliated with groups active on investment responsibility issues have served on the APIR. Students should continue to serve on these committees. First, this allows students with perhaps more awareness and an inclination for aggressive socially responsible investment policies to consistently voice their opinion and influence policy. Second, it provides a point of contact and collaboration for active student groups.

Research issues and corporations, write policies, and submit them to the investment responsibility committee or directly to the trustees.

This involves the basic process for bringing concerns of social injury to the trustees. This was done during the campaign against corporations in South Africa, corporations in Burma, and the proposal for a socially responsible endowment fund. In addition, other kinds of policies have been tried. In November of 1998, I wrote a proposal based on information disclosure and reporting and, together with other members of SEAS, presented the overarching policy and a case-study corporation—mining giant Freeport McMoRan—illustrating why the APIR needs such a policy.

This policy took a slightly different approach from those prior to it for two reasons. First, if Stanford was perennially concerned with violating its "neutrality" by making value judgments on social issues, it must be safe to make statements regarding its fundamental value: information exchange and creation. Second, I noted many of the shareholder resolutions on social issues—about 36 percent last year—were of an informational nature (and of these, Stanford abstained on 71 percent). This policy cuts across issues, because adequate information regarding corporate activities is such a fundamental concern.

The policy proposed three initiatives: (1) vote in favor all shareholder resolutions that call for the creation, retrieval, and/or reporting of information on a corporation's activities, emissions, and discharges, compliance with regulations, monetary contributions, employee composition, as well as fulfill requests for independent monitoring; (2) hire a student intern to research the corporations in which Stanford is invested and help coordinate the process of creating a set of investment guidelines; (3) occasionally disclose a list of the corporations Stanford is invested in to those participating in research for the APIR. The APIR agreed to pursue the first initiative and accept the second, but rejected the third. The APIR is still supposedly in the process of creating a more concrete policy on information disclosure (in addition to the concept being included in subsequent policies), and will be hiring a student intern.

Propose that the trustees or the trustee advisory committee create investment guidelines on categories of social issues.

Rather than address one shareholder resolution or one corporation at a time, working toward investment responsibility would be much more effective with policy guidelines that tell the trustees how to vote on any given social issue. That way, when proxy season rolls around, the investment responsibility committee just has to funnel shareholder resolutions into its corresponding investment guideline to be voted. Some of these possible social categories include human rights, labor standards, environment, diversity issues, and so forth. One simple example is adopting a policy that says the trustees will always vote for shareholder resolutions requesting that a corporation adhere to the Ceres Principles (a set of environmental principles). With this policy in place, the advisory committee must not deliberate and vote every time such a resolution comes before them. Fortunately, with the guidance of its chair, the APIR has taken it upon itself to begin developing these guidelines. It has broken down into subcommittees creating guidelines on human rights, labor standards, environmental, and diversity issues.

Propose that the trustees enter into dialogues and write letters to irresponsible and responsible corporations.

The subcommittee on environment has already developed a policy on climate change, passed it through the APIR, and presented it to the SCIR. The policy is primarily concerned with the efforts of oil corporations in the Global Climate Coalition (GCC) to subvert the scientific consensus regarding human influence on climate change, and prevent ratification of the Kyoto Protocol (reminiscent of the tobacco industry's calculated deceitfulness towards the public). Recognizing the weight an institution such as Stanford can have when it raises concerns with corporations, the policy proposes that the university begin with a dialogue, and by voting shareholder resolutions dealing with emissions, emission reduction plans, actions on climate change, and potential liabilities in regards to climate change.

Given final approval by the trustees, the chair of the SCIR will send letters to both those oil corporations active in the GCC and those corporations actively reducing emissions. The letter to those corporations in the GCC asks what evidence supports the inactive position they are currently taking on climate change, attempting to begin a dialogue. The letter to those corporations taking action to address climate change (those involved in the Pew Center on Global Climate Change) ask them for their help with regard to those corporations in the GCC, and praise them for their direction. While dialogue with corporations causing social injury has very limited effects, it has its merits as well.

Engage in stakeholder activism with the corporations your university is invested in.

It is our universities and not ourselves who are shareholders in the corporations we are deeply concerned about. As members of university communities, however, we are indeed stakeholders in these corporations. We don't own shares, but we do have a stake in their activities. As such, we can use this relationship in approaching corporations ourselves.

For example, through SEAS, another student and I accepted an invitation to speak at an alternative shareholders meeting for those invested in Freeport McMoRan (operating the largest gold mine in the world in Irian Jaya, Indonesia, at enormous social cost). In May of 1998, the alternative shareholders meeting—organized to provide a forum for discussion regarding social and environmental concerns—brought together concerned shareholders and, surprisingly, two Freeport vice presidents. I gave a speech claiming some level of responsibility for my university's two hundred thousand shares in the company, and thus for the social injury being committed. Following this speech and a demonstration displaying Stanford students' disgust in front of Freeport's corporate high rise, top executives definitely appeared concerned.

Engage faculty in the research on corporate irresponsibility, and support for those attempting to correct and prevent social injury.

This recommendation might seem like a given. Not only do faculty play integral roles in campus campaigns, but they also have the ability to aid in the correction of social injury itself. For example, in the case of Freeport, two lawsuits were filed in U.S. state and federal court by indigenous leaders living near the Freeport mine. This is one of only a handful of such environmental cases where foreigners are suing U.S. corporations in the United States for damages they caused abroad (under the Alien Tort Claims Act). Thus, the indigenous plaintiffs' lawyers necessarily had to break new legal ground with little precedent to follow.

At some point in our trip to the Freeport shareholders' meeting, the plaintiffs' lawyer asked if we knew anyone who might be able to offer legal assistance in the realm of the Alien Tort Claims Act. It just so happens that the professor sponsoring the corporate responsibility course I had taken that winter specialized in environmental law, and was in the process of coauthoring an article for the *Stanford Law Journal* on the Alien Tort Claims Act. I told the lawyer I might know someone who could help, and gave this professor the lawyer's contact information. They are now corresponding with each other on the subject, and I have no doubt that the advice and information exchange is indeed valuable.

While scholars have discussed the importance of separating professors from investment decisions, they should have the opportunity to participate because some will have expertise on investment-related issues, and all have a share in the investments themselves. Another possibility for a socially responsible investment campaign related to faculty that has yet to be tried at Stanford is to target the university's pension fund. The fund is owned by the faculty, and thus might have a greater chance of supporting a socially responsible investment policy.

Develop community investment projects.

One social investor advisor said that the three pillars of socially responsible investing include screening investments, shareholder activism, and community investing.[22] Students have put requirements for community investing in proposals to the Stanford trustees, but have yet to succeed. While this approach to community investment has proven difficult, it is by no means the only one out there. Students have investigated the possibility of establishing a community bank in the city of East Palo Alto, a low-income minority community near Stanford. A more developed community investment is Stanford's public service honors program that directs student research toward specific community needs. One student began a business partnership with a local homeless artist, who is now selling her paintings. As mentioned earlier, we must look toward alternatives for our universities, both in their financial and intellectual investments.

RIPE FOR RESPONSIBILITY

Where is Stanford University's investment responsibility headed in the future? The APIR's work on policy guidelines and broadening the pool of students contributing to research is encouraging. However, this process is still slow and resources to carry out these initiatives slight. In addition, Stanford does not have the ability to address what happens when these efforts fall through. Both the processes for "constructive engagement" and divestment could use some help: More resources are needed to make the APIR/SCIR process more efficient, and a more practical divestment policy is needed when dialogue and voting don't accomplish anything.

Furthermore, the APIR must find a way to begin affirmative invest-ing—investing a given fraction of the endowment in socially responsible funds. This means revising the University's Statement on Investment Responsibility, which currently prohibits investing "for the primary pur-pose of thereby encouraging or expressing approval of a company's activ-ities." If Stanford can praise a corporation's behavior in a dialogue, there is no reason it cannot do so through its investments. The easiest way to address would be to include this affirmative duty in the university's pri-mary fiduciary responsibility. Stanford should rewrite its responsibility to be one that is dual in nature: to maximize the financial return on resources and to minimize social injury that might result from these resources.

Our experiences at Stanford offer some insight into investment responsibility activism today, and the potential in the future. Though far from complete, some of the critical themes present in the above recom-mendations include: (1) flexibility—while activists often have strong preferences, we must be prepared to both dialogue and demonstrate at any given time; (2) diversity in approaches—similar to flexibility, we must apply creative and multifaceted campaigns that employ the resources and strategies available to us; (3) coalition building—we must be able to bridge interest with other groups and students; (4) validating activism as education—we must institutionalize our concerns and action on social and political issues; and (5) continue to pursue democracy—democratic participation is crucial both within our organizations, our universities, and our nation.

The barriers we encounter in activism toward investment responsi-bility begin to illuminate the ways in which the corporate consciousness is undermining our universities. University ideals are defined in a way that maximizes returns and minimizes social concerns. A more funda-mental argument than students' social concerns, the trustees' maximum return, and institutional neutrality revolves around the economic status quo that fails to recognize adverse consequences in economic transac-tions. Within this status quo that values profits, externalized costs, and free trade over basic tenets of freedom, justice, and democracy, all of President Casper's arguments make complete sense. Within this status quo, investments are financial transactions, not anything with moral or ethical repercussions. This explains why it is difficult for our administra-tion and much of the Stanford community to feel any sort of responsi-bility for the impact of our investments. When you look beyond the status quo, it is apparent that, based on Jane Stanford's commitment to the bet-terment of society, the university should really reflect commitment on every possible level of university operation—even beyond. Perhaps this disconnect is to be expected; as activists we must also consider our contribution to the fundamental system of shareholder ownership (as opposed to employee ownership). Focusing solely on investment responsibility and leaving other issues behind will continue to validate the current corporate structure and status quo.

Not only is an economic status quo defining the boundaries of dialogue and the realm of the possible in our educational institutions, but this growing corporate consciousness benefits from, and contributes to, the political disenchantment felt among students across the nation. This disenchantment and its ability to remove us from responsibility for healthy social and natural environments is the real tragedy. Bok said that "the fabric of trust, so essential for a democratic nation, rests on the reciprocal expectation that persons and institutions will take responsibility for the social consequences—intended or unintended—of their acts."[23] When the most prized of our institutions break this trust by denying responsibility for contributions to social injury, it contributes to the breakup of our democracy. Restoring this democracy will depend upon fulfilling our responsibilities, and by making universities more democratic themselves.

NOTES

1. Stanford University, Annual Report, 1998.

2. Social injury is defined as "particularly including activities which violate, or frustrate the enforcement of, rules of domestic or international law intended to protect individuals against deprivation of health, safety or basic freedoms." John G. Simon, Charles W. Powers, and Jon P. Gunnemann, *The Ethical Investor: Universities and Corporate Responsibility* (New Haven: Yale University Press, 1972), p. 21.

3. Ibid., p. 65.

4. As is often the case, leaders such as President Casper are criticized for decisions within and outside of their control. I recognize this tendency, but argue based on statements President Casper has made. He presumably has at least some level of influence in the matters he argues.

5. Gerhard Casper, personal communication with the author, April 23, 1998, and May 20, 1999.

6. Derek Bok, *Beyond the Ivory Tower: Social Responsibilities of the Modern University* (Cambridge: Harvard University Press, 1982), p. 255.

7. Simon, Powers, and Gunnemann, *The Ethical Investor*, p. 72.

8. Gerhard Casper, "Minds Moving: Welcome to New Students and Their Parents," Stanford University, September 19, 1997.

9. Bok, *Behind the Ivory Tower*, p. 79.

10. Jane Lanthrop Stanford, "The Founding Grant of November 11, 1885," Stanford University.

11. Simon, Powers, and Gunnemann, *The Ethical Investor*, p. 87.

12. Bok, *Behind the Ivory Tower*, p. 5.

13. Ibid, p. 10.

14. The Statement on Investment Responsibility reads: "The primary fiduciary responsibility of the University Trustees in investing and managing the University's endowment securities is to maximize the financial return on those resources, taking into account the amount of risk appropriate for University investment policy. However, when the Trustees adjudge that corporate policies or practices cause substantial social injury, they, as responsible and ethical investors, shall give independent weight to this factor in their investment policies and in voting proxies on corporate securities. . . . Substantial social injury is defined as the injurious impact on employees, consumers, and/or other individuals, or groups resulting directly from specific actions or inactions by a company. Included in this category are actions that violate, subvert, or frustrate the enforcement of rules of domestic or international law intended to protect individuals and/or groups against deprivation of health, safety, basic freedoms or human rights. Only actions or inactions by companies that are proximate to and directly responsible for identifiable social injury will be regarded as falling within these guidelines."

15. Randy Schutt, "A Powerful and Inspiring Campaign: A Short History of SCRIP's Efforts to End Stanford University's Support of South African Apartheid in 1977," February 3, 1998.

16. Ibid., p. 2.

17. While divestment is often the most appealing action to students, we must continue to evaluate the relative value in the spectrum options we have with investments, including dialogue, shareholder activism, and divestment.

18. Bob D., "Students Organize Against Stanford's Investment Policy," *Grapevine* 5 (1977): 1–2.

19. Bill Workman, "Taco Bell Won't Run Stanford Restaurant," *San Francisco Chronicle,* April 19, 1996, pp. A19, A23.

20. Beth Berselli, "Socially Responsible Investments Debate Enters Third Decade," *Stanford Daily* [online], dailystanford.org/Daily96-97/2-24-97/NEWS/index.html [February 24, 1997].

21. "SRI Index Funds Beat S&P," *Hope* (1999): 2–3.

22. Marjorie Kelly, "A Social Investor's How-To: An Inside Look at the Mechanics of Socially Responsible Mutual Funds." *Hope* (1999): 1–2.

23. Simon, Powers, and Gunnemann, *The Ethical Investor*, p. 64.

30

TAKE THE PLEDGE
*A Promise of Social and
Environmental Responsibility*

Neil J. Wollman

Since 1996, Manchester College has coordinated the national efforts of the Graduation Pledge Alliance. Founded in 1987 at Humboldt State University in California, the pledge has been adopted at dozens of schools around the country. The pledge reads: "I, _____, pledge to explore and take into account the social and environmental consequences of any job I consider and will try to improve these aspects of any organizations for which I work." (Some have modified the pledge wording to suit the needs of their school.) Taking the pledge is voluntary and allows students to determine for themselves what they consider to be socially and environmentally responsible.

Instituting the pledge gets at the heart of a good education and can benefit society as a whole. Not only does it remind students of the ethical implications of the knowledge and training they have received, but it can help lead to a socially conscious citizenry and a better world. And it can serve as a focal point for further consciousness raising around campus. Each year, well over a million students enter the workforce. Think of the impact on our society if even a significant minority of applicants and job holders inquired about or influenced the ethical practices of their potential or current employers. And shouldn't a job represent more than just a paycheck? Shouldn't it be a place where a worker can feel good about his or her own assignments and the general practice of the company?

Setting up the pledge varies from school to school. At Manchester

College, soon-to-be graduates receive an explanatory letter. Supporters receive a wallet-sized card that states the pledge. About 50 percent of students typically make the commitment, and they and supportive faculty wear green ribbons during commencement. The pledge also appears in the printed commencement program.

To ensure continuity, and to make the pledge a campuswide project, we have also found it beneficial to gain endorsements annually from a wide variety of campus groups, including student government. We have a pledge committee comprised of students, staff, and faculty. It helps to get sophomores and juniors, who can carry on the project the following year, involved. Continued support from the college is guaranteed if the project is housed within an official administrative office. Such actions will assure that the pledge doesn't come and go with one dedicated graduating class.

You can promote the pledge and social and environmental responsibility through Web sites, mailing lists, relevant local or national college-related or political activist groups, the media, public announcements, and friends or colleagues at other schools. Consider getting the word out to friends who might start the pledge at a high school, professional school (for example, law or medicine), or foreign university.

You may find that if you take the lead, others will follow your efforts. If necessary, start small—for example, start the project within a department, division, or organization until the whole school adopts it. If you can't organize at that level yet, take the pledge yourself or with friends, wear ribbons if you can, and seek publicity. Media coverage will further the campaign, no matter what its stage of development. (The pledge has appeared in national media like the Associated Press and the USA Radio Network.) Such coverage will probably appeal to your school's administration, which can assert that the pledge both betters the world and fits within the mission of the institution. *If you are working on a campaign project at your school, please do keep us informed so we can keep track of the effort.*

Manchester College has learned of inspiring examples concerning student commitment to the pledge after graduation. One graduate says, "I told my boss of the pledge and my concerns. He understood and agreed . . . and the company did not pursue the [chemical warfare] project." Another supporter says, "Now I make an effort to teach and think about social and environmental responsibility on a daily basis." And one woman helped establish a recycling program at her workplace. Some have turned down potential jobs with which they did not feel morally comfortable.

For additional materials, visit our Web page at ARES.manchester.edu/ department/peacestudies/gpa.html; write GPA, MC Box 135, Manchester College, 604 E. College Ave., North Manchester, IN 46962; or send e-mail to NJWollman@manchester.edu.

BUSINESS SCHOOL
An Interview with Noam Chomsky
Geoffry D. White

I interviewed Noam Chomsky in his office at MIT on December 10, 1999, with the understanding that the interview would be included in *Campus, Inc. : Corporate Power in the Ivory Tower.*

I began the interview by referring to *Newsweek*'s December 13, 1999, coverage of the WTO (World Trade Organization) meeting in Seattle, Washington. It is well known that the corporate-controlled media ignore and exclude Chomsky's analysis of our political system. As an expert in propaganda, I thought Chomsky would be interested to know that he was referred to in a sidebar titled "The New Anarchism" in the *Newsweek* coverage. Specifically, it said, "The movement's roots reach back to turn of the century radical Emma Goldman but it owes its current revival in large part to the influence of punk bands like Rage Against the Machine and Chumbawamba, whose latest album includes a CD featuring linguist Noam Chomsky." There was also a photo and reference to the Unibomber Ted Kaczynsky.

GW: I noticed that you made *Newsweek.*

NC: Right, they had me with Ted Kaczynsky.

GW: The interesting thing is that now America will think of Noam Chomsky as the lead singer for Chumbawamba.

441

NC: What does it say?

GW: It says, "Chumbawamba . . . last album includes a CD featuring linguist Noam Chomsky." So it looks like you're the lead singer.

GW: Today, as you know, is Human Rights Day.

NC: December tenth. It's the anniversary of the UD [Universal Declaration of Human Rights].

GW: That makes this conversation a little more special. I'd like to first mention that I first became acquainted with you when I was in graduate school in psychology at University of Oregon in the late sixties. I read *The Chomsky/Skinner Debate*, which was presented in the *New York Review of Books*.

NC: I remember writing about Skinner's book, *Beyond Freedom and Dignity*.
        Did you stay in psychology?

GW: Yes, I was in academia for ten years and then into private practice. About ten or fifteen years ago, I started getting actively involved in political and social issues.

NC: It's never too late.

GW   That's what I'd like to think.
        The first question I'd like to ask is, What is the proper role or function of a university in a democracy? What part should the university play ideally?

NC: Well, democracy or not, the integrity of the university and, in fact, its social role, depends on its functioning as basically a subversive institution. That is, raising questions, challenging received ideas, seeking to gain truth and also understanding in any domain, and that usually does lead to a subversive character. In the core sciences that is just taken for granted. It's been talked about for hundreds of years. Since the Galilean Revolution, it's been understood that core natural science is a subversive activity. You're discovering that commonsense beliefs and ideas are not accurate, that you have to look at things in new ways. Students at any decent university are encouraged to question, to be skeptical, to find alternatives, to come up with new ideas. Students are not supposed to copy down what's said in a lecture. They're supposed to try to figure out what's wrong with whats being said. That's just taken for granted.

As you move farther from the core natural sciences, this attitude tends to decline and when you get to the more ideological subjects, it virtually disappears. For the universities to maintain their function, not only for their own internal integrity but for their social value, to maintain that is a difficult thing to do. Universities are economically parasitic, they don't generate their own resources. They are dependent on external institutions for survival and here the situation becomes complex and different in different societies. So, in a society that's run by the church, let's say, the university's going to be under pressure to subordinate itself to church doctrine.

In the United States, for a long time the universities were kind of peripheral to society. The United States was not a major intellectual center until the Second World War. If you wanted to study physics, you went to Germany. If you wanted to study philosophy, you went to England. If you wanted to be a writer, you went to Paris. The United States was kind of like central Iowa with regard to the rest of the world, but that changed with the Second World War. Not 100 percent, of course, but it changed radically. In fact, during the Second World War the United States become the overwhelming world dominant power, was planning to run the world, had half the world's wealth, most of the power and was very triumphalist.

The university system changed radically. In fact, the whole economy changed. The economy had always been pretty heavily based on state initiative. That's standard for every industrial society: The state intervenes to socialize risks and costs. That's the way so-called market societies work and that was also true of the United States. The American system of mass production, which astonished the world in the nineteenth century, was primarily an outgrowth of the military system—armories, military ordnance departments which had organizational capacities, and so on. Also take agricultural, for example. The U.S. had a tremendous spurt in agricultural production, primarily after the Second World War, which was relying on practically a century of extensive state initiative at the federal and state level and partly in universities, land grant colleges, researchers, and so on. Then it sort of turned into a major growth of agri-business. But after the Second World War, there was, nevertheless, a very considerable shift and the economy shifted radically to state centered. So virtually every dynamic component of the U.S. economy today is based on state initiative, funding, organization and so on, which often works right through the university system.

You can see the change at a place like MIT [Massachusetts Institute of Technology]. It was an engineering school when I got here and within a few years it was a major science center, largely through federal funding. That happened after the Second World War. When people talk about the "miracles of the market" in computers, electronics, information technology, the Internet, and so on, they are referring to developments that came straight out of the taxpayer's pocket, including much of the initiative, the funding, and the long development time. That's even true of the few things that developed in so-called private laboratories, such as transistors. "Private" [labs] in a funny sense. It was a monopoly. The usage of transistors and the technology for them, again, mostly relied on procurement in the state sector.

Now, the universities play a central role in that, and therefore, they were nourished. The private sector is extremely happy to have cost socialized, paid for by the general public through taxes. They want profit privatized, but they want costs and risks socialized. So, vast state subsidies develop the technology and the science of the future, and also, of course, risk protection. For example, the IMF [International Monetary Fund] is basically a taxpayer-subsidized risk-protection agency for investors. They don't bail out countries, they bail out investors. And these systems are very significant in any modern economy and dramatically in the United States, and the universities are right in the center of it. They're part of the funnel through which public funds end up in private pockets. As a result, the corporate sector has been quite willing to allow the universities to fulfill their subversive function in areas of science and technology, which will ultimately, it is assumed, yield private profit. So someone, say, like Newt Gingrich—he's supposed to be the leader of the "Conservative Revolution"—he regularly brought back more federal subsidies to his rich district than any comparable district in the country. And when the heads of major universities go down to lobby Congress for more funding for the National Science Foundation, probably the first office they went to was Newt Gingrich's, because he's very sympathetic. He understands that it's poor mothers with children who are supposed to learn to get off the cycle of dependency but rich people have shelter under the wings of the Nanny State. So, in that framework, the universities did receive large scale subsidies, quite often under the cover of defense.

I happened to be on a committee that was set up to investigate these matters about thirty years ago. It was the first such committee for me as a result of student activism that was concerned about the reliance of MIT on military spending, what it meant, and so on. So there was a faculty/student committee set up and I was asked to be on it, and I think it was the first review ever of MIT funding. You can get the exact date. My memory is that at the time, about half of MIT's income came from two military laboratories. These were secret laboratories. One was Lincoln Labs and one then called the I Labs, now the Draper Labs, which at the time was working on guidance systems for intercontinental missiles and that sort of thing. These were secret labs and that was approximately half of the income. And, of course, that income in all kinds of ways filtered into the university through library funds and health funds and so on. Nobody knew the bookkeeping details and nobody cared much, but it was an indirect subsidy to the university.

The other half, the academic budget, I think it was about 90 percent Pentagon funded at that time. And I personally was right in the middle of it. I was in a military lab. If you take a look at my early publications, they all say something about Air Force, Navy, and so on, because I was in a military lab, the Research Lab for Electronics. But in fact, even if you were in the music department, you were, in effect, being funded by the Pentagon because there wouldn't have been a music department unless there was funding for, say, electrical engineering. If there was, then you could dribble some off to the music department. So, in fact, everybody was Pentagon funded no matter whatever the bookkeeping notices said.

Well, it's important to recognize that during that period, the university was extremely free. The lab where I was working, the research lab for electronics, was also one of the centers of anti–Vietnam War resistance. We were organizing national tax resistance and the support groups for draft resistance were based there to a large extent. I mean, I, myself, was in a jail repeatedly at the time. It didn't make any difference. The Pentagon didn't care. In fact, they didn't care at all as far as I know.

Their function, they understood very well, is to provide the cover for the development of the science and technology in the future so that the corporate system can profit.

GW: So they were just too big and powerful to be threatened. You were too minor of a threat?

NC: They just didn't care. What happened at the administrative level
        I don't know, but nothing ever got to us. I had perfectly good
        relations with the administration. In fact, I'd tell them if I knew I
        was going to get arrested. I had no particular interest in embar-
        rassing them, but it didn't matter.

        On the other hand, as the university has, over the years since
        that time, shifted toward corporate funding, the atmosphere has
        changed. Corporate funding is more restrictive, more secretive,
        less concerned with nourishing the subversive function of the
        university and more interested in short-term applied gain, and
        that's for perfectly natural reasons. A corporation is not in the
        business of creating the science and technology of the future for
        the business sector to profit from thirty years from now. They're
        in the business of raising their profits and market share in the next
        quarter. That's the job of the corporation. Now you know, this
        again, it's not 100 percent.

GW: Okay, but before things started shifting more and more to corpo-
        rate funding, are you saying that when the funding came from the
        Pentagon it was completely "free"?

NC: Overwhelmingly it was free. You could do pretty much what you
        wanted. And there was nothing secret on campus. In fact, we
        investigated secrecy specifically in the committee. Although it
        was regarded in the government as military-related work, there
        was virtually nothing that was secret. In fact, the parts that were
        secret were mostly an impediment to research. It wasn't because
        anybody wanted it (secrecy), it was just some technical detail that
        hadn't been ironed out. You could do what you wanted in your
        personal and political life, and also in your academic and profes-
        sional life, within a broad range. It [MIT] must've been one of the
        most free universities in the world.

GW: Who had access to the results of all this work and research?

NC: But that's a joke. I remember a discussion once with the head of the
        instrumentation lab, which was the lab that was working on guid-
        ance systems for intercontinental missiles. Of course it was all clas-
        sified, but he said that from his point of view, he would be perfectly
        happy to declassify everything and give the books to the Russians
        and the Chinese. He said they can't do anything with them anyway.
        They don't have the industrial capacity to use the technology that
        we're developing. So the whole effect of the classification system
        was to impede communication among the American scientists.

GW: With what result?

NC: Well, nothing. I mean, they kept that system classified and sort of spun it off, it's now a secret lab, independent of MIT. But, in answer to your question, right now, for example, there's an agency in the Pentagon, DARPA, the Defense Advance Research Project Agency, which has been the center of innovation for many years. It's where the Internet comes from. It's where a good deal of modern technology comes from. Right now they're also involved in highly innovative support for research. But just to go back a step, that's where a good part of Silicon Valley comes from. They [DARPA] were funding small start-up companies and supercomputers and parallel processing, fifth-generation computers in the 1980s, and out of that came spin-offs that are rich private companies.

GW: Those are former faculty?

NC: A lot of it's former faculty. So Route 128 in Boston in the 1950s, this is the big industrial, high-tech corridor around Boston. There were two major centers of high tech. By now there are several. But for a long time, there were two major centers of high tech in the country. One was Route 128, which is this highway that goes around Boston, which has big, high-tech corporations on it. That's largely a spin-off from MIT, including MIT faculty who started businesses that were later taken over by big corporations when they became profitable. The other major one is around Stanford and Berkeley, and that's the whole Silicon Valley complex. Again, this is largely based on government funding, both federal and state. State government, both here and in California, puts in plenty of money. The state college systems are the level right below the big research universities in training and research and so on. So it's all a big public complex that ends up spawning what's called "private industry." Private is a funny word for it. Most of these private industries—their market and their subsidies—are very often public.

So these [Route 128 and Silicon Valley] were the two big centers. Now there are others. For example, if you take a walk to Kendall Square here in Cambridge, you'll notice a big high-technology development. It's mostly biotech centers going up. It's another spin-off from MIT with extensive government funding. A very substantial part of it has always been public and remains there.

To go back to DARPA; as I say, they're famous for having carried the Internet from the very beginning up through the first ten or twenty years of difficult, experimental, innovative work. Then they handed it over to National Science Foundation. In fact, it was just commercialized about four years ago after about thirty years in the public sector.

Now DARPA is devoting work to other long-term developments. One of them is "Nano-Technology." They're trying to devise computers that will work with elements at the scale of an atom, basically, which will make them super fast and immensely powerful. This is cutting-edge technology. Industry doesn't want to fund it. They want the public to fund it, so a lot of it's going through DARPA. One other major project of theirs has to do with the rapid mutation of bacteria. This is now a major problem because they become, very quickly, drug resistant. New diseases are extremely hard to keep up with new drugs fast enough to kill off the mutating bacteria. That's one of the reasons hospitals are quite dangerous places. So they're working on new ideas which may work out or may not, nobody really knows. Researchers are trying to see if we can prevent bacterial mutation. It's at the very edge of the understanding in biology. Nobody knows if this is possible or not. But again, that's the kind of thing that would be publicly funded. If it works out, it'll be a huge bonanza for the pharmaceutical corporations. But that's coming out of DARPA and that's what the military's been doing for years. I mean, that's why you have a computer.

GW: It's all research and development from public funding?

NC: Yeah, by the 1950s computers were developed mostly at two labs at MIT and Harvard. Lincoln Labs in the 1950s was theoretically working on air defense systems. This was the beginning of an era of intercontinental missiles. I presume that hardly anybody there thought there was going to be a feasible defense against World War II bombers, or that it mattered much. But under the cover of air defense systems, they were developing modern computers.

When I got to MIT, a computer was something in large rooms with vacuum tubes overheating and papers spewing out all over. I mean, it was nothing that anybody could use. But over this period of working on things like air defense, theoretically, they got computers down to the point where you could make a mainframe that would be usable by a corporation and, in fact, corporations spun off from Lincoln Labs by the time that happened.

Meanwhile, IBM was shifting from typewriters to computers, largely by using the MIT Whirlwind, Lincoln Labs, or the Mark series at Harvard.

This went on for years when the private corporations started developing what they called "their own computers" in the early sixties. One major IBM innovation was designed for the National Security Agency, the Stretch computer. It goes on like that. Now, in this context, universities are very attractive to the major centers of power in the country, because they are a crucial part of the funnel by which public funds end up in private pockets somewhere down the line after science and technology develop. And that's one of the reasons why in this era of so-called cutting down government, funding for science and technology has not suffered. Take a look at the National Science Foundation or the National Institutes of Health budget. The National Health budget is going way up, in fact. The cutting edge technology of the postwar period was electronics. Now it's biotechnology and genetic engineering. So the National Institutes of Heath budget is shooting up, and the university's right in the middle of it, so they get protected. On the other hand, as you move to corporate funding, federal funding naturally declines. So federal funding has declined for the universities. It's a smaller part of the total. Back to MIT, there's much more corporate funding than there was several years ago.

GW: And where does that go? What can you predict from that?

NC: Well, you can predict pretty much what the effect is going to be. By and large a corporation is not interested in producing things that can be used by its rivals. It wants them for itself. The Pentagon and the federal system have the general interests of the business world at heart, not the particular interest of one corporation. The same is true in foreign policy. In foreign policy, the government doesn't respond to the particular interests of IBM, it responds to the generalized interests of the business world. That's why in the chief executive positions, like the state department and so on, you typically find corporate lawyers from a half a dozen major Wall Street firms that cater to corporate interests. They have the generalized concerns of the business sector at heart, not the local concerns of one particular subpart of it.

Well, as you shift to specific corporate funding, of course, that changes. So, a particular corporation is likely to be interested in something it can use and in the short term. It doesn't care about something that may or may not work out thirty years from now, like, say, the Internet in the 1960s. That's for the public to pay for. They want something that they can use tomorrow. So there's pressure, and again, this not 100 percent, it varies. For instance, Merck [a major pharmaceutical company] will give a grant to the biology department for general research, but there's a marked tendency, and a very understandable one, for research to be shifting toward more narrow, applied concerns and also to be more secret. Now, there is no way that a corporation can enforce secrecy; they can't put a stipulation into a contract saying, "You're not allowed to talk about it." But that doesn't matter, people understand that you're not going to get refunded if you talk about it. So in effect, you get kind of an atmosphere of secrecy. Actually, this comes out of the faculty too. The faculty becomes more commercial oriented. I mean, it always was to an extent. So at MIT, for example, on your contract it says you have one day free from university duties. That means for consulting or running your business or something like that.

GW: One day a week?

NC: Yeah, it's supposed to be one day a week. Anyway, it's recognized that you're going to have another life, which is the business world, but that's increasing and it's increasing to the extent that it sometimes . . . one example is a scandal that actually made the *Wall Street Journal* this summer. Something like this, I think it was an undergraduate student refused to answer a question on an exam in the computer science department and when he was asked why, he said that he was under a condition set by a professor with whom he was working. He knew the answer, he said, but the answer was worked out in some project on which he was working under some professor who was intending to begin a startup company which would use the research they were doing and didn't want anybody to know about it. So therefore, the kid couldn't answer the question on the exam. It's an extreme case.

GW: This is the kind of thing that becomes an apocryphal tale.

NC: It's a real one, and, in fact, it was reported in, I think, the *Wall Street Journal*. But people in the sciences, especially the engineering departments, talk more and more about the pressure towards short-term applied work and secrecy.

But if you think about the context in which the universities are permitted to serve their subversive function, that's restricted. It's restricted to service to the outside institutions. That's the dilemma that universities face. They are parasitic, they do not generate their own resources, they're within a framework of existing systems of power and authority, Their function is to challenge those systems, but they live in a difficult relationship with them.

GW: Let me ask you this. I hope I'm not interrupting.

NC: No, go ahead.

GW: On this particular point, Leonard Minsky has written a chapter in the book which is about the effects of the Bayh-Dole Act of 1980. You're familiar with that?

NC: Mmm hmm.

GW: Minsky's view is that The Bayh-Dole Act has changed the nature of the university in a short space of time, more radically than any other time in history. This is because the act transferred ownership of patents resulting from federally funded research to universities, making them patent holding companies.

NC: It's part of the same thing. However, remember that in the 1950s the same thing was happening in a different way. Route 128 is the prototypical example. These were spin-offs from mostly the MIT electrical engineering department, private spin-offs. It wasn't a matter of the patent being held by the university, it was a matter of a faculty member starting a small company which, if it prospered, was then taken over by a major corporation or grew into a major corporation.

GW: Okay, but now universities are patent holding [in other words, they have ownership of products]. Some of the contributors to *Campus, Inc.* are very critical of this because they see that as an increasing commercialization of the university.

NC: That's a different kind of commercialization of the university.

GW: Right, but from what you're saying, there's another side to be argued too.

NC: The other side is, in fact, this has also being discussed, if the university has the patent, it does mean that the university has, to some extent, independent resources, which could, in principle, free them from outside pressure. It's a very mixed story.

GW: Could this produce some balance?

NC: The effect is meretricious. It turns the university into something which is commercially oriented, rather than committed to its primary function of expanding understanding and that means being primarily subversive. You can't both be a stockholder in the system and be trying to undermine it. Or, you can, but it's hard. And that's the constant tension that universities have always been in. I mean, it was the same in the medieval period when individual scholars were trying to escape church control.

GW: Is it possible to have a healthy and equitable relationship between the university and corporations? If so, what might it look like?

NC: Suppose we think of a society run by a dictator, or a slave society. You could ask how a more "healthy and equitable relationship" might exist between the dictator or slave owner and his subjects. The answer would be that the rulers could become more benevolent, or might be compelled to yield to the demands of their subjects in some respects. Within the framework of the institutions, it makes sense to press for greater benevolence. But the more fundamental question, plainly, is different. Is the institutional relationship legitimate? Should it survive? I think the same kinds of considerations arose here. Within the given institutional framework, it makes sense to pressure private power to be more forthcoming; in this case, to allow universities more opportunities to pursue free and unconstrained inquiry, both in teaching and research programs, even if the educational and research programs tend to undermine existing structures of power, as I personally think they would, if they are truly free. The more such goals are achieved, the healthier is the relationship. But there are plainly going to be limits, and the fundamental question of legitimacy remains.

GW: When people ask you questions about "What should we do?" you have a characteristic response—

NC: But there's no answer to those questions. There are a million different things to do, depending on what you're trying to achieve.

GW: I would like to understand more about your reaction to the "What should we do?" question.

NC: I don't think it's the right question. In fact, it's kind of interesting where I hear that question. I give talks all over the world. Like I have met with the Landless Workers' Movement in Brazil, for example, or peasant groups in India. They never ask me what to do. They tell me what they're doing. The only people who ask you what to do are the people who don't have a clue. I mean, if you're involved in something, you know what to do. There are a lot of different things to do and there is no general answer. So these questions about the universities are quite complex and you have to handle them on their own terms. In the longer term, I don't think the whole corporate system should exist, so what you ought to do is dismantle the private tyrannies [corporations]. That's one thing you should do. Then the questions wouldn't arise, at least in this form. But we're living in this world, not in some world that you might want to achieve some day. And in this world, you have to have specific goals. You have to defend the integrity of the university to the extent you can within an illegitimate framework of power and there's no general answer on how to do that. It depends on what you're facing. Like, for example, I'll give you concrete cases if you like. I guess in the mid-1970s, the MIT administration, in effect—a little bit of an exaggeration—but in effect, they sold off the nuclear engineering department to the shah of Iran. It came close to that. Well, everything's done quietly, you know, but it did sort of leak out, and when it leaked out, there was a huge protest on the part of the students. Overwhelming opposition on the part of the students. Protest demonstrations, polls, and so on. I think the students were maybe 80 percent against it. It came to big faculty meetings. Usually nobody goes to faculty meetings, but when there's a scandal, everybody goes. So there was a big issue at the faculty meetings and the faculty finally, essentially voted in favor by about the same proportion that the students were against it, something like that. Well, you know the faculty of today are the students of yesterday.

They haven't changed their genes. They've changed their institutional role. The students are in a period of life when they are relatively free. They are not managing the society. The faculty are the same people in a different status, a different institutional role: the role of supporting, managing, and so on. I mean, I'm not hiding my sympathies. I think the students were right, but you can understand why people whose institutional role has shifted would look at things differently. Okay, those are the battles you have to fight all of the time.

GW: Okay, now on the point of faculty, you were quoted as saying that faculty makes a free choice in what they do.

NC: They make a free choice, but it's a funny kind. For example, I have friends (I won't give you their names) who are faculty members in the engineering department who don't want to go along with this kind of short-term pressure. So they don't have offices. I mean, they don't have funding, they can't get students, they're not given offices. Yeah, they made a free choice.

GW: But you said that it's not so much the trustees or the administration that were controlling the content of the research and that the issue was more in the lap of the faculty about choice.

NC: It's a choice.

GW: You've said real reform comes not by imposing restrictive rules on research or closing buildings, but by constructing alternative programs inside the university which will gather towards them the better, more creative students.

NC: We tried very hard to do that at MIT; in fact, succeeded for a long time. There was a period from the sixties for about ten years. By the late sixties, over half of the undergraduate students wanted to be part of an undergraduate program of the kind that you just described. That was their choice. And we tried to set up a program. There were very few faculty—some, but not many—who were participating. There were some from various departments, and we tried very hard to set up such a program and it finally eroded over time, and I can tell you exactly why. I know, I was one of the senior faculty involved and I have a limited tolerance for meetings, bureaucracy, time wasting, and so on, since I was the one who had to go through the process in which it was obvious that over time we were going to lose. It was not the pressure of the administration or the trustees, but from the rest of the faculty who didn't want it, it was going to be an endless, recursive process of one roadblock after another roadblock and after a while I got bored with it. I kept teaching my own undergraduate courses for about twenty-five years, on my own time incidentally, within the program, what was left of the program. But finally, those, too, had to drop because access to them was simply cut off by the departments and students. Theoretically they could take the course, but on their own time and without knowing about it contributing to any program's credits. There are all kinds of ways inside the university and from commercial forces outside, to restrict the options that you have. It's a little bit like saying that the Internet is free. Well yeah it's free, but ten years from now if you want to use that freedom, you're probably going to have to go through a path that is designed by those who control the access entries, portals, which will carry you through their advertisements and what they want you to see, and so on. If you're a fanatic, you'll be able to find what you're looking for. So yes, it's free, but it's free within a system with unequal power relations.

GW: Could it have succeeded or was it doomed to failure?

NC: If we had put sufficient energy and effort into it, we probably could've sustained it. But there are a lot of things to do and there's a lot of pressures and the day is twenty-four hours long.

GW: Speaking of which, I have the feeling we're out of time.

NC: It's coming to an end. That's what the knocking on the door is about.

GW: One more question please. If you could use your time however you wanted, I assume you would devote your time exclusively to linguistics. Working in the political area is not your preference.

NC: It's not my choice.

GW: But you've ended up doing both, and there was something written about doing this difficult balancing act between the two. Many people, including myself, find ourselves in the same position. I would rather be doing psychology or art, but there are critical and pressing social problems which can't be ignored. So, what has it been like being in that difficult position?

NC: It's like having two major full-time jobs, both extremely demanding and, of course, something has to give. What gives is—

GW: A personal life.

NC: Personal life, sleep, you know, a lot of things. I mean, if my wife and I see friends twice a year, we think it's a good year.

GW: That's quite a social year!

NC: And something has to give, obviously, but people make their own choices and compromise and we've made very different ones.

GW: Your wife and kids must be very supportive of this.

NC: First of all, I did spend a lot of time with the kids when they were growing up and now with my grandchildren, so that's one thing that didn't give. But you just have to make your own choices. There's no general answer.

Appendix

ORGANIZATIONS AND PUBLICATIONS
For Further Information

compiled by
Sonya Huber and John Peck

Useful Contacts

Alliance for Democracy
PO Box 683
Lincoln, MA 01773
(617) 259-9395
www.igc.org/alliance

Campus Voice Editor
c/o Public Health Care Workers Department
Communication Workers of America (CWA)
501 Third Street NW
9th Floor
Washington, DC 20001
www3.cwa-union.org/index.html

Canadian Federation of Students
170 Metcalfe Street
Suite 500
Ottawa, ON K2P 1P3
(613) 232-7394
www.cfs-fcee.ca

Center for Campus Free Speech
c/o Public Interest Research Group's Higher Education Project
218 D Street SE
Washington, DC 20003
(202) 546-9707
www.igc.org/pirg/student/speech/index.htm

Center for Campus Organizing
PO Box 425748
Cambridge, MA 02142
(617) 725-2886
www.cco.org
cco@igc.apc.org

Center for Commercial-Free Public Education
1714 Franklin Street
Suite 100
Oakland, CA 94612
(510) 268-1100
www.commercialfree.org
unplug@igc.org

Center for Defense Information
1779 Massachusetts Avenue NW
Washington, DC 20036
(202) 332-0600
www.cdi.org

Center for Science in the Public Interest
1875 Connecticut Avenue NW
Suite 300
Washington, DC 20009
(202) 332-9110

Center for Third World Organizing
1218 East 21st Street
Oakland, CA 533-7583
www.ctwo.org/index.html
ctwo@igc.org

Corp-Focus
a moderated listserv that distributes the weekly column "Focus on the
  Corporation"
To subscribe, send an e-mail to list-proc@essential.org with the message "subscribe corp-focus <your name>."

Corporate Watch
PO Box 29344
San Francisco, CA 94129
(415) 561-6568
www.corpwatch.org

Data Center
464 19th Street
Oakland, CA 94612
(510) 835-4692
www.igc.org/datacenter/

Democratic Socialists of America–Youth Section
180 Varick Street
12th Floor
New York, NY 10014
(212) 727-8610
www.dsausa.org/youth/index.html

Earth First! End Corporate Dominance Campaign
c/o EF! Austin
PO Box 7292
Austin, TX 78713
(512) 320-0413
entropy@eden.com
Earth First! Journal
earthfirst@igc.org

Essential Action
PO Box 19405
Washington, DC 20036
(202) 387-8030
www.essential.org
Kishi@essential.org

Free Burma Movement
www.freeburma.org

Free Nigeria Listserv
FreeNigeria@listserv.butler.edu

Interfaith Center for Corporate Responsibility (ICCR)
475 Riverside Drive #550
New York, NY 10115
(212) 870-2296

Investor Responsibility Research Center (ICCR)
1350 Connecticut Avenue NW
Suite 700
Washington, DC 20036
(202) 833-0700
www.irrc.org

Jobs with Justice
501 3rd Street NW
Washington, DC 20001
(202) 434-1106
www.igc.apc.org/jwj/corepage.htm

Labor Notes
7435 Michigan Avenue
Detroit, MI 48210
(313) 842-6262
www.labornotes.org

The Labor Party
PO Box 53177
Washington, DC 20009
(202) 234-5190
lpa@labornet.org

National Association for the Advancement of Colored People (NAACP)
    Youth Section
4805 Mt. Hope Drive
Baltimore, MD 21215
(410) 358-8900
www.naacp.org/youth-college

National Association of Graduate and Professional Students
825 Green Bay Road
Suite 270
Willamette, IL 60091
(847) 256-1562
nagps@netcom.com

National Labor Committee
275 7th Avenue
15th Floor
New York, NY 10001
(212) 242-3002
www.nlcnet.org

National Wildlife Federation—Campus Ecology Program
1730 Rhode Island Avenue NW
Suite 1050
Washington, DC 20036
(202) 797-5435
www.nwf.org/campus

180 Movement for Democracy in Education (180/MDE) Clearinghouse
731 State Street
Madison, WI 53703
(608) 262-9036
www.corporations.org/democracy
www.sit.wisc.edu/~democrac

Prison Activist Resource Center
PO Box 339
Berkeley, CA 94701
(510) 845-8813
www.igc.org/prisons

Program on Corporations, Law, and Democracy (POCLAD)
PO Box 246
South Yarmouth, MA 02664
(508) 398-1145
www.poclad.org

Project Underground
1847 Berkeley Way
Berkeley, CA 94703
(510) 705-8981
www.moles.org

Rachel's Environment and Health Weekly
PO Box 5036
Annapolis, MD 21403
www.monitor.net/Rachel

Rainforest Action Network (RAN)
450 Sansome Street
Suite 700
San Francisco, CA 94111
(415) 398-4404
www.ran.org

Scholars, Artists, and Writers for Social Justice (SAWSJ)
2565 Broadway #176
New York, NY 10025
www.sage.edu/SAWSJ

Speak Out!
PO Box 99096
Emeryville, CA 94662
(510) 601-0182
www.speakersandartists.org
speakout@igc.org

Student Environmental Action Coalition (SEAC)
PO Box 31909
Philadelphia, PA 19104
(215) 222-4711
www.seac.org

Student Liberation Action Movement (SLAM!)
www.geocities.com/CapitolHill/Lobby/6353
cunyslam@hotmail.com

Sweatshop Watch
310 8th Street
Suite 309
Oakland, CA 94607
(510) 834-8990
www.sweatshopwatch.org

Teachers for a Democratic Culture
Steve Parks, Director
Department of English
Temple University
Philadelphia, PA 19118
(215) 204-1795
www.temple.edu/tdc
sparks@astro.ocis.temple.edu

United for a Fair Economy
37 Temple Place
5th Floor
Boston, MA 02111
(617) 423-2148
www.ufenet.org

United States Student Association
1413 K Street NW
10th Floor
Washington, DC 20005
(202) 347-USSA
www.essential.org/ussa

INDEPENDENT STUDENT PUBLICATIONS WITH WEB SITES

The Beat Within (a paper by incarcerated youth)
Pacific News Service, San Francisco
www.pacificnews.org/yo/beat

College Hill Independent, Rhode Island School of Design and Brown
    University
www.netspace.org/indy

The Declaration, UVA
www.the-declaration.com/

Diversity and Distinction, Harvard University
www.hcs.harvard.edu/~dnd

The Drummer, Iowa State University
www.stuorg.iastate.edu/drummer

The Free Press, University of Chicago
home.uchicago.edu/orgs/free-press/freephome.htm

The Harbinger, Mobile, Alabama
entropy.me.usouthal.edu/harbinger

Hermes, Wesleyan University, Middletown, Connecticut
www.wesleyan.edu/hermes

The Indicator, Amherst College
www.amherst.edu/~indicate

Naked Singularity, Boston College
infoeagle.bc.edu/bc_org/sup/st_org/nsing/default2.html

Oregon Student Association Newsletter
members.aol.com/commosa/index.html

Princeton Progressive Review
www.princeton.edu/~progrev

Ruckus, University of Washington
students.washington.edu/ruckus

The Student Activist
www.tao.ca/~nrsp

Student Insurgent, University of Oregon
gladstone.uoregon.edu/~insurgent

SUNY Binghamton Experimental Media Organization
www.geocities.com/SoHo/8580

The Thistle, Massachusetts Institute of Technology
www.mit.edu:8001/afs/athena/activity/t/thistle/www/thistle.html

Touchstone, Texas A&M University
www.rtis.com/reg/bcs/pol/touchstone

Unfiltered, George Washington University
www.gwu.edu/~unfilter
unfilter@gwu.edu

The Vigil, Princeton University
www.princeton.edu/~vigil

CONTRIBUTORS

MICHAEL APPLE is John Bascom Professor of Education at the University of Wisconsin–Madison. He can be contacted at applemw@macc.wisc.edu.

MEDEA BENJAMIN is founding director of the San Francisco–based human rights organization Global Exchange. She can be contacted at medea@globalexchange.org.

LISA BLASCH is a doctoral student in philosophy at the University of Oregon.

DONALD W. BRAY is emeritus professor of political science at California State University, Los Angeles. He can be contacted at dbray@calstatela.edu.

MARJORIE WOODFORD BRAY is coordinator of Latin American Studies at California State University, Los Angeles. She can be contacted at mbray@calstatela.edu.

PETER CASTER is a doctoral student in English at the University of Texas, Austin.

NOAM CHOMSKY is professor of linguistics at Massachusetts Institute of Technology. He can be contacted at chomsky@MIT.edu.

RICHARD DANIELS is associate professor of English at Oregon State University. He can be contacted at rdaniels@orst.edu.

COREY DOLGON is chair of the Sociology Department at Worcester State College in Massachusetts. He can be contacted at cdolgon@worc.mass.edu.

RONNIE DUGGER is founder and cochair of the Alliance for Democracy, founding editor of the *Texas Observer*, a Woodrow Wilson Fellow, and a research associate at the Harvard Divinity School. He can be contacted at rdugger123@aol.com.

ABIGAIL FULLER is assistant professor of sociology and social work at Manchester College. She can be contacted at aafuller@manchester.edu.

STEPHANIE GREENWOOD graduated from Harvard-Radcliffe in 1999 with an honors degree in social studies, and is currently working as an economics researcher in New York City. She can be contacted at sgreenwood@post.harvard.edu.

FLANNERY C. HAUCK is a political organizer and writer. She can be reached at Flannerych@aol.com.

SONYA HUBER is currently on a fellowship at Ohio State University, studying "Investigative Reporting in the Public Interest." She can be contacted at sawnhuber@aol.com.

KEVIN KNIFFIN is the area vice president for the Binghamton chapter of the Graduate Student Employees Union (GSEU), Communications Workers of America (CWA) Local 118. He can be contacted at kniffin@essential.org.

LARRY A. LESLIE is professor of higher education and vice dean of the College of Education at the University of Arizona. He can be contacted at larryl@u.arizona.edu.

BERT LEVY is a student at the University of San Francisco School of Law. He can be contacted at levyal2@usfca.edu.

JEFF LUSTIG is professor in the Government Department at California State University, Sacramento. He can be contacted at jlustig@ pop.igc.apc.org.

BEN MANSKI, a student at the University of Wisconsin–Madison, has been an activist since his early teenage years. He can be contacted at brmanski@students.wisc.edu.

ADAM MARTIN is an English major at San Francisco State University. He can be contacted at aclm50@hotmail.com.

LEONARD MINSKY is cofounder with Ralph Nader and David Noble of the National Coalition for Universities in the Public Interest. He can be contacted at ncupi@earthlink.net.

RALPH NADER, consumer advocate, can be contacted at ralph@ essential.org.

SETH NEWTON is a student at Stanford University studying human biology with a concentration in cultural and political ecology. He can be contacted at snewton@leland.stanford.edu.

DAVID F. NOBLE is professor in the Division of Social Science at York University in Toronto. He is on the board of directors of the National Coalition for Universities in the Public Interest.

MICHAEL PARENTI, political anlyst and author, lives in Berkeley, California. He can be reached at mc@michaelparenti.org.

JOHN PECK is a student at the University of Wisconsin–Madison and a member of the Alliance for Democracy. He can be contacted a jepeck@ students.wisc.edu.

TODD A. PRICE is a Ph.D. candidate in the Department of Curriculum and Instruction at the University of Wisconsin–Madison. He can be contacted at taprice@students.wisc.edu.

THOMAS EHRLICH REIFER is currently a research associate at SUNY Binghamton's Fernard Braudel Center for the Study of Economics. He can be contacted at consolecb@aol.com.

MATTHEW RUBEN is a Ph.D. candidate in the School of Arts and Sciences at the University of Pennsylvania. He can be contacted at mruben@dept.english.upenn.edu.

SHEILA SLAUGHTER is professor at the Center for the Study of Higher Education at the University of Arizona. She can be contacted at slaughtr@u.arizona.edu.

LAWRENCE SOLEY is Colnik Professor of Communication at Marquette University. He can be contacted at soley@execpc.com.

HENRY STECK is professor of political science at SUNY College at Cortland and SUNY Distinguished Service Professor. He can be contacted at steckh@cortland.edu.

JOSHUA WOLFSON is a journalism student at San Francisco State University. He can be contacted at wolfsonj@sfsu.edu.

GEOFFRY D. WHITE has done humanitarian projects in the Balkans and Africa and has been active in promoting health-care and campaign finance reform in California. He is a psychologist in Los Angeles and can be reached at careerpaths@pacificnet.net.

NEIL WOLLMAN is professor of psychology at Manchester College in Indiana. He can be contacted at njw@manchester.edu.

ALI S. ZAIDI has written on higher education in New York for *Monthly Review*, *Z*, *Covert Action Quarterly*, and *Against the Current*. he can be contacted at azaidi@freewwweb.com.

ZAR NI, a Burmese political exile and educator/organizer, is completing his Ph.D. at the University of Wisconsin–Madison. He can be contacted through Michael Apple at applemw@macc.wisc.edu.

HOWARD ZINN is professor emeritus of political science at Boston University. He can be contacted at hzinn@bu.edu.

MICHAEL ZWEIG is professor of economics at SUNY at Stony Brook. He can be contacted at mzweig@notes.cc.sunysb.edu.